1980

American Law Enforcement

American Law Enforcement

Police, Courts, and Corrections

third edition

VERN L. FOLLEY

University of Texas, Tyler

ALLYN AND BACON, INC.

Boston · London · Sydney · Toronto

Library of Congress Cataloging in Publication Data

Folley, Vern L
    American law enforcement.

    Bibliography: p.
    Includes index.
    1. Law enforcement—United States.   2. Criminal
justice, Administration of—United States.   I.   Title.
HV8138.F56 1980   363.2′0973   79–10175
ISBN 0–205–06651–8

Printed in the United States of America.

Production Editor: Russell Mead

DEDICATION

to my late brother

ELWIN

*who in life knew my dedication to
law enforcement, and who now, I
believe, is pleased to know this
volume is published. He yet shares
his life with me and I humbly share
this work with him.*

Contents

vii

APPENDIXES 447

INDEX 481

Foreword

As a practitioner in this professional endeavor we call law enforcement, I welcome Dr. Folley's text. The police, as the agency responsible for the enforcement of the law, are generally in the forefront of all attention directed toward the Criminal Justice System. However, the police themselves are but one part of this elaborate system of interrelated components. The effectiveness of the Criminal Justice System is dependent upon the degree of mutual cooperation and concern shared by the members of these various components. These components include the public, the police, the courts, the prosecutorial agencies, and the correctional process.

The development of our Criminal Justice System actually has its roots in old English law. However, the similarity between the two systems is lost there. The American police system, for example, is something that just happened out of a sense of need. The British police system, on the other hand, was conceived after seven years of debate in Parliament. The British system was founded upon a series of principles which are just as applicable today as they were when they were developed by Sir Robert Peel in 1829. There exists a great need in law enforcement to use a set of standards or practical guidelines to assist the police in properly serving the public. A basis for such standards can be found in the British Police Principles. For example, one of those principles states, "The basic mission for which the police exist is to prevent crime and disorder." That concept has not changed in more than 150 years. Unfortunately, we have gotten away from many of these basic concepts. Indeed, there exists a great void in knowing and understanding the specific role the police are supposed to assume.

Dr. Folley has, in this text, captured many of the principles and governing philosophies of today's police system. This text will provide the reader with an interesting and general view of the entire Criminal Justice process. After reading this text, it should be easier for the student, practitioner, or interested citizen to understand how the entire American law enforcement system operates.

Edward M. Davis
Former Chief of Police
City of Los Angeles

Preface

In our modern and ever-changing society law enforcement becomes such an increasingly important part of our life that an understanding of its development, philosophy, responsibility, function, and problems is imperative for all citizens. In fact, responsible citizens will be cognizant of their responsibility to be familiar with the practices, procedures, and activities of American law enforcement agencies. A historical and philosophical perspective of law enforcement will help citizens to better comprehend the present complicated criminal justice system, its principles, its legal authority, and its effect on society in general. Law enforcement plays a vital role in the preservation of our democratic way of life, and an understanding of this will encourage citizen support and demand for professional law enforcement services.

American Law Enforcement, third edition, is designed to serve three groups of readers: 1) those who are preparing for a career in law enforcement or criminal justice, 2) those who are presently employed by a criminal justice agency who wish to increase their professional knowledge, and 3) citizens interested in an understanding of the law enforcement function and our criminal justice system.

The content of *American Law Enforcement*, third edition, deals generally with broad conceptual and philosophical concepts as well as practical implications. The fundamental concepts, the historic perspective, trends, advancements, new approaches, and the primary problems faced by law enforcement agencies are presented in nontechnical language for clarity of understanding and ease of reading.

This third edition has been expanded considerably to include more comprehensive information on such important topics as police authority, arrest discretion, development of law, police professionalism, the police function, and corrections. It has also been updated with recent crime statistics, current problems, and innovations in law enforcement. The third edition discusses in some detail recent experimental approaches to the two basic police functions—patrol and criminal investigation. Experimental approaches discussed include Managing Criminal Investigations based on Solvability Factors, Directed Deterrent Patrol, Community-Oriented Patrol, Split-Force Patrol, and Directed Interactive Patrol.

A new Chapter, "Orientation to Administration and Organization," has also been added to the third edition. This chapter provides an overview of Administrative Climate, Principles of Administration and Organization, Leadership, and Supervision. The chapter is designed to familiarize the student with the structure and administrative climate within which he or she will be working as a police officer.

The book is divided into eleven chapters, each dealing with a major area of concern or interest. Chapters 1 through 4 provide the reader with an understanding of the nature, development, and status of law enforcement as well as the police function. Chapter 5 deals with administration, organization, and leadership. Chapter 6 discusses dilemmas of law enforcement and Chapter 7 provides information relative to career opportunities. Chapters 8 and 9 deal with the other two major components of the criminal justice system—Courts and Corrections. Chapter 10 discusses and illustrates the flow of activities once the criminal justice process is initiated. Chapter 11 discusses the important topic of government and constitutional rights.

Vern L. Folley

1

The Nature of
Law Enforcement

The enforcement of the law, a complicated process involving numerous agencies, is one of the most influential mechanisms for social control. In fact, there exists no governmental function that controls or directs the activities of the public as much as law enforcement. With the possible exception of education, law enforcement is the service with which the public has most frequent contact. Such contact and control is constant, and, if it is not experienced directly through personal contact, it is at least felt indirectly through the visible or implied presence of law enforcement personnel. And yet, inconsistent with its significance, law enforcement remains a subject that the public knows less about than any other governmental function. Although law enforcement is an often discussed issue, few people actually realize its significance.

Before the law enforcement student can fully understand and appreciate the full scope and nature of law enforcement, he must become familiar with certain basic components, terms, and concepts.

LAW ENFORCEMENT DEFINED

The phrase "law enforcement" correctly suggests the enforcement of the law or refers to the people who enforce the law. To most citizens the phrase "law enforcement" relates directly to a uniformed police officer or to police activities in the community. This relationship is not incorrect since the police are most surely involved in the enforcement of the law and, by definition, police officers are persons employed by a governmental agency and charged with the responsibility of enforcing the law and maintaining order. The blanket term "law enforcement officer" refers to those persons employed to enforce the law and maintain order at the several levels of government. The term "police" usually refers to law enforcement personnel at the municipal level.

Not entirely valid, however, is the tendency to think of

3

crime control and the maintenance of order as the exclusive responsibility of the police. This misconception is easily understood, however, when we consider the visible activities of the police. The police have the responsibility for dealing with crime on a twenty-four hour basis, are usually conspicuously visible to the public, and are the agents that immediately respond when violations of the law occur. In fact, by virtue of their continual and immediate involvement, police officers themselves often lose sight of the total system and tend to think of crime control as their exclusive domain.

This erroneous assumption of total responsibility can be detrimental to effective law enforcement and crime control. Through cooperation with other crime control agencies, law enforcement officers can insure maximum effectiveness in working toward the common objective of law enforcement. Those agencies involved in crime control and crime suppression are collectively referred to as the "criminal justice system."

CRIMINAL JUSTICE SYSTEM

The criminal justice system is the mechanism society uses to maintain the standards of conduct necessary to protect individuals and the community. This system is comprised of the governmental agencies that have been given formal responsibility to control crime: police and sheriff's departments, judges, prosecutors and their staffs, defense offices, jails and prisons, and probation and parole agencies. This system operates by discovering, identifying, and apprehending suspects, and processing them through the courts (prosecuting) with a finding of guilty or not guilty. If found guilty, those members of society violating legislated societal rules are sentenced. The system has three generalized and separately organized units consisting of *police*, *courts*, and *corrections*.

4

There are, however, broader implications of the term *Criminal Justice System*. A system is merely a group of parts operating in coordination to accomplish a set of goals. Many public and private agencies and citizens outside of *police*, *courts*, and *corrections* are—or ought to be—involved in reducing and preventing crime, the primary goal of criminal justice. These agencies and persons, when dealing with issues related to crime reduction and prevention, plus the traditional triad of police, courts, and corrections, make up a much broader concept of the criminal justice system.

A state legislature, for example, becomes part of this broader criminal justice system when it considers and debates proposed laws that might affect any area of criminal justice activities. In addition, executive agencies of the state, educational administrative units, welfare departments, youth service agencies, recreation departments, community organizations, union offices, neighborhood action groups, and employers may also be important functionaries in the broader system.

On an individual level, the criminal justice system frequently fails, yet there is no denying that it is relatively successful on a mass scale. If it had truly failed, society would be completely shattered.

The three general parts of the criminal justice system are by no means independent of each other, since the activities of each have a direct effect on the others. The criminal justice system is interrelated through a relatively smooth sequence of events usually put into motion when the police identify and arrest a violator of the law, which then necessitates court action. The court hears the case, and if a conviction results, the law violator is sentenced and referred to the proper correctional agency.

Not only is there a sequential association between units of the system, but also there are cross-directional associations. For example, the success of corrections will determine whether a convicted person will again become police business. It will also influence the courts in their sentencing. In addition, police activities and practices are subject to court

5

scrutiny, and such activities are often determined by court decision.

Generally speaking, the police are charged with the *detection, identification,* and *apprehension* of law violators; courts *hear cases, weigh evidence, interpret law, determine guilt or innocence* and when guilt is the finding, the sentence may be suspended or, if a sentence is imposed, it may be probation, a fine, incarceration, or some combination of these. Corrections is charged with *detention* and *rehabilitation* or *reintegration* into society of the offender. This is obviously an oversimplification of the process, but it does place in perspective the generalized role of each unit within the criminal justice system. Although the criminal process is a rather orderly progression of events, it is more complicated and sophisticated than the foregoing may imply.

In meeting their responsibilities the police become involved in complicated administrative and operational processes, such as crime prevention, patrol, investigation, and various tactical operations. In addition, police activities are always controlled and influenced by law and interpretations of law. The court process involves determination of jurisdiction, prosecution, defense, and procedural processes, such as filing the information, arraignment, trial, sentencing, appeal, etc. Corrections involves pretrial investigations, probation, parole, detention, revocation, and many treatment activities.

The criminal justice system will be given indepth coverage in subsequent chapters. The important points to recognize now are: 1) The police are but one of the three related units within the system; 2) The system includes police, courts, and corrections; 3) Each unit has different but related responsibilities; 4) The success of each unit influences and is influenced by the success of the others; and 5) The overall objective of all units is the control of crime and disorder.

The primary focus of this book is on the police or the law enforcement function, but this should not suggest that courts and corrections are less important. To achieve the optimum, it is obvious that efficiency in all is imperative.

POLICE

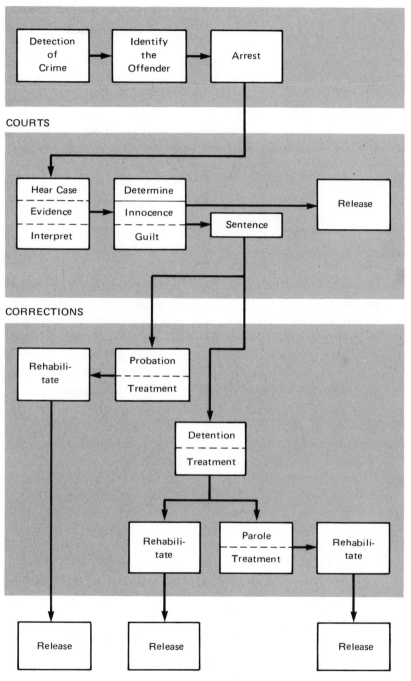

COURTS

CORRECTIONS

7

The police, however, hold a position of primary importance since they usually initiate action and are directly involved with the public. They are charged with performing their functions where all eyes are upon them. Most important, the police represent our first line of defense against criminality and disorder.

Since this is a time of increasing crime, increasing social unrest, and increasing public sensitivity to both, it is concurrently a time when police work is important, complicated, conspicuous, and delicate.

LAW

The foregoing discussion of law enforcement and the criminal justice system continually referred to *law*. In fact, the entire system evolved as a result of law, and its existence is controlled and directed by law. Therefore, to fully understand and appreciate law enforcement and criminal justice, we must have a full understanding of law, its definition, and its development.

Law is a blanket term for a far-reaching and complex concept that encompasses many types of law and relates to society, customs, and justice.

Black's Law Dictionary defines law simply as "that which is laid down, ordained, or established" and "that which is obeyed and followed by all citizens, subject to sanctions or legal consequences, is a law."[1] Certainly, this oversimplifies the concept, and we must explore its development, nature, and purposes to fully appreciate it as it relates to the role of law enforcement in our modern society.

"Law" is a general term used in several contexts. For example, there is the law of contradiction which means that

[1] Henry Campbell Black, *Black's Law Dictionary* (St. Paul, Minnesota: West Publishing Company, 1951), p. 1028.

8

a proposition cannot be both true and false, the law of gravity, and the laws of the universe. Of course, the law that concerns us does not deal with scientific principles or philosophic concepts. Instead, it deals with those principles or codes of conduct considered beneficial to society.

It is significant that the use of the word "law" always relates to what is right. The French translation of law is "droit" and is defined as right. The German word for law is "recht" which also means right. We can infer that law, like morality, tells us what is right or what is wrong. In other words, law is one means of controlling conduct and is usually supported by morality. For example, the killing of another human being, without justification recognized as acceptable, is a violation against morality as well as being unlawful.

Law is essential to society and forms the basis of a democracy. Democratic law, based on the wishes of the citizenry, attempts to balance individual freedom and the prevention of acts that infringe upon the freedom of others.

Although morality and law both relate to human conduct, they are quite different, and it is this difference that imposes the need for police or law enforcement officials. Morality is "spiritual" and not subject to man-made regulations; morality can be considered internal and law, external. If law is to create human harmony and to assure adherence to certain societal norms, there must exist machinery to effect such conduct. Law enforcement, law enforcement agencies, and the criminal justice system comprise this machinery.

Generally speaking, the laws that police are charged with enforcing can be categorized as *malum prohibitum* or *malum in se*. The former prohibits conduct even though it is not inherently immoral. There is nothing inherently immoral about driving 25 miles per hour in a 20 mile per hour zone. It becomes unlawful because a statute or ordinance makes it so. *Malum in se*, however, refers to conduct which in itself is wrong. Murder, for example, is inherently and essentially evil quite apart from whether or not it is defined as criminal conduct by the state.

ORIGIN OF LAW

The beginnings of law are lost in obscurity. Laws of some kind were necessary before historians arose, and the slow but steady growth of legal customs would in any event have been too gradual to have attracted the attention of historians even if they had existed.

The forces behind the early laws may be said to be those of custom and might. In this respect private law in its infancy bears a striking resemblance to the International Law of today. With no general tribunal to enforce the principles of this branch of law, its existence at all depends on the fact that nations will generally follow the settled customs governing relations between states. In cases of disputes the stronger nation will force its views upon the weaker.

The same situation existed among primitive people in their private dealings. It was soon appreciated that people could not live together in society without some rules governing their respective rights and liabilities and their dealings with each other. The rules arose gradually and eventually acquired the force of customs. They were generally followed by the members of the community, but when they were not, their enforcement fell upon the party injured by the breach.

As this country was being settled, we adapted from England the form of custom or case law (case law referring to laws resulting from adjudged court cases). This was the origin of American law, but certainly not of law itself. Actually, the legal tradition the settlers brought with them had evolved over a period of centuries and dated back to ancient times and early tribal customs. The customs of the early tribes, although not written, did constitute law as we define it, since the customs were a form of social control. Of course, in these early tribes, the chief was usually the strongest member, and it was his wish, whether contradictory or not, that often became the law of the tribe. This law may not have represented the will of the tribe, but conformance to the king's rule did, in effect, represent conformance to the law of the tribe.

As the tribes became more socialized and complex, there was an increased need for social control, and each member was required by custom, or chief's rule, to conform to certain standards of action which were conducive to the comfort of all. Eventually, the complexity of the society and customs necessitated the writing down of laws, so that all people would be aware of their responsibilities.

Hammurabi, King of Babylon around 2100 B.C., codified in writing customs deemed necessary for order and adherence to the king's rule. Hammurabi's Code is the oldest known form of written law. (See Appendix C.)

The Roman occupation, the influence of Norman invaders and conquerors of the eleventh century, and the subsequent development of England all influenced the evolution of law. By the seventeenth century, the basis for English law was fairly well established in both statutory law as well as case law. It was this legal tradition that the settlers brought with them as they settled in America.

The development of law in the United States was not as smooth a transition from English precedents as the foregoing might imply. English law was far too complex to be useful to our early settlers dating from 1607 to 1775. There were few lawyers and fewer law books. By and large, lawyers were distrusted and were even barred from serving in some colonial legislatures. The law as it existed then was designed to fit the relatively simple needs of the people. It was made, interpreted, and enforced by laymen. The period of the Revolutionary War (1775–1783) served to widen the gap between English and American law. In fact, citing of English court decisions was very unpopular and was even prohibited by statute in some states. It was not until some years later that the English common law achieved any measure of acceptance in America. It did come into vogue around 1820, and some states adopted it by Constitution or by statute.

The Declaration of Independence (see Appendix D) brought forward a novel idea: the notion that all people stand equal before the law. It advanced the concept that the people have certain rights, that the purpose of government is to secure

11

these rights, and that government is the agent of the people not their master. These basic concepts were incorporated in the Constitution of the United States. The Constitution was a direct outgrowth of a deep distrust which the people had in government as they had known it. The Constitution created a republic as the basic structure of government, with supreme power residing in the citizens who were entitled to vote for officials who in turn would be held responsible to the electorate. The basic standard for this structure of government is democracy, the rule of the majority.

At the same time, the founding fathers recognized the necessity for some limitation on majority rule. Otherwise, a minority would be completely at the mercy of the majority and would have only those rights allowed them by the majority. Therein lies one of the great strengths of the Constitution. It operates as a limitation on majority rule and *defines* certain fundamental rights for the purpose of maintaining and protecting those rights. It sets standards for all three branches of the republic and delineates not only what they do but what they may not do. It is the "Supreme Law of the Land," and with all its alleged imperfections, it has served this country well since it became operative in March 1789.

TYPES OF LAW

To fully appreciate the significance and complexities of law and to place the police role in proper perspective, familiarity with several types of law is important. The types listed are not conclusive, but do include those which are of interest in the study of law enforcement.

As implied previously, law can be divided into two broad general categories: 1) natural law and 2) human law.

Natural law refers to that law which is independent of enacted law or of the systems peculiar to any one society. Instead it is discoverable through man's rational intelligence and stems from his nature.[2] Natural law is a constant, unchanging concept, which exists only in pure form.

[2] Henry Campbell Black, p. 1177.

12

Human law often reflects natural law, but specifically refers to law that has been formally established by man. Human law, like human beings, is imperfect and does change as the needs or desires of people change.

Natural law is an abstract concept that has little or no applicability in our present diversified and complex society. Human law, however, is relevant as it is applied to indicate society's desires. Human law can be subdivided into additional categories. Of greatest significance to the law enforcement student are criminal law, civil law, common law, case law, statutory law, constitutional law, and administrative law.

Criminal law deals with crimes and defines actions that are contrary to the public peace and safety. Criminal law also specifies penalties or punishment to be imposed upon offenders. Obvious examples of violations of criminal law include murder, rape, robbery, burglary, and larceny, which are concurrently called criminal acts or offenses.

Civil law is commonly considered as that law governing private relationships or disputes between private individuals concerning liability. Officially, however, civil law relates to the private rights of individuals in a community and to legal proceedings in connection with these rights. In early times civil law was the law governing the citizens of the particular governmental unit in contrast to laws applied in cases between citizens. Civil law cases are usually personal actions for the purpose of compelling payment, recovery, or redress of private and civil rights. An example of civil action would be the demand that payment be received from another person or entity responsible for personal injury. A civil case is brought to court in the form of a *suit* or a legal claim in which the plaintiff pursues the redress of an injury or the enforcement of a right.

Common law originally referred to the medieval judicial concept that law administered by the king's courts was the customary law of the kingdom. As such, common law is law derived from or based upon custom rather than enactments of a legislature. The authority of common law was derived

13

solely from usages and customs, which the courts often recognized and confirmed. The American common law, derived from English law, has been modified with time to meet changing American needs.

Case law refers to that law which is established as the result of adjudged cases or judicial decisions. Case law involves the setting of judicial precedents, meaning that a principle of law has been declared by a court to serve as a rule for analogous cases or cases under similar circumstances. The English common law was built on precedent or became case law as a result of court action.

Statutory law refers to enacted legislation. To become law, a bill must be introduced and voted upon by a legislative body such as the Federal Congress or the law-making body of a state. Originating from elected officials, statutory law ideally represents the will of the public. Of course, this is not always true since pressure groups or powerful business enterprises often influence legislative bodies sufficiently to get special interests laws passed. The enactment of statutory law, though imperfect, is the best channel available to the public for fulfilling needs that can be satisfied by law.

Constitutional law, simply stated, is law or regulations found within the Federal and all state constitutions. Generally speaking, constitutional law refers to the judicial interpretations of such constitution. Constitutional law is very important to law enforcement because it places certain limitations on police precedures and defines individual rights that must be protected. Limitations refer to the Supreme Court's interpretation of such constitutional provisions as protection against unreasonable search and seizure, the guarantee of due process of law, and others. Constitutional law is fundamental, and no other law can supersede it or violate its principles and provisions.

Administrative law outlines the nature, duties, and responsibilities of offices or units of government. In the United States government there are laws that deal with such things as collection of the revenue, military regulations, and activities of all units of government. Police departments, like all organizations, have established administrative laws that prescribe certain responsibilities and prohibit certain activities. These are usually referred to as rules and regulations, but within an organization they have the same effect as law, often prescribing penalties for violators.

THE POLICE AND LAW

The primary responsibility of the police and most law enforcement agencies, and, in fact, the principle reason for their existence, is to enforce criminal law. In fact, the entire criminal justice system exists as a result of criminal law, because the system is the mechanism for handling violations and violators.

This does not mean the police are concerned only with criminal law. Traffic regulations are not normally thought of as criminal, but the police must devote a considerable amount of their time and resources to traffic control. The police, like all law enforcement agencies, are restricted by *constitutional* law, and their official acts must be able to withstand the test of constitutionality. They must conform to *administrative* law as established by the department or the government unit which they represent. Familiarity with *civil* law is imperative because all law enforcement agencies must be able to identify it as such and must not confuse it with criminal law. In addition, the police are often called upon to describe civil law to citizens and to inform them of their rights of redress and to describe legal proceedings that can be initiated. The police must also be knowledgeable in other types of regulatory law such as licensing, building codes, and health codes so that violations can be referred to the proper governmental agency.

LAW AND PUBLIC OPINION

From the foregoing, it is quite clear that law depends on custom, preserves custom, and generally has the approval of the people it serves. It stands, therefore, that for law to be effective, it must have general public support and must coincide with the customs, needs, and desires of society. A law that does not serve society *need not and should not be law.*

Public opinion should, and does, make laws effective or render them useless. An excellent and well-known example of this is the Eighteenth Amendment to the Constitution of the United States which prohibited the sale, manufacture, and transportation of intoxicating liquor. The unpopular law was widely and openly disobeyed until public opinion actually forced its repeal.

There are also many laws on the books, such as the Sunday "Blue Laws" (prohibiting hunting, spectator sports, retail sales, etc., on Sunday), which have lost much of their usefulness because, in light of present customs, beliefs, and desires, the need for them is not as great as it once was. As a result, these laws are ignored by both the public and the police. They are rendered useless because public opinion is not behind them.

Laws not related to present needs are not only useless, but they can be quite harmful. The police are placed in the position of having to decide which laws are beneficial to society and in turn enforcing only those. Not only is this a burden for the police, but also it places too much power in their hands, which may ultimately lead to dissension and disrespect for both the law and the police. The law should be influenced by public opinion, not the police. Useless, outmoded, and unpopular laws should be repealed by legislative bodies, and the police should enforce all laws. If law is to serve the public, it must relate to their needs, desires, demands, and it must be enforced by the police.

This advocacy of societal control of law should not imply justification of disobedience to the law. If we recognize and accept the need for law, we must also be willing to accept the consequences resulting from disobedience of the law. No matter how justified the cause, civil disobedience is a violation of the law, and prescribed punishment should be administered. More emphatically, *violence in protesting a law is never justified.* The society should cause the repeal or modification of undesirable laws, but such changes should result from lawful processes such as voting or peaceful persuasion.

FORMAL POLICE AUTHORITY

In the context of this book, police authority is synonymous with the term police power as both relate to the legal authority for having police and for establishing law enforcement agencies.

In countries like England and France, it is relatively simple to identify the legal basis of police authority because law enforcement operates under a centralized government and all police are under national control. In the United States, with government fragmented into various jurisdictional levels and geographical divisions, there is no general "police authority" law; we must refer to the laws and ordinances of the many jurisdictional units of government: national, state, county, and municipal.

The laws pertaining to police and police authority become particularly confusing at the local level because many states have various classes of municipalities, each with its own regulations governing the police. For example, Pennsylvania local governments are classed as boroughs; townships of the first, second, and third class; and cities of the first, second, and third class. There are state laws pertaining to police authority that are general to all local governments. Confusing, however, are additional state laws that are peculiar to each category of local government and that very frequently differ from each other.

At the risk of inaccuracy due to oversimplification, the general statement may be made that the sources of the law controlling police agencies fall into three main divisions:

1. The Federal Constitution, related statutes, and judicial decisions outline the powers, duties, and limitations of the national police agencies.
2. The state constitutions, related statutes, and judicial decisions outline the legal rights, duties, and powers of the police officer; establish the nature of his office; and govern

17

the organization and administration of state police agencies and state controlled municipal police departments.

3. In general, municipal charters and ordinances govern the organization, administration, and operations of municipal police departments.

There are numerous exceptions to these generalities, but it is relatively safe to think in terms of such divisions when discussing police authority in general.

FEDERAL LAW ENFORCEMENT

The Federal Constitution has no specific provision for the existence of law enforcement agencies at the federal, state, or local level of government. Therefore, by virtue of the Tenth Amendment to the United States Constitution, such power is reserved to the states. Because of the Tenth Amendment, we can say that the primary source for police authority is the state. (See Appendix B.)

The Federal Congress does, however, have the implied police power which authorizes the establishment of law enforcement agencies to carry out their responsibilities as outlined by the Constitution. Even though the Constitution does not specifically provide for federal law enforcement agencies, Congress can establish such agencies in order to execute or enforce the provisions of the Constitution. This implied power is derived from Article I, Section 8, of the Constitution which states:

> To make all laws which shall be necessary and proper for carrying into execution the foregoing powers, vested by this Constitution in the Government of the United States, or in any Department or officer thereof.

Therefore, since Article I, Section 8, of the Constitution established the power to coin money and punish counterfeiters, Congress was legally able to establish the Secret Service for investigative and enforcement purposes. Like the Secret Service, all other federal law enforcement agencies have evolved from the same police authority basis.

18

Other Articles deal more specifically with the authority to enforce provisions of the Constitution. For example, Article XIII, Section 2, reads, "Congress shall have power to enforce this article by appropriate legislation." Article XIV, Section 5, reads, "The Congress shall have power to enforce by appropriate legislation, the provisions of this article." Generally, however, the authority to establish federal law enforcement agencies is based on the implied power in Article I, Section 8, Paragraph 18. The Alcohol and Tobacco Tax Division was established to enforce liquor tax violations, tobacco tax violations, and the National Firearms Act. The Federal Bureau of Narcotics was established to supervise the laws governing narcotics, etc.

STATE POLICE AUTHORITY

As indicated previously, the states possess primary police authority and have established the police systems within the states. Normally, each state has created or allowed for the creation of municipal police departments for cities and sheriffs to enforce the law in the rural areas. When doing this, the state constitution or state law usually defines a police officer, outlines his powers and duties, and imposes constitutional limitations on the office. Beyond this, the state usually reserves the power of administration, organization, and operations to the local government.

There are, however, several exceptions to this rule of local control, and some states do impose strict supervision upon local police agencies. Additionally, those states that did not originally retain some supervisory control have subsequently passed legislation doing just that. A recent trend, for example, has been the passage of state legislation requiring minimum standards for selection, training, or education of local police officers. Such state control not only forces improvement but also usually provides the necessary resources for improvement.

The state, of course, also has the power to establish state police agencies and to pass legislation pertaining to the operation, management, organization, and supervision of such agencies. Some states have established state police agencies which practice full police powers throughout the rural areas of the state. Other states have established highway patrols and have made county government responsible for general policing of the rural areas. In both situations, municipalities have the responsibility for enforcement of the law within their jurisdiction.

States have also established special law enforcement agencies to enforce specific laws and to assist local law enforcement. Many states, for example, have agencies for enforcing narcotics violations, liquor violations, etc. Many states, especially those with highway patrols, have an organized criminal investigation division to enforce state laws and to assist local law enforcement.

LOCAL POLICE AUTHORITY

As mentioned previously, authority for the existence of local police agencies is found in individual state constitutions. While the state constructs the framework within which local police can exist, the local government establishes operational procedures and administration.

Some states exercise more control than others, but usually the local police officer is in reality a state officer because he derives his authority from the state. Many city or county charters detail precisely police powers and responsibilities, but in actuality the local charters merely restate or clarify the state constitution and related statutes.

Although actual operation is usually under local control, there are some cities that are directly under state control. Among such cities are St. Louis and Baltimore. Even then, however, the degree of control varies from city to city and from state to state.

LEGAL RESTRICTIONS

Police authority or power is reserved to the states, and the authority to establish federal law enforcement agencies is implied to Congress in the United States Constitution. However, such authority is not unlimited or without safeguards. Our forefathers were very concerned about the possible development of a "police state," and so certain undeniable rights of all citizens were placed in the original ten amendments to the Constitution, more commonly known as the Bill of Rights.

The Bill of Rights and related judicial decisions do limit police authority and do protect citizens against the possibility of a "police state." In addition, subsequent legislation has established additional civil rights which define or guarantee certain freedoms for all citizens.

Police power and action cannot conflict with the rights of the individual. Individual fundamental rights include such liberties as freedom of religion, speech, press, assembly, and petition; right to bear arms; due process of law; speedy jury trial; indictment only by grand jury; no excessive bail or fine; no cruel or unusual punishment; no double jeopardy by retrial for the same offense; and the right of the people to be secure in their persons, houses, papers, and effects against unreasonable searches and seizures.

Formal police authority is based primarily upon statutory law that gives the police the power to arrest. The authority to conduct investigations and the guidelines for determining sufficiency of legal cause to make arrests are typically based upon court decisions, which provide a legal framework within which the police exercise their statutory power. This combination of statutes and court decisions establishes the limits of police authority. There is no lawful basis for police action outside those limits.

At times it may seem expedient to the police to act outside these limits, but regardless of the situation they must not do so even for the purpose of restoring peace to the community. To overstep the limits encourages disrespect for the law and for the police.

The police do have the authority to use force in securing compliance with the law and this authority is, in fact, basic to their role in maintaining public order. This awesome but essential authority carries with it the responsibility of using only that force absolutely necessary in any given situation in order to achieve a legal objective.

The most frequent occasion when the police must use force is in making arrests. The potential consequence of the use of such force demands that it be exercised with the greatest degree of discretion. Unfortunately, most police organizations provide little or no guidance for their police officers relative to the manner and amount of force that should be used. For example, in most jurisdictions police officers may shoot and kill escaping felons irrespective of the actual danger the felon may impose to the officer and others. Needless to say, such extreme force, although within the legal authority of the police, should be used discriminately and dependent upon inherent danger to others.

Authority must be accompanied by accountability to insure that it remains within the limits defined in its original creation. The police are accountable in three ways: 1) they are responsible to governing bodies that provide their formal basis of authority; 2) their exercise of authority is subject to judicial review in civil damage cases arising out of police misconduct, by courts refusing to admit illegally acquired evidence in criminal trials, or through prosecution of offending officers; and 3) the unique relationship between the people and the police requires that the police be answerable to the public if their authority is to be respected and accepted by the people.[3]

POLICE DISCRETION

It is a well-known fact that the police in the United States exercise considerable discretion during their daily activities. The decisions they make actually define the limits of the

[3] National Advisory Commission on Standards and Goals, *Police* (Washington, D.C.: U.S. Government Printing Office), p. 18.

criminal justice process and have a profound effect upon the overall administration of justice as it affects individuals. Police discretion is paradoxical. It appears to flout legal commands, yet it is necessary because of limited police resources, the ambiguity and breadth of criminal statutes, the informal expectations of legislatures, and the often conflicting demands that are received from the public.

Many police administrators would like to deny that discretion is practiced within their organization. They would like the public to believe that they enforce the letter of the law equally in every situation and with every individual. It is obvious to all, however, that the police do exercise discretion based upon each situation. The police are *decision makers*, and they exercise discretion in resolving conflicts arising out of violations of the law.

The police have received little direction from either legislatures or the judiciary relative to the practice of their authority. Statutes defining police authority to arrest, for example, are couched in mandatory rather than discretionary terms in all but a few states. Judicial decisions in cases where police discretion has been at issue have been confined generally to the immediate facts of the case, and except for an occasional imprecise dicta, have ignored larger policy considerations regarding police law enforcement administration. Cases involving such issues as the interrogation of suspects, police lineups, and search and seizure of evidence frequently result in decisions in which police needs are not fully considered. Yet, in reality, they are expected to be guidelines for police activities.

Many police organizations have developed operational and procedural manuals, but these generally limit themselves to controversial or mechanical aspects of the police task. It is primarily through the allocation of available resources and unwritten policies that most police agencies establish enforcement and service objectives on a priority basis.

The decisions an officer makes on a daily basis have a profound influence upon the lives of those with whom he has official contact. For example, through his discretionary power he does make decisions on when to search, to arrest, or to do nothing. Policemen are not lawyers, but they are held accountable for complete knowledge of the law as it relates to criminal procedure. If they fail to properly apply the legal principles enunciated in myriad appellate court decisions, cases are dismissed and criminal justice resources are wasted. Worst of all, police officers may never know why cases are dismissed, as they often receive no direction to avoid future errors.

It sometimes seems that courts are generally more concerned with the rights of individual defendants than with the effect their decisions will have on law enforcement operations. While those decisions may define the limits of police authority, they are rarely structured to provide significant guidance to officers in the infinite variety of complex situations that might in some way be affected by a particular court decision.

It is obvious that police agencies should analyze court decisions and concurrently develop policy statements that define police authority and provide guidelines for the exercise of discretion. Such guidelines will better assure uniformity of decisions and should eliminate unnecessary discretion.

If police organizations fail to establish police guidelines, officers are forced to establish their own policy based on their individual understanding of the law and their individual perception of the police role. Errors in judgment may be an inherent risk in the exercise of discretion, but such errors can be minimized by definitive policies that clearly establish limits to discretion.

The task of the police executive is one of the most difficult in society. He must not only use limited resources to deal with increasing crime, but he must do so within budgetary, organizational, and legal constraints that limit his discretion in establishing objectives and departmental priorities.

The police chief would receive valuable assistance if state and local governments would determine broad policy and give the police executive the authority and administrative flexibility to establish objectives and priorities and to organize and direct his agency with the greatest freedom possible.

While it is desirable to have the criminal law clearly express effective and enforceable limits of conduct, the fact that it does not always do so requires the police to establish enforcement policies and provide some clarification to the meaning of the law. As long as those policies are openly adopted, reduced to writing, and applied in a nondiscriminatory manner, the public and governing bodies are assured that the law enforcement is being administered properly by the police.

There are also many laws in the books that are no longer enforced. In those cases, a decision to arrest after a long period of enforcement inactivity could be viewed as an abuse of discretion and could raise constitutional questions. Furthermore, unenforced yet frequently violated laws may create disrespect for all law. Police agencies, therefore, should review all criminal laws and either enforce them or seek to have them rescinded.

The police also have a role in the determination of new laws that may be passed by state and local legislatures. The police should attempt to prevent enactment of criminal laws that, as a practical matter, are unenforceable or that will unduly deplete police resources. Police executives should determine the impact that any proposed criminal statute or ordinance will have on police operations and should subsequently submit recommendations to the law-making body.

ARREST DISCRETION

It is the individual police officer who usually makes the decision relative to taking a person into custody. In the absence of departmental guidelines, the officer must rely on the language of the law as interpreted by the judiciary and refined by informal direction from the police department and local prosecutors. This authority places the individual police officer among the most important decision makers in society.

Only in the police service is such tremendous authority delegated without administrative guidelines. Such guidelines are usually not developed because of the difficulty in formulating policy or because of the belief by the police chief that unlimited discretion is preferable to written policy.

Crime does not look the same on the street as it does in a legislative chamber. It is difficult for a police organization to establish rules covering the infinite variety of situations involving criminal violations. Even more important, extensive rules that eliminate all discretion invite injustice by failing to consider all circumstances surrounding individual cases.

Unnecessary discretion should, however, be eliminated and appropriate control established to provide guidance. To eliminate unnecessary discretion, police administrators should identify situations where the officer's discretion to make physical arrests is restricted or eliminated. Alternatives to physical arrest might include citations, application for complaint, warning, or diversion to another governmental organization.

In determining discretion guidelines, it is important that situations as well as particular crimes be identified. For example, when a victim declines to prosecute in an assault case the officer may be directed not to make a physical arrest. On the other hand, the police chief may require arrest in all assault cases. Another example where discretion might be limited involves crimes where the victim's interest is primarily one of reimbursement, rather than the desire to prosecute. Examples of such crimes might include shoplifting, vandalism, bogus checks, and minor larcenies.

Policies for situations requiring application of alternatives to arrest should not, however, be rigid. It must be recognized that policy involves nothing more than *guidelines* from which deviation may be justified. Any deviation from nonarrest policy, however, should ensure that the officer who judges the arrest to be in the public interest obtain permission at the supervisory or command level.

It must be remembered that to be acceptable constitutionally, any guidelines defining arrest policy must be based upon rules that are nondiscriminatory and jurisdictionwide in application. If, for example, it is thought that rigid enforcement of the curfew law is contrary to the best interest of the community and the law enforcement organization, guidelines should be written that define enforcement criteria. Officers, for example, might be restricted from arresting a youth en route home from an organized activity, yet might be required to make an arrest in a situation where youths congregate or cause disturbances.

Of paramount importance, is that officers do use discretion relative to making arrests. Therefore, it is in the best interest of the community being served that discretionary guidelines be developed by the chief executive of the police department. Without such guidelines, discretion may become arbitrary and certain groups, persons, or businesses may be given preferential treatment. This must be avoided.

Summary

The enforcement of the law is one of the most influential mechanisms for social control in existence. Yet, inconsistent with its significance, law enforcement remains a subject that the public knows less about than any other governmental function.

Though the concept of law enforcement is most visibly manifested in the presence of the law enforcement or police officer, there are other agencies involved in crime control and the maintenance of order. These agencies are referred to collectively as the "criminal justice system." This system has three separately organized units consisting of the police, courts, and corrections. Generally speaking, the police are charged with the detection, identification, and apprehension of law violators; courts hear cases, weigh evidence, interpret law, and determine guilt or innocence; and corrections is charged with detention and rehabilitation of the offender.

The entire criminal justice system evolved as a result of law, and its existence is controlled and directed by law. Law is essential to society and forms the basis of a democracy. Democratic law, based on the wishes of the citizenry, attempts to balance individual freedom and the prevention of acts that infringe upon the freedom of others.

Law can be divided into two broad general categories: 1) natural law and 2) human law. Human law is of concern in law enforcement, and types of human law include criminal law, civil law, common law, case law, statutory law, and administrative law. The type of law of most concern to the police is criminal law and, in fact, the entire criminal justice system exists as a result of criminal law.

The authority for the existence of local and state police generally is contained in state constitutions, since the Federal Constitution makes no provision for the existence of law enforcement agencies. Federal police agencies have been established by the implied police power granted by the

Constitution which authorizes the establishment of law
enforcement agencies to carry out the responsibilities
assigned Congress.

Formal police authority is based primarily upon statutory
law that gives the police the power to arrest. The authority to
engage in police activities leading to arrest is typically based
upon court decisions. Such statutes and court decisions
provide the legal framework within which the police must
work. Although this framework does permit the use of force in
making arrests, the force permitted is only that which is
absolutely necessary.

In performing their tasks, the police exercise considerable
discretion, which actually defines the limits of the criminal
justice process. It is imperative, therefore, that police
administrators develop policy statements that define guidelines
for the exercise of discretion.

Discussion Questions

1. What is the role of law enforcement in our democratic society?
2. Define law enforcement and the criminal justice system.
3. What are the responsibilities of each unit of the criminal justice system?
4. Why does the criminal justice system owe its existence to law?
5. What are the different types of law?
6. What purpose does law serve?
7. What types of law are of concern to the police?
8. What is the relationship between law and public opinion?
9. How do the police derive their authority?
10. Discuss police discretion and its effect on citizens and the criminal justice process.

2

Development of
American Law Enforcement

Law enforcement as we know it today has its roots within the mysterious past. Law enforcement agencies evolved slowly throughout ancient, medieval, and modern history in response to the social needs of an ever-advancing civilization.

Understanding of the continuous but often haphazard development of law enforcement is important since it provides an indepth appreciation of the police role and function in modern society. Familiarity with the history of law enforcement helps emphasize that law enforcement came into existence as a social need and, concurrently, as a social function. Just as law enforcement evolved in response to past social needs, it is presently changing to meet changing social needs. Knowledge of the history of law enforcement is important because an understanding of its early development helps us to better understand and appreciate present changes.

A deep appreciation for the law enforcement heritage will also instill a feeling of pride in the profession and in its recent accomplishments. Such pride will enhance law enforcement and place it in proper perspective with other academic and professional disciplines.

ANCIENT HISTORY OF LAW ENFORCEMENT
(TO 500 A.D.)

EARLY TRIBAL LIFE

There is ample historical evidence to indicate that a form of law enforcement was familiar even to early tribal people. Of course, people at that time did not employ enforcement as we understand it, but for all general purposes they were involved in the principle of law enforcement. Archaeological findings such as cave drawings and early tablets give evidence that tribes were concerned with protection and the enforcement of social codes. Most needs were based on survival, but the concept of protection from marauders and each other can certainly be related to a form of policing.

Many ancient tribes probably looked to their chief for protection and the preservation of social order. As such, the chief's doctrines or commands were obeyed for fear of admonishment or even punishment. In this sense, the chief established law, enforced law, and also adjudicated law.

As ancient society became more complex, additional rules of conduct had to be established to promote harmony. Concurrent with the increasing size and complexity of society, it became more difficult to administer tribal custom. As a result, the chief probably designated certain individuals or groups of individuals to seek violators and bring them before him. In a sense, these military aids were law enforcement officers. Of course, the rules laid down by tribal leaders were not laws as such but were customs which law later reflected.

Law enforcement developed concurrently with law, since law had to exist before it could be enforced. In other words, enforcement methods were developed in order to achieve conformance to the emerging body of law.

FORMALIZED LAW

The existence of formal law and, therefore, the concept of law enforcement can be traced to ancient Babylon. There is archaeological proof that 2,000 years before the birth of Christ, Hammurabi, King of Babylon, compiled a legal code dealing with such things as commercial law, land law, and criminal law. More specifically, the laws dealt with such things as responsibilities of the individual to the group and private dealings between individuals. There were also provisions of penalties of the retributive type exemplifying the "lex talionis" or the law of the talon. Messengers were referred to as those responsible for carrying out the law.

Although the Code of Hammurabi shows a surprisingly high development of the law, it is far from representing the highest point reached by Babylonian law. This can be easily appreciated when we remember that the period which elapsed between the writing of this code and the final overthrow of Babylon by the Persians, is approximately equal to the total period so far included in the Christian era.

Extracts from the Code of Hammurabi will be found in Appendix C. The provisions of the code are also made use of in the treatment in the following sections of the various branches of the Babylonian law.

The adjective law of the Babylonians was always far less advanced than their substantive law. While many of the provisions of the latter may not compare unfavorably with modern legal conceptions, the former represents a low grade of legal development.

The administration of the courts seems to have been largely in the hands of the priestly class. This was perhaps largely brought about by the numerous and complicated oaths required, both in business transactions and in legal proceedings.

No scientific system for weighing the value or truth of evidence was ever devised by the Babylonians. Witnesses seem to have acted, to a certain extent, in the capacity of jurymen, as was the case in early English law. Cases, if possible, were settled upon the authority of written instruments. To prevent their alteration an ingenious system was resorted to. Legal instruments, written on baked bricks, were made out in duplicate; these duplicates were then fastened together in such a manner that the inner one could not be reached without destroying the outer one. If it was claimed by either party that the outer tablet had been tampered with, this tablet was destroyed and the inner one exposed to view.

One of the earliest, and also one of the most distinctive branches of the law to be developed in the legal history of any race or nation, is that of Domestic Relations. The first step toward the construction of a social organization was the creation of the family. The tribe or nation was later developed as an enlargement of the family, or a combination of families, and the organization of the family served as the model for the government or the larger state. Upon such organization of the state, the unit for most purposes was the family rather than the individual. Most property was held as family rather than as individual property, and each family had its own internal government, under a head, whose almost despotic power was recognized and protected by the superior government.

It is thus apparent that among primitive people, not only did the law of Domestic Relations occupy a far more important place in the judicial system than it does among more advanced people, but also that this branch of the law was, in general, the first branch of the law to take any definite shape. Furthermore, no other set of laws gives such an insight into the habits and character of people as do those laws governing marriage and regulating the mutual rights and obligations existing between the various members of the family.

The Babylonian marriage was frankly one of purchase. The daughter was considered as valuable property for which the husband paid a purchase price to the father, or to the mother if the father was a priest. The marriage contracts dealt fully with the future property rights of the parties, sometimes even containing provisions as to a possible future divorce.

The Babylonian law clearly distinguished between real and personal property, or perhaps better, between movable and immovable property. Land was only transferred by written deeds, and a complicated system of conveyancing arose. One striking peculiarity of the Babylonian law of conveyancing was the right of the vendor at any time to repurchase his land at the original purchase price. This must have had the effect of greatly unsettling titles. This right, however, could be expressly waived in the deed at the time of sale.

Personal property was naturally of great importance in such a commercial nation as Babylon. No particular form of sale was required, possession being prima facie evidence of ownership. This system of law was much in advance either of the early Roman law or the early common law.

The Babylonian Law of Contracts was the first highly developed system dealing with this branch of jurisprudence in

36

the history of the world. Many formalities were required in the making of contracts.

The lack of slaves in the country made the creation of the relation of master and servant an important branch of contracts. The times of these contracts were generally for one year, and an advance payment was customarily paid to the servant. The laborer acted as a free agent in making the contract, but the law was strict in enforcing it, and any attempt to avoid performance on the part of servants met with severe penalties.

The Old Testament also contains many provisions of law or customs relating to property, inheritance, slaves, and even crime. Of course, these provisions reflected highly religious principles rather than just the needs of society. The enforcement of such principles was obviously the responsibility of the religious leaders or their representatives rather than of organized police forces.

GREEK INFLUENCE

Near Eastern civilizations also contributed to the development of law and law enforcement. However, the real influence occurred with modification and solidification of law by the Greeks and, ultimately, the Romans.

The early Greek city-states witnessed considerable turmoil during their existence. Much of the citizen unrest resulted from a strife between powerful groups. At various stages, rulership was intermittently rotated between a king, the wealthy merchants, and participation by free citizens. It is significant that in every case rules were established to meet the needs as understood by those in control and adherence was then enforced by military units.

Eventually, as a result of continuous wars, the city-states declined and huge kingdoms came into existence. Kings ruled and carefully controlled the lives of the people. Again, a sort of military police enforced the rules of the king.

The early Greek city-states did, however, witness some development from tribal policing to more formalized policing. For example, Pisistratus (605–527 B.C.), an early ruler of Athens, established a guard system. The responsibilities of these guards included the protection of the tower, highways, and their ruler.

Solon (639–559 B.C.) probably contributed more to the development of law enforcement than any previous leader had. Solon ruled Athens democratically and devised a system by which a general assembly of freemen passed the laws, and instituted courts in which the jury was chosen from the citizenry. On the other hand, the rulers of Sparta, the other great city-state, were completely authoritarian and personally controlled matters of justice.

ROMAN INFLUENCE

During their period of expansion, the Romans finally conquered the entire Mediterranean world. Rome imposed on the newly absorbed Greek culture its own law and organization. In doing so, the Romans had considerable influence on the development of law enforcement. The Roman's attempt to secure justice for all people was reflected in its body of law referred to as *the twelve tables* which related to such things as judicial process, ownership, inheritance, and torts. (Tort refers to willful or negligent injury to an individual's person, property, or reputation.) Magistrates were appointed to adjudicate, but they were given or assumed great latitude in exercising their powers and in laying down decisions. (See Appendix E.)

Perhaps the greatest Roman contributor to law enforcement was Caius Julius Caesar Octavianus (Octavian). He was the grandnephew and heir of Julius Caesar. In 27 B.C., the Senate decreed that his name should be Augustus which meant *exalted* or *consecrated*.

Augustus (Octavian) (63 B.C.–*14* A.D.*)* utilized a military unit called a *cohort* to serve as his army and to protect the city. A cohort was comprised of from 500 to 1,000 men, and three such cohorts were assigned to the city of Rome. The soldiers of a cohort were called *praetorians*, and these praetorians were scattered throughout Rome and were probably dressed as civilians. Civilian dress was in response to the resistance to military control and was a means of disguising the praetorians as civilians.

The many large-scale disorders in Rome during the reign of Augustus evidenced the inadequacy of existing local law enforcement and forced Augustus to improve the system. Originally, slaves under the supervision of an appointed official were expected to quell riots and disorders. Not only did this system prove totally inadequate, but also its inefficiency actually contributed to the disorder.

The praetorian guard was considered an elite group in Roman society and, therefore, Augustus was reluctant to ask it to function as riot police. As an alternative, he established the *urban cohort*. Members of both groups were selected from the military units, but standards for the praetorian guard were somewhat higher than those for the urban cohort. The urban cohort had the specific responsibilities of keeping order among the slaves and of controlling unruly citizens.

Part of Roman disorder was reflected in the devastating fires that occurred throughout the city. As he had done with riots, Augustus originally expected large groups of slaves under the direction of an appointed official to extinguish fires. The use of slaves proved totally inadequate again and finally Augustus established the *vigiles of Rome*. Rather than have this new unit assume just the fire-fighting responsibility, he also assigned them the task of policing, which was previously carried out by the urban cohort. In this sense, we see the establishment of the first *police-fire integrated service*. Their function was to control fires and to exercise police functions which included the right to arrest thieves and housebreakers as well as to control and suppress riots.

The vigiles of Rome were not selected from the military legions, and were, therefore, the first nonmilitary or civilian police force. We also see the direct implementation of home rule, because the vigiles consisted of freemen appointed to serve in that capacity. Of course, this may be also the origin of the patronage system which still plagues many police departments. (Patronage is the appointment of people to jobs as a reward for their previous favors.)

Another contribution of Augustus was his organization of the city into *wards* to facilitate the operation of government which included the police function. Such decentralization was necessary not only for organizational control, but also to reduce response time in the event of disorder. Groups of vigiles were assigned to the various wards, and we see the emergence of the police administrative concept, *division by area*. The *ward system* was used throughout the early development of law enforcement, and this concept is still common to modern law enforcement. Today, however, we commonly refer to such a division as a *precinct* rather than a ward.

A later Roman contributor to law enforcement was the Byzantine emperor Justinian (483–565 A.D.) who summarized the Roman law into what is known as *corpus juris civilis* or body of civil law. This is probably the world's most famous and influential law book. Roman law more or less contributed to the concepts of fair trial, proof of guilt, and opportunity of accused to meet his accuser.

ANCIENT PUNISHMENT

As might be expected, ancient punishment was usually quite crude, cruel, and often consisted of the infliction of pain upon the offender. In early societies, offenses were often left to the family or clan group to settle as they saw fit. As a result, the degree and kind of punishment were dependent upon the personality and strength of the person or group offended, since they were the executors. In fact, it was quite common for one clan to seek retaliatory compensation from the entire clan to which the offender belonged. The practice contributed to the beginning of the so-called family or *blood feuds* since the right of one clan to punish the other was not necessarily limited to the punishment of the individual that actually committed the offense.

As defined in the Laws of Hammurabi, ancient society held to the belief of *lex talionis* which implies *an eye for an eye* or *a tooth for a tooth*. If a person inflicted a particular injury upon another individual, the retaliatory punishment would be the infliction of the same injury upon the accused.

As society developed, certain punishments became customary for certain offenses. If a person stole, for example, he might have been punished by having his hand amputated or by some other predetermined mandate. Ancient punishment may have included such things as mutilation, partial dismemberment of the body, exposure to wild beasts, burning at the stake, and stoning to death.

ENGLISH DEVELOPMENT DURING MEDIEVAL HISTORY (500 A.D.–1500 A.D.)

ANGLO-SAXON ENGLAND

The collapse of the Roman conquest of England was followed by several hundred years of confusion and increasing barbarism. Finally, during the fifth and sixth centuries, the Angles and Saxons became conquerors and settlers rather than just marauders. They brought governmental organization to England and with it the development of local law enforcement. Policing, for the most part, was delegated to the people on the basis of mutual responsibility. The king's peace was actually the promise of protection, peace, and security to the people in return for their allegiance.

King Alfred (872–901) one of the most influential Anglo-Saxon kings, held landed proprietors responsible for the members of their household. Alfred devoted considerable energy to the task of preserving peace within his kingdom.

One of Alfred's contributions was a new body of law or *dooms* which covered a variety of subjects. His code included such provisions as the declaration of forms of punishment and the sums an offender was to be fined for committing an offense.

The customs, government, and divisions of England evolved and became firmly established during Alfred's reign. This period profoundly influenced the subsequent development of law enforcement.

   Organizational structure. Most of the people of Anglo-Saxon England lived in villages, which were known as *tuns* from which we derive our word *town*. In the tun, law enforcement was everyone's responsibility. When an offense was committed, a *hue and cry* was issued, and every able-bodied man was required to take chase or help in the apprehension of the offender. In a sense, this practice represents the first use of the *citizen's arrest*. As in earlier times, when a member of one tun committed an offense against the other tun, subsequent action was retaliatory in nature. Each tun was responsible for the actions of its members and was, therefore, punishable as an entity.

As tuns became larger and more complex, it became necessary to subdivide them into *tithings*. The tithing consisted of ten families, and responsibility for protecting the tun and maintaining peace among the tun's people was rotated among the tithings. Each tithing was held responsible for the conduct of its members and if a member committed an offense, the tithing had to make retribution. One member of the tithing was elected by the group and was called the *chief tithingman*. When his tithing was providing police services, he had the responsibility of raising the hue and cry and for executing punishment when an offender was apprehended and found guilty.

A group of ten tithings, called a *hundred*, comprised the framework for accomplishing judicial work. The *hundred's court* was responsible for rendering punishments, settling land disputes, and settling disputes between groups within

42

the hundred. The head man of the hundred was called the *reeve*. Although the king could intervene, the people generally handled disputes among and between themselves. Thus, again we see the evolution of community or local rule. It is interesting, too, that cases could be appealed to the king for settlement.

A larger geographical unit comprised of several hundreds was the *shire*. The shire was governed by an *ealdorman* who was appointed by the king or by one of the king's royal officers. An ealdorman was usually a great noble who owned extensive lands in the part of the country he governed. He was sort of a governor and, when necessary, had the power to call out the fighting force of the shire. Eventually, the ealdorman became know as the *earl*, which is a more common usage today.

The ealdorman did not, however, have complete control and authority over his shire. The king appointed a *shire-reeve* and subsequently looked upon this office as the primary liaison between the crown and the shire. The word sheriff is derived from shire-reeve and to some extent our present office of sheriff is similar to the early office of the shire-reeve. The shire-reeve had the assigned responsibilities of collecting taxes, enforcing law, and attending to all affairs of the government as viewed necessary by the king. He had the power of *posse comitatus* which allowed him to command able-bodied men of the shire to offer assistance. The shire-reeve was the king's official representative, and it was natural that he became even more powerful than the ealdorman, and eventually he became one of the most powerful political figures of the time.

This tithing system of Anglo-Saxon England can be logically compared with our present day police system which includes local police, county police, and state police. Our courts are also organized under a similar arrangement, including appeal to the federal court.

Justice. From time to time the landowners and other official men of the shire would meet to discuss and resolve a variety of problems. In addition to regular business, messages from the king were announced, and lawsuits were often settled. These meetings were referred to as the *hundred's courts, shire courts,* or the *hundred* or *shire mote.*

When a person was charged with an offense within the hundred or shire, there were generally two customary methods of determining his guilt or innocence. They were the *oath* and the *ordeal.* Both were based on the premise of an appeal to God asking him to indicate which person was telling the truth.

The oath required several people known as *compurgators* to testify relative to another's innocence or veracity. The accused would furnish a certain number of compurgators and each would then take a solemn oath that the accused was telling the truth. Evidence or the compurgator's knowledge of the event was not important as long as he would support the oath of the accused. Actually, the compurgator was a character witness and, customary to the times, the value of his support became greater if he held a high social rank or position. In other words, oaths of such men were of much greater value than the oaths of men who held a lower status in the society.

In the absence of compurgators, the courts could demand *trial by ordeal.* For example, the accused would be required to carry a red hot iron in his bare hand for a specified distance. His hand would then be bandaged for a specified length of time. Upon removing the bandages, the person was deemed innocent if by divine help the hand was healed and guilty if the hand was not healed.

Ordeal by water consisted of appropriate prayers, binding the accused with rope, and then throwing him into a body of water. If he was received by the water and sank, he was deemed innocent. If, on the other hand, the water rejected him and he floated, he was deemed guilty. In either event, the accused was quickly retrieved from the water and released or punished accordingly.

Actually, this primitive trial process was not entirely unsuccessful. Certainly the fear of ordeal led many offenders to confess their sins and admit guilt. Obviously, however, many innocent people were declared guilty or confessed to something they didn't do rather than face the ordeal. Regardless of their system's inadequacies, it is important to realize that the Anglo-Saxons were interested in achieving justice, otherwise they would not have devised any method for determining guilt. Perhaps they realized the human inability to devise a system that would achieve *true justice* and thus turned to God for wisdom and power.

Capital punishment was seldom used, but branding was quite common. Branding, however, may have been more for identification of criminals rather than for punishment. The most common form of punishment was the payment of fines. Punishment was graduated to fit the crime and depended upon the position or class of the victim. As a result, a very elaborate system of fines was developed. The more severe the crime committed, the higher the fine became. At the same time, if the position or class of the victim was high, the fine would be higher than if the victim was from a lower class. The complexity of the system is illustrated in King Alfred's *dooms*. It states, for example, that a man stabbed in the thigh will receive thirty shillings from the perpetrator. A specified amount was even payable by a murderer or his family to the family of the victim.

NORMAN INFLUENCE

In 1066, William the Conqueror invaded and conquered England. William and his predecessors had an uncanny genius for government that the Anglo-Saxons did not possess. Whereas the Anglo-Saxons were committed to local government, the Normans were more interested in national control and established a highly formal centralized bureaucracy, which unified the country's law enforcement processes.

King William (1027–1087), known as William the Conqueror, maintained the same organization of shires and hundreds but appointed his own sheriffs of the shires, or counties as the shires came to be known. At the same time, he strengthened the positions of county officials and formalized centralized control. Within a very few years Norman earls, sheriffs, barons, and knights superseded the Saxon earls and shire-reeves in official positions and as landowners.

William introduced harsh *forest laws*, under which large tracts of forest were preserved for deer hunting by the King and his nobles exclusively. The severe punishment meted out to violators of these laws caused historians to judge William's reign as tyrannical.

William also introduced the concept of a *curfew*, which required that all fires be extinguished or covered at nightfall.

In the judicial system, William added to the previously developed concepts of trial by oath and by ordeal the concept of *wager of battle* or *trial by combat*. If one man charged another with an offense, the court would determine the truth on the basis of the resulting battle between the accused and the accuser. The person winning the battle was deemed in the right and the person losing was deemed to be in the wrong.

The *doomsday book* was another legal contribution of William. This book was essentially a tax roll listing the landowners and the extent of their lands. It is significant of his great authority that William was able to compel the people of England to give the kind of information that people even today frequently decline or hesitate to give census takers. His ability to put these reports into order also illustrates the establishment of a very efficient and well-organized body of government officials.

Henry I and Legis Henrici (1100–1135). The next Norman king who significantly influenced the development of law enforcement was William's younger brother, Henry I. In fact, Henry's contributions were so pertinent that he became known as the *lawgiver*. This title was primarily a result of his issuance of the *legis henrici* which established certain offenses, such as arson, robbery, murder, false coinage, and crimes of violence, as being against the king's peace. Thus,

46

emerged the concept of *disturbance of the peace* and the idea that a person should be punished by the state rather than by the victim or his group. The legis henrici also differentiated crimes as being either *felonies* or *misdemeanors*— divisions we use today. Murder, robbery, arson, and other violent crimes were felonious, while crimes of a lesser nature were misdemeanors.

Recognizing that many lawsuits could be tried satisfactorily only in the area where the matters at issue were known, Henry established roving or traveling justices. These royal justices became known as *circuit justices* because they were sent throughout the established regular circuits. This custom of circuit judges has been customary in England ever since and was utilized also in the early American West.

ANGEVIN RULE (1154–1399)

It was during the reigns of the seven Angevin kings that the foundations of national unity were laid in England. During this period laws were further strengthened, and the processes of justice were more definitely established. This period is called Angevin in recognition of Henry II, the first of the line that reigned for nearly 245 years. Henry II was one of the most able of all the English kings, and he initiated the many reforms that led to national unity such as had not been enjoyed since Alfred.

Henry II and trial by jury (1154–1188). The reign of Henry I was followed by many years of strife and turmoil that did not end until Henry II came into power. Henry II's greatest contribution to the development of law enforcement was the foundation he laid for the jury system. Henry II reinstated the circuit justices of Henry I and at the same time improved and extended them. We see during Henry II's reign, for example, the origin of *trial by jury*. The king's justices used a new form of trial rather than by ordeal, compurgation, or wager of battle. They called this an *inquisition*. At the inquisition, persons were required to give in-

47

formation under oath on any matters requested of them by the justices. When asked to hear a case, the judges would order a number of men, usually twelve, to investigate the case and give a sworn *verdict* as to which of the people had the better right in the dispute. These selected men were known as *jurors* because they had to swear to tell the truth and were required to decide in favor of one or the other of the people involved in the case. Thus, we see the beginning of trial by jury, the jurors being peers of the defendant.

The origin of indictment by jury can also be attributed to the reign of Henry II. He issued the *assize of Clarendon,* the object of which was to introduce a reform in the punishment of crimes. It provided that when the king's justices came to the hundred's mote, twelve men from each hundred and four men from each manor in the hundred would be put upon their oath and required to give the names of any men they knew who had been accused or suspected of having committed a great crime. This allowed for the punishment of all persons committing an offense rather than of just those persons that may have been reported to the sheriff.

It was during Henry II's reign also that justices began to keep a record of the cases settled and the decisions that were given. The justices were educated men and their decisions were given on principles that were quite logical, consistent, and in comformance with the customs then existing. These decisions as laid down by the king's justices became known as *common law.* The recording of decisions based upon precedent did much to bring about conformity and uniformity in both national law and customs of the age.

The church. During this period, the church had attained practically as much power as the government. The church was so powerful that it was actually immune from normal law enforcement practices to the extent that it had its own courts to try cases concerning the clergy. These church courts had been important ever since the early Norman conquest, and it was William I who stipulated that church matters should be tried by the bishops in courts of their own rather than in hundred and shire courts. The church stipulated that all cases involving clergymen, church property, marriages, wills, inheritance, and those involving a breach of an oath should be heard by the church. Thus, we see the inauguration of *benefit of clergy*, which exempted clergy from trial or punishment except through a church court. We also see the custom of *sanctuary* that provided the fugitive from justice with immunity from arrest or apprehension if he were in a church.

The evolution of such protections is easily understood when one considers the types of punishment issued by the other courts. For example, capital punishment consisted of beheading or hanging to strangulation, being buried alive, boiling, and impaling. Lesser punishments consisted of such things as the pillory, whipping, the rack, the wheel, and the strappado.

King John and the Great Charter (1199–1216). Although King John is known as one of the worst kings of English history, his seventeen-year reign did contribute to the development of law enforcement. Because of his oppressive actions and heavy taxation, he was completely disliked by both the people and his nobles. King John imposed increasingly greater taxes upon the people and demanded that the barons fulfill military services. However, he did not lead them to war but kept them waiting until they were willing to pay a fee to go home. He even used the courts to plunder the clergy. In addition to the oppressions, the king was hateful to so many that a rebellion against him was unavoidable. Finally, as a result of pressures from the church, the noblemen and the general populace, King John gave way and signed the *Great Charter* at Runnymeade on June 15, 1215. He granted the list of demands by the church, the barons, and those drawn up by townsmen. This charter became known as the *Magna Carta* and is one of the most notable documents in history. The Magna Carta is of particular importance to law enforcement because local control was restored, trial by jury was assured, and due process of law was installed as a right of all people. (See Appendix F.) These guarantees were of such importance that they are also reflected in the fifth and sixth amendments of the Constitution of the United States.

The importance of the Magna Carta relative to the democratic philosophy was illustrated quite aptly by England and her memorial to the late President John F. Kennedy. In 1965, England set aside one acre of land to be known as Runnymeade, U.S.A. By this move, one acre of English land became the property of the United States.

King Edward I and the Statute of Winchester (1274–1307). King Edward I so greatly influenced the course of events relative to law enforcement that in this respect he can be considered the equal to Augustus. Edward I probably contributed more to legal reform and law enforcement than any person preceding him.

As a result of the increasing frequency of robberies, murders, and arsons, coupled with the reluctance of officials to arrest and prosecute, Edward issued the *Statute of Winchester.* Juries were not suppressing crime, and citizens were reluctant to convict each other or were afraid of retaliation if they accused the lords. Edward's statute dealt with this problem by making it illegal for people to conceal committed felonies or to harbor felons.

The Statute of Winchester also required that the hue and cry be raised when felonies or crimes were committed in counties, hundreds, markets, fairs, or any place where a large number of people were grouped. The statute further stipulated that ignorance of the law was no excuse, and that every county had to be efficiently governed. In conjunction with this, when a felony was committed, immediate pursuit was required that would continue from town to town and county to county until the offender was apprehended.

Of great importance to local control was a provision that held people dwelling in the county answerable for robberies and resulting damages within their area. Local responsibility was demanded, in that the whole hundred where a robbery was committed was liable for the crime. This gave additional

50

impetus for local policing since the people of the hundred needed a means to prevent crimes now that they were held responsible.

Other provisions required large towns with walls to close their gates at night and forbade persons from lodging in the suburbs or near the town except during the daytime and only then if a host vouched for him. From this evolved our concept of vagrancy and loitering laws. *Bailiffs* were mentioned as having the responsibility of checking for such people and taking appropriate action.

Watches were required to be assigned to the gate of every borough or town within the country. The statute was so specific as to say that every city would have six men at every gate, every borough would assign twelve men, and every town, six or four depending on its population. Strangers were to be arrested and delivered to the sheriff. The *night watchmen* or *bailiffs* were selected from the ranks of able-bodied citizens within the community and were required to serve but were paid for their services. On some watches, the watchmen grouped themselves together and roamed throughout the city thus forming a *marching watch* which may very well have been the first known patrol activity of a law enforcement agency. Another unique characteristic of the night watch was the eventual addition of a specialized police unit called *police des mouers* that was responsible for regulating prostitutes throughout the cities.

Another provision of the statute required that highways leading from one market town to another be cleared to a width of two hundred feet on each side so there was no place of concealment for criminals. Landlords were required to clear the roads on their land and if they did not, they were held responsible for crimes committed and required to pay a fine to the king.

The Statute of Winchester also commanded that every able-bodied man arm himself to the degree that his station in life allowed. Such ability, of course, ranged from the most sophisticated of weapons possessed by the richer people to the least sophisticated of weapons available to the poor peo-

ple. To initiate control over this army, the king stipulated
that weapons be inspected two times every two years and
that every hundred assign two *constables* to handle and inspect the weapons.

Other reforms of Edward I dealt with offenses of royal
servants, forbade the corrupt maintenance of lawsuits by
judges or sheriffs, and ordered free elections. In an attempt
to bring reform in the justice system, Edward more than
once replaced all of the sheriffs, removed many judges from
the bench, and accused nearly eight hundred officials. These
events actually were forerunners to the establishment of a
justice of the peace who was to supersede the sheriff.

The reign of Edward I marked a definite trend in the
history of common law. Previously, law had been flexible and
judges used wide and varying discretion when making decisions. Now law was developing from the decisions of justices
and from new writs issued by the chancellor. Edward's
statutes gave law order and organization and at the same
time made it more rigid. This rigidity actually paved the way
for equity in the laws of the land, replacing arbitrary decisions by justices.

Edward III and justices of the peace (1327–1377).
Under Edward III, justices of the peace were appointed to
assist itinerant justices, to help maintain the peace, and even
to try cases themselves. The office of sheriff still existed but
the justice of the peace took over much of the sheriff's former
responsibilities, and in time became much more powerful
than the sheriff. The justice of the peace could punish petty
offenses brought to his attention by an accuser, a constable,
or the policemen of the village. He could punish drunkenness
or card playing on the sabbath or the refusal to work at
harvest time. He could order a vagabond whipped. He could
force suspected persons to give bond to keep the peace or
appear in court, or he could hold them in jail until they were
tried. It was his duty to stop a riot before it became dangerous although he could not punish the rioters.

Edward III's act relative to the justice of the peace actually combined in that office the police function with the function of a judge. In fact, the justice of the peace had the power to inquire into the activities of sheriffs and punish them if they had violated the law.

Justices of the peace, who were usually country gentlemen, were required to be learned in the law since such knowledge was deemed necessary to carry out their responsibilities. We, therefore, see the emergence of the belief that in order to fulfill their responsibilities, police officers must be competent and trained.

King Edward III also issued the *Statutes of Treason* which made giving aid and comfort to enemies of the land the offense of treason. The same statute also contained provisions against counterfeiting and indicated that those engaged in such activity were also guilty of treason.

DEVELOPMENT OF ENGLISH LAW ENFORCEMENT DURING EARLY MODERN HISTORY (FROM 1500)

The reign of King Charles I (1625–1645) was marked by his constant dispute with Parliament and by his belligerent attitude toward Parliament and its members. Because Parliament would not provide him with funds, Charles initiated illegal actions and forced loans which created great resentment on the part of Parliament and lords of the day. Charles totally ignored Parliament and all previous rights afforded the people by past rulers. He tried to operate on the basis of absolute rule by the king.

Court of Star Chamber. In conjunction with his high-handed methods, Charles forced compliance by the subversive use of the *Court of Star Chamber* which was actually instituted by Henry VII in 1487 for the purpose of trying special cases such as bribing sheriffs or jurymen. The members of the court were appointed by the king, and, in reality, the court was a means by which the king could demand his will while under the disguise of judicial authority.

The court charged persons, and then the same body heard the case and pronounced sentence. The court called witnesses but did not allow the defendant to be represented or to present his case. Actually, to be charged by the court was the same as being condemned.

In reaching their preconceived decisions the high justices frequently resorted to the *third degree* or torture to induce a confession. Obviously, many defendants would confess rather than suffer continuous third-degree tactics. The court could find the accused guilty without the confession, but securing it probably made the judicial process seem more legitimate. In essence, the Court of Star Chamber by virtue of its authority derived from the king was a form of *legalized third degree*. The court enjoyed complete freedom to try cases arbitrarily and was not committed to limitations imposed upon other judicial systems or processes.

The court also imposed cruel punishments which often consisted of heavy fines, flogging, the pillory, imprisonment, and the cutting off of the ears of the convicted person. For example, a lawyer by the name of William Prynne was charged with libel because a book he had written charged sinfulness in drama. Charles enjoyed the theatre and saw this as a reflection upon his character. Prynne was, therefore, charged with libel, convicted, and sentenced to the pillory, loss of ears, fined five thousand pounds, and imprisoned until the king would wish to release him.

In reality, the Court of Star Chamber was exploited by Charles and was a threat by which he could demand his will while under the auspice of the court. Men would yield to his demands rather than face certain conviction and harsh punishment by the court. Charles was achieving forced cooperation by using the Court of Star Chamber as a tool which instilled fear of judicial retaliation if demands were not met.

Petition of Right. (See Appendix G.) In 1628, the problems between Parliament and Charles came to a head when Parliament refused to grant revenue to Charles until he signed the "Petition of Right." This petition was intended to end Charles' complete disregard for Parliament and his illegal activities. Actually, this document reaffirmed many of the provisions of previous concessions agreed to by former kings. For example, many of its provisions were a repeat of agreements found in the Magna Carta signed by King John in 1215.

The Petition of Rights specifically stated that no man could be compelled to make loans to the king against his will, to give gifts, or pay any tax not stipulated by Parliament. It also provided that freemen could not be imprisoned or detained without observance of the law and the land and without due process of law. This petition again indicated that the will of the people was above that of the king and, therefore, gave local control back to the people.

Charles signed the document but had no intention of abiding by it. He continued his devious methods and uitilized the Court of Star Chamber even more. Finally, demands were such that, along with other constitutional reforms, Charles was forced to sign a measure in 1641 that abolished the Court of Star Chamber.

Finally, as a result of his tyrannical methods, civil war broke. Charles was finally beaten, tried, and was beheaded in 1649.

OLIVER CROMWELL AND MILITARY RULE (1653–1658)

Following the execution of Charles, Oliver Cromwell assumed leadership of the country under military rule. Cromwell was a good administrator who managed to raise England to a position of international prominence while maintaining law and order. For all purposes, Cromwell was king, but he refused the title and became known as *Lord Protector* instead. The country was divided into twelve districts and a general or *provost marshall* was placed at the head of each. The provost marshalls held arbitrary powers in enforcing the law.

Although law and order was maintained successfully under martial law, the techniques involved total political suppression. The people resented the power of the army and their rule by a dictator. This attitude was reflected in the desire for safeguards against military rule carried to America by the English settlers.

It must be remembered, however, that he was able to keep peace and order in England which was a demoralized state. Perhaps, due to the chaotic problems, this was about the only means available for controlling crime and disorder.

KING CHARLES II AND HABEAS CORPUS (1660–1684)

Following Cromwell's death in 1658, his son became protectorate for a short time, but due to his inability, Parliament asked Charles II, son of Charles I, to take the throne. Charles II was given restricted powers, and he accepted the throne on conditions which included adherence to the Magna Carta, Petition of Right, and other statutes that limited the power of the king. Parliament had emerged as the governing body of England and the king could not rule in opposition to its wishes.

The emergence of this democratic ruling philosophy has great significance for law enforcement. Responsibility for making or approving law was taken from the absolute whims of the king, and the function was placed with Parliament. Since people could now influence those laws that governed them, laws would better reflect social or community needs. This is the essence of law and the philosophy we have adopted in the United States.

Charles II's primary direct contribution to law and law enforcement was the passage of the *Habeas Corpus* Act of 1679. This act required law enforcement officials to bring a prisoner before a judge and explain why he was being held.

If there was, in the opinion of the judge, good reason for keeping the prisoner in custody, the judge was required to establish a trial date. If, on the other hand, good reason was not given, the prisoner would be released.

Although the entire importance of habeas corpus may not have been recognized then, it still is an important part of judicial processes in the United States. Like many provisions of these early petitions or acts, habeas corpus appears in our own Constitution.

During the reign of Charles II, in response to increasing crime, the Common Council in 1663 introduced a force of paid constables who became known as *charlies*. Because they checked the doors of businesses, they also became known as the *shiver and shake watch*.

SOCIAL CHANGE AND CRIME

During this period, along with changes in the processes of lawmaking and implementation, the nature of the social order itself was being completely transformed. Throughout the middle ages England had been predominately rural, and most of its people were either farmers on small tenant farms or were farm laborers. However, the country was becoming urbanized, which created vast social problems. There were many influences at work in creating a new and different society. New lands were being discovered that provided fresh avenues for trade. Technology was advancing, new inventions were being developed, and mass production was coming into existence. In conjunction with this, the demands for goods were ever increasing, and the emerging capitalists were interested in making England more productive.

Enclosures. The changing times and the eagerness of lords to capitalize on the demands for goods were exemplified in the development of *enclosures*. Wool was in demand, and the large landowners began to convert farm land to pasture for the grazing of sheep. Sheep grazing not only re-

57

quired large tracts of land, but at the same time it required little help. As a result, tenant farmers were evicted, and farm laborers were put out of work. Thousands of rural people were without a means of support. In desperate hope of improving their situation, they migrated to the rising urban and industrialized centers.

Urbanization and crime. During the industrial revolution, the displaced rural people as well as other poor people were employed by urban industries, whose owners' only interest was production. They had total disregard for the safety and welfare of employees and exploited them without mercy. Men, women, and children were paid starvation wages, kept at their jobs sixteen hours a day, and worked until they were physical wrecks and unable to continue. When no longer productive, employees were fired and replaced by younger and stronger persons.

Unemployment grew by leaps and bounds, while the rich became richer and the poor became poorer. The squalor and filth of the developing slums were unbelievable and much worse than anything seen since that time. The worst slums or ghettos of today cannot begin to match the conditions then existing in England.

Faced with starvation and with no hope for help, the people obtained money or food in any way possible. The crime rate rose at an alarming pace and was uncontrollable. Youth stole goods to sell to the hundreds of fences (a fence refers to a person or business that buys and sells stolen goods). The fence would actually instruct the children on how to steal and designated goods they could best peddle. This may very well be the real beginning of *juvenile delinquency.* Thousands of women and young girls became prostitutes and roamed the streets in search of customers. Men resorted to every conceivable type of crime, primarily as a means of survival.

The cities, London in particular, were not safe, and men of means dared not walk the streets even during the day. The watch and ward, somewhat successful in the past, was not capable of handling the increased population or crime. Contributing to their ineffectiveness was the rebellion of people against serving on the watch and their practice of employing vagabonds to replace them. These hired substitutes were not only incapable of doing the job, but their actions added even more chaos to the situation. They now had a legitimate reason for being on the streets, which made it easier to steal or pilfer.

Attempts to combat crime. Many schemes were tried in response to the enormous crime problem. Penalties were made severe to the point that practically all crimes were punishable by death. However, the opposite effect was realized since more severe penalties tended to make crime seem more profitable since a greater risk was involved. In addition, a man with a starving family in search of survival did not consider the consequences of being caught.

Rewards were offered for information leading to the apprehension of criminals in an attempt to gain public participation in crime control. This, however, merely encouraged citizens to falsely accuse a neighbor in hopes of gaining the reward. This also encouraged constables to ignore minor violations in hope that success would lead the violator to a more serious offense that would carry a larger reward.

Eventually, many forms of private police came into existence. *Merchant police* were employed by merchants to protect their places of business. *Parish police* consisted of church members serving in rotation to protect members of · the congregation. *Dock police* or police employed by shipping companies concerned themselves with protecting goods on the docks. Needless to say, none of these proved capable of handling the problem, and, in fact, their inefficiency and disorganization probably contributed to the problem.

HENRY FIELDING AND BOW STREET RUNNERS

During this period of turmoil and lawlessness, a lawyer-novelist was appointed principal magistrate of Westminster in 1749. Henry Fielding is best known as a novelist, but his contributions to law enforcement are also of great significance. Fielding's concern for lawlessness is typified by his 1750 publication, "An Enquiry into the Causes of the Late Increase of Robberies."[1] This document is an indication of his literary ability as well as a survey relative to the problem of robberies. In fact, Fielding can be credited for having conducted the first actual police survey, which included recommendations for the improvement of law enforcement in London.

As principal magistrate, Fielding took over the police station located on Bow Street and with the help of his blind brother, John, proceeded to establish an improved police force. As part of the improvements, he established what has become the first known detective unit. Men of this unit wore no uniforms and responded quickly to the report of a crime in an attempt to quell the situation or apprehend the criminal. The members of this unit, which became known as *the Bow Street runners*, were entitled to rewards that were offered.[2] The Bow Street runners were not readily accepted by the people, but as they proved themselves successful, the public gradually accepted them and became more and more dependent upon them as law officers.

The runners were disbanded for awhile, but John Fielding, who succeeded his brother as principal magistrate, revived them during his administration. Henry Fielding did not live to see the real success of his efforts, but his brother continued the police reform movement. John's longer administration actually gave him time to make advances beyond the accomplishments of Henry. John developed crime prevention programs such as caring for prostitutes and misguided children, implemented better street lighting on a larger scale, instituted foot patrol, and established horse patrol in order to cover a greater area.[3]

[1] Douglas G. Brown, *The Rise of Scotland Yard* (New York: G. P. Putnam's Sons, n.d.), p. 27.

[2] Douglas G. Brown, p. 28.

[3] Douglas G. Brown, p. 28.

ROBERT PEEL AND THE NEW POLICE

Although many improvements were being made, the real beginning of the modern police system did not take place until 1829 when Sir Robert Peel established a new metropolitan constabulary under the command of a commissioner. Sir Robert Peel was the Home Secretary at the time and the new constabulary derived its existence and authority from a Parliamentary bill which he pushed through to passage.

The significant features of the new metropolitan police were: 1) adherence to semimilitary principles, 2) the quality of the men employed, 3) the discipline that prevailed, and 4) the fact that one man was in charge and responsible only to the national government.

Specifically, some of the principles under which the police force was established were: [4]

1. Police officers must be under strict discipline to ensure the necessary high standard of behavior.
2. The absence of crime is an index of efficiency.
3. The force should be territorially distributed.
4. The force should be divided by hours and shifts.
5. Higher positions should be filled by men from the lower ranks.
6. Police officers should wear a uniform and that a good appearance commands respect.
7. Applicants for the police force should be judged on their own merits.
8. Training of police officers assures greater efficiency.
9. The principle object to be attained is the prevention of crime.
10. A perfect command of temper is an essential quality.

It is interesting that these principles are as applicable today as they were in 1829. This portrays the farsightedness of Peel as well as his genius in police reform. It also illustrates

[4] Douglas G. Brown, pp. 82–86.

Original Scotland Yard building

By kind permission of the Commissioner of
Police of the Metropolis, New Scotland Yard,
Broadway, London, W.W.I., England

the weakness in many of our present day American police
departments and their failure to learn from history. Some
police administrators have yet to recognize the value of these
principles developed over 140 years ago.

The headquarters for the new police force was a small
side street called Scotland Yard, thus the origination of the
name attached to the London police and their famous address.

The constables for the new police force were drawn from
the retired military ranks, thus insuring good discipline and a
willingness to don the police uniform. The constables wore top
hats and blue coats and were armed with nightsticks. They

62

The first Peelers

By kind permission of the Commissioner of
Police of the Metropolis, New Scotland Yard,
Broadway, London, W.W.I., England

carried no firearms, and this custom still prevails in England today.

At first, the citizens were contemptuous of the constables and were apprehensive of their authority. This is easily understood since the people were generally distrustful of the military and saw Peel's force as a tool for government control. In other words, the citizens were fearful of martial law. However, as the police proved their effectiveness, the people not only accepted them but placed them in a position of high esteem and respect.

In respect for Sir Robert Peel, the constables became known as *peelers* or *bobbies*. The term bobbies is still used in England to identify their police officers or constables.

DEVELOPMENT OF LAW ENFORCEMENT IN THE UNITED STATES

THE ENGLISH COLONIAL PERIOD

The beginnings of American law enforcement can be traced to the period of English colonization. Early law and governmental structure were dictated by the king's charters, under which the colonies were established and ruled. These charters formally confirmed English tradition already customary to the English settlers in America.

The charters of both the London and Plymouth companies reflected England's philosophy of government and law enforcement. There was some provision for home rule, but always with national control. The colonists were allowed to administer local matters but only as long as they did not conflict with English law or beliefs. In other words, all governmental activities were subject to the approval of the king and were held within the confines of English tradition and legality.

The London Charter of 1606 typified such control. It stipulated that each colony was to be governed by a resident council appointed from among the residents of the colony. Although this reflected local control, national authority was maintained by having members of the resident council appointed by a superior council whose members were appointed by the king. In terms of local control, the resident council was authorized to: 1) establish ordinances that did not conflict with English law, 2) act as a court, 3) appoint colonial officials such as law and judicial officers, and 4) administer the government of the colony.[5]

Control changed hands frequently as the colonists progressively demanded more control over their affairs. Slowly, after much struggle, democratic self-government became a reality. The emerging country had to pass through much

---

[5] John Spencer Bassett, *A Short History of the United States* (New York: The Macmillan Company, 1939), p. 46.

turmoil which included indian wars, the Revolutionary War and the events leading to it, the Declaration of Independence, and, finally, the ratification of the Constitution of the United States.

Southern law enforcement. The agricultural nature of the South practically dictated the type of government and law enforcement to be established. The South's relatively flat, sparsely populated land with its fertile soil and favorable climate made it natural farm country. The people attracted to the South were largely the farming class from the rural areas of England. As they settled, they naturally adopted the county form of government because of their familiarity with it and because the county unit lended itself to the sparsely populated rural area.

As in rural England, the office of sheriff was established as the primary law enforcement official. The county court was established, and this court originally made the ordinances, directed the sheriff in enforcing them, and handled all judicial matters. Although the county court had great influence, the sheriff was without a doubt one of the most, if not the most, influential and important man in the county. He had full police powers and exercised his authority throughout the county.

Northern Law Enforcement. Although counties were established in New England, the primary government unit was the town. New England was as opposite the South as opposites can be. The North's soil and climate were not as favorable for farming, and because of the fear of Indian attacks, the people settled close together forming clusters of populated areas. It naturally followed that the town became the primary governmental unit. As the problem of Indian attacks subsided, the inhabitants began to move to outlying districts, but by habit they clustered in groups, thereby establishing new towns.

In conjunction with their form of government and urban English background, the colonists established the office of

65

town constable or watchman. As the towns grew larger, the town officials established the watch and ward, patterned after the English system.

As this country grew in both population and area, the North became more dependent upon the office of county sheriff, while at the same time the growing southern cities had to utilize the town constable and watch and ward system. However, even today the office of sheriff in the South practices broader law enforcement functions than his counterpart in the North. Again, the role of the southern sheriff indicates the tradition that was established in rural England and reinforced during colonial times.

Far western and southwestern law enforcement. Although migration to the far west and southwestern United States took place after considerable settlement of the Atlantic regions, mention should be made of Western law enforcement. Actually, the West had characteristics of both the North and the South. The area was vast, but much of it was good for ranching rather than farming. This rural character lended itself to the utilization of the county sheriff and, in fact, this office emerged as the most important.

At the same time, however, the western pioneers had to originally settle in groups in order to protect themselves from the Indians. Therefore, the town also emerged as an important governmental unit and the town marshall became an important law enforcement official.

To encourage the development of both officers was the fact that northerners as well as southerners were moving to the West and bringing with them the tradition of their areas. Those people settling in towns demanded the town constable or marshall, and those settling in the more rural regions demanded the sheriff.

By virtue of the predominately rural character of the West, the sheriff emerged as the primary law enforcement official. Even today, the Western and Southwestern sheriff and his deputies practice full police powers and provide law enforcement services throughout their respective counties. In

Wyatt Earp, well-known early Western law enforcement official

U.S. Signal Corps Photo number 111-SC-94117
in the National Archives

fact, the sheriff and his deputies may be the only significant law officers serving large areas within their county.

FURTHER DEVELOPMENT OF MUNICIPAL POLICE

As stated previously, the first American police officers were parish constables appointed during the colonial period. Originally, the town probably appointed one constable and added others as the population increased. The first constables were most concerned with the hours of darkness, and night watches

67

were eventually established to patrol the streets. With the continued population growth, night patrol proved quite inadequate, and some cities established a separate day watch.

Growth of cities. Since the United States was primarily rural, forces developed rather slowly. Not until the late 1700's and early 1800's were there any cities of significant size. In fact, in 1760, Boston and Philadelphia were the largest cities, each with a population of approximately 20,000. New York was the third largest with a population of about 10,000, and Charleston came next with 9,000.[6]

In the 1800's population growth surged significantly, due to both a high birth rate and mass immigration. The growth of manufacturing and the resulting need for labor encouraged immigration. Hardships of life in Europe, as well, caused many to leave for a land of greater opportunities. Immigration records show that from 1820 to 1860 over five million aliens immigrated to the United States.[7]

Conflict in the growing cities. Most of the immigrants were laborers for whom the South—with its tradition of slave labor—held little opportunity for settlements. Generally, the immigrants moved to the northern cities, took what employment was available, and resided in areas that were within their financial means. This migration created many social problems, some of which caused a substantial increase in crime and the concurrent need for more and better law enforcement.

Conflicts that frequently resulted in riots arose between the immigrants, especially between the Irish and native-born Americans. Actually, an organization called "Native Americans" was formed which expanded to incorporate chapters within many cities. A riot occurred in Boston in 1837 as a result of conflict between the Irish and the "natives." In

[6] John Spencer Bassett, p. 142.
[7] John Spencer Bassett, p. 461.

1884, a prolonged riot occurred in Philadelphia as a result of the Catholics' opposition to using the Protestant Bible in the public schools.[8] Of significance is the resemblance these riots have to race riots involving black suppression that occurred during the 1960's.

As industrialization increased, the cities became larger and more complex, thus causing even greater problems for law enforcement. At the time of the Civil War, the country's labor force was quickly changing from one of an agricultural nature to one of an industrial nature. These industrial laborers began to organize into unions for purposes of negotiation with factory owners. Since employee demands were not always granted, mass strikes and sometimes riots resulted.

In 1886, the Knights of Labor union called for a strike by railroad employees because a fired foreman was not reinstated. This strike became quite violent with the result that federal troops were called in to quell it. Special constables were not able to control it. Buildings were burned, and innocent people were killed during mob violence. In the same year a labor riot occurred in Chicago with the result that seven police officers were killed and sixty were injured. Of course, there were mass arrests and considerable property damage.[9]

Patterns of development. As stated previously, the rural character of the United States up to the present century inhibited the growth of municipal police departments. As the cities grew, however, they had a greater need for protection and an increasing demand for not only a larger police force but also for a more effective one.

The pattern of development of the police department in most cities was from military protection or martial law to the appointment of a single watchman, to a constable or marshall, to a night watch, to a separate day watch, to the combina-

[8] John Spencer Bassett, p. 462.
[9] John Spencer Bassett, pp. 741–742.

tion of both the day and night watch which was eventually subdivided into wards, and finally to the establishment of a formal police department under the direction of a chief of police or commissioner. Such development was not usually smooth but rather was haphazard and confusing. More often than not the organization, supervision, and control of the law enforcement agency shifted frequently. For example, many police departments would first be under the control of the mayor, and later under the control of the commissioner. Similar shifts back and forth can be found in many other areas as well.

The first night watch in American history was instituted in Boston in 1636. It was formed at sunset and initially consisted of an officer and six men who formed a kind of military guard. Later the night watch was staffed primarily by citizens, rather than soldiers, who were appointed by the town council.

New York (New Amsterdam) and Philadelphia soon followed Boston's lead and established night watches in 1658 and 1700. New York's night watch was referred to as the *rattlewatch* because the watchmen used rattles to announce their presence and to communicate with each other. The slow growth of cities and, consequently, police departments was evidenced by the lapse of over one hundred years before there was a need for night watches in cities such as Cincinnati and New Orleans. Cincinnati established its night watch in 1803 and New Orleans in 1804.

As in England, the early night watches were anything but effective. They had the appearance of vigilantes and were often lazy. Usually, members of the watch were citizens who had to rotate the responsibility among themselves. Like their counterparts in England, these citizens frequently hired substitutes who often were less than respectable citizens. It was also not uncommon for a court to sentence a minor misdemeanor to be a watchman as a form of punishment.

Daytime policing did not come into existence until 1833 when the city of Philadelphia established a day watch, followed by Boston in 1838, Cincinnati in 1842, and New York in 1844. As the first, Philadelphia had twenty-four day watchmen and one hundred twenty night watchmen who were all under the command of a captain. Later, Philadelphia went back to a separate night watch, and in 1854 the then existing force was directed by a marshall who was elected for a two-year term. A few years later, the office of marshall was abolished, and the police agency came under the direction of a chief of police who was appointed by the mayor.

During this same period of time Boston was in a period of tumult. The publisher William Lloyd Garrison was assaulted in his offices by a crowd infuriated by his antislavery writings. The Broad Street riot of 1837 pitted volunteer firemen against mourners in an Irish funeral procession, and the military had to be called in to quiet it. These events led to the hiring of Marshal Francis Tukey, who in time managed to build a competent and efficient police force. He expanded the night watch to 22 men and they arrested more criminals than the entire day watch of more than 200 volunteer watchmen. Tukey established police divisions and eight precinct stations were opened throughout the city. Although Tukey was later discharged for malfeasance in office, police reform had caught on and police operations continued to improve significantly.

New York in this same period of time had a police force with three separate components. Rivalries existed among the units, and each force was supervised by a separate authority. In 1844, finally recognizing the problem, New York followed the successful pattern set in England fifteen years earlier by Sir Robert Peel, and became the first city in the western hemisphere to establish a modern police department. New York, by adopting Peelian principles years before other cities, proved itself to be one of the most energetic American cities in terms of law enforcement. In fact, there are still cities today that may be further behind times than Peel was in 1829.

Other cities, to mention a few, that followed New York with the establishment of formal police agencies included Chicago in 1851, Cincinnati in 1852, Philadelphia in 1855, Baltimore in 1857, and Detroit in 1865.

American police agencies were slow also in comparison to London's bobbies in adopting official police uniforms. Un-

71

fortunately, the early watchmen, constables, and police officers saw the uniform as a symbol of degradation and refused
to wear it. In fact, when New York first suggested uniforms,
the police officers protested vigorously and actually refused
to wear them. Finally, in 1856, twelve years after the establishment of the department, New York police adopted a full
police uniform and became the first such uniformed officers
in the country. Even then, however, the problem of identification was not fully solved, as each ward of the city was
allowed to adopt a uniform of their choosing.

Although Henry Fielding established the Bow Street
runners around 1750, it was more than one hundred years
later before American police agencies recognized the need
for and significance of a detective unit; it was not until 1866
that Detroit established a detective bureau as one of the
early ones in the United States. New York established a detective bureau in 1882, and Cincinnati established one in
1886.

The primary method of patrol in the early days was by
foot, and it was not until the late 1800's that horses were
used to any great extent. Generally, the cities were rather
concentrated, but as they began to spread over a larger area,
mounted patrol became a necessity. In 1873 Detroit established one of the earliest mounted units to patrol the city's
outskirts. Philadelphia began its mounted patrol in 1889 with
the purchase of ninety-three horses.

The use of horses as the chief means of patrol was relatively short-lived. With advent of the automobile, police on
foot or horseback found themselves unable to apprehend
motorized law violators. Philadelphia began using motorcycles in 1906, and Detroit modernized with the installation
of their motorcycle patrol in 1909. In that same year, Detroit's police commissioner, at his own expense, purchased an
automobile for patrol. The Commissioner was reimbursed,
however, after the automobile proved itself, and, in fact,
other autos were added to the force shortly afterwards.

Other municipal police developments during the early
twentieth century included the adoption of the telephone,

the use of radio-equipped police cars, the installation of teletype systems, the use of fingerprint systems, and the employment of policewomen, etc. These and many more advances were occurring at an accelerated pace. Cities were growing rapidly and by necessity were becoming more dedicated to providing efficient law enforcement services. The conflicts of the times such as race riots, labor riots, and general rise in crime forced additional developments in law enforcement.

Horse-drawn police wagon in Philadelphia in the late 1880's

Courtesy of the Philadelphia, Pa.
Police Department

73

LEADERS IN THE DEVELOPMENT OF MUNICIPAL LAW ENFORCEMENT

Professions develop primarily as the result of the foresight, wisdom, and energetic efforts of select people. The field of law enforcement is no different, as certain individuals can be identified who led the way in the development of law enforcement. Just as Augustus and Sir Robert Peel were leaders in their time, there were Americans who stood above others as law enforcement developed in the United States. Most notable were Allan Pinkerton, August Vollmer, Orlando Winfield Wilson, and William H. Parker.

Allan Pinkerton (1819–1884). Allan Pinkerton was born in Glasgow, Scotland, on August 25, 1819, the son of a local police officer who was disabled during the Chartist riots and died four years later. Due to the family's poor financial situation, Allan was apprenticed as a cooper (barrel maker) at the age of 12.

As a young man, Allan Pinkerton was active in the Chartist movement, which was a widespread attempt to improve the conditions of the laboring classes and to bring about political reforms. His role in this movement led him to fear political reprisal, and he therefore migrated to the United States in 1842. Initially he lived in Chicago, but within a year he moved to the Scotch settlement of Dundee, a small farming town 38 miles northwest of Chicago, where he established a cooper's shop.

The primary event that destined Allan Pinkerton to become a detective was his role in the capture of a counterfeiting ring. While cutting hoop poles on an isolated island, he came upon an obvious meeting place of counterfeiters. He led a party of men who captured the entire ring, and as a result earned a reputation as a crime fighter and detective among the townspeople and businessmen. When any illegal activities were suspected, the townspeople would call upon Pinkerton to solve the case and apprehend the criminal(s). In 1846 he accepted an appointment as a deputy sheriff for Cane County, and his subsequent activities enhanced his reputation even

Allan Pinkerton (1819–1884)

Courtesy of Pinkerton's, Inc.

further. His outstanding work for Cane County earned him an appointment as deputy sheriff for Cook County, Illinois in 1850.

Pinkerton's demonstrated ability led to his appointment as a special agent for the United States Post Office Department. He investigated cases of fraud, extortion, and other crimes involving the use of mail. When the City of Chicago disbanded its inadequate Constable Corps and established a regular police department, Pinkerton became the city's first and only detective.

75

These were the years when the railroads were at their financial pinnacle. Although there were many benefits from the rise of the railroad empire, its existence provided new opportunities for the criminal. Troubled with the ever-increasing number of train robberies and crimes directed against the railroads, several railroad presidents requested Pinkerton's help. In response, Pinkerton formed a partnership with a lawyer, E. G. Rucker, and established a private detective agency. Within a year he resigned his city position and assumed full control of the agency, which became the most famous private detective agency of all time. Many books, articles, and movies include the exploits of "Pinkerton men." In all instances, these stories depict the Pinkerton detective as a "master sleuth."

The success of the agency gained national recognition for Allan, which led to General George B. McClellan's request that Pinkerton organize and administer a secret service operation for the Ohio Department. The secret service organized by Pinkerton was highly efficient, and when McClellan became Commander-in-Chief, Pinkerton moved his headquarters to Washington, D.C., where he subsequently became involved in the direction of counterespionage during the Civil War. He resigned his post when General McClellan was removed in 1869, but continued to serve as investigator of numerous claims against the government.

In 1869, Pinkerton suffered a slight paralytic stroke and had to give up his actual field investigation activities. He left the field work entirely to his employees and sons, devoting his full attention to administrative duties and those investigative techniques that could be handled in the office. He directed most investigations from his office and can be considered the mastermind behind most apprehensions.

It is certain that many law enforcement officials learned from Allan Pinkerton's investigative methods and adapted his techniques. In fact, his techniques of surveillance are still widely used by police agencies throughout the United States.

It is significant to the study of law enforcement that many communities and business agencies relied upon private

76

detective agencies rather than on the public police departments. This reliance can be attributed to two things: first, only a few communities had a publicly supported law enforcement organization to provide such services; and second, existing police organizations did not have the manpower or expertise necessary to handle criminal investigations effectively.

Certainly, *Allan Pinkerton can be considered the first professional detective in the United States.*

August Vollmer (1876–1955). August Vollmer contributed more to the early development of American law enforcement than any other person. His innovations and administrative concepts received worldwide attention and the Berkeley, California police department, over which he was Chief of Police for 32 years, became the model for others to emulate.

August Vollmer (1876–1955)

Courtesy of the Berkeley, California Police Department

August Vollmer was America's foremost pioneer in the application of modern police administrative principles, and he is known as the *Dean of American Chiefs of Police.*[10] Others have referred to him as *America's greatest cop* or the *father of modern police science,* but the most fitting title is that of Dean.

Vollmer's distinguished law enforcement career began in 1905 when he was elected Town Marshal for the City of Berkeley. Vollmer immediately recognized the need for additional manpower to deliver adequate police services for the City of Berkeley. Fourteen days after Vollmer's appointment, the Board of Town Trustees appointed six police officers. Within two years Vollmer had increased the size of the force to 26 regular officers and one special officer, and had created the position of detective.

In 1909, August Vollmer, under the provision of a new charter, was appointed Chief of Police. Shortly after his appointment he established the first known police training school in the United States. Vollmer had become convinced that the major problem of all police departments throughout the United States was inefficiency, resulting from ignorance on the part of police officers, and he concluded that the only solution to this problem was adequate police training.

August Vollmer expressed this philosophy when he wrote:

Those authorized and empowered to enforce the laws, rules, and regulations which are intended for the better protection of the public, should have some knowledge of the fundamental principles underlying human action, more especially those actions which are commonly designated as criminal or contrary to law and order.[11]

[10] V. A. Leonard, *The Police of the 20th Century* (Brooklyn: The Foundation Press, Inc., 1964), p. 135.

[11] August Vollmer and Albert Schneider, "The School for Police as Planned at Berkeley," *Journal of the American Institute of Criminal Law in Criminology* (March, 1917), p. 878.

During the nine years prior to 1917, the police department of Berkeley offered courses in police methods and procedures, anthropometry, and fingerprinting. In addition, authorities on criminology, psychiatry, anthropology, and many other related subjects would periodically lecture to the department's personnel. August Vollmer continued his efforts at upgrading the police through training and education. For example, in 1916 he initiated the first classes in law enforcement at San Jose State College. Courses of various types were offered through the years, and in 1931 San Jose State College awarded its first Bachelor of Science degree in Police Science and Criminology. During this period of time August Vollmer worked with the University of California, which offered courses in criminology for his police officers. This leadership led to his appointment in 1929 as a full Professor of Police Administration at the University of California. He served in that capacity until 1938, when he found it necessary to resign and devote more time to writing.

Vollmer took innovative action in 1911 by introducing the use of the bicycle in patrol, soon to be followed by the use of motorcycles. In 1913, some officers were placed in radio-equipped police cars. By 1917 the entire police department was completely motorized with automobiles. Each police officer furnished his own automobile, and was reimbursed for its use by the city. This resulted in a large fleet for the size of the force and provided great flexibility in police operations. Eventually the practice was ended with the City of Berkeley purchasing distinctly marked vehicles that were used on an around-the-clock basis.

August Vollmer was responsible also for the police telephone callbox system. This system in Berkeley was known as a red light signal recall system. Red lights were mounted strategically throughout the city where they could be observed by officers assigned to specific beats. When an officer observed the red light flashing signal he would go to a telephone and call central control who would relay the message.

Vollmer pioneered the idea of an effective records or accounting system for the police business. This was at a time when very few departments kept any records at all. He saw the need for organized, factual data concerning the nature, extent, and distribution of the police problems of crime, vice, and traffic. It was his belief that no intelligent approach to police operations was possible without factual data.[12]

Vollmer also pioneered in the field of identification. He established one of the early fingerprint bureaus in the United States by purchasing Bertillion fingerprint equipment.

The significance of the modus operandi system was recognized by Vollmer. Although this procedure for establishing the method of operation by which various criminals worked was first implemented in England, August Vollmer was quick to realize its application to law enforcement in the United States. Certainly, he was a man ready and willing to implement and try procedures that were being tested by other countries and police organizations.

He was also interested in state-level operations that could aid and assist local police agencies. For example, he was instrumental in the development of a central identification bureau at the state level. This bureau later became known as the State Bureau of Criminal Identification and Investigation, and is now known as the California State Bureau of Investigation. Nationally, Vollmer urged the U.S. Congress to establish a national bureau of fingerprint records to be located within the Bureau of Investigation of the Department of Justice. Upon the recommendation of Vollmer, J. Edgar Hoover established the fingerprint identification section in the Federal Bureau of Investigation.

Vollmer, in 1914 one of the first to officially recognize the police role in crime prevention, established a juvenile division as an official administrative unit in the Berkeley police department. He brought in Elizabeth Lossing, a psychiatric social worker, to head up the new division and to develop a program designed to coordinate the resources of the community on behalf of youngsters who were in difficulty.[13]

[12] V. A. Leonard, p. 140.
[13] V. A. Leonard, p. 140.

During his long career, Vollmer served as a consultant to survey and reorganize police departments in 75 American and foreign cities, including Los Angeles, Portland, Minneapolis, Kansas City, Detroit, Chicago, Syracuse, Dallas, Havana, Honolulu, and Peking. In the Los Angeles police reorganization of 1925, he inaugurated for the first time in police history the use of automatic tabulating machinery to marshal the facts of crime, vice, traffic, and other police departments. What he did in Los Angeles and Berkeley in this respect, set the stage for the introduction of computerized equipment and techniques for American police practice. During the reorganization of the Los Angeles department, he also created the tactical unit or mobile task force. He found that with this mobile striking power, the police could saturate an area in terms of time and place, as shown by the records, and liquidate the problem.[14]

Chief Vollmer's interest in using the physical and biological sciences in the criminal investigation and evidence technology led him to establish in Berkeley the first scientific crime detection laboratory in police history. This was the nucleus for the era of scientific crime detection.[15]

From the foregoing it is quite obvious why August Vollmer can be considered the Dean of American Police Chiefs. He received many honors within the state, nationally, and throughout the world. His contributions significantly assisted in the development of modern law enforcement in the United States. He was and continues to be an inspiration for police officers and administrators.

Orlando Winfield Wilson (1900–1972). Orlando Winfield Wilson is probably the best-known expert in police administration in the United States. Of course, one must recognize that Wilson was influenced significantly by August Vollmer, since he served as a patrolman under Vollmer in the Berkeley Police Department.

---

[14] V. A. Leonard, p. 140.
[15] V. A. Leonard, p. 141.

Orlando W. Wilson (1900–1972)

Courtesy of the Chicago, Illinois Police Department

During his youth, Wilson attended the local schools of San Diego, California. After completing high school, he attended the University of California at Berkeley, where he majored in criminology in the Department of Political Science. His first police experience was as a patrolman with the Berkeley Police Department from May 1921 to April 1925. During his tenure as a police officer, he attended the University of California, and in 1924 received his Bachelor of Arts degree. Wilson was persuaded by August Vollmer to consider criminology as a career. As a direct result of this influence, his academic qualifications, and practical experience, Wilson at the age of 25 was appointed Police Chief of Fullerton, California in April 1925. He was with Fullerton for a very short time and then assumed the position of Chief Investigator for the Pacific Finance Corporation.

In March 1928, Wilson was appointed to head the police department in Wichita, Kansas. Within five years Wilson attracted nationwide attention by his success in reorganizing what once was a department with great internal problems. He introduced such things as conspicuously marked police cars, lie detectors, mobile crime laboratories, and, as did Vollmer, he hired college students as part-time policemen. In 1936, he received a leave of absence from Wichita to serve as an instructor in the Bureau for Street Traffic Management at Harvard University. He ended his career as Chief with the City of Wichita in May 1939.

In July 1939, Wilson returned to Berkeley, California where he was appointed Professor of Police Administration at the University of California at Berkeley, succeeding August Vollmer who had retired. In January 1943, his academic career was interrupted when he entered the United States Army as a Lieutenant Colonel in the Military Police Corps, serving as a Chief Public Safety Officer in Italy and England. During this time he earned the Bronze Star Medal in the Legion of Merit. After his discharge with the rank of Colonel, in November 1946, he remained in Europe as a civilian employee with the United States War Department. He was the Chief Public Safety Officer in charge of de-Nazification activities in the United States zone. He planned and played a major role in the rapid development of civilian policing in West Germany. In 1947, desiring to contribute more to the field of police administration, he returned to his position as Professor of Police Administration, and from 1950 to 1960 served as Dean of the School of Criminology.

Wilson served as a consultant for many police organizations throughout the United States. It was in this capacity as a consultant that Wilson eventually became the Police Superintendent of the City of Chicago. He was named Chairman of a five-man committee with the responsibility of choosing a new Police Chief to replace the Commissioner in Chicago. After about a month of screening during which almost 100 persons were considered, the other members of the committee recommended to Mayor Richard J. Daley that the post of Police Commissioner be offered to Wilson. Wilson accepted the post, after he was assured a free hand in running the department, full support by the Mayor, and complete separation of the police force from any political pressures. In spite of much opposition to his "academic reputation," he turned the Chicago Police Department into one of the finest major city police departments in the world.

Perhaps Wilson's greatest contribution to the police administration field was his writings. His best-known book, *Police Administration*, published in 1950, has gained nation-wide acceptance and has been translated into many foreign languages. This book has been used for many years by universities and police departments throughout the United States. Obviously, his writings have greatly influenced the type of administration that exists in police departments throughout the United States. In a sense, his book became the "Bible" for police administration. There is hardly a student of law enforcement who does not know of Orlando Winfield Wilson.

William H. Parker (1902–1966) is another outstanding individual who made significant contributions to the field of police administration. He was born in the town of Lead, South Dakota on June 21, 1902. His first job was that of a hotel detective, which helped him earn his way through high school in Deadwood, South Dakota where he graduated with honors and was a leading debater. It is apparent that his ability in this area helped in achieving the success he did as an outstanding public speaker.

The Parker family moved to Los Angeles, California during the 20's and Parker enrolled at the Los Angeles College of Law in 1926. He received his appointment to the Los Angeles, California Police Department on August 8, 1927 and three years later earned the Bachelor of Laws degree. In that same year, the State Bar of California admitted him to membership, and on April 26, 1956 he was admitted to the practice of law before the United States Supreme Court.

William H. Parker

Courtesy of the Los Angeles, California Police Department

He served the City of Los Angeles for 39 years; 15 as Chief of Police, having been appointed to that position on August 9, 1950. His tenure as Chief was the longest tenure in the department's history. Today, Parker is recognized as one of the leading architects of that city's world-famous police organization. This organization best reflects the semi-military organization as recommended by O. W. Wilson in his book, *Police Administration*.

His organization and tenure as Chief of Police of the Los Angeles department earned Parker professional recognition and status in history as one of the foremost police administrators in the world. In recognition and memory of Parker, the

City of Los Angeles has named the new modern multi-storied police headquarters building *Parker Center.*

During World War II Parker entered the military service and served in the Military Government Branch of the United States Army, where he rose to the rank of Captain and was under the command of Colonel O. W. Wilson. He was directly responsible for the development of the Police and Prisons Plan for the European invasion and later in prompting the closer relationships between the police of both continents. Parker introduced democratic police systems into the cities of Munich and Frankfurt, and those systems are still in operation today. During his service life, Parker received the Purple Heart Medal, the European Campaign Medal with two stars, the American Campaign Medal, the Victory Medal, and the Occupation Medal. From the Free-French government, he received the Croix de Guerre with the silver star. The Italian government also awarded Parker the Star of Solidarity for his work in restoring civil government in Sardinia.

Upon returning to the Los Angeles Police Department in 1945, Parker served in the Traffic Enforcement Division and was later appointed Director of the Bureau of Internal Affairs which he developed and organized. After his appointment as Chief of Police he immediately reorganized the department to assure his control over its operations and to facilitate the attainment of police objectives. Parker initiated sweeping changes within the department, which were met with considerable resistance. Parker persisted, and with great courage put his intentions and philosophies into practice. Like many other pioneers in the professionalization of law enforcement, Parker was confronted by endless obstacles and many scoffers. Parker's great qualities of leadership evidenced by his patience, diplomacy, sound judgment, moral courage, and great emotional strength contributed to the success he enjoyed throughout his entire career of law enforcement.

Parker always insisted on police professionalism and insisted that the profession be free of political control. Attesting to this is the fact that his continuing service took place under three mayors and 23 prominent citizens serving as Police Commissioners. Parker is recognized throughout the

United States as one of the leading exponents of professionalism in police work.

Parker's dedication to the Los Angeles Police Department
and law enforcement in general kept him in the Chief's chair
in spite of health problems. Chief Parker died with his boots on.
That is, he died while sitting in the chair of the Chief of Police
for the City of Los Angeles. Chief Parker exemplifies true
police professionalism and dedication and will long be remembered as one of the most outstanding police administrators in
the United States.

THE STATE POLICE

In comparison with municipal police, state police agencies
are of relatively recent origin. As the United States continued to grow and expand, the need for law enforcement
services also grew. In many instances, the existing municipal
agencies could not adequately handle crime, since criminals
were not confining their activities within the municipality
but were operating throughout the state. Corruption and
political patronage also existed in some police agencies to the
extent that the broader governmental unit had to develop a
more centralized arm of the law. All things combined, crime
was continually increasing, and there was a definite need for
the state to become directly involved in providing law enforcement services.

Although corruption and inefficiency at the local levels
of law enforcement were sometimes factors in the development of state police, another influential factor was that the
state did not have an agency to enforce rules and regulations
deemed necessary by it. Instead, the state had to rely completely upon the municipal or county law enforcement officials to carry out the state's sanctions. If a particular law was
unpopular, the sheriff and other officials were likely to ignore
its enforcement rather than cause unrest among constituents.
The local law enforcement officer identified much more
closely with his local situation and had little concern for the
desires of state government.

87

Officer Walter Stick, May 1921, with the first radio-equipped patrol car in the United States

Courtesy of the Detroit, Mich. Police Department

State police forerunners. The first agency similar to our present day state police was the Texas rangers. This force was established by the Texas provisional government in 1835 when Texas was still a republic. It was actually a military unit under the direction of military authorities. The act of 1835 established three ranger companies with the primary responsibility of border patrol. One of the major border problems concerned the rustling of Texas cattle by Mexicans who took the cattle back to Mexico; consequently, the apprehension of rustlers became one of the rangers' primary tasks. They also investigated crimes within the state, and today the Texas rangers have confined themselves primarily to investigations and to assisting other law enforcement agencies within the state.

Massachusetts was the next state to recognize the need for a state-wide enforcement agency. The appointment of a small force of state officers or constables in 1865 was in direct response to the need to control vice within the state. The constables were also given general police powers, and, therefore, Massachusetts can rightfully claim the establishment of the first law enforcement agency with general police authority throughout the state. This unit did not last long as such and was replaced in 1879 by a state investigation unit called

Texas Rangers, Company G, at Alice, Texas, in 1903

Courtesy of the Texas Department of Public Safety

89

The Arizona Rangers, 1901–1909

Courtesy of the Arizona Department of Library and Archives
Phoenix, Ariz.

the district police which was later incorporated in the state
police established in 1920.

After a lapse of thirty-eight years following the establishment of the Massachusetts state constables, Connecticut
established (1903) a state detective force patterned after the
Massachusetts district police. This force also was primarily
concerned with vice control, such as gambling and enforcement of liquor laws. The force was also too small and unsta-
ble to accomplish much and was finally absorbed into a more
effective organizational unit.

Next to be established were the Arizona rangers in 1901
and the New Mexico mounted police in 1905. Like the Texas
rangers, they were more or less a border patrol rather than a
state police agency. Their fate, however, was not as good as the
Texas rangers, and they both eventually ceased to exist.

Emergence of the state police. The first modern state
police agency was the Pennsylvania constabulary, established in 1905. The ill-conceived state police agencies established prior to 1905 were created in response to limited
needs, such as frontier problems or the enforcement of usually unpopular vice laws.

The Pennsylvania constabulary, on the other hand, originated to serve multiple needs: 1) to provide the governor

90

an executive arm to assist him in accomplishing his responsibilities, 2) to have a means of quelling the riots that were occurring during labor disputes in the coal regions, and 3) to improve law enforcement services in the rural portions of the state where county officials had been less than successful.

The first reason is clearly illustrated in Governor Pennypacker's statement relative to the establishment of the agency:

> In the year 1903, when I assumed the office of chief executive of the state, I found myself thereby invested with supreme executive authority. I found that no power existed to interfere with me in my duty to enforce the laws of the state, and that by the same token, no conditions could release me from my duty so to do. I then looked about me to see what instruments I possessed wherewith to accomplish this bounden obligation—what instruments on whose loyalty and obedience I could truly rely. I perceived three such instruments—my private secretary, a very small man; my woman stenographer; and the janitor, . . . So I made the state police.[10]

The second reason, to quell riots and disorders, resulted from labor disputes primarily between coal miners and the mine administrators. The local sheriffs and constables were unable to cope with such massive disorder, making a larger and more centralized police agency essential.

The third reason is somewhat typical of the times and again illustrates the then existing problems related to local law enforcement. The primary characteristic that set Pennsylvania off from its earlier counterparts was the concept of rural law enforcement and its organization. From its inception the Pennsylvania state police was under the administrative control of a superintendent appointed by the Governor. It was a uniformed mounted force that operated from an

[10] Katherine Mayo, *Justice to All: The Story of the Pennsylvania State Police* (New York: G. P. Putnam's Sons, 1917), pp. 5–6.

arrangement of troops and troop substations situated throughout the state so that protection was afforded in even the most remote areas. This force was well organized and served as a blueprint for other states to follow. With the establishment of the Pennsylvania state police, modern state policing had emerged.

FEDERAL LAW ENFORCEMENT

Federal law enforcement agencies, like the state police, emerged as a result of the many problems faced by a fast

Pennsylvania State Troopers on strike duty in Chester, Pennsylvania, in April 1908

Courtesy of the Pennsylvania State Police

growing country. The fantastic increase in population, urban growth, the rise of industrialization, technological advances, and the broadening of the country by ratification of new states all contributed to the need for controlling legislation that could only be enforced by the centralized government. For example, the advent of the automobile made it possible for criminals to commit a crime in one jurisdiction or state and be in another within a relatively short time. Advances in communication allowed the planning of a crime in one jurisdiction with its perpetration in another. In addition, communications media also aided specific crimes such as gambling and fraud. Local police, ununited as they were, found it virtually impossible to prevent such crimes or apprehend criminals from within the confines of their bailiwick.

Actually, the Constitution of the United States, by virtue of its many provisions, made it imperative that investigative and enforcement agencies be established at the federal level. Although the Constitution did not specifically establish law enforcement agencies, Congress does have the implied power by virtue of Article I, Section 8 (see Chapter 1) authorizing them to enforce or carry into effect provisions of the Constitution and its amendments. For example, the Constitution provides authority to lay and collect taxes (Article XVI) and, therefore; Congress has the authority to establish the Internal Revenue Service as an enforcement agency. The Constitution stipulates that Congress has power to coin money and punish counterfeiters (Article I, Section 8) and, concurrently, Congress also has the authority to establish an agency to detect and arrest counterfeiters. Without such agencies to enforce laws of such magnitude to the entire country, counterfeiting would run rampant, and there would be no means to effectively collect taxes.

Unlike the states, who required a police force with broad general powers, federal law enforcement agencies resulted from the passage of specific laws, and, therefore, they had somewhat limited functions. Federal agencies did not come into existence in an orderly manner, but instead they developed haphazardly as a result of the passage of controlling legislation. This does not mean, however, that enforcement agencies were established concurrent with legislation. In fact, enforcement agencies usually were established several years after the legislation went into effect and only then when the law was proven ineffective without enforcement.

Actually, Congress purposely avoided the establishment of such centralized law enforcement agencies. The Constitution reserved police power or authority to the states, and the consensus of opinion was that this right should not be infringed upon. In addition, citizens generally were in fear of a federal police force as this suggested a "police state." Therefore, the development of federal law enforcement agencies was slow; agencies were usually not established until mass violations made them absolutely imperative.

The forerunners. The forerunner of federal law enforcement was the office of United States marshall, established by Congress in 1789. As the first federal law enforcers, marshalls were appointed to federal districts throughout the United States. In this capacity they functioned as the only existing enforcement arm of the United States government. It was not until 1861 that Congress placed the marshall under the administrative control of the attorney general along with United States district attorneys. The early years of the marshalls were quite colorful, as they were often assigned to the frontier areas of the country. Today their functions are primarily connected with judicial processes. Generally speaking, United States marshalls have responsibilities similar to those of sheriffs, but they are concerned with federal rather than local law.

Also, in 1789, in reaction to the growing problem of smuggling, Congress inaugurated a Revenue Cutter Service. Following this, Congress did not establish additional law enforcement agencies for forty years. Finally, the government became concerned with mail robberies and frauds. The Postal Act was passed, authorizing postal agents to enforce

94

the Act's provisions. Enforcement of postal laws was again strengthened in 1836 when Congress authorized the post-master general to pay agents for investigating postal mat-ters.

In 1842, the counterfeiting act was passed, and three years later the secret service was organized to enforce its provisions. Between the years 1882 and 1886, the problems of immigration and smuggling led to the establishment of the U. S. border patrol within the customs service. In 1906, the pure food and drug regulations were established to combat the unhealthful ways that foods were being processed within many factories. This regulation, of course, necessitated spe-cial agents for enforcement. This pattern of passing legisla-tion and then establishing enforcement agencies persisted throughout the years until a multitude of federal agencies were in existence. The one agency that added great impetus to the development of federal law enforcement was the secret service, and it deserves additional mention at this time.

Secret service. During the Civil War, counterfeiting became so prevalent that Congress was forced to recognize the need for a law enforcement branch of the Treasury De-partment. The counterfeiting law was passed in 1842, but of interest is the fact that the secret service was not established until 1865. This agency's primary responsibility was to re-store faith in United States currency by detecting and arrest-ing counterfeiters.

The secret service proved to be exceptionally effective, but they were certainly not without their problems. Origi-nally, the agents carried as identification only a written letter of appointment which did little to dispel the suspicions of citizens and businessmen who questioned the agents' authority and who were reluctant to cooperate in investigations. This identification problem continued for approximately eight years until in 1873, the Treasury Department issued all agents printed credentials and a badge.

The main significance of the secret service is that it was the first general investigative agency of the federal government. In fact, for years it was the primary law enforcement

Three U. S. Marshals of the San Antonio, Texas District in the early 1880's: "The Kid," Tom O. Bailes, and Sam Walker

U.S. Signal Corps Photo number 111-SC-93366
in the National Archives

agency of the United States, and other federal departments frequently borrowed secret service agents to conduct investigations for them.

Federal Bureau of Investigation. The best known of the federal law enforcement agencies is the Federal Bureau of Investigation. The history of the FBI is quite colorful and reveals a great deal relative to the times. It specifically illustrates the legislature's reluctance to organize a central police agency.

Although the office of Attorney General was established in 1789, it was not until 1870 that the Department of Justice was created with the attorney general as the chief administrator. The creation of the Justice Department is attributed to the post-Civil War reconstruction problems and the need for the centralization of legal activities at the federal level. By this action, the attorney general assumed the tasks of prosecuting federal violators, formerly handled separately by the various governmental departments. During the early years of the department, the attorney general had only one "special agent" to conduct investigations. For most of such work, he expected his attorneys and marshalls to act as investigators in addition to their other responsibilities. He also hired detectives for specific investigations or borrowed secret service agents. Actually, this practice of borrowing secret service agents was followed by many other departments. Congress would authorize money for the borrowing of secret service agents, but it would not authorize money for Justice investigators.

Finally, after much effort by the Justice Department and much resistance from Congress, Attorney General Bonaparte was given sufficient appropriations that allowed him to establish a permanent force of detectives within his department. Bonaparte acted swiftly by having able secret service agents who had worked for him from time to time transferred to his department. This force worked relatively well, but as the department grew, unsound practices crept into the emerging organization. Finally, in 1924 the FBI was established and placed under the able leadership of J. Edgar Hoover, then a young attorney. Under his leadership, the FBI quickly became the most efficient and respected law enforcement agency in the United States.

J. Edgar Hoover (1895–1972). In the United States the name that is synonymous with federal law enforcement is that of J. Edgar Hoover, Director of the Federal Bureau of Investigation from its inception until 1972, when he died. In fact, J. Edgar Hoover probably is the best-known American-

John Edgar Hoover (1895–1972)

Courtesy of the Federal Bureau of Investigation

98

born police official in the country's history. He directed the Federal Bureau of Investigation within the United States Department of Justice for 48 years, serving eight presidents. Like William H. Parker, he remained on the job until his death. Perhaps the best description of J. Edgar Hoover was made in a short statement by former President Richard M. Nixon when he said of him: "J. Edgar Hoover was one of the giants in the Nation's history. Let us cherish his memory and be true to his legacy. Without peace officers we can never have peace. He was a peace officer without peer. He richly earned peace through all eternity."

Hoover was born in Washington, D.C. on New Year's Day, 1895. Little is known of Hoover's very early years in Washington, D.C., but history records that he was a serious and academically successful student at Central High School. Deeply involved in debating and athletics, he showed unusual leadership in both. He was chosen to be the valedictorian of his high school class, which exemplifies the kind of man he was, even during his early life. He enrolled in George Washington University, attending night classes and working by day until he received his LL.B. degree with honors, and a year later his Master of Laws degree. Although Hoover never entered the practice of law, he was admitted to practice law before the Bar of the District Court of the United States for the District of Columbia, the United States Court of Claims, and the United States Supreme Court. Later in life, Hoover received honorary degrees of every type from well-known universities throughout the United States.

Upon completing college, Hoover obtained a position with the Department of Justice. During World War I his capable handling of cases involving counterespionage came to the attention of the Attorney General who appointed him, at age 22, as a Special Assistant to the Enemy and Alien Registration Section, on July 26, 1917.

On May 10, 1924 Attorney General Harlan Stone selected Hoover to head the Bureau of Investigation in the Department of Justice. He thus became the federal government's top policeman at the age of 29. This assignment came at a time when the Bureau was under severe criticism, but Stone believed that Hoover could restore public confidence.

During the turbulent years that followed, the agency became the FBI. Hoover and his agents gained nationwide praise as "G-men," helping to rid the nation of such notorious gangsters as John Dillinger, Ma Barker, "Creepy" Alvin Carpis, and George "Machinegun" Kelley. Kelley is credited with labeling the hated government men "G-men."

When Hoover accepted his assignment from Stone, he did so upon two conditions. First, he must be assured a free hand in personnel selection and policy, and second, he be responsible only to the Attorney General. With these guarantees accorded to him, he began a complete reorganization of the agency. As a result of the reorganization, many employees left the agency, and "The Director," as he was later affectionately called, combed the country for competent, conscientious men who could be depended upon for hard work and efficient service. In his recruitment program he announced that the promotion system that he would utilize would be one where the employee would be judged only by performance. This, of course, was a relatively innovative comment to be made during a time of high patronage within the federal government.

The Federal Bureau of Investigation grew under Hoover's leadership and direction from 441 special agents in 1924 to 8000 special agents and more than 1100 civilian employees in 59 field offices located throughout the United States and Puerto Rico.

Although recent critics of J. Edgar Hoover and his organization have raised serious doubts about the role and activities of the Bureau, he did build an organization that was highly efficient and held in high regard. Although one may question the appropriateness of some of the methods of the F.B.I. and their image, it must be admitted that by Hoover's conscientious efforts, the organization earned a place in history and contributed to the evolution of law enforcement within the United States.

Summary

Archaeological findings give evidence that some form of law enforcement existed even during ancient times. Such law enforcement was, of course, based primarily on the need for protection against marauders or for the enforcement of elementary social codes. As society became more complex, so did the type and degree of enforcement policies and principles.

Generally speaking, law enforcement developed concurrently with the development of law. The first known codification of laws was that of Hammurabi, ancient king of Babylon. This legal code was concerned with such matters as responsibilities of the individual to the group and private dealings between individuals. The existence of law naturally required the existence of a mechanism for enforcement. As law developed, the mechanism became continually more elaborate.

Law enforcement developed rather slowly during ancient and medieval history, but many events during that time influenced the emergence of law enforcement as we know it today. To appreciate and understand current law enforcement, it is imperative that one be familiar with the contributions of such people as Pisistratus, Solon, Augustus, and the English kings during medieval history.

A very critical need for effective law enforcement came into existence in London when, as a result of the industrial revolution, the city became urbanized. In response to the concurrent crime problem, Sir Robert Peel created the first modern police organization: the new metropolitan constabulary. This new police agency became the model for those that were eventually established in the United States.

Law enforcement in America developed in a rather haphazard manner, with the Southern colonies adopting the English sheriffs system, and the North their constable or town system. Municipal police systems evolved further with

101

the growth of cities. As the cities grew, the demand for
police services multiplied. In the United States, police
departments in most cities developed from military protection,
or martial law, to the appointment of a single watchmen,
to a constable or marshall, to a night watch, to a separate
day watch, to the combination of both the day and night
watch, and finally to the establishment of a formal police
department.

State police agencies came into existence for a variety
of reasons, such as the inability of municipal agencies to
handle mobilized interstate crime activities and corruption
in some local agencies. Others were created to meet the need
for an executive arm to enforce state laws. Federal law
enforcement agencies, like the state police, emerged as a result
of the many problems faced by a fast growing country.

Some of the early leaders in the development of American
law enforcement were Allan Pinkerton (first detective),
August Vollmer (Dean of American Chiefs of Police), O. W.
Wilson, William Parker, and J. Edgar Hoover.

1. Discuss the relationship between the development of law and the development of law enforcement agencies.
2. Discuss the early Greek and Roman contributions to the development of law enforcement.
3. Discuss the Anglo-Saxon contributions to the development of law enforcement.
4. Discuss the governmental structure of Anglo-Saxon England and its influence on law enforcement.
5. What were the contributions of King William toward the development of law enforcement?
6. What is Henry I famous for relative to law enforcement?
7. What was the Court of Star Chamber?
8. What effect did the Industrial Revolution have on law enforcement?
9. Discuss the development of municipal law enforcement in the United States.
10. Discuss the development of state and federal law enforcement agencies in the United States.

3

State of the Art

Police agencies in the United States—with its rapid and erratic growth—developed in a rapid, haphazard, and sometimes contradictory manner. This statement is not necessarily critical of the police, but rather is critical of local government wherein the police have developed.

By tradition, law enforcement is a local matter, and, therefore, the development of the police naturally reflects the quality of local government. Police efficiency, quality, image, and prestige are clearly dependent upon the quality of local government and reflect the attitudes of those representatives administering government.

Early police departments, like local governments, were often inefficient and incompetent. Most, if not all, early police departments were traditionally impregnated with political appointees who were often corrupt and who were not necessarily concerned with individual rights. Even today, there are departments so ingrained with such traditionalism that appointments and promotions are still politically made. In many cities such patronage exists throughout the ranks, and a complete reorganization occurs with the election of succeeding mayors. However, even though such problems still exist, the police have advanced considerably.

LAW ENFORCEMENT AS A PROFESSION

Recognized professions include such fields as law, medicine, theology, and education. Can the police service join their ranks and also be considered a "true" profession? This question has been debated for several years, and debate will undoubtedly continue for several more. Actually, however, those who claim a professional status for the police service are being unrealistically optimistic.

There has been much said about what is required for professional status, and there is ample literature that lists the criteria or characteristics of a profession. However, these

107

lists often have little in common and are often contradictory. It would seem, therefore, that professional status is a broad term which means different things to different people.

Police officers are eager for professional recognition, and they have devised numerous supporting rationales. In supporting their claim they often point to such things as amount of recruit or in-service training, efficiency, appearance, and an elaborate organizational structure. These are all elements or criteria for professionalization, but by themselves they do not justify the claim.

Unfortunately, much of the effort toward achieving professionalism has been directed toward the total organization rather than the individuals within it. Certainly, administrative concepts and organizational designs are important, but more important are the individuals working within that framework. Before the police service can be considered a profession, each and every person involved must be a professional. Each police officer must be totally dedicated, possess a healthy attitude, be interested in self-improvement, and have a firm grasp of that field of knowledge peculiar to law enforcement.

Perhaps a reasonable approach is to identify the common characteristics of the identifiable professions and then determine if law enforcement possesses these elements. If law enforcement does, perhaps it can lay claim to professional status. If it does not, then it may not justifiably make the claim.

In comparing the accepted professions, those characteristics that seem to be common to all are: 1) ample professional literature, 2) research, 3) the existence of and participation in professional organizations, 4) an ethical code of conduct sworn to by all, 5) a devotion by all members toward self-improvement, and 6) the existence of an identifiable academic field of knowledge peculiar to that profession in conjunction with a formulized educational prerequisite.

Progress, although slow, has accelerated recently as a result of societal demands. The police have had to struggle to merely keep pace with technological advances and social change.

As will be recalled, law enforcement is a blanket term that includes enforcement at the federal, state, and local level. The various law enforcement agencies are striving toward professionalization at varying rates. Generally speaking, federal law enforcement agencies better reflect professionalism than do most local agencies. This is not to imply that federal law enforcement is alone in such an accomplishment, nor is it to say they have actually reached the "true" professional level. State and local police agencies have also, in varying degrees, advanced toward the goal. Some are within reach, some have exceeded federal agencies, but most have lagged behind.

The greatest encouragement can be derived from the fact that the police are involved in all the criteria believed necessary for professionalization. They have not sufficiently progressed in any one of the areas, but progress is constant in all areas. The federal government should be credited with providing the necessary impetus for the improvement in local and state law enforcement agencies.

FEDERAL INFLUENCE

In recognition of the nation's crime problem and the need for improving law enforcement, the federal government initiated several programs to study the problem and to assist local law enforcement. This participation by federal government initiated a surge forward toward professionalization. Federal interest was best typified by the creation, in 1965, of a Commission on Law Enforcement and Administration of Justice, the passage of the Law Enforcement Assistance Act of 1965, and the passage of the *Omnibus Crime Control and Safe Streets Act of 1968*. These programs were of such significance and influenced the professional criteria so greatly that they need to be discussed fully as a prelude to the present involvement of law enforcement in the professional criteria.

Commission on law enforcement and administration of justice. This commission was established on July 23, 1965, in recognition of the urgency of the nation's crime problem

109

at that time. The Commission was instructed to inquire into the causes of crime and delinquency and to issue recommendations for preventing crime and delinquency and improving law enforcement and the administration of criminal justice.

The work of the Commission was initially divided into four major areas: 1) police, 2) courts, 3) corrections, 4) assessment of the crime problem. As the Commission's work proceeded, special task forces were formed to study organized crime, juvenile delinquency, narcotics, and drunkenness. Finally, a task force in science and technology was also organized.

The Commission's research and inquiries took many forms and included broad-scale surveys, analysis of data available from federal law enforcement agencies, and conferences. Advice was sought at every step from experts in law enforcement, criminal justice, and crime prevention. Finally, the results of the Commission were published in ten documents, each covering a task force subject.

The mere formation of the Commission created nationwide interest that directed attention to the criminal justice system. Police were looking critically at their own department. The public became painfully aware of police problems and the apparent ineffectiveness of the criminal justice system. Legislatures began reviewing laws with an intention of improving them, and many states established similar commissions. All in all, everyone became more aware of the law enforcement problems and more concerned with solutions.

The published task force reports were a hallmark in police literature. They attacked the issues, discussed without reservation the failure of criminal justice, and offered recommendations for improvement. The reports provided guidelines for improvement. Criminal justice leaders pored over the reports and implemented many changes which did improve criminal justice.

A primary value of the Commission and the resulting reports was that the issue of criminal justice was forced upon legislatures and local politicians. No longer could they avoid the issue. It was before them, demanding subsequent action.

Law Enforcement Assistance Act. The Law Enforcement Assistance Act of 1965 also resulted from the federal government's concern with the problem of crime. This act which created the Office of Law Enforcement Assistance (OLEA) was signed by the President on September 22, 1965. The act made funds available to states, localities, and private organizations to improve methods of law enforcement, court administration, and prison operation. Briefly, the act authorized federal grants to public or nonprofit agencies to improve training of personnel, to advance the capabilities of law enforcement bodies, and to assist in the prevention and control of crime. The Law Enforcement Assistance Act also authorized the United States Attorney General to conduct studies, render technical assistance, evaluate the effectiveness of programs undertaken, and disseminate information on the projects.

Under this act, which concluded June 19, 1968, federal support was given to 359 separate projects. The projects included training, research, demonstration efforts to prevent and control crime or to improve criminal justice agencies, and the giving of assistance in upgrading personnel. Four hundred twenty-six grants and contracts were given, totaling 20.6 million dollars, to grantees or contractors in all fifty states, thus causing national influence on criminal justice.

The act was the first federal law giving money to local government for improvement of law enforcement. The accomplishments under it were quite significant to law enforcement. For example, during the act's duration, 2.5 million dollars were allocated for general recruit and in-service training, and .8 million dollars for higher education. Like the Commission on Law Enforcement and Administration of Justice, this act and resulting activities were without precedence and added great impetus to the achievement of professional law enforcement. OLEA was also influential in that moneys from it supported much of the work done by the

111

Commission. In reality, the two were partners to some extent, and their concurrent roles strengthened each other. The Commission identified weaknesses in criminal justice to which OLEA could direct its attention and OLEA provided financial assistance to the important work of the Commission.

Omnibus Crime Control and Safe Streets Act. This act, commonly referred to as the *Safe Streets Act* became effective on June 19, 1968. The Safe Streets Act repealed the Law Enforcement Act of 1965 but was committed to fulfilling the existing obligations of OLEA. The new act established the Law Enforcement Assistance Administration (LEAA) which was responsible for carrying out the provisions of the bill.

The Safe Streets Act was a milestone for the nation and addressed itself to some of the most urgent problems in criminal justice. It offered federal funds to help states and local communities plan, coordinate, and attack the crime problem. The origins of this bill can be found in the studies conducted by the previous President's Commission on Law Enforcement and Administration of Justice, some of which was funded by OLEA. The Safe Streets Bill incorporated recommendations made by the Commission and reflected the experiences of OLEA.

Title I of the Safe Streets Bill provided funds for planning and initiating action programs to strengthen law enforcement. More specifically, it provided funds for 1) the creation of state planning agencies, 2) action grants to improve and strengthen all aspects of criminal justice, 3) academic assistance grants to encourage higher education, and 4) the establishment of a National Institute to conduct research relative to crime prevention.

The Safe Streets Bill provided impetus for the creation of state planning agencies and subsequent state comprehensive law enforcement plans. It also provided funds, channeled through the state agency, which improved police operations throughout the United States. The bill also caused many law enforcement personnel to seek additional education by providing grants and loans for such purposes. In addition, the act allowed pre-service students of law enforcement to obtain loans which were excused when they became employed by a law enforcement agency.

The Safe Streets Bill was obviously the culmination of all federal programs for local law enforcement and has had, by far, the greatest impact. As a result of such federal interest, law enforcement has improved, is continuing to improve, and such improvement moves law enforcement toward becoming a profession.

National Advisory Commission on Criminal Justice Standards and Goals. This Commission was appointed by Jerris Leonard, Administrator of the Law Enforcement Assistance Administration (LEAA), on October 20, 1971. The purpose of the Commission was to formulate for the first time national criminal justice standards and goals for crime reduction and prevention at the state and local levels. The work of the Commission was supported by a discretional grant from LEAA in the amount of $1.75 million. Although it represents only one of many grants awarded by LEAA, its significance to law enforcement in the United States merits comment in any discussion of federal influence on local law enforcement.

Commission members were drawn from state and local government, from industry, and from citizen groups. Commissioners were chosen, in part, for their working experience in the field of criminal justice. Represented were police chiefs, judges, correctional leaders, and prosecutors.

Other recent commissions, such as the Commission on Law Enforcement and Administration of Justice, have studied the criminal justice system. The purpose of this Commission was not to duplicate past significant activities, but to expand their work and build upon it by developing clear statements of priorities, goals, and standards to help set a national strategy to reduce crime through the equitable administration of justice; the protection of life, liberty and property; and the efficient mobilization of resources. It was hoped that state and local governments would evaluate their present status and implement those standards and recommendations that were appropriate.

In many instances the Commission recommended specific guidelines for evaluating existing practices or for setting up new programs. In some areas, however, there was a lack of reliable information that would justify specific recommendations. In these cases, the Commission urged additional professional research.

The National Commission appointed six different task forces that were each responsible for a specific area of study. This organization resulted in six separate reports: 1) *A National Strategy to Reduce Crime*; 2) *Criminal Justice System*; 3) *Police*; 4) *Courts*; 5) *Corrections*; and 6) *Community Crime Prevention*. Each report contains valuable recommendations relative to standards and goals.

These publications are extremely valuable and relevant to all segments of the criminal justice system. Professional criminal justice administrators will undoubtedly find the reports helpful as they attempt to improve their delivery of services. These reports represent the most up-to-date and proven experience in the criminal justice field today.

PROFESSIONAL LITERATURE

For years there was a definite lack of good professional literature in the fields of police administration, police technology, and law enforcement in general. Books were the exception rather than the rule, and the number of law enforcement periodicals were few.

In recent years publishers have become increasingly interested in publishing books and periodicals in the police field. Probably the most influential factor in increasing the availability of professional literature has been the growing number of college-level law enforcement programs. Not only have these programs created the need for textbooks, but also

114

Police officers from various police agencies in library

Courtesy Harrisburg Area Community College
Harrisburg, Pa.

they have provided police educators with an opportunity to publish and share information.

There is still a need for quality professional literature, but that need is being met.

PROFESSIONAL ORGANIZATIONS

Perhaps one of the most influential professional law enforcement organizations is the International Association of Chiefs of Police (IACP) which has a membership exceeding six thousand. The IACP has been very active in upgrading law enforcement across the country, has encouraged cooperation between police agencies, and has disseminated professional information to all police agencies.

The IACP has been particularly active in the areas of developing training standards, developing instructional materials, encouraging education, and providing consulting services on a fee basis to law enforcement agencies. In fact, endorsement by IACP has resulted in the acceptance by police agencies of many modern innovations. The results of this organization's efforts are highly visible throughout the law enforcement field.

Not all law enforcement agencies in the United States are represented in the IACP membership, and in all probability some never will be. However, membership representative of the greatest possible number of agencies is highly desirable in furthering professionalization of law enforcement.

One limitation of the IACP is that active membership is limited to chiefs of police or law enforcement executive officers. It is an organization for management personnel and does not necessarily represent the lower echelon within the law enforcement ranks. This is not to suggest that membership should be open, but illustrates the need for professional organizations for the lower ranks.

A recently chartered organization that has the potential of playing an extremely important role in the improvement of policing is the Police Executive Research Forum (PERF). This organization was established in 1976 and its membership is limited to chiefs serving populations of 100,000 or more persons or having at least 200 employees. PERF is dedicated to the comprehensive improvement of policing through research, debate, and professionalization of police leadership.

PERF has already issued many policy statements related to the improvement of policing. For example, they have pledged to work to remove the roadblocks which keep police executives and officers from advancing their careers through transferring from one agency to another, they have called for a four-year degree for all police chiefs, and have recommended that state and local jurisdictions consider ways of

116

establishing a fair tenure system for chiefs. It can be expected that PERF will play an increasingly important role in the future of policing.

The population limitation for membership is justified on the basis that the larger cities have common problems, that they face the nation's truly intensive crime problems and the other complicated issues of police service, and that most of the nation's police officers are represented by the larger cities that qualify for membership. However, it is believed that chiefs of smaller jurisdictions should have some official association with PERF. Certainly the larger cities have severe problems, many of which are a result of poor planning or the lack of vision a few years ago that would have permitted preparation for solving them. A vehicle should exist whereby executives of the larger communities identify their problems so that chiefs of the smaller, but growing jurisdictions, can develop appropriate plans so that the problems will not arise at a later time. At least, problems related to growth can be minimized with the help of PERF.

Another recently established national organization is the National Organization of Black Law Enforcement Executives (NOBLE). NOBLE was established in 1976 to improve the nation's system of criminal justice and to promote a better understanding of crime and its causes in urban areas. This organization will also be very influential in the future development of policing and criminal justice in general. In fact, NOBLE has already taken some very important stands relative to police practices.

The Academy of Criminal Justice Sciences (ACJS) is an organization comprised primarily of criminal justice educators. The purpose of this organization, according to its constitution, is to foster excellence in education and research in the field of criminal justice in institutions of higher education, to build cooperation between criminal justice agencies, and to provide a forum for the exchange of information. ACJS was established in 1963 as the International Association of Police Professors and later changed its name to better reflect the broad concept of criminal justice. This association has been

117

becoming increasingly active and will definitely influence the development and improvement of criminal justice across the nation.

Most states have statewide as well as local law enforcement associations. It is common, for example, to find state associations of chiefs of police, training officers, juvenile officers, investigators, and others representing a specific police activity. Most state groups also have highly specialized committees and subcommittees and sponsor annual conferences and professional seminars. Some associations are more active than others, but all are concerned with upgrading police service.

Lambda Alpha Epsilon is another national association that exists for the purpose of upgrading criminal justice. This association's membership is limited to police officers and police aspirants who are enrolled in college law enforcement programs. The association began in California, but as more colleges have adopted law enforcement programs the membership has grown significantly. In recent years Lambda Alpha Epsilon has regionalized its organization and has chapters throughout the United States. The prerequisite for membership is advanced education, and therefore, it would seem the organization can become significantly influential.

Another national organization is the Fraternal Order of Police (FOP) which has chapters throughout the United States. Membership consists primarily of patrolmen, and hundreds of municipal police departments have their local chapter.

Although considerable activity exists, there are still many directions these associations can take that will provide impetus for better law enforcement. They need, for example, to become more actively involved in training programs, work more closely with colleges and universities, and encourage professional standards for all law enforcement personnel.

RESEARCH

Research is a vital part of all professions, but until recent years little research was conducted in law enforcement. In fact, for years law enforcement existed on pure traditionalism with little emphasis on experimentation or attempting to determine better and more rewarding techniques. Actually, little research was done until 1965 and then it was a result of the critical crime problem throughout the United States. At that time, and also as a result of the crime problem, the Federal Law Enforcement Assistance Act was passed which provided additional impetus for research.

A giant stride in research was made with the passage of the Safe Streets Bill of 1968 which, among other things, established a National Research Center. This center, in Washington, D. C., has conducted a great deal of research which has been quite enlightening to law enforcement nationally.

The National Research Center was later named the National Institute of Law Enforcement and Criminal Justice, the research arm of the Law Enforcement Assistance Administration. To study, evaluate, and inform is the threefold mission of the Institute. The Institute's goal is to develop useful ways to reduce crime and promote justice. Since its establishment, the Institute has sponsored imaginative and useful research which has had a significant impact on criminal justice practices. Research efforts have focused on new approaches in the areas of community crime prevention, police, courts, corrections, advanced technology, patrol, and criminal investigation. The emphasis has been on meeting pressing needs in these areas and providing information that is helpful and practical. Hopefully, from this research will come insights and methods to improve the effectiveness of the entire criminal justice system.

The Law Enforcement Assistance Administration has committed the Federal government to provide substantial financial assistance to the police and other criminal justice agencies. Local governments have also demonstrated their willingness to provide additional financial support to the police by enlarging their police budgets. Most of this local money, however, has gone to support increases in manpower and increases in police salaries. There will, in the years to come, be a massive infusion of new funds into police activities.

119

The private sector is also providing additional support for the police. For example, the Ford Foundation established the Police Foundation which has already put considerable money into police operations.

Regardless of all the financial assistance, if the country is to benefit the funded programs must be carefully analyzed and researched. Unfortunately, increased spending for police, for the most part, is proceeding without the benefit of analysis relative to how the program is better achieving goals and objectives.

If ultimate police efficiency is to be realized, a portion of the available financial resources must be directed to supporting experimental and evaluative programs designed to improve the accomplishment of police objectives.

CODE OF ETHICS

A hallmark of a profession is a code of ethics that is adhered to by all within that profession. There is a Law Enforcement Code of Ethics which very adequately depicts the ideals and common goals of the law enforcement officer. Unfortunately, however, many police officers are unaware of this formalized code. Therefore, they do not realize that the ideals set forth in the code should be an integral part of their lives. This does not mean that officers do not live by its standards. By virtue of dedication to service most officers do live by the code even though they may be unfamiliar with it.

Regardless of conduct, however, all officers should be familiar with the Law Enforcement Code of Ethics, and let it serve as a framework within which to direct their lives. Devotion to the code is absolutely necessary since it pertains directly to each and every individual. Only professional individuals make a profession.

SELF-IMPROVEMENT

Dedication to self-improvement by every law enforcement officer is imperative before professionalism can be realized.

Law Enforcement Code of Ethics

As a Law Enforcement Officer, my fundamental duty is to serve mankind; to safeguard lives and property; to protect the innocent against deception, the weak against oppression or intimidation, and the peaceful against violence and disorder; and to respect the Constitutional rights of all men to liberty, equality and justice.

I will keep my private life unsullied as an example to all; maintain courageous calm in the face of danger, scorn, or ridicule; develop self-restraint; and be constantly mindful of the welfare of others. Honest in thought and deed in both my personal and official life, I will be exemplary in obeying the laws of the land and the regulations of my department. Whatever I see or hear of a confidential nature or that is confided to me in my official capacity will be kept ever secret unless revelation is necessary in the performance of my duty.

I will never act officiously or permit personal feelings, prejudices, animosities or friendships to influence my decisions. With no compromise for crime and with relentless prosecution of criminals, I will enforce the law courteously and appropriately without fear or favor, malice or ill will, never employing unnecessary force or violence and never accepting gratuities.

I recognize the badge of my office as a symbol of public faith, and I accept it as a public trust to be held so long as I am true to the ethics of the police service. I will constantly strive to achieve these objectives and ideals, dedicating myself before God to my chosen profession . . . law enforcement.

Officers must have inquisitive minds, must question aspects of law enforcement, and must exploit every possible opportunity to improve themselves. This improvement, of course, is usually best achieved by participating in training and education programs. Therefore, it is necessary that law enforcement officers extend themselves to make such opportunities available. Many departments have initiated pre-service and in-service training programs during the last few years, but there is still room for improvement. All departments must become involved with or make available self-improvement programs in such areas as supervision, middle management, management, community relations, and in specialized techniques. Law enforcement will become a profession only after such programs are available and utilized nationwide.

Perhaps this is the area of most concern for many police administrators. Many chiefs are questioning the interest of line level police officers in improvement. It seems that many officers have lost a sense of direction and purpose relative to their role as police officers. Some chiefs are asking, for example, what has happened to commitment, dedication, and loyalty? Are police officers interested in serving their community or are they only interested in higher pay, fewer working hours, more vacation, and payment for any extra commitment? How can officers swear to enforce the law and then threaten to strike?

In any event, many believe that there is a different kind of person entering the law enforcement vocation today. Somehow police administrators must not only find answers to these questions, but must restore the commitment of employees to public service. Of primary concern is that we have made many strides toward becoming a profession, but the changing attitude of line officers has taken a step backward. This is not to imply that there are not dedicated police officers, but there certainly seem to be increasing numbers of officers more interested in personal comfort than in serving mankind. For example, many chiefs have made training programs available to police officers, but the officers refuse to attend unless time-and-a-half pay is given. It would seem that a professional person would be willing to devote some of his or her own time to training, since both the officer and the profession would benefit.

The recognition of the need for law enforcement educational programs and their subsequent development has been the most encouraging step in the climb toward professionalization and is, perhaps, the key to achievement. Sound educational programs not only reflect their field of knowledge, but as more and more officers attain degrees, their excellence will give strength to the other professional criteria. Such men will, by virtue of their education, be prone to become concerned with and involved in all those activities that reflect a profession. The growth of law enforcement education programs in our colleges and universities can be considered the most significant development in law enforcement since the existence of the police service. In view of such prominence, the law enforcement student should be knowledgeable of the development of this role.

POLICE TRAINING

Probably every chief of police in the United States pays lip service to the need for police training; yet some of these same chiefs are not exploiting the available training possibilities. This was clearly evident in 1959 when a survey of the present status of police training in the United States was conducted. This survey indicated that out of 1,105 cities reporting, more than 43 percent did not have any form of training program. All cities over 250,000 population reported that they had a recruit training program of one type or another, while only 42 percent of the cities in the 10,000 to 250,000 population group had some type of recruit training. This indicates that most cities with populations less than 10,000 do not maintain

123

any recruit training, although they did indicate that they periodically send some personnel to state-sponsored schools.[1]

In 1967, the President's Commission on Law Enforcement and Administration of Justice in the *Challenge of Crime in a Free Society* recommended that an absolute minimum of 400 classroom hours be established for basic police training. An IACP survey in 1970 disclosed that 33 states had laws requiring basic police training, but that only 19 states required 200 or more hours of instruction. The hours of required training ranged from 72 to 400.[2]

Although it is true that many police departments have established training programs, it is being increasingly recognized that training facilities and opportunities should be available to all law enforcement personnel.

Many departments lacking recruit training justified the circumstances on the basis of inadequate resources, citing a lack of facilities, money, time, or know how. Most often, however, each of these excuses serves primarily as an attempt to rationalize a more subtle resistance.

Every police department has some room or office that could be used for training for at least part of the day. Chairs, a table, a blackboard, and chalk are standard equipment everywhere and can be easily moved from place to place. If the problem of space actually does exist, it is often possible to hold meetings in other community buildings. Public school officials often are willing to loan the use of their buildings from time to time at little or no cost to the police department. Various businessmen often have room that they are willing to donate. The National Guard Unit or Reserve Centers usually have space that may be available for the asking. Obviously, lack of facilities for the training is not a valid excuse.

[1] International City Managers' Association, *The Municipal Yearbook—1959* (Chicago: International City Managers' Association, 1959), p. 402.

[2] National Advisory Commission on Criminal Justice Standards and Goals, *Police* (Washington, D.C.: U.S. Government Printing Office, 1973), p. 392.

124

Shortage of funds is a common and convenient excuse for not providing training. Yet, training need not cost anything except for the time and personnel involved and an incidental outlay for textbooks, some of which can be borrowed from public libraries.

Availability of time may pose a problem, but it is believed that a sufficient number of officers will be willing to attend class on their own time if they believe the program to be worthwhile. Many of these officers will be so career-minded that they will be willing to spend some off-duty time on additional training. Vollmer's men back in 1907 believed it desirable to attend training classes on their own time. There is no reason to doubt that modern officers lack this desire for learning. At least some of the officers will voluntarily attend training sessions if they are made available. Persons capable of acting as instructors may be obtained from sources such as police academies of larger cities, universities, the Federal Bureau of Investigation, community colleges, and the local school system.

Four principal types of training programs can be identified from available literature: 1) local programs, which include recruit training and department in-service training; 2) zone schools, which include short courses offered by the Federal Bureau of Investigation; 3) specialized police schools, which include institutes and short courses offered by colleges and universities; and 4) extended college and university programs in police administration, criminology, and specialized fields.

PRE-SERVICE RECRUIT TRAINING

Pre-service recruit training is the foundation for good patrol service and for the continuation of specialized training. It is essential that the recruit training be for a period of no less than three months. During the recruit training, the recruit should receive considerable supervised street experience in addition to the classroom instruction. Upon completion of the

Firearms training

Courtesy of the Police Training Institute, University of Illinois, Champaign, Ill.

recruit training school, the officer should receive additional supervised street experience. This supervised training is essential in determining if the new officer can put into practice those things he has learned in the recruit school. Very often it is necessary for the street supervisor to clarify many things that were taught in the classroom situation.[3]

[3] O. W. Wilson, *Police Planning* (2nd ed.; Springfield, Ill.: Charles C Thomas, 1962), p. 149.

126

Instructors. An analysis of law enforcement indicates that there is a large amount of practical knowledge and technical information that should be acquired by an officer before he is qualified to serve as a functioning member of a police agency. Officers should receive organized instruction in the elements of their job. For each phase of the training, a highly qualified instructor is the best assurance that the student officer will receive the type of training and education necessary to tackle his task as an officer. The instructor of law enforcement groups should be thoroughly experienced in law enforcement work and should have demonstrated that he can measure up, in all important aspects, to the demands of the job.[4] In addition, he should: 1) understand and appreciate the difficulties of the learner, 2) have an appreciation of what the teaching job consists of and its importance, and 3) have a clear knowledge of reliable, effective teaching methods and be able to apply them.[5]

In addition to using those qualified individuals within the department as instructors, the department can utilize available resources of the community and nation. In some states, boards for vocational education provide this type of assistance and also provide teacher training. The Federal Bureau of Investigation in its regional and local training programs provides both organization of subject matter and instruction. There are also many people within the community who, although they have no police experience, are more competent to provide instruction in subjects not of an exclusive police nature than are the police themselves. Such subjects include legal medicine and toxicology, criminologic psychiatry, first aid, public speaking, report writing, typewriting, self-defense, public relations, and photography. In addition, it is usually quite easy to get the legal staff of the city or county to assist in teaching subjects related to their field of endeavor.

---

[4] *The Operation of a Local Program of Trade and Industrial Education with Emphasis on Improving Instruction Through Supervision,* Bulletin 250 (Washington, D.C.: United States Office of Education, 1953), p. 122.

[5] Samuel G. Chapman, *Police Patrol Readings* (Springfield, Ill.: Charles C Thomas, 1964), pp. 459–461.

127

Training in use of Prosecutor

Courtesy of Harrisburg Area Community College, Harrisburg, Pa.

Quite obviously, there should be no problem in obtaining the necessary instructors for the recruit training school.[6]

Subject matter. In developing the curriculum for the pre-service police recruit school, it is extremely important to select courses that will contribute most to the development of the recruit. If careful selection of subjects is not exercised, it is likely that relatively insignificant subjects will be overemphasized while the more important ones are neglected.

In 1969, the New York City Police Department conducted a study relative to the curricula content of training programs

[6] From *Police Administration* by O. W. Wilson (New York: Mc-Graw-Hill Book Company, Inc., 1950), p. 383. Used with permission of McGraw-Hill Book Company.

within 60 various-sized police departments. Although the New York study might tend to discourage attempts to develop an ideal basic police curriculum, several broad areas can be identified as basic. Individual agency training programs could expand from this base by adding areas and concentration to meet local police, government and community needs. This base should include topics similar to the following:

1. Introduction to the Criminal Justice Systems: an examination of the foundation functions of the criminal justice system with specific attention to the role of the police in the system in government:
2. Law: an introduction to the development; philosophy; types of law; criminal procedure and rules of evidence; discretionary justice; application of the U.S. Constitution; court systems and procedures; and related civil law;
3. Human Values and Problems: public service and non-criminal policing; cultural awareness; changing roles of the police; human behavior and conflict management; psychology as it relates to the police function; causes of crime and delinquency; and police public relations;
4. Patrol and Investigation Procedures: the fundamentals of the patrol function including traffic, juvenile, and preliminary investigations; reporting and communications; arrest and detention procedures; interviewing; criminal investigation and case preparations; equipment and facility use; and the other day-to-day responsibilities and duties;
5. Police Proficiency: philosophy of when to use force and the appropriate determination of the degree necessary; armed and unarmed defense; crowd, riot, and prisoner control; physical conditioning; emergency medical services; driver training; and
6. Administration: evaluation, examination, and counseling processes; departmental policies, rules, regulations, organization, and personnel procedures.[7]

[7] National Advisory Commission on Criminal Justice Standards and Goals, p. 394.

DEPARTMENTAL IN-SERVICE TRAINING

Officer continuation training is the next vital step after the recruit school. Each year there should be at least one full week of training for each member of the force. The course of instruction should be redesigned each year in order to meet current needs arising from changes in policies and procedures, the adoption of new techniques, and weaknesses detected in the recruit program.

In addition to this one week a year instruction, it is also important that the officers receive continuous instruction on new developments throughout the year. Many current issues cannot be postponed until the yearly school is in session and must be presented to the men as quickly as possible.

The officer continuation training program can be broken down into three distinct areas: 1) new laws, ideas, and techniques; 2) repeat information; and 3) manual skills.[8]

New laws, ideas, and techniques. It is essential for police efficiency and effectiveness that every officer be familiar with new laws and ordinances that affect his work. Under law, every man is presumed to know the law. Although this is not literally true, it is true that the police officers should be more familiar with the law than the average citizen.

To keep up with the changing world, it is necessary that any new ideas be passed on to every officer. The beat officer is at the execution level of the police organization, and he is the only man that can put new ideas and techniques into operation. Any new idea or technique of the administrator must be tested by the beat officer at the execution level. It is, therefore, absolutely essential that the men at the execution level have complete understanding of any and all new ideas or techniques.[9]

[8] Robert Matt, "Officer Continuation Training," *Police*, V (September–October, 1960), p. 6.

[9] *Ibid.*

Breath alcohol testing training

Courtesy of the Police Training Institute, University of Illinois,
Champaign, Ill., and Professor Walter Ziel

Repeat information.   A great many things given in the
recruit training school will be forgotten unless the information
is periodically repeated. Such things as departmental policy,
rules and regulations, and general orders come within the
realm of repeat information. These are things that directly
influence the efficiency of the department. Retention can be
more assured if the information is repeated from time to time.
The officers must be constantly aware of their responsibilities,
and only repetition on these vital points can produce the constant awareness that is necessary.[10]

Manual skills.   Such things as techniques and mechanics
of arrest, firearms training, manual traffic control, self-

[10] *Ibid.*, p. 7.

defense tactics, search and seizure, and other related law enforcement physical skills fall into this area. Manual skills will decrease in efficiency if constant practice is lacking. It is unlikely that an officer will remain a sharpshooter without constant practice. It is also unlikely that the officer will become effective in self-defense techniques unless he practices on a continuous basis after the pre-service recruit training school.[11]

What methods can a department use to offer continuous in-service training? One worthwhile method that should be used is "roll call training." Almost every police department in the country has a briefing period prior to each shift. This period can be used for training purposes. The first two areas of continuous in-service training: 1) new laws, ideas, and techniques, and 2) repeat information can easily be accomplished through this method.[12]

Bulletins can be distributed periodically to the officers to supplement the instruction at roll call. The information on the training bulletins can be discussed in detail, and the supervisors can clarify the content.[13]

Police departments should periodically offer one- or two-day training sessions throughout the year. At these refresher courses the department can cover material that they believe is pertinent to the efficient operation of their particular department. This type of training can be very beneficial to those officers working toward promotions and those who are desirous of receiving some advanced police education. The training enables the police department to cover material that is of special importance at that particular time. Very often incidents will occur, such as passage of the civil rights laws, which necessitate the training of officers in their role as it is affected by the new laws.

[11] *Ibid.*, p. 8.

[12] International City Managers' Association, *Municipal Police Administration*, 5th ed. (Chicago: The Institute for Training in Municipal Administration, 1961), pp. 189–190.

[13] *Ibid.*

Manual skills training

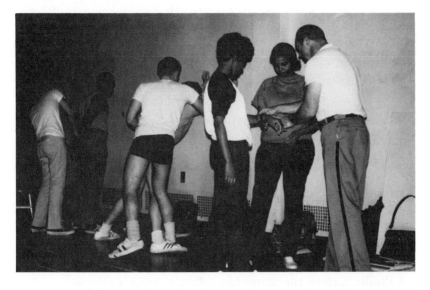

Courtesy of the Police Training Institute, University of Illinois,
Champaign, Ill.

In all instances of in-service training, instruction should be of the same caliber as that received at the pre-service recruit training school. Since the same resources are available for both, there is no reason that this cannot be the case.[14]

SPECIALIZED POLICE SCHOOLS

So far the material presented has dealt only with those training programs that should be provided by the police department, but many other significant training opportunities are available to interested police officers.

As officers develop in experience, some will demonstrate an interest and aptitude for special phases of police work, or they might demonstrate their potentiality as future police administrators. These men should take advantage of any train-

[14] *Ibid.*

133

ing program that will be of assistance to their careers. It will benefit the department to be sure that such opportunities for potential specialized personnel are used.

There are many diversified advanced police training programs that are available for such use. Some of the most noteworthy are:

- Northwestern Traffic Institute, Northwestern University
- Bureau of Police Science, University of Iowa
- Delinquency Control Institute, University of Southern California
- Center for Police Training, Indiana University
- In-Service Training Program, Michigan State University
- Southern Police Institute, University of Louisville
- Southwestern Center for Law Enforcement Education, University of Oklahoma
- Public Safety Institute, Long Beach State College
- Federal Bureau of Investigation National Academy

There are also numerous programs offered by the more than 300 colleges and universities with academic programs in criminal justice. These colleges recently have begun to respond to the training needs by offering specialized courses of varying natures. Typically, if a police department contacts an area community college, state college, or state university with the request for specialized training, these institutions will respond.

THE REGIONAL TRAINING CONCEPT

The regional school type of organization relates specifically to providing training opportunities for law enforcement agencies in small cities, towns, and counties which employ comparatively few police officers.

The regional school idea actually originated in 1934 when several large cities began the practice of offering basic courses for the smaller communities in the surrounding area.

134

A prime example of the regional school system at the state level is found in the state of California. California was divided into a number of zones, each comprising a number of small communities where it was found desirable for officers to go to a central training center for instruction. Special consideration was given to the location of the school, so that adequate training facilities would be available to officers who lived within practical and easy commuting distance of the training center.

Historically, police training in the United States has been primarily a local responsibility. While some state and national efforts existed, the training of local police depended on local initiative. It is agreed that training of local police is rightfully a local responsibility, but complicating the achievements of any success is the fundamental problem of the large number of uncoordinated local governments and law enforcement agencies. It is common, for example, to find within metropolitan areas several small police departments, none of which have sufficient resources to establish and administer an adequate police training program.

This is further complicated by the fact that throughout the nation nearly 90 percent of all police agencies consist of less than 10 personnel. It can, therefore, be assumed that, due to lack of resources of smaller departments, nearly 90 percent of the police departments in the United States are using police officers with little or no training at all. Conversely, in larger cities (i.e., 500,000 or more) several weeks of training may be required.

There are two alternatives to the resolution of this particular problem. One is development of the regional school training concept, whereby training is available at various locations throughout the state. Typically, the locations are geographically distributed so that they are within easy commuting distance of any police department.

This is certainly not a new concept. In 1937, as a result of the George Dean bill, a number of states became active in the police training field. Even two years before this 1937 bill, the zone school idea made its appearance, when several large municipalities began the practice of providing police basic training for smaller communities in the surrounding areas.

In developing regional schools, the local governmental units should look to existing resources that may be utilized in their implementation. For example, in most states there exists a system of community colleges with readily available facilities for training purposes. California community colleges for some time have offered such facilities with considerable success. Thus, a significant capability already exists, namely the community college, for the establishment of regional police officer training schools throughout the United States.

The other alternative for the small police jurisdiction is police training provided at the state level. A single administration at the state level could provide the necessary coordination and program consistency that is generally needed with training programs. Under such a system, the centralized training facility could provide all basic/recruit level training for the state's law enforcement officers. In addition, the centralized training facility could be supported by regional training offices, staffed by personnel from the central facility, which would have the responsibility of providing the majority of the advanced/specialized training within the state. In this manner, regional training programs could be tailored to meet the various individualized needs of the regions.

One such state that has a system of this nature is Illinois. In 1955 the legislature of that state passed an act establishing a school to provide training. This led to the establishment and growth of the Police Training Institute at the University of Illinois in Champaign-Urbana, Illinois. In this system the Police Training Institute provides training for all police organizations—excluding the State Police and police of the City of Chicago—located throughout the state of Illinois. Funds for the training are provided by another act passed in 1965, which provided for the establishment of a Board that would disburse funds to local jurisdictions for their participation in training programs. Typically, jurisdictions would receive one-half the cost incurred as a result of their participating in various courses offered by the Police Training Institute or other schools that may be certified by that particular Board.

136

Police officers attending a college-level class in police adminis-tration

Courtesy Harrisburg Area Community College
Harrisburg, Pa.

In conclusion, there is little excuse for municipalities not to have training available for their police officers. All it takes is initiative on the part of the police administrator, and his willingness to reach for those resources that may be available to him within his community and throughout his state. It is imperative for police professionalism that police administrators respond in this way.

POLICE EDUCATION

The very nature of the police function demonstrates the importance of providing educational opportunities to police officers. The police are charged with safeguarding the lives and property of all citizens, the prevention and suppression of crime and delinquency, and protection of individual rights. Such vast responsibilities definitely demand all police officers be intellectually aware of their responsibilities and possess the ability to perform accurately and efficiently.

In performing their duties the police must be able to act without hesitation and very often make instantaneous and legal decisions that would take a court months to reach. Individual constitutional rights of all citizens are also realized through the actions of the police, and, in effect, people realize their rights through the interpretive actions of the police. To a large degree, therefore, our democratic way of life is dependent on the ability and effectiveness of the police in upholding and administering the laws of the land.

In the present era of sociological change, scientific development, and technological advance, the field of police service has widened tremendously. For example, with the rapid growth of urbanization, police responsibility has proportionately increased. Each year police take on more and more responsibility which greatly increases the complexity of their task.

Another major factor which demands police education is the increased need for effective administrative techniques that are necessary to cope with the increasing size of police agencies. In fact, many of our present police departments are comparable in complexity to our largest business enterprises which demand highly effective and creative administrative ability.

In view of the need for police education, it is believed that the colleges of this country, if they are to serve the educational needs of the community, have the responsibility for providing law enforcement programs. In fact, if the police service is to maintain merely its present level of efficiency, the colleges must provide such educational opportunities. Each year a higher percentage of high school graduates go on to college. Normally, in the absence of a police curriculum, students will prepare themselves educationally

138

for employment in other areas. If police programs are not established, the source of supply of qualified police officers will increasingly shrink in terms of highly qualified individuals; it can be assumed that the shrinking source of supply of police officers will consist largely of those who lack the ability or the initiative to attend college.

RESISTANCE TO POLICE EDUCATION

Resistance to police education is weakening in most parts of the country as more and more chiefs are practically demanding that programs for their officers be established. In fact, most of the law enforcement programs that have come into existence during the past few years are a result of their efforts.

Perhaps the only real remaining obstacle to program development is some lack of mutual understanding on the part of the police chief and the college administrator. The educators and law enforcement officials must meet as equals for discussion and must erase any misconceptions or suspicions that may exist. The police need to realize that the college is a service institution with no other interests beyond that. The college administrators must recognize and appreciate the practical needs of law enforcement and must attempt to establish programs that meet these needs.

IMPETUS FOR POLICE EDUCATION

Although we can trace police education back to 1907 when the University of California at Berkeley established a program for law enforcement officers, the actual impetus for the development of police education did not really occur until a much later date. In 1963, the Ford Foundation provided a grant to the International Association of Chiefs of Police for the purpose of improving standards for police education. As a result of this grant and the work in conjunction with it, many community colleges and universities throughout the

139

country established law enforcement programs. Prior to IACP's work there were fewer than one hundred such programs, most of which were in California. By the end of the four-year grant period there were over two hundred such programs throughout the United States.

The next boost to police education occurred with the passage of the Law Enforcement Assistance Act of 1965. Among other things, OLEA offered financial aid to several colleges so that they could establish programs in law enforcement. Generally, the grants were given to colleges in states where no such programs existed. With the establishment of these programs, other colleges were encouraged to embark upon similar programs. The recent rapid growth of police programs can be largely attributed to the influence of the Ford Foundation grant to the IACP and to the establishment of the Office of Law Enforcement Assistance.

Another boost was provided by the passage of the Omnibus Crime Control and Safe Streets Act of 1968. This act covered many areas of concern to law enforcement throughout the United States, but of importance to education was the appropriation of funds to assist police officers and police aspirants in achieving a law enforcement education. The bill provided loans and grants to police officers and police aspirants enrolled in law enforcement programs. It further authorized the total cancellation of any such loans at the rate of 25 percent for each complete year of law enforcement service after graduation. Quite obviously, this bill encouraged hundreds of police officers to pursue college-level work.

It is expected that the trend toward higher education will continue, and will continue to exert an influence in all areas necessary for police professionalization.

PHILOSOPHY OF LAW ENFORCEMENT

As in all academic or professional areas, the evaluation of a law enforcement education philosophy has not been smooth

140

and without controversy. Also, as in all professions, such differences of opinion will continue to exist.

In reviewing the development of police education, it appears that three distinct philosophies exist. For purposes of clarification, they can be identified as vocational, humanistic, and professional.

Vocational. The curriculum established within the framework of the vocational philosophy has an emphasis on the tools, skills, and techniques of police work. In essence, the primary thrust is to train men how to do their job. In conjunction with this emphasis, the curriculum is geared very closely to the local situation and may include skill-oriented courses such as radio dispatching, firearms training, defensive techniques, pursuit driving, state vehicle code, state criminal code, and first aid. The individual completing such a curriculum is in a position to don a police uniform and go directly into the field. Such a curriculum often replaces the need for the police academy and may, therefore, be very beneficial to those departments that may not possess the resources necessary for such training.

Humanistic. A program within the humanistic philosophy is usually typified by a pure liberal arts education with emphasis on the social or behavioral sciences or is based on a sociology curriculum. This philosophy indicates that the law enforcement task or function is such that there is no need or justification for more specific courses in law enforcement.

The curriculum may, however, have a strong correctional emphasis and may concern itself with the relationship between the police function and the activities of correctional agencies such as parole, probation, or penology. Examples of humanistic programs are often difficult to illustrate, since they are often not identified as such and may be identified synonymously with "liberal arts."

Professional. The professional philosophy seems to be the most prominent and probably has had the greatest impact on law enforcement. This philosophy recognizes that there is a field of knowledge intrinsic to law enforcement in which the police officer should be conversant and knowledgeable. The curriculum, like the humanistic approach, is also concerned with behavioral sciences, but recognizes a value in their immediate relationship to law enforcement.

The professional curriculum should provide a broad intellectual and professional background that will help the officer better utilize communicative skills in writing reports and expressing thoughts, to more efficiently and effectively accomplish his task, to be conversant with the structure of government and its philosophies, to understand and appreciate the managerial functions of police departments, and to be well grounded in psychology, criminology, and human relations in order to understand the ramifications of the problems which confront him daily.

The professional courses or those specifically related to law enforcement are also of an academic nature and are designed to expand the student's knowledge of the actual implementation of psychological and sociological concepts. In essence, the professional philosophy includes the offering of professional courses taught in conjunction with the liberal arts, communicative arts, and behavioral sciences. This philosophy recognizes the existence of a definite field of knowledge peculiar to the law enforcement service and includes such knowledge along with general education. Such professional courses are not technique or skill oriented, but are of a broad academic nature. The curriculum is constructed to develop the student's intellect and also to improve his professional competence, which will ultimately help him to more efficiently fulfill his responsibilities as a law enforcement officer.

The objectives of such a philosophy might include:

1. Development of competencies that will enable students to gain employment with the various law enforcement agencies.

142

2. Development of leadership qualities that will help the student to progress through the higher positions in his agency.
3. The fostering of ideals of professional achievement in the police service.
4. The provision of a broad intellectual framework within which the student can direct his efforts, both personally and professionally, in a more intelligent and meaningful manner.

LAW ENFORCEMENT:
AN EDUCATIONAL DISCIPLINE

The foregoing discussion on police education provides the necessary background information necessary to determine whether law enforcement is an *academic discipline* or a *professional discipline*. However, before discussing law enforcement and its adaptability as an academic discipline we must first define the words *academic* and *discipline*. *Webster's New Collegiate Dictionary* defines *academic* as "pertaining or belonging to an academy, college, or university, or to colleges." A second listed definition is "literary, classical, or liberal rather than technical or professional." *Discipline* defined by *Webster* in the instructional or educational sense is a "branch of knowledge involving research" and "training which corrects, molds, strengthens, or perfects."

Combined, the definition of an academic discipline would be "literary, classical, or liberal education combined with research and offered at the college or university level." It would seem that this definition in its present form would exclude law enforcement from the ranks of the traditional academic family. In its strictest sense, the definition requires constant involvement in research and excludes those subject areas that are professionally or technically oriented. Law enforcement is becoming more and more involved in research, but most of the research is conducted by social scientists rather than law enforcement academicians. Certainly, most

143

law enforcement educational programs have a professional or technical orientation. Because of these orientations, law enforcement cannot be considered an academic discipline in the strictest interpretation of what an academic discipline is.

In the strictest sense, law enforcement education must be considered as a professional discipline rather than as an academic discipline. This, however, is not a dilemma since there are many other prestigious professional fields under the same heading. By this definition in the academic world, law enforcement is placed side by side with law, medicine, engineering, and education. They, like law enforcement, cannot be called academic disciplines because they are professionally or technically orientated rather than being of a classical or literary nature. Educationally speaking, law enforcement is a professional discipline rather than an academic discipline and is a respected and accepted college or university level program.

If one were interested, however, a good case could be presented to claim law enforcement as an academic discipline. Degrees issued by colleges and universities reflect the nature of study pursued and, in effect, the degree identifies the "academic discipline" from that of the "professional discipline." Good's *Dictionary of Education* defines a degree as "a title bestowed by a college or university as official recognition for the completion of a course of study or for a certain attainment." The same source defines an *academic* degree as "(1) a degree offered for attainment in liberal education, (2) more broadly, a degree conferred by an institution of higher education, regardless of the field of study." It is in the second and broader sense that the term is most commonly used today, and, therefore, almost all degrees are generally thought of as *academic*.

As in the case of academic degrees, the academic disciplines are also thought of in broader terms. This broader and commonly accepted definition would include law enforcement and the other "professional disciplines" which involve some technical or professional education.

144

It should be restated, however, that technically speaking law enforcement is a "professional discipline" rather than an "academic discipline." There is no stigma to such a classification and law enforcement officers should stand proud of such professional education and their professional degrees.

TECHNOLOGY AND LAW ENFORCEMENT

Technology has played an important role in law enforcement for some time, but recent years have seen greater emphasis in this area. Technological improvements have been made especially in the areas of computerization of records, communications, transportation, weaponry, criminal investigation, and crime detection. The greatest improvement has been in the area of the application of science to crime detection, but in recent years there has been an increased interest in other areas as well.

Some important possibilities that were reported by a federal task force include:

1. Electronic computers for processing the enormous quantities of needed data.
2. Police radio networks connecting officers and neighboring departments.
3. Inexpensive, light, two-way portable radios for every patrolman.
4. Computers for processing fingerprints.
5. Instruments for identifying criminals by their voices, photographs, hair, blood, body chemistry, etc.
6. Devices for automatic and continuing reporting for all police car locations.
7. Helicopters for airborne police patrol.
8. Inexpensive, reliable burglar and robbery alarms.
9. Nonlethal weapons to subdue dangerous criminals without inflicting permanent harm.

10. Perimeter surveillance devices for prisons.
11. Automatic transcription devices for courtroom testimony.

All of these devices are not "of the future" since many are already in operation and others are being developed. In addition, as law enforcement turns to technology, there is no question that other innovations not presently envisioned will come into existence.

All of these, of course, are in addition to those devices already in general use among most police agencies. For example, there are many instruments that can measure the

Modern police equipment

Courtesy of the Cleveland, Ohio Police Department

blood-alcohol content of a person in determining whether he can be prosecuted for drunk driving. The lie detector is in general use in most police agencies and has aided in hundreds of criminal investigations. The lie detector has also been widely used in selection of personnel as well.

Computers are being used in our large departments, and they can retrieve information on stolen vehicles or wanted persons within seconds. These computers can also predict crime incidence by area, which allows a more efficient assignment of personnel.

Administration of lie detector examination

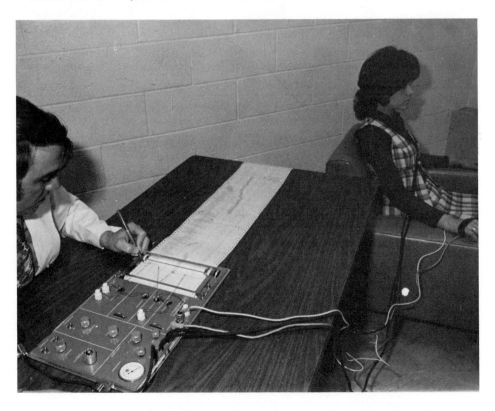

Courtesy of Harrisburg Area Community College
Harrisburg, Pa.

Mobile crime laboratory

Courtesy of Public Safety Department, Metropolitan-Dade County, Florida

In the laboratory, many kinds of analyses are made in conjunction with criminal investigations. A narcotic or dangerous drug can be identified within minutes. A fiber can be identified as similar to comparable fibers from a suspect's clothing. Microscopic dust from the cuff of a suspect's pants can be compared with dust at the scene. Bullets can be matched with a certain gun, etc. The crime laboratory plays an important role in crime detection.

A recent trend in crime detection has been the "mobile" laboratory, a van-type vehicle equipped to provide scientific instruments and technicians directly on the crime scene. The mobile laboratory team may evaluate and determine the potential of evidence left at the scene. The mobile team may also conduct field-test or preliminary examinations at the scene to reveal, immediately, important clues to the solution of a crime. The mobile laboratory technician will then transport the evidence to the main crime laboratory for a more detailed examination.

148

The use of laboratory-analyzed physical evidence, how-ever, does not replace the work of the investigator. Information and other forms of evidence must be gathered from witnesses, suspects, and victims before the investigation is complete.

In many cases of hit-and-run accidents, there are no eye-witnesses and the victim is past talking, so physical evidence becomes very important, and the solution to the crime depends on recognition, protection, collection, and identification of articles left at the scene. As in other types of criminal investi-gations, the police officer seeks to identify the criminal and place him on the crime scene through something he takes from the scene or something he deposits while on the scene.

In addition to the above, the forensic, or crime, laboratory is concerned with the elimination of certain physical evidence. Through examinations of evidence, a material submitted as evidence to a crime may be rejected because it has no relation to the crime, or the evidence may render facts to show the innocence of a suspect.

There is certainly a defined need for the crime laboratory, either fixed or mobile, to be included in the investigations of criminals and crime scenes. This fact is underscored by its proven value in the past and its potential for greater usefulness in the future. This phase of scientific investigation has grown from the "crime laboratory" to "forensic science" or "criminal-istics."

Summary

Police agencies in the United States developed in a rather haphazard manner and were often inefficient. Many agencies were staffed with political appointees and were corrupt. Even today we find police departments so ingrained in traditionalism that appointments and promotions are still politically made.

There is much controversy over whether or not law enforcement has reached a professional status. Generally, law enforcement is involved in all the characteristics that are common to accepted professions, but not to the extent to justify a professional status. Great strides are being made, however, and professional status is within reach.

The need for college-educated police officers is becoming more obvious every year. The importance and diversity of the police function demands that police officers be better prepared to assume their tasks. Police education generally is new on the national scene, but there are now over three hundred colleges with law enforcement programs.

It appears that three distinct philosophies of law enforcement exist: 1) vocational, 2) humanistic, and 3) professional. The vocational approach stresses skills and techniques and relates to training rather than education. The humanistic approach can generally be equated to a liberal arts education. The professional approach stresses a field of knowledge that is intrinsic to law enforcement.

Many technological improvements have been introduced to law enforcement in recent years. These improvements have been most obvious in the areas of computerization of records, communications, transportation, weaponry, criminal investigation, and crime detection.

150

Discussion Questions

1. Is law enforcement a profession? Discuss.
2. What influence has the federal government had on local police during the past few years?
3. What is the importance of police education?
4. What has been the primary impetus for police education during the last decade?
5. Describe the police training program that should exist within every police department.
6. Is law enforcement an academic or professional discipline?
7. How will technological advances affect the police service?
8. What were some of the problems of early law enforcement agencies?
9. What is the relationship between the police department and the city it serves?
10. What is the status of research in law enforcement?

4

The Police Function

The municipal, county, and state police of the United States are charged with responsibilities which rank second to none in importance in our democratic society. The police service is that branch of government that is assigned the awesome task of securing compliance to the multitude of laws and regulations deemed beneficial to society. Since law is society's means of achieving conformance to desired norms, the police are society's agents for the maintenance of harmony within the community. Within this broad context, the police are charged with the safeguarding of lives and property, the prevention and repression of crime, the prevention of delinquency, and the protection of individual rights.

The police have not always had these broad responsibilities. For years the police, and even the public, generally believed the police were fulfilling their full responsibility by investigating crime and attempting to apprehend criminals. There was little thought given to the concept of prevention, and most certainly citizens did not expect the police to intervene in domestic disputes or problems related to their youngsters. The problem of raising youth was a family responsibility and was kept within the family.

In our rural past, conformity to the social norm was achieved through *folk-policing.* That is, people refrained from certain activities for fear of being admonished by neighbors. In our present mobile and urbanized society *folk-policing* is minimized, and the public depends upon the police to fill the gap. The fear of admonishment no longer prevails and, therefore, people are less restrained from deviating from society's demands.

Although the police function is old, it has, of necessity, changed to meet changing needs. The process of law enforcement has gone through a gradual development along with the country's urbanization which has enlarged the police role significantly.

The police resisted change, but the forces of time were unrelenting, and their role widened to meet the new needs of each new generation. Even today the police resist change, but they are becoming more and more open-minded, and as a result are able to more readily assume additional and different responsibilities.

The police of this country have very admirably met the challenge of changing times, but there are certain societal expectations beyond their capability. For example, even under the most favorable conditions the police cannot eliminate crime. The police do not create the social conditions conducive to crime nor can they resolve them. The police do not enact the legislation that they must enforce. They do not adjudicate the offenders they arrest, and they are only one of the agencies of criminal justice.

In order to appreciate what the police do to achieve the complex objectives of law enforcement, it is necessary to review the "line" functions or methods which directly attack the problems.

PATROL

Patrol refers to the moving on foot or by vehicle around and within an assigned area for the purpose of obtaining information relative to serving the police function. Officers are usually in uniform, and when a vehicle is used, it is usually conspicuously marked. The marked vehicle is often referred to as a "uniformed unit" since, like an officer's uniform, the markings identify it as a police car.

The purpose of patrol is to distribute police officers in a manner that will eliminate or reduce the opportunity for citizen misconduct and to increase the probability of apprehension if a criminal commits a crime. These are the two primary concerns of the potential criminal, and where effective patrol minimizes his chances of success, he will refrain from committing the crime.

The patrol function is the backbone of police operations and has the broad basic responsibility of public protection and service. The patrol force is on twenty-four hour surveillance and should be able to respond quickly to all situations requiring police attention. The most important police operation is patrol, and its effectiveness will determine the success of the entire police agency.

The patrol function is so basic to fulfilling the police responsibility that its goals are essentially synonymous with the total police objective. These objectives include the prevention and suppression of crime, the safeguarding of lives and property, the apprehension of criminals, the control of traffic and noncriminal conduct, and the provision of public services. In achieving these objectives, the patrol force checks buildings, surveys possible incidents, questions suspicious persons, gathers information, regulates traffic, enforces traffic regulations, responds to reports of crime, conducts preliminary investigations, and arrests violators of the law.

Before discussing fully the activities involved in the achievement of patrol objectives, the organization of patrol must be made clear.

GEOGRAPHICAL DISTRIBUTION OF PATROL

In order to be effective, the patrol force must be geographically distributed so that response time to crime incidents is minimized. Vehicles and men must be assigned to definite geographical areas that will assist them in the achievement of the patrol responsibility. Such geographical breakdowns are referred to as beat, sector, and precinct.

Beat. The fundamental unit of patrol is the beat. The beat is that area within which patrol officers are assigned either on foot or within a marked unit. The officer assigned to a beat is responsible for all activities within the area and must provide continuous surveillance throughout his tour of duty. All calls originating within his beat are referred to him and he makes the original contact.

Since the beat is the fundamental unit of police patrol and, in fact, the entire police organization, it is important

157

that it be constructed properly. Unfortunately, many police departments arbitrarily design beats without regard to the needs to be met.

Beats cannot be constructed solely on the amount of ground to be covered and the number of people in the area, but on a combination of many factors. If properly designed, the beat will vary in size and shape according to such factors as population density, the type of area, the crime problem, topography, past called-for services, and geographical characteristics. An ill-conceived beat will not only disproportionately distribute the workload, but will also contribute to the ability of criminals to commit violations.

The manner of determining beats is not always given the attention it deserves. Quite frequently the same beats are used throughout the twenty-four hour day and year after year. Not only do changes in need occur from year to year, but the needs may very well be different throughout the day. Beat arrangements demand constant evaluation and should be changed as conditions change.

Sector. A patrol sector consists of several beats and is so divided to facilitate proper supervision. The patrol supervisor usually holds the rank of sergeant and is often referred to as the "line supervisor." His task is to coordinate activities of the several beats and to assist patrol officers when needed. One of his major tasks is to instruct beat officers or correct patrol techniques and to subsequently see that such techniques are practiced. For general purposes, therefore, the sector is a division for supervision.

Precinct. Larger cities have so many beats and sectors that it becomes necessary to have another larger division. The precinct relates to a large district which is comprised of several patrol sectors. Like the sector, the precinct is a geographical division that facilitates coordination of the activities of the smaller geographical units. Usually, the only justification for a precinct is an area too large to be handled by smaller divisions. Like beats, the precinct should be so located that it facilitates the accomplishment of the police objective.

THE PATROL OFFICER

The patrol officer is not only the most important police position in the police department, but it is the most challenging. The patrol officer is responsible for all activities within his beat and must patrol continuously throughout his tour of duty. He must practice proven patrol techniques, be alert to all situations, and respond to all calls within his area. This means he will become involved in activities ranging from looking for lost children or writing a traffic summons to conducting the preliminary investigation of a murder. He has the greatest responsibilities of all police positions, and he must be able to cope intelligently with them.

His importance is obvious when it is realized that he is at the implementation level of the police function. The best-conceived plans of executive officers are entirely dependent upon the patrol officer's ability to put them into practice. In addition, the patrol officer is at the grassroots level and is the one in direct contact with society's problems. He makes the physical arrest, he stops the traffic violator, and he prevents crime.

Many departments throughout the United States have adopted the "generalist" theory which places the major emphasis of police service on the patrol officer. The generalist theory minimizes the specialist and requires the patrol officer to accomplish as much of the police task as possible. The generalist patrols the streets, issues traffic violation notices, investigates accidents, and conducts preliminary investigations of all crimes within his beat. In fact, where feasible, the generalist will investigate a crime to its conclusion with the resulting arrest of the offender. In most cases, the generalist conducts the entire crime scene investigation so that the detective merely picks it up at that point and carries it onward.

159

PATROL DISTRIBUTION BY TIME

Another important factor in patrol is the distribution of manpower according to the time of day. Like the determination of beats, many police departments have arbitrarily divided the patrol officers into three "platoons" with each working on one of three "shifts." A platoon refers to the group of men working a particular shift and shift refers to a division of the day.

In determining shifts, the police must consider such criteria as the times of called-for services and the workload over certain blocks of time. The shift change should occur when there are the fewest calls and when police activity is at a minimum. The shift hours should, as nearly as possible, equalize the workload on each shift.

During shift changes, police availability is significantly reduced, and the opportunities for criminal activity are increased. Traditionally, police departments have thought in terms of three shifts which has necessitated almost total inactivity by police during certain hours. To illustrate, assume the shift changes at twelve midnight. Since police vehicles are usually used around the clock, the officers on the previous shift will need to start to headquarters prior to midnight. For example, they may leave their beat at approximately 11:40 PM. Those officers going on duty will pick up the car at midnight, but it may take them until 12:20 AM to reach their assigned beat. Therefore, the police have been absent from that beat for forty minutes.

This problem has existed for years, but police departments have finally begun to rectify it. One solution is to have overlapping shifts. This merely entails dividing each platoon in half with one group coming in an hour earlier than usual and the other half coming in an hour later than usual. The following illustrates this arrangement:

OVERLAPPING SHIFTS

Normal shift hours All officers	Overlapping shifts	
	1st platoon	*2nd platoon*
8 AM–4 PM	7 AM– 3 PM	9 AM–5 PM
4 PM–12 midnight	3 PM–11 PM	5 PM–1 AM
12 midnight–8 AM	11 PM– 7 AM	1 AM–9 AM

160

Another method has been to add a fourth shift which may overlap two other shifts. For example, if the traditional 8:00 AM–4:00 PM, 4:00 PM–12 midnight, 12 midnight–8:00 AM were used, the fourth shift may work 6:00 PM–2:00 AM or some other overlapping combination.

Another method of patrol distribution by time that is working well is the *ten–four* (10–4) plan. This plan replaces the traditional eight-hour shift with a four-day week of ten hours each day. This system permits a shift overlap potential of six hours and an increase in the number of patrol beats. More important, the *ten–four* plan permits the department to deploy manpower so it is greatest during the busy hours. Another advantage may be the possible increase in morale due to three days off each week.

Following is an example of a time schedule utilizing the *ten–four* plan. It must be remembered, however, that each department must tailor its time schedule to meet its specific needs.

TEN–FOUR SHIFT SCHEDULE

Shift	Hours
I	7 AM–5 PM
II	4 PM–2 AM
III	9 PM–7 AM

It will be noted that this time schedule provides extra manpower and patrol coverage during the hours of 4:00 PM to 5:00 PM and 9:00 PM to 2:00 AM. The assumption with this time schedule is that the overlapping hours represent the time of greatest workload.

The number of men on each platoon must also be given serious consideration. It is virtually impossible to equalize the workload on each shift and at the same time have low activity shift change times. Invariably, one eight-hour period will vary in workload from another. Traditionally, police departments have mistakenly divided the men into thirds with one-third assigned to each shift. Frequently, this means that one platoon has a greater or lesser workload than another, even though the manpower is the same. Obviously, this

161

should be avoided, and the number of men assigned should be in accordance with the workload of each platoon.

TYPES OF PATROL

The two basic types of patrol are walking and the well-marked automobile. The foot beat is the oldest form of patrol, but the advent of the automobile has made foot patrol less useful. There are still some cities in the United States utilizing foot patrolmen, but generally, most police departments have abandoned this practice in favor of motorized patrol.

As a result of the automobile, the population has become less concentrated and has spread over a larger area. It is, therefore, virtually impossible for the police to patrol on foot the vast area within which the people live.

Additionally, of course, the automobile itself became a police problem that could only be solved with the use of police cars. If police officers were on foot, the motorized public could generally drive as they pleased with little chance of a policeman catching them.

Generally speaking, in a motorized age it is impossible to police the mobile public while on foot. The police must be motorized in order to adequately fulfill the police responsibility.

This is not to say that foot patrol cannot be used effectively. In highly populated business areas a foot officer may be very effective. There may be areas, for example, where a car cannot patrol because of heavy traffic or because of narrow alleys and walkways between buildings. Foot patrol is also useful to regain citizen support simply by personal contact, since motorized patrol has taken much of the human perception of the police officer away from the public. However, before using foot patrol officers, the police department should be sure that a more effective means of patrol is not available. Generally, foot patrol is only justified in a highly populated business district where there is pedestrian and vehicle congestion as well as an abundance of crime. Of in-

162

Mounted Texas Rangers on manhunt, supported by modern communications equipment and Department of Public Safety helicopter

Courtesy of the Texas Department of Public Safety,
Austin

terest is the fact that many police departments are motorizing their foot patrol officers by putting them on motor scooters. This decreases response time and also allows more coverage by each officer.

Other types of patrol include the use of horses, motorcycles, aircraft, and boats. In many instances a combination of two or more of these patrol methods, in conjunction with modern communications equipment, are required to meet

163

specific needs. For example, the police may utilize horses, jeeps, walking men, and a helicopter when searching for lost hunters or a lost child. They may use the patrol car in conjunction with directions from observers in a helicopter when searching for a criminal suspect or chasing a fleeing felon.

Many cities have large harbors or waterways within their jurisdiction and, therefore, utilize boats. In such cases they have highly trained officers commanding the boats who are engaged in activities ranging from enforcing boating regulations to investigating smuggling activities. They usu-

Patrol boat of the Detroit Police Harbormaster Division

Courtesy of the Detroit Police Department
Detroit, Mich.

ally work quite closely with the United States Coast Guard as well as pursuing their own responsibilities.

The helicopter is probably the most recent development in police patrol. During the last few years many police organizations have adopted helicopters. State police organizations and highway patrols use the helicopter for traffic control and for emergency medical treatment at accident scenes. The helicopter is also very useful when searching large areas and for transporting emergency medical supplies to hospitals. Municipal police agencies use the helicopter quite effectively in patrol since they can observe rather large areas with

Air medical evacuation helicopter used for transporting victims of accidents

Courtesy of the Arizona Department of Public Safety

165

clear visibility. They can, for example, direct a ground patrol car when chasing escaping felons. These are just a few examples of the use of the helicopter, as it can be adapted to many policing situations very effectively.

TEAM POLICING

Because of changes in the social climate and the trend toward complete mobilization of patrol forces, many police organizations have become isolated from the community. The face-to-face relationship that existed between foot patrolmen and citizens was replaced by having a police vehicle cover a large geographical area. The concept of the neighborhood policeman was lost, and the familiarity a policeman had with the people on his beat was no longer possible. In reality, the motorized patrol officer was isolated, insulated, and separated from the people he was supposed to serve. This made effective crime control extremely difficult. The need to regain the close citizen-police relationship became evident to police administrators across the United States, especially those of the cities.

Team policing is a modern police technique developed to reduce the isolation and to involve community support in the fight against crime. Team policing is the assignment of a team of police officers to specific geographical areas. The officers work as a team on an around-the-clock basis in their assigned area. In this way, officers can become more familiar with the area, its people, and existing problems so that they can better provide police services. In essence, it is the extension of the "cop on the beat" concept brought up-to-date with more men and modern police services.

The first experiment in team policing took place in Aberdeen, Scotland in 1948. It was terminated in 1963. In 1966, a new modification known as the "unit beat policing" appeared, also in Great Britain. This concept combined patrol and investigative personnel and stressed public cooperation. It is this form of team policing that was experimented with in the United States.[1]

By 1973 several cities in the United States had experimented with team policing, but with varying success. In theory, the patrol force is reorganized to include one or more quasi-autonomous teams, with a joint purpose of improving police services to the community. Each team has responsibility for most police services in its neighborhood, and each is expected to work as a unit with the assistance and cooperation of the community. Team policing has been experimented with in such cities as Dayton, Los Angeles, Detroit, and New York, to mention a few.

Although not proven as the answer to patrol, team policing is a step in the right direction and has great promise. Whatever the outcome, the experiment with team policing is proof of police administrators' attempts to improve service to their communities.

PATROL AND CRIME PREVENTION

The primary means by which patrol prevents crime is through being conspicuous and available. The obvious presence of the police discourages the criminal from committing a crime for fear of being caught. This indicates the importance of the conspicuously marked vehicle. Not only does this show their presence, but it also gives the impression of police saturation.

The appearance of police saturation is a result of the noticeability of the police unit. Every time it passes, the citizenry will see it, whereas a less conspicuous car would be

[1] National Advisory Commission on Criminal Justice Standards and Goals, *Police* (Washington, D.C.: U.S. Government Printing Office, 1973), p. 154.

167

observed less frequently. The public identifies the car rather than the driver and, therefore, assumes a different car has passed each time, when it is actually the same vehicle. In other words, the citizen thinks he has seen fifteen different police cars, rather than having seen the same car fifteen times.

The uniform car also tends to gain voluntary compliance to the law from motorists. The sight of the police unit causes them to be more observant of traffic laws. Of importance too is the fact that the uniform car is observable from great distances and over a wide area. Therefore, its presence will affect many people at the same time. The more conspicuous the police unit, the more people it will affect at any given time.

Patrol officers can prevent crime by becoming familiar with juveniles within their patrol area or beat. A healthy relationship built on mutual respect between the patrol officers and juveniles will do more toward the prevention of delinquency than any other police activity. The patrol officer is the man the juveniles see and identify as the authority symbol. Respect for the officer promotes respect for the law, and such respect will discourage aggression.

A very important role of patrol in crime prevention is the securing of information that can be passed to other units of the police department. With such information the specialized units can work on a potential problem prior to its actually becoming a problem. The patrol officer is on the street and is in the best possible position to gain information on such things as the formation of a juvenile gang, the underlying frustrations of the community, the use of narcotics, etc. By virtue of his closeness to the community, the patrol officer must keep alert to anything and everything that might indicate a potential problem.

APPREHENSION OF CRIMINALS

When prevention fails, apprehension during or immediately after commission of the crime becomes the next objective of patrol. Alertness on the part of patrol officers leads to the

168

apprehension of a large number of criminals who are: 1) about to commit a crime, 2) committing a crime, or 3) escaping after the commission of a crime. In fact, the large proportion of police arrests are made by patrol officers.

The ability to make these apprehensions is directly related to proper beat layout and chronological distribution of the patrol force. In other words, to increase the potential for making arrests the patrol areas must be designed as a result of an analysis of called-for services, crime patterns, and crime frequency. This coupled with continuous patrol will allow the observant officer to make apprehensions before and during the commission of a crime.

Directly related to apprehension is quick response to calls. Generally, patrol should be able to respond to all calls within a maximum of five minutes and much quicker to calls of "crime in process." Frequently, businesses that are prone to robbery or burglary will have an alarm system which notifies the police upon the initiation of a crime. Certainly, with proper response time the police can often arrive before the perpetrators have left the scene. Of course, like everything else related to patrol, adequate response time is dependent upon proper beat determination.

To facilitate the capture of criminals after the commission of a crime, it is often necessary to have formalized tactical response plans. Tactical plans include standard operating procedures relative to the proper approaches and precautions to be utilized when responding to certain calls. Examples of this are the nonuse of sirens when answering a prowler call, and approaching a building from corners in order to cover all four sides.

More formalized tactical plans are those that are specific to certain offenses or to certain locations. For example, the police should identify potential robbery victims such as banks and develop a plan to be initiated if a robbery occurs. This might entail the assigning of quadrants surrounding the scene, the establishment of roadblocks to seal off the area, and the coverage of probable escape routes. Such precon-

169

ceived plans will allow quick implementation, which will enhance the probability of success in apprehension.

Unfortunately, many police departments do not have such formalized plans, and this often allows the offender to escape. In fact, the lack of tactical plans may very well contribute to criminality and the probability of escape because of the lack of coordination.

REGULATION OF TRAFFIC AND NONCRIMINAL CONDUCT

The traffic role of patrol is quite obvious and is the most familiar to the public. Traffic control includes the direction of traffic; traffic enforcement through the use of verbal and written warnings; the issuance of citations; and the investigation of traffic accidents. The traffic task is very demanding, and a great deal of police time is devoted to it.

There are police administrators who would like to disclaim the traffic responsibility on the basis that the police job should be crime control rather than traffic control. They believe another city department should assume the traffic responsibility, thus allowing the police to devote full attention to crime prevention and control.

There are many reasons why this is not feasible. If the police accept their primary responsibility of safeguarding lives and property, they must accept the traffic responsibility. Since traffic accidents are a major "killer" in our modern society and since property damage is a result of traffic accidents, traffic control must be accepted as a police responsibility.

It must also be remembered that motor vehicles are used in most crimes. The automobile is used to go to and from the crime scene, it is used to transport stolen property, and auto theft itself is a crime. Because of such use, it is impossible to divorce crime from traffic and traffic from crime.

Additional support for the police handling of traffic control is the large number of criminal arrests resulting from

170

traffic activities. Frequently, a vehicle is stopped for a minor infraction, but when the driver is checked, it is found he is wanted by the police. Quite frequently, also, the police find stolen goods or contraband within violators' vehicles.

Traffic involvement by the police also will help prevent crime. Constant traffic surveillance and frequent stopping of cars may very well discourage the would-be burglar from committing an offense. He may be on the way to commit a crime, but if stopped by the officer, he will realize a better chance of police identification if he commits the crime in that area.

Involvement in traffic will also aid the officer in becoming familiar with people on his beat. Although he may not always be stopping cars, he will as a result of his traffic role pay more attention to all vehicles and, therefore, be somewhat familiar with cars common to his area. A strange car may quickly come to his attention.

A very important benefit from traffic involvement is the frequent opportunity for contact with the public. The police come in contact with the public more often in pursuing traffic activity than in any other police function. This is their greatest opportunity to demonstrate efficiency and to create a good image. Of course, the violator dislikes being stopped, but the employment of proper tact even in this type of contact will do much toward creating an image of professionalism.

PROVISION OF SERVICES

One role of the police is the provision of services ranging from giving directions to answering questions relative to points of interest. This role is inescapable due to the twenty-four hour availability of the police and their easy identification as a representative of that jurisdiction.

Rendering assistance is perhaps one of the best opportunities to improve or maintain the police image. Seemingly little problems are of great importance to the troubled person, and understanding help in time of stress is greatly appreciated. The police should give particular attention to rendering assistance, and they should do it with courtesy and demonstrate real concern for each person's problem. The po-

Highway patrol officer assisting the injured at an accident scene

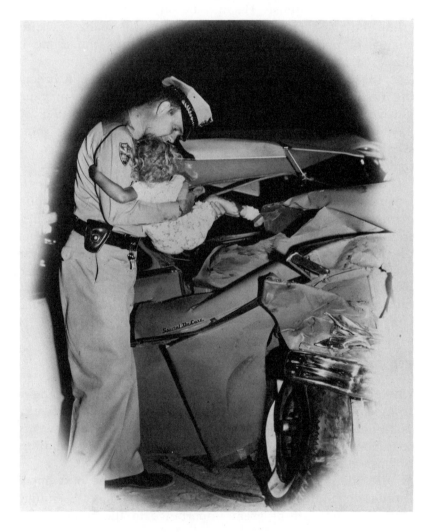

Courtesy of the Arizona Department of Public Safety

lice should realize that a visitor's impression of a city is often synonymous with his impression of the police.

There are those who believe the police should direct their total efforts toward the important activities of crime prevention and crime suppression. However, the provision of services provides the police their best opportunity for achieving many of the crime preventative activities with which they are involved. Provision of services would include such things as providing information, directions, advice, general assistance, and special services.

Information can refer to the routine duties of providing motorists directions and finding locations within a municipality, or it can refer to the more sophisticated reports of crime data and other statistics with which the police are involved. The police are also in a unique position to provide assistance in the form of advice to other governmental agencies as well as private agencies within the community. For example, the police, by virtue of their presence in the field, are in a unique position to detect deficiencies in control devices and report such deficiencies to the traffic engineering or maintenance division of the city. In addition, they are in a position to detect hazardous conditions which may exist within the public realm of the city as well as with private agencies who seek such cooperation.

General assistance, of course, refers to any and all activities which are provided as a courtesy by the police department. General assistance should not infer special privileges to members of the community, but merely refers to services that can justifiably be related to safety in the community.

PATROL EFFICIENCY

The foregoing very aptly demonstrates the importance of the police patrol function. Actually, by virtue of the broad involvement, if patrol were 100 percent successful, there would be no need for specialized activities such as criminal investigation, traffic, or crime prevention bureaus. In fact, the degree of specialization in a police department is dependent

173

upon the success of the patrol function. The police only need to specialize to the extent that patrol is unsuccessful. If patrol prevents all crime, there is no need for detectives, jails, photography specialists, juvenile officers, etc.

Of course, it is virtually impossible for patrol to be 100 percent successful. Even if there were policemen on every block, there are certain crimes that would be committed. For example, murder is often a family affair, in that most are committed within the family unit. Additionally, a large number of murders and assaults are "lovers' quarrels" which are usually within the confines of private homes.

In any event, because of its importance, it is imperative that patrol operate as efficiently as possible in order to minimize other needs within the department. Personnel for specialized units comes from the patrol force, and it is, therefore, necessary that such depletion be carried out with caution. Before strengthening specialized units, for example investigation, the administrator must be assured that the patrol operation cannot be improved to lessen the need for additional detectives. In addition, caution must be exercised in such reassignment, since patrol efficiency may be reduced to a greater extent than what is achieved by the added detective strength. For example, the detective workload may justify another detective for forty hours weekly. The addition of the forty hours in investigation commensurately reduces the man-hours of patrol. Perhaps this loss to patrol reduces efficiency to the extent that forty more hours are needed in investigation to offset the loss.

The important thing is not to weaken the patrol strength unjustifiably in order to strengthen other specialized units. The patrol force is the backbone of the police agency, and its strength should be depleted only when adequate justification exists.

Lately there has been some question as to the real efficiency of police patrol. The Kansas City, Missouri Police Department conducted an experiment from October 1, 1972 through September 30, 1973 designed to measure the impact routine patrol had on the incidence of crime and the public's fear of crime. The experiment, funded by the Police Foundation, used a methodology which determined that the traditional preventative patrol technique had no significant impact on the level of crime or on the public's feeling of security.

A great deal of caution must be used, however, to avoid the error of believing that the experiment proved more than it actually did. It would be a grave error to assume that the cities throughout the nation should forego their patrol activities in favor of another approach. What occurred in Kansas City during the period of the experiment might be different than what would happen in other cities with a different societal and geographical configuration. In addition, this one experiment certainly would require followup programs to determine the actual result of preventative patrol.

This study must be considered a milestone in police research, but police administrators throughout the nation must use caution in interpreting the study and certainly should not overreact by eliminating their patrol activity. In fact, there is much controversy relative to the experiment, and many questions concerning its implementation have been raised by professional police administrators throughout the United States. Of importance is the fact that there may be new and innovative approaches to crime prevention and control that might achieve better results than the normal practices. Some innovative experimental approaches to patrol are: 1) Directed Deterrent Patrol in New Haven, Connecticut; 2) Community-Oriented Patrol in San Diego, California; 3) Split-Force Patrol in Wilmington, Delaware; and 4) Directed Interactive Patrol in Kansas City, Missouri. Success has been enjoyed in all of these approaches and it is certain that patrol of the future will have a completely different complexion than that of today.

DIRECTED DETERRENT PATROL

The objective of *directed deterrent patrol* is to focus upon suppressing crime through directed police visibility. The

175

directed deterrent program was a product of growing crime problems, financial constraints, and a belief among police officials that the traditional method of random preventative patrol was not very effective in deterring crime. The directed deterrent program is directed by detailed crime analysis rather than by the *seat-of-the-pants* decisions of individual police officers.

The program contains three important components:

1. Identification through crime analysis of the places and times when crimes are occurring and are likely to occur in the future.
2. Development of written directions describing in detail the way problem areas are to be patrolled.
3. Activation of these patrol directions at specific times as determined by crime analysis.

The directed deterrent runs (D-runs) are performed during time that was formerly devoted to random preventative patrol. When assigned a D-run the officer follows the specific instructions provided. Each plan is extremely detailed and deviation can only occur under extraordinary circumstances. D-runs are assigned the same priority as dispatched calls for service and can only be cancelled under emergency conditions.

These directed activities have enabled police administrators to use patrol time more effectively and to achieve saturation levels of patrol in problem areas without increasing the number of patrol personnel or vehicles.

COMMUNITY-ORIENTED PATROL

The community-oriented policing program (COP) in San Diego was a direct outgrowth of deteriorating police/community relations in the late 1960s and early 1970s. In an attempt to solve this problem the department developed COP, since it was applicable to both the improvement of police/community relations and to crime control, order maintenance, and social

176

Directed patrol pattern sheet

RUN NUMBER:___82___
SECTOR:___RICHARD___

PROBLEM: COMMERCIAL BURGLARY

Step 1: LOCATION: Sixth and Grant
TACTIC: Park car. Check fronts and backs by walking to Calvert and back to car.

Step 2: LOCATION: Sixth and Speedway
TACTIC: Park car at Stone. Check fronts and backs by walking one side of street to Front Street and back to other side of street.

Step 3: LOCATION: Sixth between Congress and Browning
TACTIC: Park at George Street and Sixth Avenue and walk to the temple between Winchester and Remington Street and back to car; check fronts and backs of buildings.

Step 4: LOCATION: Sixth between Wildwood and Pennington
TACTIC: Ride entire length at 5 mph., checking fronts and backs as appropriate. One swing in each direction.

Step 5: LOCATION:
TACTIC:

SPECIAL NOTES:

ESTIMATED TIME REQUIRED FOR RUN: 45-50 mins.

Amber lights will be used by the officer while assigned to a deterrent run.

INSTRUCTION SHEET ORIGINATED BY: _____

APPROVED BY: _____

DATE: _____

service issues faced by patrol personnel. The primary objective of the project was to develop ways by which patrol officers would become closely attuned and accountable to the people and problems of their beats, thereby improving the quality of police services.

In essence, community-oriented policing is based upon an effort to decentralize patrol decisions from command levels to individual police officers. The program is based upon the assumption that each patrol beat within a city has unique social and law enforcement problems that can only be adequately addressed when patrol officers have a clear understanding of these problems. Officers are provided with appropriate information (census data, crime trend analysis, traffic information, etc.) so they can analyze and develop patrol tactics that address specific beat conditions and problems.

In support of the program the department established policy that provided long-term assignments to a beat, responsibility for clearing most service calls, and performing directed patrol assignments on that beat. In a sense, the beat is the officer's domain and he or she is held accountable for developing appropriate approaches and solutions to problems.

SPLIT-FORCE PATROL

The basic goal of the Wilmington split-force patrol program has been to increase police productivity by providing concentrated patrol coverage in areas of the community experiencing high crime rates. To achieve this goal, the department launched a two-part program that involved major changes in the deployment of patrol officers and the implementation of new patrol tactics. The result has been an increase in patrol productivity and a decline in criminal activity throughout the city.

Like most directed-patrol programs, the Wilmington experience was affected by the Kansas City preventive patrol experiment and by the belief that random preventive patrol was not doing the job. In addition, departmental administrators believed that patrol operations should be organized to reflect the dual nature of patrol work. As a result, the patrol force was divided into two groups:

1. A *basic patrol* force that responds to calls for service, conducts random patrol, and performs limited amounts of directed activity.
2. A *structured patrol force* that engages almost exclusively in directed crime prevention, deterrence, and apprehension activity.

178

Basic patrol units, when not busy with answering complaints or requests for service, are assigned fixed post duties that require only short blocks of time and can be interrupted to respond to calls for service. These fixed post responsibilities are determined by crime and work analysis and include such things as operating radar, checking parking violations in problem areas, monitoring schools at opening and closing times, observing disorderly and nuisance locations, and conducting property checks.

The activities of *structured patrol units* are based upon detailed crime analysis and involve some plain clothes, covert activities. High visibility saturation patrols are the primary deterrence tactics used, but covert patrols have been used against commercial and residential burglary and robbery. Officers use civilian clothes and unmarked vehicles, and in some instances act as decoys. The structured units have also been assigned suspect and location-oriented surveillance missions.

DIRECTED INTERACTIVE PATROL

The Kansas City directed patrol program is in response to the question of how patrol time can be most effectively used. A workload analysis indicated that as much as one-third of all patrol manhours could be used for directed purposes. It was decided that the implementation of preplanned directed activities would have a greater impact upon crime than the traditional random preventive patrol operations of the department.

The Kansas City program also represents an experiment in decentralized decision making. However, rather than focusing upon individual officer initiatives, as in San Diego's COP, the patrol sergeants became responsible for planning and implementing directed patrol activities.

It should also be noted that, whereas COP in San Diego has emphasized the importance of the beat, Kansas City made the sector or the area patrolled by a sergeant and several officers the focus for planning activities. Under their program, beat boundaries are regarded only as administrative districts and sergeants are free to redeploy officers within sectors according to short-term service demands and crime trends.

CRIME PREVENTION

Traditionally, the police role has been the apprehension of law violators, but the prevention of crimes has also become generally recognized as an equally necessary and important police function. In fact, apprehension of law violators automatically prevents crime by deterring many who might believe that the opportunity to successfully commit a crime does exist. There has been some resistance to the police crime prevention role, and even today there are a few who believe the police should not concern themselves with formalized crime prevention activities. These people, however, fail to recognize that the traditional activities of police have not been entirely successful. Crime has increased tremendously in recent years. Realizing that traditional methods have not been entirely successful, the police must, of necessity, look to other supporting methods to better reach their goals.

It should be realized that attention to the crime prevention role of law enforcement is not entirely a new concept. In his book published in 1920, Fosdick devoted a full chapter to crime prevention. He said, "All police work has as its goal the prevention of crime." Fosdick also pointed out: "There is as much room for crime prevention in our communities as for fire prevention or the prevention of disease, and in this endeavor to limit the opportunities of crime and keep it from claiming its victims the police department must take a leading part."[2]

2 Raymond B. Fosdick, *American Police Systems* (New York: The Century Company, 1920), p. 356.

180

Unfortunately, the police field has been slow in accepting such responsibilities. Like all social institutions, the police have resisted change and have maintained the traditional view which imposes few administrative problems. Such agencies must recognize their broader responsibilities and assume an active role in crime prevention.

In reality, although they may fail to recognize it as such, the police have always been involved in an elementary role of crime prevention. The attention to apprehension may very well discourage others from committing crime for fear of their own apprehension. The presence of police, whether organized or not, tends to discourage potential violators. Of course, these activities are not sufficient in themselves, and more formulized action is imperative.

Earlier we discussed the role of patrol in crime prevention. This role cannot and should not be minimized since crime prevention can best occur at that level. There is, however, the need for other crime prevention activities that supplement the patrol function. These activities include working with juveniles, improving community relations, becoming involved in community organizations, educating the public, and cooperating with other public service agencies.

JUVENILE UNIT

Juvenile delinquency is definitely a problem with which the police must be concerned. The involvement of children in crime is becoming greater each year to the extent that the commission of certain crimes is dominated by juveniles. For example, the 1973 Uniform Crime Reports published by the Federal Bureau of Investigation indicated that young persons under eighteen accounted for 54 percent of all arrests for burglary, 56 percent of all arrests for auto theft, and 34 percent of all arrests for robbery.[3]

[3] Federal Bureau of Investigation, United States Department of Justice, *Uniform Crime Reports for the United States, 1970* (Washington, D. C.: Government Printing Office), pp. 17–28.

181

Nearly every police department needs a working unit staffed with carefully selected and qualified officers who will devote nearly all of their working time to the juvenile problem. These men should have special training and education in such things as crime causation, adolescent psychology, child growth and development, human relations, and the handling of juveniles. They must also, of course, have a sincere interest in children and be dedicated to helping them. The need for such a unit will depend not so much upon the size of the department, but instead upon the number of juveniles who come to the attention of the department. Influential also is the severity and frequency of the offenses committed by them.

Juvenile problems encountered by patrol officers should be referred to the juvenile bureau for additional followup. The juvenile officer should take full charge at this point in terms of working with the juveniles, the juveniles' parents, and with the other public service agencies that may be involved. Although juvenile officers must be concerned with possible criminal charges, they should also be very actively concerned with rehabilitation. Juvenile officers are in a good position to make recommendations to juvenile courts, and it is, therefore, important that their primary concern be with reintegration.

It is very important that the juvenile bureau does not isolate itself from other public service agencies. Juvenile delinquency is a community problem, and as such community involvement can best achieve results. Juvenile officers should coordinate their work with other juvenile authorities and share with them all information that is available. Full cooperation by all will certainly strengthen the juvenile delinquency prevention effort. Working in isolation not only achieves less, but it builds animosity from other agencies, which contributes to a lack of achievement.

COMMUNITY RELATIONS

Citizen hostility toward the police is every bit as disruptive of peace and order as police indifference to or mistreatment of citizens. Citizens, particularly those of the ghetto, will not receive adequate police protection until the police accept them as true citizens and appreciate them as individuals. Conversely, the police will not be able to achieve any kind of success unless the citizens appreciate the police role, trust them, and cooperate toward the achievement of the police goal. Basically, both the citizens and the police must recognize that the police goal is really a community goal.

It is quite obvious that this cooperative atmosphere does not exist and, in fact, that a great deal of hostility and distrust between the police and ghetto residents does exist. The responsibility of improving this state of affairs must rest with the police as public servants, it is their responsibility to do all that is possible to control crime and protect the community.

Community relations is, of course, the responsibility of every police officer. Every officer must perform his duty with the interest of every citizen in mind without showing favoritism or animosity. Every officer must be knowledgeable in human relations, respect his fellow man, and conduct himself in a manner that enhances mutual respect.

However, the police officer cannot do the job by himself. This problem is so urgent that a specialized unit, where department size allows, is a valuable asset to meeting the police responsibility. The community relations unit should be an integral part of the department and should have a voice in decisions affecting the community. The community relations unit should be a full-scale operation, and it should concern itself with long-range plans that will reduce racial tensions within their communities.

It is also very important that the community relations unit become involved with the community, gain their respect, and become a respected friend to the residents. Only total involvement by the unit with both the police agency and the community will lead to any degree of success.

COMMUNITY ORGANIZATIONS

There are many community or civil organizations whose primary interests are to improve the community within which they live. As such, their basic concerns are somewhat synonymous with the concerns of the police. It is, therefore, reasonable to expect the police to become actively involved in such organizations. This does not merely mean a response to give a speech and then fade from the scene. It means involvement in the organization to the extent of participation in its activities and perhaps the provision of leadership from time to time.

There is probably no better way for the police to relate to the community than through membership in local organizations. Whether this membership is as a citizen or as a police officer, the police organization is represented and a better understanding and appreciation of the organization will prevail.

Participation in community activities also gives the police officer an opportunity to be a citizen as well as a policeman. Too often the police isolate themselves from their citizen role and consequently fail to appreciate the concerns and beliefs of most citizens.

It is a well-known fact that police effectiveness is highly dependent upon public cooperation in reporting crimes and serving as witnesses. A better understanding between the two establishments will certainly encourage a climate of participation.

PUBLIC EDUCATION

Unfortunately, a large segment of our population is totally unaware of the police role, how it affects them, and what their responsibilities as citizens are relative to crime control. Quite definitely, if the public were knowledgeable about law enforcement, they would better appreciate the police and their problems. Better understanding should ultimately improve citizen-police relationships, and a combined effort would aid the fight against crime.

The police are responsible for the publics lack of understanding and awareness of the law enforcement role. Public education can occur through various media such as television, radio, newspapers, pamphlets, and presentations to schools, civic organizations, and professional groups. This responsibility may very well be assigned to the community relations unit, but all other units of the police department should participate as well. For example, the community relations unit should have a speakers' bureau that utilizes many officers in many divisions of the police agency. The traffic unit should develop special safety programs for school children, and the juvenile divisions should participate in recreational programs.

A good means of public education is a yearly "open house" that allows the public to tour the police facilities. Of course, the facilities should always be open to public tours, and the police should encourage groups to visit. There are many means by which the police can educate the public, and every police department should use every means that is applicable to its situation.

COORDINATION WITH OTHER PUBLIC SERVICE AGENCIES

There are many public service agencies and functions that are directly involved in crime-curbing activities. However, like the police, they resist change. These agencies do not tend to coordinate their activities. The police may look upon the parole people with distrust. The parole people accuse the police of harassment of their charges. The police charge the courts with too much leniency. Social welfare agencies are accused of coddling, etc. All of this leads to dissension, and very little is accomplished for their clientele. The police work with the same people as do parole agencies, probation agencies, and to a large degree social welfare agencies. All are after the same result: the reduction of the number of individuals involved in criminal offenses.

It would seem obvious that these agencies should work in close cooperation with each other rather than in isolation. Each must understand and appreciate the role of the other,

185

and all must recognize the similarities of their roles. It might be wise for these agencies to form a council with representation from all to discuss how coordination and cooperation can better exist. This council could also discuss specific problems and strive toward solutions collectively.

What must be recognized is that all public service institutions to a large degree serve the same clientele with the same objective in mind: to help each citizen be a respectable member of society. Isolation of the many agencies will accomplish little, but coordination will increase the efficiency of all.

CRIMINAL INVESTIGATION

The investigation of crime becomes necessary when the penal and criminal laws fail to deter persons from committing crime or when patrol has failed as a deterrent, or has been unable to apprehend the criminal immediately after the commission of a crime. The purpose of investigation is to identify, locate, arrest, prepare the case for court, and assist in the prosecution of the offender. Generally, the detective goes to work *after the fact* and must rely on such things as physical evidence, witnesses, and information obtained from various sources. As a general rule, the detective works in civilian clothing so that he is inconspicuous as he moves about the community in the pursuance of his task.

Unlike patrol officers, detectives are not usually involved in crime prevention but with the repression of crime through subsequent arrest of offenders. Briefly stated, the detective becomes involved in such activities as searching crime scenes, securing physical evidence, interviewing witnesses, interrogating suspects, obtaining warrants of arrest, arresting suspects, preparing written reports for prosecution, and testifying in court.

The effectiveness of the investigative forces in a police department and compliance with the legal safeguards imposed

186

Burglary investigation in progress

Courtesy of Harrisburg Police Department
Harrisburg, Pa.

by the Constitution are problems of great concern. Almost daily, the judicial and legislative branches of government evaluate the operational tactics of the criminal investigators. Many questions have been posed as to strategies used by detectives, regarding such issues as: confessions and detentions; revealing confidential informants; search and seizure; and legislative investigations. Consequently, investigators have to withstand critical inquiry, and the effectiveness of criminal investigation depends on the caliber of police officers selected to carry out the varied duties of an investigator.

187

THE DETECTIVE

The term *detective* is used to identify that police officer who has been assigned the specialized task of investigating crimes that have been committed. In most cities, the detective is selected from the patrol force as a reward for good service as a patrol officer. In many police departments it is considered a promotion and quite often the position of detective is a rank and may demand a higher salary. By having rank the detective achieves tenure and thereby cannot be removed except for gross misconduct. These practices are unsound for several reasons.

Success as a patrol officer does not necessarily indicate proficiencies that are necessary to be a good detective. It may very well be that the good patrol officer will not be a good detective. It is also true that a poor patrol officer may possess attributes that would make him a good detective. The police should ask themselves what it is that a man learns on patrol that would make him a good detective. There may be little relationship between the two tasks. Detective work must be analyzed, and patrol officers selected who possess the necessary attributes to be successful detectives.

To carry the point a little further, it may be that a man need not be a patrol officer first before becoming a detective. Perhaps a man right out of the academy possesses attributes that justify his immediate assignment as a detective. Traditionalism is the only real reason that patrol service is a prerequisite to becoming a detective.

By bestowing the rank of detective, the police department becomes unduly rigid. The position of detective should be considered an assignment for only an indefinite period of time. The need for detectives can vary from time to time, and this arrangement would allow needed flexibility. When the demands are great for detectives, a few could be temporarily assigned and then reassigned to patrol when the workload becomes normal again. Conversely, detectives could be temporarily assigned to patrol when that division has an unusual need.

Another justification for abolishing the rank of detective is that the consequent effect would allow for the men to rotate various functions. This keeps interest high among the personnel and also develops potential executives who have knowledge of the total police operation. Another advantage is that rotation of the detective function may possibly cut down on the corruption that plagues various police departments throughout the United States. The shorter tenure of detectives may not provide sufficient time for them to develop those contacts that may lead to corruption.

With the crime costs in the United States rising to billions dollars annually and with the role of the detective investigator posing a significant need, the lack of a comprehensive method of detective selection is remarkable. Related to the problem of selecting detectives is the problem of training detectives. Generally, most federal agencies require that potential detectives undergo some form of training *before* selection, while municipal police agencies have no such requirements. Some departments provide training after the selection, but the most common method of familiarizing the new investigator with his task is through *on the job training.*

In reviewing the specialized functions of a detective, it appears as a full-time job to:

Ascertain information relating to criminal offenses and obtain evidence for arrest.

Visit crime scenes and search for evidence and apprehend violators.

Interview witnesses and suspects.

After investigation is complete, prepare the case for court.

Make specialized investigations on vice, narcotics, and raids.

Check pawnshops for stolen property.

Appear in court to give testimony.

Investigate reports of missing persons.

Inspect businesses requiring certain city licenses for operations.

189

Maintain surveillance over known criminals and other suspects.

Prepare written reports.

All of this requires full knowledge of modern methods and techniques of criminal investigation; a knowledge of rules and regulations and law; a knowledge of the city geography; ability to withstand and execute oral and written reports; and ability to deal firmly, but courteously, with the public.

Every member of the police department, regardless of rank or position, should possess these traits and should have the opportunity to use them in the community.

MANAGING CRIMINAL INVESTIGATIONS

The 1966 report of the President's Commission on Law Enforcement and Administration of Justice emphasized the need to upgrade the performance of criminal investigations, but by a decade later little improvement had occurred. Fortunately, however, recent years have witnessed attention by police administrators in this most important area.

Perhaps the doubling of crime rates, the slower rise in the number of arrests, the declining levels in clearance rates, and growing community dissatisfaction with police effectiveness in criminal investigations during the past few years has spurred administrators to address the issue. In addition, studies funded by the National Institute of Law Enforcement and Criminal Justice have provided information that was necessary before new and different approaches to criminal investigation could be taken.

The most notable study of the investigation process was conducted by the Rand Corporation through a grant received from the National Institute of Law Enforcement and Criminal Justice. The major findings of this two-year research project were as follows:

1. Differences in investigative training, staffing, workload, and procedures appear to have no appreciable effect on crime, arrest, or clearance rates.

2. The method by which police investigators are organized cannot be related to variations in crime, arrest, and clearance rates.

3. Substantially more than half of all serious reported crimes receive no more than superficial attention from investigators.

4. An investigator's time is largely consumed in reviewing reports, documenting files, and attempting to locate and interview victims on cases that experience shows will not be solved. For cases that are solved, an investigator spends more time in postclearance processing than in identifying the perpetrator.

5. The single most important determinant of whether or not a case will be solved is the information the victim supplies to the immediately responding patrol officer. If information that uniquely identifies the perpetrator is not presented at the time the crime is reported, the perpetrator, by and large, will not be subsequently identified.

6. Of those cases that are ultimately cleared but in which the perpetrator is not identifiable at the time of the initial police incident report, almost all are cleared as a result of routine police procedures.

7. Most police departments collect more physical evidence than can be productively processed. Allocating more resources to increasing the processing capabilities of the department can lead to more identifications than some other investigative actions.

8. Latent fingerprints rarely provide the only basis for identifying a suspect.

9. In relatively few departments do investigators consistently and thoroughly document the key evidentiary facts in order to reasonably assure that the prosecutor can obtain a conviction on the most serious applicable charges.

10. Police failure to document a case investigation thoroughly may have contributed to a higher case dismissal rate and a weakening of the prosecutor's plea bargaining position.

191

11. Crime victims in general strongly desire to be notified officially as to whether or not the police have "solved" their case and what progress has been made toward convicting the suspect after his or her arrest.

12. Investigative strike forces have a significant potential to increase arrest rates for a few difficult target offenses, provided they remain concentrated on activities for which they are uniquely qualified; in practice, however, they are frequently diverted elsewhere.

The findings of this research project certainly indicate that traditional approaches to criminal investigation by police departments do not significantly affect the rate at which cases are solved. If this be true, then several policy changes are needed. The recommendations of the Rand project, based on the findings, are as follows:

1. Reduce follow-up investigation on all cases except those involving the most serious offenses.

2. Assign generalist-investigators (who would handle the obvious leads in routine cases) to the local operations commander.

3. Establish a Major Offenders Unit (depending on the size of the department) to investigate serious crimes.

4. Assign serious-offense investigations to closely supervised teams, rather than to individual investigators.

5. Strengthen evidence-processing capabilities.

6. Increase the use of information-processing systems in lieu of investigators.

7. Employ strike forces selectively and judiciously.

8. Place postarrest investigations under the authority of the prosecutor.

9. Initiate programs designed to impress on the citizen the crucial role he or she plays in crime solution.

In response to the findings and recommendations of the Rand study and workshops on managing criminal investigations funded by the National Institute of Law Enforcement and Criminal Justice and conducted by University Research Corporation, an increasing number of police organizations are critically examining the organizational structure and effectiveness of the resources allocated to the criminal investigative process. As a result of this critical analysis, changes are being made in the placement of investigative responsibilities and in the establishment of investigative priorities as well as other substantive actions affecting investigative operational tactics and strategies.

In most instances, as recommended by the National Institute of Law Enforcement and Criminal Justice, the departments are developing approaches to managing criminal investigations that lead to:

1. An increased participation by patrol personnel in a comprehensive initial investigation at the time a crime is reported.
2. The establishment of a case-screening system that will remove nonsolvable cases from the investigative process at an early point.
3. The development of a police/prosecutor relationship that will result in better case investigation and preparation and greater likelihood of successful prosecution.
4. The establishment of a management information system that provides agency administrators with appropriate information for managing the criminal investigative process and alerts them to emerging problems.
5. A reexamination of agency structure in order to maximize the use of all personnel (both patrol and investigative).
6. The development of investigative management techniques for the improved use of detective personnel.

The foregoing clearly illustrate the changing role and approach of managing the investigative process. The coming years may very well see a drastic departure from the traditional approach to criminal investigation. In fact, if police organizations are to keep pace with the ever-changing problems of crime, it is imperative that they develop programs and approaches that will maximize results and minimize costs.

CRIMINALISTICS

Criminalistics may be defined as the science of crime detection, also known as forensic science. Criminalistics is based upon the application of mathematics, physics, chemistry, and the biological sciences and medicine to the study of physical evidence. Recently, forensic pathology and forensic psychiatry have become important elements of criminalistics. It is, fundamentally, a physical science, with much of its success depending on general science knowledge and the ability to develop new methods of applying scientific techniques to crime detection.

As all students of law enforcement know, repetition and compulsion are elements considered in criminal investigations; thus, the criminalist locates the arsonist through physical evidence left at the scene of the fire, the check-writer through his signature on a forged check, and the burglar through his tools and toolmarks remaining at the burglary.

Broadly speaking, the criminalist is concerned with the criminal "deed" and not the causation or the motivation for the crime.

The criminalist is prepared to assist law enforcement agencies in investigations of murder, rape, hit-and-run traffic accidents, and many other crimes of violence. In studying and presenting the available evidence, the criminalist may clear innocent suspects as well as convict the guilty. The criminalist will use many scientific instruments to demonstrate certain characteristics of physical evidence, such instruments as the spectroscope, phase microscope, the x-ray and x-ray diffraction, gas chromatography, microphotography, and many others. In using these instruments, the scientist will analyze soil samples, blood stains, firearms, questioned documents, glass fragments, hairs, fibers, building materials, tool impressions, etc. The criminalist must also know how to effectively process evidence that will serve as a development tool for the solution of crimes; to preserve the evidence safe from change and contamination so that the peculiar features of the evidence are not destroyed or damaged for courtroom testimony.

194

Criminalist at work

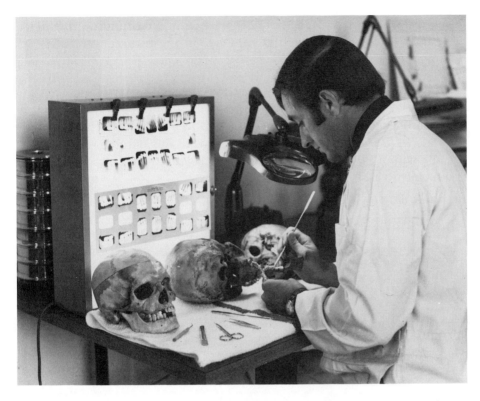

Courtesy of Ronald Eltzeroth, Police Training Institute, University of
Illinois, Champaign, Ill.

One of the important aspects of the criminalist's function is to translate complicated scientific data into reasonable and everyday language, comprehensible to the average jury. The more complicated the science and the more incomprehensible the classifications of evidence, the more the criminalist is vulnerable to cross-examination by the criminal defense. The criminalist speaks in court as an "expert witness" and is given the opportunity for full expression of his scientific findings and opinions regarding the conclusions of his analysis.

The criminalistic laboratory is very important to the detective because it can often place the suspect at the scene,

195

prove he left something from his person at the scene, prove he took something from the scene, and so on. Criminalistics is a relatively new field, but the science is continually growing and will assume a much greater role in the future.

SPECIALIZED OR AUXILIARY SERVICES

Many specialized and auxiliary services must exist to assist the important line functions of a police department, only one of which is the crime laboratory or criminalist unit—existing solely to assist in criminal investigation.

Voiceprint identification in police crime laboratory

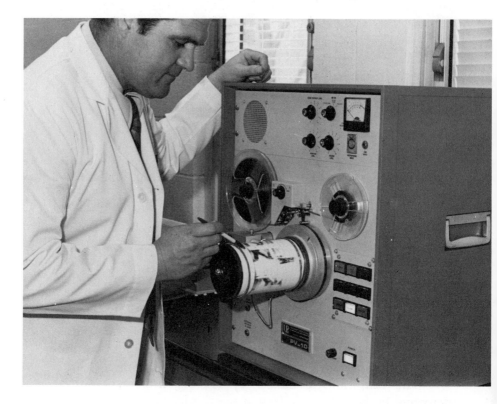

Courtesy of the Harrisburg Area Community College
Harrisburg, Pa.

The growth in complexity in police agencies has been in response to certain needs as they became obvious. When the need for follow-up investigation became apparent, the detective came into existence. When we became a nation on wheels, traffic units were established. When science became useful to police work, laboratories were established. Obviously, such development was haphazard, and the simple organizations became somewhat disorganized. The primary problem was the depletion of patrol as these specialized areas developed. This, as we know, must be guarded against. However, these are definite needs that must be met that necessitate specialization or the provision of certain auxiliary services.

Necessary auxiliary services include such things as the crime laboratory, records, juvenile bureaus, jail maintenance, community relations units, communications, identification, transportation, etc. Some of these have already been discussed, while the need for others are quite obvious. Of those not previously discussed, the most important are records and communications, since the success of line functions such as patrol and investigation are completely dependent upon them.

RECORDS

Accurate, comprehensive, and detailed records are absolutely necessary for effective police administration. If a police agency expects to provide maximum police service, a records system must exist that will allow careful and detailed collection and analysis of facts and information. Such information should include such things as calls for police service, crime activity, arrests, traffic statistics, etc. In addition to the input, the information must be easily retrieved and be accessible for rapid and efficient compilation, computation, and analysis.

Centralized records not only help coordinate and direct criminal investigation but also provide information necessary for adequately determining such things as the distribution of manpower, determination of patrol areas, and determination of shift changes as they relate to called-for services. It is imperative that all incidents reported to the police be promptly and correctly recorded for current reference and review or subsequent analysis.

Records should also be kept on personnel and other administrative activities. Personnel records are of prime importance when assigning men, evaluating men for promotion, determining training needs, and improving selection procedures. Cost records are absolutely necessary in preparing future budgets. Inventory records are necessary when projecting equipment needs. Equipment performance records are helpful when determining the kind or quality of equipment to purchase.

Records systems of today have become so complex that computers and other innovative mechanisms are in broad use. In fact, records systems utilizing computers can quite accurately project future crime areas and trends which will allow better distribution of personnel. Such records can also determine within seconds if a car is stolen or if a man is wanted in conjunction with a crime.

Records are so important that the success of today's police agency is largely dependent upon their availability.

COMMUNICATIONS

Actually, there are few, if any, police activities that are not dependent upon communications of some form. For example, most citizen complaints are reported to the police by the telephone which is a basic communication medium. Patrol response to citizen complaints is a result of the receiving of such information over the two-way radio. Information from the field for specific information from records is transmitted over the radio. Communication between staff members is often via the telephone.

As can be seen, communications by mechanical means plays a very prominent role in law enforcement. In fact, a

Dispatcher communicating with officers in the field

Courtesy of St. Louis Police Department
St. Louis, Mo.

centralized radio communication system is an absolute necessity for effective patrol and coordination of effort by patrol. Quick response to crime scenes is dependent upon fast radio communication. The coordination of patrol officers engaged in a tactical approach or coverage of a crime scene is dependent upon instruction required by radio. The supervisor would find it impossible to coordinate patrol activities without the radio.

Proper supervision is also dependent upon the radio, since the first line supervisor must be able to communicate

199

with his men. Many departments have also initiated command frequencies to facilitate the supervisory function.

Like records, modern communication systems have become very complex to meet the challenging demands of modern law enforcement. Great strides are still being made in improving communications systems, and as such improvement is made the police become even more dependent upon it.

POLICE ROLE IN THE PROTECTION
OF INDIVIDUAL FREEDOM

The police, by virtue of their activity, have a very important role in the protection of individual freedom. In fact, the previously mentioned Law Enforcement Code of Ethics says specifically, "and to respect the constitutional rights of all men."

In effect, people of the community realize their civil rights through the interpretive actions of the police. In other words, police procedures and policies are in a sense telling the public what they can or cannot do. There are, of course, many controls from the federal level relative to civil rights, but implementation is the major responsibility of the local police departments, and they must be totally cognizant of the ramifications and importance of these rights.

In addition to interpretive actions defining civil rights, the police have the responsibility to instruct citizens in regard to their duties, obligations, rights, and privileges in reference to the law. They might, for example, publish pamphlets which describe the citizens' rights under the Constitution of the United States, the state, and the municipality within which they live. The police might also stress the public's responsibility in relation to those protective privileges that they have under the law.

In the past, the police preferred that the citizenry remain ignorant of certain rights since this provided great lati-

200

tude for accomplishing the police task. There is no question that the police frequently denied basic rights to the accused in order to facilitate prosecution and conviction. In fact, there are those who believe such unprofessional conduct was the rule rather than the exception. Anything goes if it builds a case and convicts a violator.

As a result of such conduct, the courts—although they may have overreacted—issued decisions which placed certain legal limitations upon the police. These decisions have had an effect. They obviously limited police action, but at the same time they caused the police to take a critical look at past practices.

It is agreed that the courts have limited police operations, but *it was probably the best thing that ever happened to law enforcement*. The decisions caused the police to seek better and more efficient methods of achieving the police role, while at the same time preserving individual rights. For many years, the police had sat placidly, satisfied with age-old practices and procedures. Now to get the job done with any degree of success at all, the police had to improve themselves. The police were challenged, and it should be added that they have met this challenge and have conquered it.

The police are now concerned more than ever with individual rights, and they have accepted preservation as a primary responsibility of the police function.

Summary

Police responsibilities are more important than those assigned to any other agency within our governmental structure. The police are actually society's agents for the maintenance of harmony within the community. They are charged with the safeguarding of lives and property, the prevention of delinquency, and the protection of individual rights.

In order to meet these complex responsibilities, the role of the police has become quite broad. The most important activity is patrol, as its effectiveness will determine the success of the entire police agency. The patrol function is so basic to fulfilling the police responsibility that its goals are essentially synonymous with the total police objective .

Other important line activities of the police include crime prevention and criminal investigation. Crime prevention includes all those activities that help discourage the commission of crime. Crime prevention includes working with juveniles, special community relations programs, participation in community organizations, public education, and working with other public service agencies.

The purpose of criminal investigation is to identify, locate, arrest, and help prosecute offenders. Generally, the detective goes to work "after the fact" and must rely on such things as physical evidence, witnesses, and information obtained from various sources.

Specialized and auxiliary services must be provided by the police department to assist or support the line functions. The most important of these services are records and communications.

202

Discussion Questions

1. Define the police function.
2. Why is patrol considered the "backbone" of police operations?
3. What things must be considered when determining the geographical boundaries of beats?
4. What things must be considered when determining shift hours?
5. What is the relationship between patrol and crime prevention?
6. What is the role of the police in traffic regulation and control?
7. What is the relationship between patrol and the need for specialized services?
8. What is the purpose of criminal investigation, and when does it become necessary? Explain some of the new approaches to managing criminal investigations.
9. To what extent should the police be involved in the problem of juvenile delinquency?
10. What is criminalistics, and what is its role in law enforcement?

5

Orientation to Administration and Organization

During the last several decades law enforcement has been surveyed by numerous agencies, committees, and individuals, beginning with the Wickersham Commission in 1929, which was anything but complimentary about the status of law enforcement in the United States. The United States Congress, state legislatures, and many local, public, and civic bodies have been greatly concerned about lawlessness and the police ability or inability, as the case may be, to provide adequate protection and services. Most of the discussions and findings have been justifiably critical of the police and in recent years the reaction has been almost at a panic level.

This panic is clearly evidenced by the recent trend of federal involvement in and assistance to local law enforcement agencies. Federal interest, or perhaps we should say concern, was very graphically illustrated by President Lyndon B. Johnson when, in 1965, he reacted to public concern by establishing the Commission on Law Enforcement and Administration of Justice. The membership of this commission was comprised of outstanding men in law enforcement and other related disciplines. The commission was subdivided into several task forces, each with the necessary funds for staffing, and in-depth studies were conducted. Recommendations from the task force were numerous and many of those from the "Police Task Force Report" related directly to principles of police organization and administration. For example, to mention only a very few, the report recommended:

1. The establishment of community relations units in departments serving substantial minority populations.
2. The establishment of citizen advisory committees in minority group neighborhoods.
3. More active recruitment, especially on college campuses and in inner cities.
4. Modification of inflexible physical, age, and residence recruitment requirements.
5. The stressing of ability in promotional consideration.

6. The encouragement of lateral entry to specialist and supervisory positions.
7. The strengthening of central staff control.
8. The provision of areawide communications and records coordination.
9. The pooling and coordination of crime laboratories.
10. Consideration of pooling or consolidation of law enforcement in all counties or metropolitan areas.

The list enumerates only a few of the recommendations made by the Police Task Force, but it does indicate the many problems that must be attacked.

The implications of so many recommendations from the Commission are obvious. Apparently police departments in general were not practicing modern administrative, organizational, and operational procedures and principles. There was a need to analyze past practices very critically with an eye toward improvement. The police were becoming painfully aware, and still are, of the inadequacies that were prevalent, and the publicity of the report provided the necessary impetus for improvement.

As is always the case, of course, the paramount problem was one of financial ability to initiate changes and implement improvement. Local, municipal, county, and state governments complained that they did not possess the financial capability to make needed improvements in their law enforcement agencies. To a large degree this was true, since the tax base at the local level may be quite limited for many jurisdictions. Recognizing this as a practical obstacle for improvement, the federal legislature passed the Law Enforcement Assistance Act of 1965, which established the Office of Law Enforcement Assistance (OLEA); later it passed the "Omnibus Crime Control and Safe Street Act" of 1968, which established the Law Enforcement Assistance Administration to replace OLEA.

As a result of federal support, law enforcement has already improved, is continuing to improve, and will eventually reach a high professional level. Federal interest and support have created an enthusiasm for improvement and efficient law enforcement that has affected the citizenry, public officials, and law enforcement leaders. The combined effort of äll three groups will hopefully continue so that optimum police service will be available to every citizen regardless of his or her location within the United States.

ADMINISTRATION

The term *administration* is frequently used rather loosely and means different things to different people. Its definition is also dependent upon the context within which it is used. Reference is frequently made to the "administration" when one is discussing those within an organization responsible for its operation. For example, we frequently hear of students protesting against the administration of a college or university. This use of the term is incorrect, as administration is a process rather than a thing or a group of people. The students, within the true definition of the term, should be protesting against either the process of administration or those people doing or responsible for administering. Of course, it has become quite common to refer to the administrators as "the administration."

Administration is a complicated and complex process involving numerous variables. It involves human factors such as: 1) honesty, 2) integrity, 3) discretion, 4) human relations, 5) compassion, and 6) an appreciation of the needs and desires of others. It also involves nonhuman or material aspects such as providing a service, producing a service, producing a product, and either making a profit or providing a public service with the stress of economy.

Administration relates to the establishment of goals and their achievement. Administration exists in every human activity from the very simple to the most complicated. For example, when an individual leaves for work in the morning, he has established the goal of reaching work and then determines the means by which he will get there.

Generally, however, we do not think of administration in this manner but rather in terms of the achievement of goals in an organization. For our purposes administration deals with *institutional goals and objectives and the process or techniques utilized in their achievement.* It is a process that involves leadership and the control or direction of the efforts of individuals toward the common goals. Administration involves the tasks and duties of people placed in a position of responsibility within an organization. It is the job or task of the person or persons charged with the operation of a phase or unit of the organization. The police chief is the primary administrator of the police organization because he is charged with the operation of the police department. There are additional subordinate administrators who are charged with the operation of segments of the police department under the broad office of the chief.

ORGANIZATION

Administration is dependent upon the ability to organize—in other words, the organization. Like administration, organization can be either simple or complex. When two people combine their efforts to move a table from one place to another, they have established a goal and will usually organize to achieve that goal. In large organizations the same principle is used, but the involvement is much more complex and complicated. Here we may be speaking of several hundred people who must organize to fulfill numerous functions whose achievement will accomplish the stated goal of the organization. Perhaps the best definition of organizing or organization is that given by Pfiffner and Sherwood:

> Organization is the pattern of ways in which large numbers of people, too many to have intimate face-to-face contact with all others, and engaged in a complexity of

tasks, relate themselves to each other in the conscious, systematic establishment and accomplishment of mutually agreed purposes.[1]

The definition of organization given by the American College Dictionary provides additional insight relative to this concept. It defines organization as follows:

> . . . to form as or into a whole consisting of interdependent or coordinated parts, esp. for harmonious or united action . . .

By these definitions organization entails units and subunits each with specific objectives that, combined, will accomplish the achievement of the organization's broad objective. Like all organizations, police departments are organized into various divisions, units, and sections each with assigned specific responsibilities or objectives. The number of subunits, of course, is dependent upon the size of the police department. The larger the department, the more complicated and complex the organizational structure will be. *Regardless of size, however, if each unit accomplishes its assigned responsibility, the combined success of all units will achieve the broad goals of the agency.*

To follow and understand police organization fully it is necessary that the student be familiar with several organizational and operational terms, some of which are peculiar to law enforcement. Although terminology and its usage do vary across the country, the following definitions are generally accepted and will be applicable throughout this chapter.

Organizational units in a police department can be classified into three broad areas: 1) functional, 2) geographical, and 3) chronological.

[1] John M. Pfiffner and Frank P. Sherwood, *Administrative Organization* (Englewood Cliffs, N.J.: Prentice-Hall, Inc., 1960), p. 30.

Functional. Functional units of a police organization are designed or adopted primarily to perform some specific operation or duty. It refers to the organization into subunits to facilitate functions in the accomplishment of assigned tasks. Normally this consists, in descending order, of the *bureau, division, section,* and *unit or office.*

Bureau—The bureau is the largest organizational unit within a police department and is comprised of a number of divisions. Bureau commanders usually have the rank of deputy or assistant chief and report directly to the chief of police. Smaller police departments will have a captain in charge. The function of the bureau is primarily administrative in nature, dealing with policy formation and coordination.

Division—The division is the primary subdivision of the bureau, and its commander, who usually holds the rank of captain (perhaps lieutenant in smaller departments), reports directly to the bureau head. The divisional function provides either general police service or a specialized activity. The function of the divisional commander can be described as mid-management and deals with operational aspects of management or administration. Examples of the divisional level, again dependent upon the size of the department, would be the Investigation Division, the Services Division, and the Uniformed or Patrol Division.

Section—The section is a subdivision of the division and is usually commanded by a lieutenant who is responsible to the divisional head. The section level has a more specialized function defined by specific duties. In a large investigation division there may be various sections investigating specific types of crime—for example, the homicide section, the burglary section, the auto theft section, and the robbery section. Smaller departments may combine some of these areas—for example, the assault and homicide section. In the uniformed division we may find the traffic section, the patrol section, and the maintenance section.

Unit or Office—Units usually exist when further specialization is needed but not to the extent to justify the size of a section. An example may be the accident investigation unit within a traffic section.

It must be realized that the examples cited are merely an attempt to clarify and place in perspective the terms relative to functional organization. The organization of a police department is dependent upon its size. It may be justifiable to have a traffic division in larger organizations while only a section within a division may be justifiable in smaller departments. Ranks attached to the commanders of each functional unit will also depend upon the size and complexity of the organization as well as the degree of specialization.

The following simplified organizational chart illustrates the various levels in the hierarchical functional pattern.

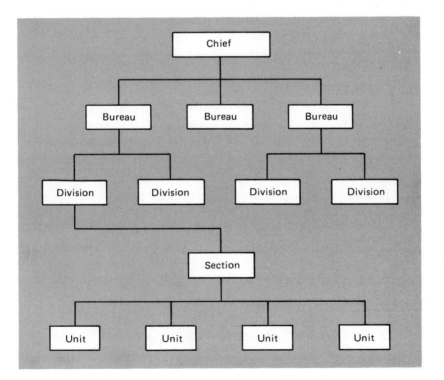

213

Geographical. Geographical units of a police agency related to the subdivision of the jurisdiction serve to facilitate total police coverage. The generally accepted terminology used to identify geographical units from the smallest to the largest is as follows:

Post—The post is a fixed point or place where a police officer may be assigned. An example is the traffic officer who is assigned to a specific intersection to direct and control traffic movement. Other examples would be the school crossing officer and the traditionally known desk sergeant.

Route—This term refers to the assignment of an officer along a stretch of street. Examples are the traffic officer assigned to a length of street and the foot patrolman. The route has no corners and the area of patrol is confined to one length of street.

Beat—The beat is the fundamental unit of patrol and is that area within which patrol officers are assigned either on foot or within a marked unit. The officer assigned to a beat is responsible for all activities within the area and must provide continuous surveillance throughout his tour of duty. All calls originating within his beat are referred to him and he makes the original contact.

Sector—A patrol sector consists of several beats and is so divided to facilitate proper supervision. The patrol supervisor usually holds the rank of sergeant and is referred to as the "line supervisor." His task is to coordinate activities of the several beats and assist patrol officers when needed. For general purposes, therefore, the sector is a division of supervision.

Precinct—Larger cities consist of so many beats and sectors that it becomes necessary to have another larger division. The precinct relates to a large district comprised of several patrol sectors. Like the sector, the precinct is a geographical division that facilitates coordination of the activities of the smaller units. Usually the only justification for a precinct is an area too large to be handled by smaller divisions.

Area—An area represents the major and largest geographical subdivision of a large jurisdiction served. For example, to facilitate administrative efficiency the city may be divided into two or more areas with an administrative officer assigned to each. State police agencies usually are divided into areas and a high-ranking officer such as a major is assigned to coordinate and administer activities in his area.

Chronological. Chronological division refers to the division of the day for purposes of assigning personnel. Following are the common terms utilized:

Shift—The shift is a time division of the day to which personnel are assigned. The shift is usually eight hours in duration, and traditionally there are three shifts to each day to cover the twenty-four–hour span. However, it is quite common to find more than three shifts in order for them to overlap and, therefore, to have personnel available at all times. The shift is also called a *watch* in some cities.

Platoon—This refers to the men assigned to a specific shift. The platoon is normally commanded by a lieutenant and may serve the entire city. In the case of larger cities with several districts, the platoon will serve only one district.

Following are the traditional ranks, from the highest to lowest, used throughout the United States. However, depending on individual situations, not all departments use all ranks.

Chain of command

Common to all agencies	Interchangeable	Primarily in large departments
Chief of Police	Chief of Police	
	Deputy or Assistant Chief	Deputy or Assistant Chief
	Chief Inspector	Chief Inspector
	Inspector	Inspector
Captain	Captain	
Lieutenant	Lieutenant	
Sergeant	Sergeant	
	Corporal	
Patrolman	Patrolman	

PRINCIPLES OF ORGANIZATION

Although it is impossible and impractical to identify absolute principles of organization that will apply to every police organization, there are some terms that are somewhat universally acceptable. It is, therefore, important that the student of law enforcement have some familiarity with them. These are: 1) Hierarchy of Authority, 2) Delegation of Authority, 3) Span of Control, and 4) Unity of Command.

HIERARCHY OF AUTHORITY

Hierarchy of authority refers to the arrangement, up or down the organizational structure, of classes of positions that have various degrees of authority. The higher a person is in the organizational structure, the higher his or her level of authority. Authority, in other words, is commensurate with an individual's position within the hierarchy. Typically an organizational structure takes the shape of a pyramid; as one nears the top of the pyramid the number of positions is decreased while the level of authority is increased. The Chief of Police is located at the top of the pyramid and authority flows from the top down.

DELEGATION OF AUTHORITY

As stated above, authority emanates from the Chief of Police and he grants authority to those lower in the pyramid as it relates to their area of responsibility. In conjunction with this, the chief must formulate the proper balance between responsibility and authority. In other words, if he assigns a subordinate the responsibility of fulfilling a task, he must give him or her the authority necessary to accomplish it.

SPAN OF CONTROL

Span of control refers to the number of subordinates one person can effectively supervise. This principle is based on

216

the fact that if a supervisor is given too broad a span of control (too many subordinates) he or she will be unable to provide the leadership necessary to accomplish the task. At the same time, if the span of control is too limited, the supervisor will not be used to the fullest capacity.

There is no magic number relative to span of control, as it relates to three primary factors: 1) nature of the work being performed, 2) ability of the supervisor, and 3) ability of the subordinates. Generally, however, the span of control in most police departments will range from three subordinates up to seven.

UNITY OF COMMAND

Unity of command is very closely linked to the *chain of command* as illustrated. Simply stated, unity of command means that each individual in the organization reports to just one superior officer. This minimizes confusion and facilitates more efficient operations. Under this principle each officer has an immediate superior to whom he is responsible and through whom all authority, communications, orders, and directives pass.

LEADERSHIP AND SUPERVISION

Leadership and supervision in the police organization can be considered the most important single factor relating to the success or failure of the achievement of police objectives. It is important, therefore, that all personnel understand what effective leadership is and how it can be exercised. Unfortunately, this type of understanding is not easily accomplished, as leadership is a very complex concept. Leadership and the ability to exercise it cannot be learned in a short time, but is something the administrator and the supervisor must strive toward every working day of their lives.

217

THE CONCEPT OF LEADERSHIP

It is a common belief that leadership can be equated with a person's position in an organization or that power endowed upon the person by virtue of his position is leadership. It is certainly advantageous if a leader has power, but this does not mean that leadership and power are the same thing. Leadership basically involves the ability to influence, and this ability is not necessarily endowed in a person's position or the power that goes with the position. Positions of hierarchical importance are inextricably bound to leadership, but they are not synonymous.[2] The administrator who understands this distinction will perceive his role more clearly than one who does not. He will know that his high position and the authority by virtue of that position alone are not sufficient to lead his subordinates effectively. He will know that he must possess other personal attributes and that he must exercise wisely all that he has learned about leading his men.

The administrator should also understand that the exercising of command power, which is granted because of his position in the hierarchy, may not be real leadership. It may be that his exercising of command power generally operates in routine situations and that it is constant and regular. It is usually sufficient to get the job done, but only because the subordinates *expect* and *accept* such commands. In contrast to this, leadership is needed in the nonroutine activities or when the subordinates may challenge the official command. In perceiving his role, the administrator should not waste too much effort with routine orders that are expected and accepted. He should, rather, devote his major energies to the difficult and more complicated tasks that may arise from time to time.

Probably the best definition of leadership is given by Lipham, who states that leadership and administration are two different concepts. Leadership pertains to the initiation of a new structure or procedure for accomplishing an organiza-

[2] Pfiffner and Sherwood, op. cit., p. 35.

218

tion's goals and objectives or for changing an organization's goals and objectives. Administration relates to the utilization of existing structures or procedures to achieve an organizational goal or objective. In other words, leadership suggests change while administration suggests maintaining the status quo.[3]

Another assumption that seems to be prevalent among police executives is that leaders are born, not made. This type of thinking has resulted in many attempts to ascertain what qualities make one man a better leader than another. Research has been conducted on these significant traits and has suggested such possibilities as: 1) physical and constitutional factors, 2) intelligence, 3) self-confidence, 4) social ability, 5) will (initiative, persistence, ambition), 6) dominance, and 7) surgency (talkativeness, cheerfulness, geniality, enthusiasm, expressiveness, alertness, and originality). So far no constant pattern of traits has emerged and researchers have found that individuals can possess the same traits but not achieve similar success in their roles as leaders. In short, the behavior of leaders varies widely from one leadership situation to another.[4]

We have heard a person described as "a natural leader." This claim may be true, but rather than being a result of traits, it may be the result of the social and psychological climate in which the supervisor-subordinate relationship exists. Leadership takes place in an environment and is relative to that environment.

It is believed that leadership, although limited to some degree by character and personality, can be learned and improved through instruction and education. It is also believed that the existing situation has a direct influence upon it.[5]

---

[3] Willard R. Lane and others, *Foundations of Educational Administration* (New York: The Macmillan Company, 1967), p. 312.

[4] Fred D. Carver and Thomas J. Sergiovanni, *Organizations and Human Behavior: Focus on Schools* (New York: McGraw-Hill Book Co., 1969), p. 288.

[5] *Ibid.*

219

CLIMATE FOR LEADERSHIP

The style of leadership certainly affects the psychological and sociological environment of the working situation. Essentially, there are three basic leadership styles. They are 1) authoritarian, 2) laissez faire, and 3) democratic or participative.

Authoritarian. The authoritarian leader can be described as directive and production centered. Basically, and unfortunately, the police have all too frequently relied upon this type of leadership. Authoritarian leadership attempts to dominate the subordinates and force them rather than lead them to the attainment of their goals. In the authoritarian environment the supervisor relies upon the philosophy that he is the *boss* and his task is merely *telling* or commanding the subordinates what they are to do. All communication is from the boss to the subordinate without any opportunity for feedback. The subordinate's role under the authoritarian style is merely to respond in a given way when specific orders are issued. It is not his role to question, suggest, or attempt to improve techniques as described by the supervisor or administrator.

Laissez faire. With the laissez-faire style of leadership the philosophy is one of providing little or no direction to the subordinate so that he more or less does as he pleases. Supporters of this view believe that if personnel are left alone, they will work for individual satisfaction and a job well done, while with the autocratic approach they will revolt by doing only what they have to do and no more.

The primary and basic problem with a laissez-faire leadership is that no common direction exists. Because of lack of direction, subordinates may be uncertain as to their role and what they are trying to accomplish. Such uncoordinated effort is certainly not conducive to the concept of a *team* working toward common goals. Simply stated, the usual result of laissez-faire leadership is mass confusion, which is unlikely to be efficient or effective.

Democratic. The philosophy of the democratic leader is one of everyone working together to achieve the stated goals of the police service. Rather than telling subordinates what to do, the supervisor explains why certain things should be done and how the subordinates can help in the achievement of the objectives. He sees that every person under his direction realizes his place in the organization and has an appreciation for the contributions he can make. The democratic approach is the real test for the supervisor or administrator, and achievement of goals will pay the biggest dividends.

For leadership purposes, it is believed that the democratic style is best. It is definitely the most difficult to achieve, but its benefits over the other styles demand that all supervisors wholeheartedly strive toward it. Generally speaking, democratic leadership gives great emphasis to the importance of the subordinate's individuality through functional and shared leadership, permissive participation, open council, and free communication.

In support of this contention Halpin stresses two major dimensions of leadership behavior: *initiating structure* and *consideration.*[6]

Initiating structure refers to the leader's behavior in delineating the relationship between himself and members of the work group and in endeavoring to establish well-defined patterns or organization, channels of communication, and methods of procedure. Consideration refers to behavior indicative of friendship, mutual respect, and warmth in the relationship between the leader and his subordinates.[7]

Halpin goes on to explain:

Practical men know that the leader must lead—must initiate action and get things done. But because he must accomplish his purposes through other people, and without jeopardizing the intactness or integrity of the group,

[6] Carver and Sergiovanni, p. 290.
[7] *Ibid.*

221

the skilled executive knows that he also must maintain good *human relations* if he is to succeed in furthering the purposes of the group.[8]

Simply stated, this means that the administrator or supervisor must show consideration toward his subordinates. Jack Gibb adds support to this by stating, "The leader is present, available, and with the group as a person, not as a role."[9] He goes on to say that the key to leadership centers on the high degree of trust and confidence in people. Valid, direct, and open communication among all segments of the organic institution is the central process of effective leadership.[10]

DEVELOPING A PARTICIPATIVE CLIMATE

The function of the administrator or supervisor is not to do the entire job himself but to energize the group, encourage initiative, and use the resources that all have to offer. Too often the police administrator or supervisor tries to do the work rather than leading others to do it. For example, there may be a sergeant who is nothing more than a glorified patrolman. He continues to perform the tasks of the patrol-man, but has not been able to adjust to his new role as a first-line supervisor.

To be successful the police administrator must rely on more than his formal status or rank in the organization. He must develop a climate that provides for genuine participation on the part of subordinates. The best means of achieving this is by making sure all subordinates have a complete under-standing of the goals of their unit and believe they are im-portant members of the team. Each subordinate's contributions must be encouraged, and each should be allowed to express

[8] *Ibid.*
[9] Carver and Sergiovanni, p. 316.
[10] Carver and Sergiovanni, p. 324.

222

his or her ideas freely. It is important that there exist joint, interdependent, and shared planning by all people concerned with the accomplishment of the task.

Perhaps the most important benefit of a participating climate is that it better assures that all the capabilities of the group are harnessed. In such an environment the subordinate will want to perform to the limit of his or her capacity because the objectives of the police department have also become personal objectives. Another benefit is that the supervisor's workload will be considerably reduced. Since the subordinate fully understands his job and appreciates his position, he will require less of his supervisor's time for routine directions.

A third benefit involves personal satisfaction in that the subordinate recognizes himself as an important segment of the team. This creates good morale and is conducive to motivation.

LEVELS OF LEADERSHIP

There are actually two levels of leadership within the police organization. They are *managerial* leadership and *operational* leadership.

MANAGERIAL

Managerial leadership relates to those functions and responsibilities of the top administrators within the hierarchy. These people would be the chief of police and his immediate subordinates, who may have the title of deputy chief, assistant chief, or captain. The primary responsibility of the managerial leader includes such things as budgeting, coordinating, public relations, and stimulating his immediate subordinates to accomplish their tasks as efficiently and effectively as possible.

The managerial leader should have some general knowledge of operational tactics and procedures within the police department, but he need not be an expert in this area. His function is well above the operational aspects, which are

223

better left to lower executive and supervisory positions within the police organization. For example, the managerial leader need not be completely familiar with the techniques of searching a house. He must recognize there are definite patterns that should exist relative to specific situations, but he should be able to rely upon executive and supervisory personnel for effecting the necessary leadership at that level.

Again, the managerial leader will deal in abstract, conceptual, and rather sophisticated needs of the police organization. He will be the primary policy maker of the department and will rely heavily upon operational personnel for developing procedures and tactics that will most effectively accomplish the objectives of the department.

OPERATIONAL

At the other end of the continuum is the operational leader. Operational leadership potential must be inherent in both the first-line supervision (sergeant) and the executive level (lieutenant or captain). It is the responsibility of the operational leader to energize his work group in accomplishing the many tasks of the police organization. Whereas the managerial leader exercises influence on the overall operation of the police department, the operational leader must influence the accomplishment of specific tasks. In other words, the operational leader (perhaps a sergeant) encourages and energizes his work group to proceed correctly in specific situations. An example would be the efficient utilization of proper procedures during the search of a burglary scene.

This implies that the operational leader needs considerable police knowledge so that he fully understands the operational aspects of the police department. On the other hand, the managerial leader (chief of police) need not necessarily have extensive knowledge in the various ranks of the police organization. The requirements for the chief would primarily be an academic preparation in management, public administration, business administration, or some other related ad-

224

ministrative area. It would also be beneficial, of course, if he had experience in a top managerial position. This, of course, supports the view that the top administrator can be a layman who is well versed in management, rather than a person with extensive years of experience as a police officer. In fact, the transition from an operational leader to a managerial leader might be so difficult that it may be best that the chief of police not come from the ranks of the police organization.

SUPERVISION

The supervisor is an extremely important person within the police organization. His significance can be appreciated when we visualize what would happen to a police organization if the supervisor were suddenly removed from the scene. In no time, what we think of as a smoothly functioning system would deteriorate into one of individual action without direction or control. Confusion would reap chaos and the entire system, as we know it, would break down.

Supervision is probably the weakest link in most police organizations. Unfortunately, most departments pay little attention to selecting supervisory personnel possessing the potential for adequately accomplishing the task. In addition, little attention is generally paid to the effective training of a person once he or she is selected to be a supervisor.

Since the supervisor is such a vital link in the chain of command, it is imperative that he or she be an operational leader. It is an indisputable fact that the mere donning of a pair of chevrons does not automatically make a person a leader. In other words, as stated previously, the position within the hierarchy does not necessarily mean that the person holding that position is a leader.

Most people who have attained positions of authority and have exerted strong positive leadership, have made a strenuous and conscious effort to become leaders. They realize that the performance of others whom they direct is a constant reflec-

225

tion upon their own ability. With this realization in mind, supervisors should consider their duties and responsibilities and periodically review the manner in which they fulfill them. Self-improvement should be a continuous goal and one should ask himself many times throughout his career whether or not he is effectively accomplishing the assigned objectives.

As stated previously, so far no constant pattern of traits of effective leaders has emerged and researchers have found that different individuals can possess the same traits but not achieve similar success in their roles as leaders. In short, the behavior of leaders varies widely from one leadership situation to another. Simply stated, this means that there are no identifiable traits that a person must possess in order to be or have the potential for being a leader. However, we can assume that certain traits will at least not inhibit one's ability to be a leader. In addition, some traits are believed beneficial for a person to possess if he is to accomplish an operational leadership role effectively.

TRAITS OF A LEADER

KNOWLEDGE

Knowledge is a most essential quality. In and of itself, it will not make a person a leader, but it is certain that no one can be a leader without possessing specific knowledge relative to his job and his surroundings. It is a fair assumption that the supervisor has acquired a large fund of knowledge in order to reach his present position within the hierarchy. This knowledge is probably based largely upon experience as a patrol officer. Such experience is not sufficient, but should be supported by academic pursuits during or before employment.

Knowledge has many dimensions and in order to function properly one should have a knowledge of the things not necessarily connected with formal study. Specifically, he should know the abilities and limitations of his subordinates. Knowing this enables the supervisor to assign the best personnel to a particular job, thereby ensuring its completion without serious complication.

In reality, the sergeant should be fully and completely knowledgeable about each person for whom he is responsible. This means that he be familiar with the man not only as a worker, but as an individual, a husband, a father, etc. In other words, he should be well aware of the man's special interests, wants, desires, and aspirations. Only in this way can a sergeant be in a position to fully energize his personnel toward the accomplishment of the police task. Without such knowledge operational leadership is difficult to effect.

The sergeant should also be well versed academically. He should not be satisfied just to be familiar with the operations and activities of his own police department. He should pursue other academic subjects that will provide knowledge relative to advances being made in law enforcement throughout the United States. With this kind of knowledge he will be in a position to recommend or suggest improvements within his own organization.

All this should be a part of the supervisor's knowledge, but no easy formula exists for its acquisition. He will come by this knowledge only when he studies the departmental records, engages in active and alert supervision, makes visits and inspections, submits reports, and follows up all complaints —not once a week, or every other day, or occasionally, but every single day that he performs a tour of duty. In addition, as stated above, he must pursue other studies on the side so that he is completely familiar with what is occurring within the profession.

It was mentioned previously that the supervisor must know the capabilities and limitations of his men. The only way to acquire this knowledge is to engage in intensive supervision by visiting the patrolmen on their beats and by responding to calls as an observer so that he can see how they react in particular situations. It also means that he should

227

develop opportunities for meeting with the men during hours of duty on an informal basis. For example, he might meet a man for coffee to discuss what is taking place within his area and other items of interest.

INTEGRITY

Integrity must be a part of every police officer's makeup, and this is especially true of the supervisor by the very nature of his task. It is he to whom the patrolmen are closest. It is he who must set a good example for his men. He need not go about beating his own breast or uttering sentiments to get the message across that he is a man of honor. The old maxim that "actions speak louder than words" should be enough to convince one and all that he takes his oath of office seriously and he expects others to do the same.

Integrity should extend even beyond the boundaries of morality. For example, he should never require a person to do something that he himself would be unwilling to do nor should he ever forget that his subordinates possess a god-given quality called dignity—that this dignity should never be tampered with by demeaning or ridiculing an individual.

The quality of integrity, more than any other quality, breeds respect—there is no middle ground. He either has it or he does not. If he has it, he is well on his way to a satisfying career. If he lacks it, he is courting disaster.

LOYALTY

Loyalty is a "must" quality in a leader. To the supervisor it has specific application to his relationship with superiors. Out of the maze of orders, directives, and individual personalities, occasions will arise when he will find this quality strongly tested. In these situations, he should be mature enough to realize that his superiors, just as he, are human beings with human feelings, and if at times he is not in agreement with certain policies or pronouncements, he should not manifest this to his men either explicitly or implicitly. There is nothing that can destroy a good opinion of a person more quickly than the discovery that the person is disloyal. On the other hand, when one demonstrates his loyalty, he can usually be sure of a vote of confidence from his superior officer.

Aside from specific consideration in dealings with his superiors, the supervisor, like every member of the department, should exhibit his loyalty to the profession by defending it against unjust or unfounded attraction. In his social relations with people outside the department he should evince his loyalty by having enthusiasm for his calling. After all, how can one expect others to be enthusiastic if he is not enthusiastic himself?

EMPATHY

Empathy is a quality relatively new in the field of superordinate-subordinate relationships. The supervisor can enhance his leadership by exercising it prudently. We say "prudently" because this particular quality, important as it is, can make a leader ineffectual if used to the extreme.

Empathy, simply defined, is the act of putting yourself in the other fellow's shoes. For the supervisor it can be the key that will unlock the bulk of individual motivation and help him to understand his men. When he understands his men, he is in a better position to direct, instruct, and control. He should make it clear to them, however, that his empathy is not to be mistaken for weakness or exaggerated sympathy. The mere fact that he can understand why a mistake was made or a rule violated should not suggest to anyone that he approves or condones the violation. The supervisor, in displaying his empathy, should leave no doubt in anyone's mind that he is doing it for constructive purposes such as correcting a grievance, a misconception, a misunderstanding, or an outright mistake.

Empathy can be an important factor in strengthening morale. It is proof of the supervisor's approachability. When

229

he is approachable, his men will not fear him nor will they want to let him down. Rather, they will come to the superior, express their feelings willingly, and do all in their power to accomplish the task for him.

RELIABILITY

Reliability refers to "doing first things first" and never losing sight of the value of routine. The supervisor who is reliable has a strong sense of responsibility. He takes his job seriously and realizes its ramifications. If he is a stern taskmaster with himself, his men will have little reason to complain about the goals and responsibilities he sets for them. On the other hand, if he believes in the double standard, whereby he can be a shirker but his men cannot, he will be faced with a granite wall of resentment.

FLEXIBILITY

Flexibility is another very important attribute of the supervisor. He must understand and appreciate the nature and the reason for change and be prepared to recognize and accept it. In addition, he must be prepared to suggest change in either the goals of the organization or the means by which those goals are achieved.

The police supervisor must realize that he lives within a changing society, that he is working with a younger group of men, and that their aspirations might be different from his own. Only by being flexible and understanding can he fully energize the group toward the accomplishment of their task.

The flexible supervisor knows that the "good old days" are usually good only in retrospect. Problems are a constant reality, whether in the past, present, or future, and flexibility is one of the means of coping with them.

When working conditions or procedures change, it is the supervisor's duty to discourage any lethargy that might arise. He should instruct his men carefully and precisely, and should follow up on the way those instructions are carried out.

230

FAIRNESS

Fairness must take a leading position when considering the qualities important in a supervisor or leader. A subordinate can overlook certain idiosyncracies or weaknesses in a supervisor, as long as they have no direct effect on personnel. However, the supervisor's fairness, or lack of it, is a special concern to every man in the field. Most police personnel do not mind pitching in when there is a job to be done, nor will an individual complain when he is told to perform a task that lies within the area of his responsibility. But no person takes kindly to being assigned a task that he knows would have been assigned to another individual had not that other individual been the so-called "fair-haired boy." There are also many occasions when one is made the whipping boy simply because he is not a member of the clique.

Situations of this type are most unfortunate, since all too often they are the result of a supervisor's ignorance or prejudice, and if not corrected they can play havoc with the efficiency and morale of the entire police organization. Simply stated, fairness implies objectivity and a single standard.

ENTHUSIASM

Enthusiasm can motivate men to advance from levels of mere acceptability to heights of merit. Enthusiasm means having zeal-fervor-commitment to a cause. It involves group identification and "esprit de corps." It is an essential ingredient of teamwork and cooperation. The enthusiastic leader is a secure leader, a plugger, a doer, a man with a goal. The supervisor who is endowed with enthusiasm can infect others by his spirit. His enthusiasm brings a feeling of well-being and will cause his subordinates to respond with the same attitude. The enthusiastic supervisor creates competence in his men. He has the necessary facility for getting men to do just that extra little bit which so often ranks a performance "excellent" instead of merely "satisfactory."

THOROUGHNESS

Thoroughness is usually indicative of a well-organized mind that is directed to detail as well as to the overall picture. Thoroughness is extremely important when conducting an investigation, when answering a communication, or when engaged in making an inspection. A supervisor's thoroughness can rather easily be ascertained by a superior. All the superior need do is scrutinize the written reports or study the group's progress and accomplishments.

Thoroughness is also important when a supervisor is evaluating his men. All people resent a cursory evaluation of their performance. They believe firmly that they should be totally evaluated in terms of their total commitment and performance within the police organization. A lack of thoroughness will cause the men to lose respect for their supervisor and this will adversely affect their performance on the job.

Thoroughness will deter a supervisor from making false assumptions regarding his men. It will aid him in getting at the root of a specific problem. It will discourage people from hoodwinking him or attempting to sell him a false bill of goods.

DEVELOPING PROBLEMS IN SUPERVISION AND ADMINISTRATION

During the past several years, changes have taken place that have greatly complicated the work of the police administrator and supervisor. If they are to work effectively they must be aware of these changes so that they can adjust their approaches and techniques accordingly. Some of these changes that influence supervisory techniques include: 1) the increasing size of the police organization; 2) the emphasis toward better educated and trained police officers; 3) the increasing growth of specialization; 4) less unemployment; and 5) the growing emphasis on individual participation in the social group.

INCREASING SIZE OF POLICE DEPARTMENTS

It is a well-known fact that this country is rapidly becoming an urban society. Our society, since World War I, has shifted from one of a rural nature to one of an urban nature and the speed with which this revolution has taken place is increasing each year. As this urban society develops, there is an ever-increasing demand for governmental service, which includes the police. Conversely, in order to meet this demand, the police departments have grown proportionately with the population.

With this rapid growth come additional problems that are of a completely different nature than those that existed before. If increased population merely created more of the same police task there would be little problem. Unfortunately, this is not the case. Along with increased population comes a complexity of police management problems that never before existed. For example, the small town police department may have experienced some traffic problems twenty years ago, but today they are a major police responsibility. This is true of other specialized services as well.

The days when the chief of police was responsible for all supervisory tasks are rapidly disappearing. In their place is a complicated organizational structure that contains many levels of supervision. As a result of the necessary organizational structure, the role of supervisors has become much more complicated. Today the police supervisor must be familiar with these complications and be able to work within the framework of a large organizational structure. Principles of organization are varied and many, and the supervisor must be completely familiar with all of them. Simply stated, supervision is no longer the single relationship between the chief and a few patrolmen, but is much more complicated because of the size of the department.

Another problem created by the rapid growth of police departments is the use of relatively young men as supervisors. This may be a problem for several reasons, among which are: 1) because of such early success the young supervisor may become a "prima donna"; 2) the young supervisor may lack the necessary police experience to appraise a police problem properly and react accordingly; 3) he may lack the human understanding that can only be learned with maturity; and 4) he may find it difficult to lead men who are older and who have more police experience.

This does not mean, however, that the chief of police should avoid promoting young police officers. It merely means that he should consider many factors before doing so. It should be kept in mind that a police officer may have one year's experience twenty times. Conversely, an officer with five years, or even three, of well-rounded experience is better qualified for promotion than one who has one year's experience twenty times.

The increase in size of the police department also complicates the social environment in which the officers work. With increase in size, homogeneity among the men is replaced by heterogeneity. As a result, the supervisor must be more flexible in his relationship with subordinates.

HIGHLY EDUCATED POLICE OFFICERS

In the past it was not uncommon for most police supervisors to be authoritarian. That is, they forced compliance by so-called "strong-arm" methods. A subordinate did what he was told or disciplinary action was taken. This system was probably successful because the subordinate accepted it as a way of life. Today such harsh supervision is not tolerated primarily because of the increased social and academic education among subordinates. They recognize authoritarian supervision for what it is—a cover-up for inadequacy on the part of the supervisor.

College programs for police officers are creating supervisory problems along this line. Graduates often possess more knowledge relative to their chosen profession than do many of the supervisors for whom they will work. They are academically knowledgeable in police administration, criminal law, criminal investigation, traffic administration, criminalistics, and other such areas. The police supervisor and administrator must recognize this fact and provide an environment within which the full resources of the individual are utilized. He cannot restrict a free flow of information, but must encourage it. The wise supervisor is one who teaches the subordinates all he knows and at the same time learns all he can from them.

SPECIALIZATION

To begin with, let us define police specialization. It is all operational activities that are not performed by the patrol division (photography, fingerprinting, traffic, investigation, etc.).

Specialization in the police service occurs for two reasons. First, because of departmental size, the work must be divided and then assigned to employees. An attempt is then made to direct the efforts of all units in such a manner as to achieve the final product. Thus, as the police agency becomes larger, it is inevitable that greater specialization will occur.

Secondly, as a reply to new inventions and scientific advances, more emphasis is placed on specialists than on generalists.

Whatever the causes, the important thing is that specialization has created very serious supervisory problems. Gone is the day when the policeman can see the end result of his labors. He merely does his part of the job and at a certain point turns it over to the specialists. This situation is obviously not conducive to a sense of responsibility and, therefore, it is difficult to motivate the officers in their work.

Specialization also creates a poor environment for producing competent supervisors. Specialization tends to keep the potential supervisor within definite areas. Conversely, when he becomes a supervisor he does not possess a generalized view. This provincialism may very well remain with him as he advances through the ranks. This is why we find that many of our police executives are oriented in one particular area. Rather than having a well-balanced organization, he may stress his particular area of interest to the detriment of other areas.

FULL EMPLOYMENT

Gone are the days when the police officer must bow down to unreasonable demands for fear of becoming unemployed. With our present era of full employment for the qualified, job mobility has increased. Police officers have less to lose in changing jobs and, therefore, will not remain with an organization that makes unreasonable demands or where adverse conditions exist.

In the past few years there has been a tremendous emphasis on finding highly qualified and educated individuals to fill the available police jobs. The trend is definitely toward the college-trained police officer, as is evidenced by the many cities that require degrees for entrance into the police service.

As the result of their education and intelligence it would pose no problem for young people to obtain another position. In fact, many of our qualified police officers could very likely find other employment at a higher salary. Again, in order to retain these badly needed people, the police supervisor must see that a good working environment exists.

INDIVIDUAL PARTICIPATION AND SOCIAL GROUPS

Educators are constantly stressing the development of the individual within his social environment. Great emphasis is placed on the individual's ability to think and to participate openly in his group. The education system in our country also attempts to create and encourage creativity among the students.

The police supervisor must recognize this new individual for what he is and not allow, but encourage subordinate participation and the activity of group effort. Creativity must not

236

be suppressed but must be openly encouraged. The authoritarian supervisor must step aside for the democratic or participative one.

As is obvious from the foregoing, the task of supervision and administration is not a simple one. The supervisor's job in our present diversified society is challenging, interesting, rewarding, but at the same time occasionally frustrating.

Summary

During recent years law enforcement has been surveyed by numerous agencies, committees, and individuals, which indicates the present concern for the way criminal justice agencies are administered and operated. This concern demands that administrators evaluate their methods with a view toward improvement.

Administration relates to the establishment of institutional goals and objectives and the process or techniques utilized in their achievement. It is a process that involves leadership and the control or direction of the efforts of individuals toward the common goals.

Administration is dependent upon the ability to organize or, in a broader sense, the organization. Organization entails units and subunits each with specific objectives that, combined with accomplishment, result in the achievement of the organization's broad objective. Police departments are organized into various divisions, units, and sections with specific responsibilities or objectives. Organizational units in a police department can be categorized into three broad areas: 1) functional, 2) geographical, and 3) chronological.

Leadership and supervision in the police organization can be considered the most important single factor relating to the success or failure of the achievement of police objectives. The three leadership styles are: 1) authoritarian, 2) laissez faire, and 3) democratic. The two levels of leadership are 1) managerial, and 2) operational.

Supervision is probably the weakest link in most police organizations. Unfortunately, most departments pay little attention to selecting supervisory personnel possessing the potential for adequately accomplishing the task.

Some of the developing problems in supervision and administration include the increasing size of organizations, increased education of police officers, increased specialization, full employment, and individual participation in social groups.

238

Discussion Questions

1. Discuss the need to improve the management of police organizations.
2. Define administration.
3. Define organization.
4. Define and discuss leadership.
5. Define and discuss the three styles of leadership.
6. Define and discuss the two major levels of leadership.
7. Explain why supervision may be the weakest link in a police organization and indicate how this link can be improved.
8. Identify and discuss five (5) traits of a good leader.
9. Identify and discuss four (4) developing problems in supervision and administration.
10. What is meant by situational leadership? Cite an example.

6

Dilemmas of
Law Enforcement

There are two broad, general categories of problems that relate to law enforcement agencies. First, there are the basic problems that necessitate law enforcemnt agencies: primarily the existence of crime and traffic congestion. Secondly, there are the multitude of problems that hamper the police as they attempt to resolve crime and traffic problems. These problems include such things as a fragmented police system, adverse political influence, confining legal restrictions, social disorder, a poor police image, and the ever-existing threat of police corruption.

In a sense, by trying to resolve the first category of problems, the police are actually striving to work themselves out of a job. Of course, such success is virtually unachievable in a society of increasing complexities and commensurate problems. *Man being what he is, there will always be a need for the police.* Even if the police were able to completely resolve existing problems, man would probably create new ones, and assign the task of solving them to the police.

Those problems that created and support the need for the police are a tribute to man's inability to handle his own affairs and to live in harmony with his neighbors. The existence of law enforcement agencies and their size are actually a measure of man's failure. In reality, Americans should feel embarrassment over the need for and reliance upon the police. The larger the police agency in relation to the size of the community, the greater the indication that man has relegated his own responsibilities and, concurrently, the greater his failure. This is true whether size is a result of the amount of crime or a result of police inefficiency in combating it, since the public must be interested in their police and must insist on efficient police service.

All this does not mean that the people should avoid having police agencies, because they are a necessary segment of our increasingly complex society. Just as the police cannot be entirely successful, it is also impossible for man to manage his affairs to the extent that enforcement agencies are not necessary. There are too many people and too many problems to permit this achievement of Utopia. It does mean, however, that man should be concerned with this yardstick of his failure and cooperate more fully with the police in keeping crime and disorder at a minimal level. The more fully the people cooperate, the more successful and less needed will be the police.

In addition to giving their cooperation, citizens must also demand efficiency of the police. Citizens should be aware of police practices, evaluate them, and offer criticism when necessary. In our dynamic society debate and controversy are indications of health, since conflicting ideas are the very essence of a free society. Of course, this is not an endorsement of illegal demonstrations, and such criticism must be of a constructive nature and voiced through the legitimate channels. Dissenters must be willing to compromise and pool their ideas through cooperative and intelligent thinking.

The police cannot completely fulfill their major function unless the people they serve act as catalysts, forcing the police to reevaluate their philosophies and formulate new viewpoints that are appropriate to the times. This citizen-police cooperative technique will help destroy outmoded customs and techniques. There must exist an ever-evolving synthesis of old and new so that harmony will exist along with progress.

Many of the problems that hamper the police in the achievement of their objectives are also a result of man's nature. Man's desire for power has often led politicians to inaugurate and perpetuate undesirable practices in the police agency. For example, to gain votes the politician may obtain help from many people and then reward them by appointments to the police force. Man's greed for money has also allowed graft and corruption to exist. And, finally, man's disinterest in basic concepts of democracy has allowed some police agencies to become lawless and careless in their activities.

THE CRIME PROBLEM

The word *crime* is somewhat of a blanket term and can be subdivided into several different parts depending upon the situation and the subject under discussion. There are basically three broad identifiable types of crime: 1) *street crime*, 2) *white collar crime*, 3) *organized crime*. Crime is also categorized into two classifications: 1) *misdemeanors* and 2) *felonies*. Street crime can again be subdivided into: 1) *crime against the person*, and 2) *crime against property*. Crime can also be broken down into specific crimes such as robbery, murder, rape, etc. The following definitions will clarify these divisions and subdivisions.

1. *Street crime* refers to those crimes that are most obvious and troublesome to the citizens of the community and, therefore, those the police most vigorously attack. Street crimes are those usually thought of when the crime problem is discussed. This category includes all crime not specified as white collar or not committed on an organized basis.

2. *White collar crimes* are crimes that are related to the occupational positions that people have. They are committed in the course of performing activities of particular occupations and exist as opportunities available only to people of those occupations. Usually white collar crime is thought of as being committed by persons of high social status as differentiated from those committed by lower social class persons.[1] Examples of white collar crime includes such things as misappropriation of funds by an executive, the use of defective materials by a contractor, and price fixing.

3. *Organized crime* bears a resemblance to the workings of a business operation. It involves a large number of crimi-

[1] President's Commission on Law Enforcement and Administration of Justice, *The Challenge of Crime in a Free Society* (Washington, D. C.: Government Printing Office, 1967), p. 47.

nals working in well-organized, highly structured operations engaged in activities involving the supplying of illegal goods and services to cooperative customers. Organized crime is the organizing of illegal operations involving such things as gambling, narcotics, and prostitution. Frequently, it also involves infiltration into legitimate business and labor unions.[2]

4. *Felonies* are the most serious crimes and usually impose penalties of death or one or more years imprisonment in a state or federal prison. Murder, forcible rape, robbery, aggravated assault, burglary, grand larceny, and auto theft are all examples of felonies.

5. *Misdemeanors* are all offenses of a less serious nature than the felony. This classification includes such misdemeanants as petit larceny, disorderly conduct, traffic violations, etc. Punishment is usually a fine and/or confinement in a city or county jail for periods not exceeding one year.

6. *Crimes against the person* are crimes of a violent nature and impose physical harm or force upon a victim. Crimes within this category specifically include murder, negligent manslaughter, forcible rape, aggravated assault, and robbery.

7. *Crimes against property* are directed toward the illegal acquisition of property rather than the infliction of injury upon a person. Crimes against property specifically include burglary, larceny, and auto theft. Although the criminal's purpose is not to inflict injury upon a person, such potential is always imminent.

In addition to these categories or broad classifications, there are a multitude or specific offenses ranging from murder to drunkenness. In fact, there are so many offenses that the Federal Bureau of Investigation (FBI) in reporting crime on a national level has developed a measurement index that includes only seven of the most frequent and serious street crimes which are known as *Part I* offenses. These are

---

[2] President's Commission on Law Enforcement and Administration of Justice, *Task Force Report: Crime and Its Impact—An Assessment* (Washington, D. C.: Government Printing Office, 1967), p. 100.

murder, forcible rape, robbery, aggravated assault, burglary, larceny $50 and over in value (referred to as grand larceny in this book), and auto theft. The definitions of these offenses may vary from state to state, but the following definitions seem to be as nearly uniform as possible. Definitions of other offenses appear in the appendix and should be reviewed.

1. *Murder* is the unlawful and willful killing of a human being by another with malice aforethought, either expressed or implied.
2. *Forcible rape* is the unlawful carnal knowledge of a woman by a man forcibly and against her will. For reporting purposes, the FBI also includes assault to rape and attempted rape.
3. *Robbery* is the felonious taking of personal property in the possession of another from his person or immediate presence and against his will, accomplished by means of force or fear. Specifically, this includes strong-arm robbery, stick-ups, armed robbery, assault to rob, and attempt to rob.
4. *Aggravated assault* is assault that is more serious than common assault. Assault is defined as an intentional, unlawful offer of corporal injury to another by force or force unlawfully directed toward the person of another under such circumstances as to create well-founded fear of imminent peril coupled with apparent present ability to execute attempt if not prevented. The FBI Uniform Crime Report specifically defines aggravated assault as assault with intent to kill or for the purpose of inflicting severe bodily injury by shooting, cutting, stabbing, maiming, poisoning, scalding, or by the use of acids.
5. *Burglary* is the breaking and entering or any unlawful entry of a building or dwelling with the intent to commit a felony or theft therein.
6. *Grand larceny* is the felonious stealing of another's property when the value of such property is $50 or more. For FBI uniform crime reporting purposes, grand larceny also includes the theft of bicycles, automobile accessories, shoplifting, and pocket-picking. The Federal Bureau of Investigation includes larceny of $50 or more as a Part I offense. In differentiating between a felony and a mis-

247

demeanor, some states use the figure of $100 or more, while others use the figure of $50.

7. *Auto theft* is the stealing or driving away of an automobile belonging to another person. This usually excludes the taking for temporary use when actually returned by the taker or unauthorized use by those having lawful access to the vehicle.

STREET CRIME

Crime on this nation's streets is one of the most critical problems Americans have ever faced. Certainly, a certain amount of crime is seemingly unavoidable and has always been with us. Alarming, however, is disproportionate increase in incidents of violence and criminality. The risk of falling victim to a criminal act is greater with each passing year, and the ratio of crimes per population category has continually increased.

A quick glance at any newspaper will illustrate not only that crime is prevalent but also that citizens are justifiably concerned. Every day these papers carry a multitude of stories with headlines such as "Two Men Face Narcotics Charges," "$130 Taken in Finance Holdup," "Juvenile Arrested after High Speed Chase," "City Hit by Racial Unrest," "More Crime—Fewer Convicts," "Fifteen Indicted by Grand Jury," "Youth Sentenced for Rape," "Man Is Convicted for Murder," "Troops Patrol City," etc.

The prevention and control of crime is one of the many responsibilities assigned to the police. We might infer from this that the extent of street crime is a measure of police efficiency. If crime is rampant, then police efficiency and effectiveness must be improved. Conversely, the absence of crime or a low crime rate is an indication of police success. Of course, crime control is not only a police responsibility. It is also a function of the entire criminal justice system and of all people. However, the police are much closer to the problem since they are on the streets and will usually make the first contact with a crime or with the criminal. They play a paramount role, and to do their job adequately, they must be knowledgeable about crime, its extent, and related sociological factors.

Extent of crime. The exact extent of crime in the United States is impossible to determine. Many police departments compile crime statistics, but there are many offenses that never come to their attention. Complaints received directly by prosecutors may not become part of statistics gathered by the police. Many crimes are not reported by citizens. Available police statistics are also not always reliable since a department may adjust their figures to present a favorable picture. And, finally, not all police departments compile statistics and, therefore, an overall national picture may be impossible to obtain.

The most reliable crime statistics are those gathered by the Federal Bureau of Investigation and published in their Uniform Crime Report (UCR). The need for a nationwide view of crime was recognized many years ago and the UCR program was initiated in 1930 on the basis of uniform classification developed by the International Association of Chiefs of Police. The FBI has since served as the national clearinghouse for the program and has yearly compiled the extent and distribution of crime in the United States. The UCR statistics are, of course, dependent upon the information provided by local police agencies and reflect voluntary reports provided by them.

The UCR is incomplete also because only seven types of serious crimes are reported. As previously stated, these crimes are murder, forcible rape, robbery, aggravated assault, burglary, larceny $50.00 and over, and auto theft.

The ever-increasing occurrence of reported crime is clearly illustrated by the following table that reflects information from the 1973 UCR reports.

TABLE 1. COMPARISON OF REPORTED MAJOR CRIMES FOR THE
YEARS 1967 THROUGH 1976 AND CORRESPONDING RATE
PER 100,000 INHABITANTS[3]

Year	Total crimes reported	Rate per 100,000 inhabitants	Crimes against persons	Crimes against property
1967	197,457,000	2,989.7	499,930	5,403,500
1968	199,399,000	3,370.2	595,010	6,125,200
1969	201,385,000	3,680.0	661,870	6,749,000
1970	203,235,298	3,984.5	738,820	7,359,200
1971	206,212,000	4,164.7	816,500	7,771,700
1972	208,230,000	3,961.4	834,900	7,413,900
1973	209,851,000	4,154.4	875,910	7,842,200
1974	211,392,000	4,850.4	974,720	9,278,700
1975	213,124,000	5,281.7	1,026,280	10,230,300
1976	214,659,000	5,266.4	986,580	10,318,200

Although the information in Table 1 may not be statistically pure due to limitations in the collection of data, it is sufficiently complete to indicate the trend of increasing crime. In fact, the table illustrates that the crime rate per 100,000 inhabitants increased from 2,989.7 in 1967 to 5,266.4 in 1976.

More revealing is the relationship of crime to population which indicates that crime is increasing faster than the population. For example, from 1960 to 1973 the population of the United States increased by about 10 percent while the percentage change in crime was 157.6+. During the same period, the national crime rate, or the risk of falling victim to a crime, had a percentage change of 120.2+.[4] The greatest and most frightening concern of citizens is this probability of being personally attacked. In the United States the risk of being a victim is better than one in four hundred. The risk is much greater for people living in urban areas, as crimes per unit are highest in the larger population centers.

[3] Federal Bureau of Investigation, *Uniform Crime Reports*—1976 (Washington, D. C.: U. S. Government Printing Office, 1976), p. 37.
[4] Federal Bureau of Investigation, p. 59.

Unreported crime. Although available crime statistics indicate considerable crime, they do not begin to indicate the full amount. UCR totals are based on reported crimes, but there are many crimes that are not reported to the police. The extent of unreported crime is impossible to determine, but surveys conducted by President Johnson's Commission on Law Enforcement and the Administration of Justice revealed that the actual amount of crime in the United States was several times that reported in the UCR.

These surveys indicated that the amount of personal injury crime was almost twice the UCR rate and the amount of property crime more than twice as much as the UCR rate for individuals. Forcible rapes were more than three and one-half times the reported rate, burglaries three times, aggravated assaults and larcenies of $50 and over more than double, and robbery 50 percent greater than the reported rate.[5]

Even these rates probably do not illustrate the actual amount of crime. The surveys were conducted by contacting a single member of households who answered for the whole family. Conceivably, unknown to the respondent, there may have been other family members victimized. It is likely that the combination of UCR and results of these surveys still underestimates the actual amount of crime.

Of interest are the reasons given for not reporting crime to the police. The most frequent explanation was that the police could not do anything anyway. This could indicate that the citizens had little faith in their police, but also it may be rationalization as well. In any event, it does indicate that the police must demonstrate an ability to handle reported offenses and must also educate the public about their availability and willingness to help. The second most frequent reason given was that it was a personal matter, or that

[5] President's Commission on Law Enforcement and Administration of Justice, *The Challenge of Crime in a Free Society*, p. 21.

the victim did not want to get the offender in trouble. This reason is quite understandable in those cases where the crime involved other family members or close associates of the victim.[6]

Crimes against the person. The most serious crimes and those for which we show most concern are those involving violence against the person (murder, rape, robbery, assault). These crimes involve the infliction of bodily harm or the threatened use of force with the ability to carry out the threat.

Murder is usually considered the most serious crime, and in 1976, there were an estimated 18,780 *murders* in the United States or 8.8 victims per 100,000 population. Firearms are the most predominant weapons used in murders and have been almost since their invention. Seemingly, firearms usually account for over half of all murders.[7]

Generally speaking, the police are powerless to prevent a large number of the murders, since most of them are committed by relatives or acquaintances of the victim. The police, powerless to influence family situations, are unable to prevent such violence. A large percentage of murders result from romantic triangles or lovers' quarrels, and such problems are usually not a police concern until the actual crime is committed.

The police are more successful in clearing or solving a higher percentage of murders than any other crime index offense. This is partially due to the high percentage of family unit murders, since the murderer is frequently readily identified. In addition, since there are so many romantic triangle murders, the police can direct their efforts toward such a possibility and frequently locate a suspect. The great success in solving murders must also be attributed to the seriousness of the offense which dictates full police action and interest.

[6] President's Commission, *The Challenge of Crime.*
[7] Federal Bureau of Investigation, p. 7.

252

The public is much more concerned with this type offense, and, therefore, the police react by devoting considerable time and energy to such cases.

Forcible rape is the crime which is ranked second only to murder in seriousness. As with all crimes, the reported number of rapes has continually increased and in 1976 56,730 such offenses were reported. In relation to population, a reported 27 out of every 100,000 women fell victim to a rapist.[8]

Aggravated assault, which includes unsuccessful murder attempts, accounts for the second largest number of offenses against the person. Most aggravated assaults also occur within the family unit or among acquaintances and are, therefore, difficult for the police to prevent. Again, a firearm is the weapon most frequently used. The use of personal weapons such as hands, fists, and feet usually account for about one-fourth of the offenses. Law enforcement agencies frequently have difficulty getting conviction for this crime because of the close family relationship between victims and assailants and, consequently, the victim's frequent unwillingness to cooperate or testify for the prosecution. In 1976, there were an estimated 490,850 aggravated assaults, a crime rate of 228.7 per 100,000 population.[9]

Robbery is the most frequent of the crimes against the person, and involves the stealing or taking of anything of value from the person by use of force or threat of force. This offense usually comprises more than one-third of the crimes of violence, and robberies seem to occur most frequently during the winter months. Like other crimes of violence, robbery is primarily a big city problem, with the largest increases occurring within the urban centers. In 1976, 50 percent of the robberies were committed on the street. Bank robbery is also increasing at an alarming rate, as evidenced by a 74-percent increase since 1972. During 1976, the average bank rob-

[8] Federal Bureau of Investigation, p. 15.
[9] Federal Bureau of Investigation, p. 12.

bery dollar loss was $3,190. Between 1972 and 1976, gas or service station holdups increased by 11 percent, and chain store robberies increased by 58 percent. More than half the robberies involved the use of firearms. During 1976, the average loss in all robberies was $338 for a total loss of approximately 142 million dollars. The police were successful in solving about 27 percent of all robberies committed in 1976.[10]

Crimes against property. Generally speaking, crimes against property, or theft, are crimes of opportunity and are committed when criminals think they can get away with it. The police are not as successful in clearing crimes against property as they are in clearing crimes of violence. There are several reasons for this. Probably the most influencing factor is the lack of face-to-face confrontation between the victim and criminal in property crimes. In violent crimes, the victim is usually able to provide a description of the criminal and his actions which will aid the police, while property crimes involve the "sneak" element since the perpetrator is usually not seen. A second factor is that property crimes are considered less serious by both the public and the police. The police, therefore, direct less attention to property crimes and more attention to the violent crimes. Because of these and other factors, the odds of getting away with a theft are quite good. It is for this reason that some men become professional criminals and make their living from stealing. These criminals are well aware of the odds in their favor, and become very competent in their profession.

Burglary is the most frequently committed of the three property crimes and is the one most troublesome to the police. This crime is one of stealth and opportunity, and the burglar usually directs his attention to unattended apartments, houses, and businesses. The extent of daytime burglaries is steadily increasing but over half are committed

[10] Federal Bureau of Investigation, pp. 19–20.

under the cover of darkness. Because of the volume of burglary and the fact that such crimes occur almost anywhere, the police experience great difficulty in its suppression and prevention. Property loss to burglary is quite high and according to the UCR amounted to over 1.4 billion dollars in 1976—an average dollar loss of $449 per offense.[11]

Larceny over $50 is the second most frequently occurring crime of the crime index, and in 1976 the crime rate rose to 2,921.3 offenses per 100,000 population. The average value of property stolen in 1976 was $184 for a total loss of 1.2 billion dollars.[12] As with burglary, the police experience difficulty in suppressing and preventing the offense of larceny. The crime is one of opportunity and is usually perpetrated when the chance of apprehension is low. At the same time, many people do not report the theft or do not provide "full" information because insurance usually covers the loss. In fact, it is often the case that the victim does not want the property returned but would prefer the insurance payment. They, therefore, are likely to withhold information and not assist the police.

Auto theft is the property crime against which the police enjoy the greatest recovery success. This is largely due to the temporary theft of many automobiles and the visible means of identifying motor vehicles. Many police administrators claim the increase in auto thefts is due solely to the continually growing number of vehicles. This assumption is refuted by statistics which indicate that the percentage increase in auto theft has continually been greater than the percentage increase in automobile registrations. Like most other crimes, auto theft is also primarily a city problem since the highest rates occur in the heavily populated or urban areas of the nation. Like the other property crimes, auto theft is also a crime of opportunity, and, therefore, the police have difficulty in apprehending auto thieves or in preventing

[11] Federal Bureau of Investigation, p. 23.
[12] Federal Bureau of Investigation, p. 27.

the crime. In 1976, 957,600 motor vehicles were reported stolen, for a rate of 446.1 victims per 100,000 inhabitants.[13]

Other offenses. In addition to crimes against persons and property, there are a myriad of other offenses that also create adverse social problems and take up considerable police time. These offenses are reflected in the literally hundreds of city ordinances and state laws. They range from special ordinances relative to excessive noise, to juvenile hangouts, curfews, malicious mischief, washing cars on public streets, parking regulations, and then to more serious offenses such as arson and vice.

The UCR identifies these other crimes as *Part II* offenses, which include:

> Assaults other than aggravated
> Arson
> Forgery and counterfeiting
> Fraud
> Embezzlement
> Buying, receiving, or possessing stolen property
> Vandalism
> Carrying or possessing weapons
> Prostitution and commercialized vice
> Sex offenses other than rape and prostitution
> Narcotic drug laws
> Gambling
> Offenses against family and children
> Driving under the influence
> Liquor laws
> Drunkenness
> Disorderly conduct
> Vagrancy
> All other offenses
> Suspicion
> Curfew and loitering law violations
> Runaways

[13] Federal Bureau of Investigation, p. 31.

The thousands of arrests made for public drunkenness and disorderly conduct place an extremely heavy workload on the entire criminal justice system. These offenses take up considerable police time, clog the courts, and crowd the penal institutions. The irony is that in such offenses the only victim is the offender, and there is considerable question as to whether drunkenness should be a police concern. The emerging contention is that drunkenness is a medical or psychiatric problem, and that the police are not equipped to handle it. Rather, these people should be turned over to another authority for treatment and, hopefully, cured. The same holds true for the offense of drug abuse, which is taking more and more police effort and time to control.

Crime clearance. A crime is cleared when the offender is identified, there is sufficient evidence for prosecution, and the police actually take him into custody. A crime is also considered cleared when something beyond police control prevents formal charges against the offender even though sufficient evidence is available. Such is the case when a victim refuses to prosecute or the prosecutor's office declines to charge because a man is already being charged in another jurisdiction. In discussing crime clearances it must also be kept in mind that there is not a one-to-one relationship between persons arrested and crimes cleared. The arrest of one person may clear several cases, and conversely several persons may be arrested for involvement in the same crime.

As with crime statistics, it is impossible to accurately determine crime clearance. This is because there is no reliable way of associating the number of crimes committed with the number of offenders processed at the various stages in our criminal justice system. These proportions vary considerably, and for most of the Index crimes at least, they are quite low.

Identification and apprehension by the police is not necessarily followed by prosecution. The prosecutor may be reluctant to prosecute for a variety of reasons. The case may appear weak for prosecution purposes, the offender may be under prosecution in another jurisdiction, or other extenuating circumstances may make it impractical to try a case. Frequently, also, the prosecutor will accept a plea to a lesser offense. This complicates the crime reporting procedure and breaks down the relationship between crimes committed and convictions. In these cases, which are exceptionally frequent, the crime cleared is the one the person was arrested for rather than the one for which he was convicted.

Effects of crime. There are many varied direct and indirect effects of crime, but the primary effects include: 1) injury to the victim, 2) hardships to the victim, 3) economic cost, and 4) fear. The most serious and direct of these is the effect on the victim of a violent and injurious attack. The likelihood of becoming a victim of a criminal attack is continually increasing. Statistics on reported index-crime occurrences indicate that the probability of being victim to a criminal attack in a given year is about one in four hundred. Of course, the potential of criminal assault varies dependent upon where a person lives. Such crimes as rape, murder, and aggravated assault are more frequent in slum areas, and, therefore, the risks of personal harm are greater than for the middle-class family living in suburban areas.

Actually the total impact on these victims is impossible to determine. Factors involved are varied in both type and degree. However, all victims suffer in terms of pain, misery, financial loss related to the period of hospitalization and treatment, cost of treatment, and psychological ramifications from the crime. On top of this must also be stacked the inconvenience and hardships of trial in the event the offender is identified, arrested, and prosecuted.

Although some crimes do not necessarily inflict physical injury to a victim, serious hardships still result. A person may be deprived of his automobile through auto theft and, consequently, be without transportation to and from work. In fact, in our mobile age the automobile is so relied upon that it can be considered an actual necessity. The loss of today's automobile can be equated in seriousness to the loss of one's horse in the early years of the West. The loss of money due to robbery or burglary also can impose considerable financial hardships upon a family that may take years to overcome. Radiating from this are also the psychological effects related to financial problems within the family unit. And there is always the inconvenience of trial in the event the offender is apprehended and prosecuted.

A third major effect of crime is its economic costs. According to the 1976 UCR Report, for example, property worth more than $2.7 billion was stolen as a result of robberies, burglaries, and larcenies.[14] Of course, cost to the victim is not the only factor involved in determining the actual cost of crime. Not only does crime impose an economic burden upon individuals, but also it places a burden upon the community as well. The economic impact of crime must also include the cost involved in operating police agencies, insurance premiums paid by individuals and business enterprises, damage to property in perpetrating the crime of burglary, etc. Also to be considered are such things as consumer fraud that runs into the millions and such offenses as employee theft, shoplifting, arson, vandalism, embezzlement, and tax evasion.

Perhaps the heaviest impact of crime is fear. Because of the extent of crime in the United States and the citizens' awareness of the risk of becoming victim to a criminal attack, literally thousands of people are living in constant fear. There are many repercussions of fear, and we find homeowners arming themselves and equipping their homes with anti-burglary devices. We find women and men locking themselves in at night rather than enjoying the freedom of evening walks or attendance at recreational events. The worst effect of fear is the development of mistrust and suspicion among people. An unfriendly atmosphere has developed,

[14] Federal Bureau of Investigation, pp. 19–27.

particularly in urban areas, and such an environment is actually conducive to criminality.

Crime trends. As indicated by the above, crime is increasing in both volume and rate, which means that the risk to any citizen of becoming involved as a victim constantly increases. Regardless of the many factors influencing the statistical data, crime is increasing and the risk of becoming involved in or in observing a crime is greater today than it was yesterday and will be greater tomorrow than it is today.

CRIME AND THE YOUNG

Perhaps the most shocking and distressing element of the crime picture is the ever-increasing involvement of this nation's youth. In 1976, for example, 40 percent of all UCR crime index offenses solved involved juveniles (children under the age of 18). Of interest and concern also is the revealing fact that the arrests for female juveniles has been increasing disproportionately to that of juvenile boys. While male arrests still outnumber female arrests, the trend indicates that these two groups are drawing more closely together in their involvement in crime. This is another indication of our troubled times.[15]

It is difficult to measure accurately how much juvenile delinquency there is, and most figures must be general estimates. However, it is estimated by many that approximately one percent of the nation's children under eighteen come to the attention of the juvenile court each year. It is further estimated that 5 percent annually come to the attention of the police.[16]

[15] Federal Bureau of Investigation, p. 215.

[16] John P. Kenney and Dan Pursuit, *Police Work with Juveniles* (Springfield, Ill.: Charles C Thomas, Publisher, 1962), p. 10.

260

Whatever the estimates, it is obvious that juveniles are far too involved in the commission of crime. Although this is a problem of several public service agencies, the police must play a paramount role. Police juvenile bureaus must be established, policewomen must be employed, and liaison must exist between all agencies concerned and involved with children. This list would be quite exhaustive, but it would include scouting groups, boys' clubs, YMCA, YWCA, YMHA, YWHA, athletic leagues, juvenile courts, schools, church groups, and the police.

Cooperation among agencies is essential, since children of concern to one agency will also be of concern to another. For example, frequently children who come to the attention of the police are the same ones that are truant from school. It is ridiculous for each of these two publicly financed agencies to work with the child in isolation from the other agency, when so much more could be accomplished by working together.

CAUSES OF CRIME

"What causes crime?" "Why does man commit murder?" "Why does a juvenile steal an automobile?" "Why does a woman become a prostitute?" "Why do several juveniles attack and rob an old man?" There are no single or correct answers to any of these questions. Crime is the result of a complex interaction between an individual and his environment. What motivates one individual to commit a specific offense—perhaps murder—may be completely different from what influences another person to commit a similar offense. Generally speaking, to determine crime causation is to determine individual human motivation.

Many crimes are caused by the victim, his activities, and his availability. Often it is said that "there is a victim for every crime." A common example is the con artist's victim who thought he had the opportunity to get rich quick. There is also the woman who, by her activities, makes herself readily

261

available for attack and rape. The assault victim is often the person who started the fight or who agitated the offender to the point of striking. Anyone who leaves keys in his automobile for the auto thief and any homeowner who leaves his house unlocked for the burglar encourages crime. All of this means that many crimes would not have been committed were it not for the existence of an available, and oftentimes willing, victim.

Social and economic conditions are responsible for some crime. The statement "remove the slums and we will eliminate crime," though not completely true, has some merit. Crime reports indicate that crime particularly flourishes in the urban areas and especially within the slums of urban areas. It is reasonable to assume that slum characteristics such as overcrowding, poverty, and racial discrimination are conducive to criminality.

The present unequal distribution of wealth in our country contributes to crime. Since social class and values are determined by the possession of material things, people strive for possession of these goods by any means at their disposal. Thus, those who are fortunate can purchase them, but the less fortunate must either go without or obtain them illegally. This problem is further aggravated by store display windows and by television. Store displays make such goods easily available to steal, and television commercials make possession of certain things even more desirable. In addition, poverty-stricken people are well aware of what other people have, and this creates some animosity that often justifies in their minds the right to steal from the more wealthy.

Mention must also be made that many crimes are committed because some law enforcement agencies do not operate effectively. As stated before, many offenses are *crimes of opportunity*. Due to lack of effective police patrol, opportunities will be greater. In addition, many potential criminals are really gamblers. If the law enforcement agency is ineffective, they will believe the odds are in their favor relative to the police being efficient enough to prepare adequate prosecution.

262

As can be seen, crime causation is a complicated phenomenon, and it involves many defined and some undefined
elements. Perhaps with a better understanding of crime and
its causes we could better prevent, combat, and control it.

THE CRIMINAL

A criminal is a person who is responsible for having committed a crime. He cannot be identified by appearance or by
any other descriptive characteristics. Criminals represent all
walks of life, age groups, and social classes. They may be
eighteen or fifty, men or women, wealthy or poor, black or
white, ghetto or suburban residents, laborers or professional persons, etc. The only thing criminals may have in
common is the fact that they have committed a crime. However, even those having committed the same crime may not
be similar in any other way whatsoever. In addition, what
motivates one man to commit an offense may be completely
dissimilar to what motivates another man to commit the
same offense.

It is likely that everyone has the capacity and perhaps
from time to time the desire to commit a law violation that
would place him in the criminal category. This is especially
true in our present diversified society with its multitude of
laws. Generally speaking, maintaining a good law-abiding
reputation is largely the ability to refrain from criminal desires and tendencies. Actually, the separation between the
criminal and the mass of citizens is not distinct. The criminal
has been discovered; others have committed crimes without
being caught; and still many others think or have had criminal thoughts but have controlled overt acts of crime.

Criminality is really measured by degrees. A person
guilty of a few minor offenses should not necessarily be considered a criminal. If this were not the case, practically all
citizens would be considered criminals. As implied previously, our thousands of laws, ordinances, and regulations
make it virtually impossible for a citizen not to commit a
violation during his lifetime. To define criminality otherwise

would classify the violator of a minor traffic offense as a criminal. On the other hand, persons who commit more serious crimes, especially felonies, would be considered criminals. The point where criminality begins is very hazy, and the obvious determinations are only at the extreme ends of the continuum.

Actually, when a person becomes a criminal, society as a whole must take some of the blame. Certainly the individual, unless mentally incapacitated by insanity or other reasons, is responsible for his actions. At the same time, however, society certainly failed to prevent the crime and has tolerated or allowed those conditions which are conducive to criminality to exist.

Most people believe that this country's population consists of a rather large group of law-abiding citizens and a very small group of *criminals*. This assumption or belief is totally inaccurate for several reasons. If we consider index crimes alone, the fact must be accepted that there is far too much crime and far too many criminals. Although the index crimes are the only ones for which we have measurements, there are also the thousands of "other offenses" that must be considered when determining the degree of criminality in this country. There are the unreported crimes that people observe and the crimes people have committed but which have not come to the attention of legal authorities. Recent surveys have shown that most people, when they are asked, remember having committed offenses for which they might have been sentenced if they had been apprehended. A study involving almost 1,700 people revealed that 91 percent of the respondents had committed one or more offenses for which they might have received jail or prison sentences.[17]

Although the criminal cannot be identified by individual characteristics, national arrest statistics do provide a general profile of offenders. Generally speaking, the offender is likely

---

[17] President's Commission on Law Enforcement and Administration of Justice, *The Challenge of Crime in a Free Society*, p. 43.

to be a member of the lowest social and economic classes, poorly educated, unemployed, unmarried, and from a broken home.[18] One of the most significant factors affecting crime rates is the age composition of the population. For as long as national crime statistics have been compiled, they have shown that males between the ages of fifteen and twenty-four are the most crime-prone group in our population. Of course, the age of criminals varies considerably in relation to the type of offense. For example, offenders over twenty-four make up the great majority of persons arrested for fraud, embezzlement, gambling, drunkenness, offenses against the family, and vagrancy. For many other crimes, such as burglary and auto theft, the peak age of criminality occurs below twenty-four.[19]

The race factor is quite important in a discussion of crime and the criminal. Many more whites than blacks are arrested every year, but blacks have a significantly higher rate of arrest in every offense category except certain offenses against public order and morals.[20] Many studies have been made relative to these differences in arrest rates, but it is difficult to reach any valid conclusions.

Another important factor in criminality is the comparison between the arrests of males and females. Males are arrested nearly seven times as frequently as females for index offenses plus larceny under fifty dollars. However, this difference seems to be diminishing, and since 1960 the arrest rate for females has been increasing faster than the arrest rate for males.[21] There are many reasons for this, but one of the most influential may be that the police are less controlled by the "double standard" between male and female than they once were.

As women gain equality, the police tend to treat them as equal. In other words, the police are less likely to ignore a

[18] President's Commission, *The Challenge of Crime*, p. 44.
[19] President's Commission, *The Challenge of Crime*.
[20] President's Commission, *The Challenge of Crime*.
[21] President's Commission, *The Challenge of Crime*.

woman's illegal acts today than they did in past years. This is not to say that females are not continually becoming more involved in crime. However, it does mean that the increase in female arrests cannot be equated with the increase in their commission of offenses.

RECIDIVISM

The single most striking fact about offenders who have been convicted for crimes against the person and property is that a large proportion of them repeat their crimes or commit other serious offenses. Arrest, court, and prison furnish insistent testimony to the fact that these repeated offenders constitute the hard core of the crime problem. A review of several recidivism studies in the federal and various state prison systems lead to the conclusion that roughly a third of the prisoners released will be reimprisoned, usually for committing new offenses, within a five-year period. Recidivism is most frequent in property crimes such as burglary, auto theft, forgery, or larceny, and least frequent with crimes of violence.[22]

According to the 1969 UCR, of the 18,567 offenders released from the federal criminal justice system in 1963, 65 percent had been rearrested by the end of the sixth calendar year after release.[23]

All of this indicates the seriousness of recidivism and its relationship to the extent of crime on our streets. Apparently, the criminal justice system has not been effective with those persons convicted of crime, and little real rehabilitation is achieved. Not only is the system unable to prevent crime from originally occurring, but it is unable to sufficiently influence criminals to the extent that they will reform to the degree necessary.

[22] President's Commission, *The Challenge of Crime*, pp. 45–46.
[23] Federal Bureau of Investigation, p. 38.

266

WHITE COLLAR CRIME

Thus far we have primarily discussed those crimes that more or less directly affect the citizen as he goes about his day-to-day activities. These are the crimes easiest for citizens to commit, and, therefore, they have the greatest visibility to all people. Concurrently, they are also the most troublesome and are the crimes to which the police direct most of their efforts. Most of the cases flowing through the courts are the result of street crimes, and the perpetrators of such crimes represent the clientele for correctional agencies.

White collar crime does not directly involve or affect people of the community, but it does have a great impact on the total assessment of crime. White collar crime is associated with a person's profession and the opportunities for criminal acts that the profession presents. Generally, white collar crime designates occupational crimes committed by persons of high status or social repute during the course of their work.

The white collar criminal is the contractor who uses cheaper materials than specified by contract, the politician who purchases land because he has prior knowledge of future purchases by his administration, the legislator who sells his vote, or the business executive who collaborates with other companies to fix prices. The list of such possible activities is quite inexhaustive, and there are practically no limitations.

Available criminal statistics give little information on the extent of white collar crime, but it is believed to be enormous. Edwin H. Sutherland conducted a study involving the corporate life histories of seventy of our largest corporations in relationship to decisions of courts and regulatory commissions under the antitrust, false advertising, patent, copyright, and labor laws. He found that 980 adverse decisions had been rendered against these corporations. His study, which included a forty-five year period, indicated that the organizations had an average of fourteen adverse decisions each.[24] This is but one study of white collar crime, but this and others indicate that white collar crime is prevalent throughout the United States. The exact amount is unknown, but its cost in dollars is probably greater than all street crimes combined. Where burglaries and robberies may involve a few hundred dollars each, white collar crimes involve many thousands of dollars. In 1974 the Chamber of Commerce of the United States, after surveying various sources, came up with a figure of approximately $41 billion annually, not taking into account the cost to the public of price-fixing illegalities and industrial espionage.[25]

Cost in dollars is not the only cost imposed upon society by white collar crime. In addition to financial loss, there is the cost measured in physical injury or death. The use of defective materials may cause a building to collapse, thus injuring or killing several people. Food sold in violation of the Pure Food and Drug Act may result in painful illness, which may lead to permanent disabilities or death.

Another cost attributed to white collar crime is the loss of social relations among business and individuals. Those business enterprises that flout the law set an example for other businesses to follow. It is reasonable to suspect that one corporation's involvement in illegal acts may force competitors into similar practices if they are to survive. In addition, if businessmen who are leaders in the community become involved in "shady" activities, the youth of the community may begin to believe it acceptable behavior to deviate from the law. This later situation is exemplified by the common comment that a person is a "shrewd" businessman rather than a criminal.

Finally, white collar crime violates trust among individuals and between businesses and consumers. Such mistrust demoralizes the entire community and actually perpetrates community or social disorganization.

[24] Edwin H. Sutherland, *White Collar Crime* (New York: Holt, Rinehart and Winston, Inc., 1949), p. 20.

[25] Chamber of Commerce of the United States, *White-collar Crime: Everyone's Problem, Everyone's Loss*, 1974, pp. 4–6.

ORGANIZED CRIME

One of the greatest, if not the greatest, problems facing the United States today is the extent of organized crime and its damaging effects on our society. If organized crime continues unchecked as it has in the past, it may very well be the element that will decay and eventually destroy our democratic heritage. Organized crime is a common enemy to all citizens from all walks of life, and its immunity from detection and prosecution must cease to exist. Citizens and the police must create a united front and an all-out war on organized crime to eliminate it from the American scene.

Organized crime is the most menacing purveyor of crime in the United States. According to the late J. Edgar Hoover, "Organized crime is filth with a vile stench. It is the personification of every lawless evil. It is a cancer in our society which is being allowed to grow by some people and actively nurtured by others."[26]

The term organized crime tends to be equated with the Mafia. This is true only in part, for organized crime encompasses a far greater area than that controlled by the Italian-Americans. Indeed, the Mafia is a substantial, if not dominant, part of organized crime, yet many other groups belong to this loose confederation.

The Mafia, La Cosa Nostra, the Syndicate, the Organization, the Mob, the Office, the Arm, and the Crime Confederation—these are just a few of the labels given to organized crime. These terms are misleading either because they pertain to only one segment of organized crime or because they are too general in their connotation.

"La Cosa Nostra" translated literally means "the our thing." When Joseph Valachi referred to his crime family as "our thing" law enforcement officials jumped to the false conclusion that this was the real name of the organization that for years the public had called the Mafia. The "La" (an Italian pronoun meaning "the") was simply added to give the name a

[26] J. Edgar Hoover, "War on Organized Crime," *DePaul Law Review*, Vol. 16, No. 2 (1964), p. 195.

more euphonic sound for press releases. The fact is that members of the Mafia do not have a specific name for their organization. They may refer to themselves as being in Carlo's *famiglia*, Vito's *brigata*, or Salvatore's *regime*; which simply means that they belong to a particular group headed by Carlo, Vito, or Salvatore. Just as a Chief of Police might be obliquely referred to as "the Old Man" by members of his department, so members of the Mafia on the East Coast referred to their organization as "our thing." Prior to the Valachi hearings in 1963 the term "cosa nostra" would not have been understood by Italian-American crime families in Chicago, Detroit, or Kansas City.

The term "Syndicate" has a variety of meanings depending on where and how it is used. In Chicago the word connotes an organized criminal gang whose leaders are Italian-Americans. In other cities the word "Syndicate" refers to the local criminal group in power, be it Irish, Jewish, or Polish in character.

"The Organization" and "The Mob" are simply convenient labels used by the news media when referring to groups of organized criminals.

"The Office" is the Kansas City and New England equivalent of "cosa nostra" while "The Arm" is a colloquial term utilized in Buffalo, New York.

"The Crime Confederation" is the result of the Oyster Bay conference on organized crime. The conference (by invitation only) was held at a secluded Long Island estate and was attended by approximately forty experts on organized crime. This term has proven to be rather meaningless, however, because it is unknown and unrecognized by the vast majority of citizens in the United States.

Although often misused and frequently overworked, the term "Mafia" is probably the most applicable when referring to those organized criminal gangs wherein membership is limited to Italian-Americans. Those favoring this term will argue that "Mafia" is generally understood by most Americans, and since it has meaning to most people, it is the term that should be used. Those opposed to the term hold that "Mafia" connotes a Sicilian origin, and that while a majority of mem-

270

bers are of Sicilian ancestry, membership includes others of Italian (but not necessarily Sicilian) background. Two classic examples are Al Capone and Vito Genovese—neither of whom were Sicilian, but Neapolitan. They further argue that the word "Mafia" suggests that the American Mafia is a branch of the Sicilian Mafia, or merely the Sicilian Mafia transplanted; whereas in truth Italian-American organized crime is uniquely American. Furthermore, there is an ethnic slur inherent in the word "Mafia," implying that all Italian-Americans belong to the Mafia. Nothing could be further from the truth—out of approximately twenty million Italian-Americans in the United States, only about five thousand belong to the Mafia.

Admittedly, the opponents to the term "Mafia" have valid arguments, but they have failed to come up with a better term. Therefore, the term "Mafia" appears to be the most fitting, as long as those employing the word realize that Mafia is only a part of organized crime.

What, then, is organized crime? Perhaps it can be best described as *a loose alliance of autonomous organized gangs whose operations are based on corruption, force, and fear.*

According to this definition, organized crime could include Cuban narcotic traffickers, Chinese-American tongs, certain labor unions, the Unione Corse (often incorrectly referred to as the Corsican Mafia), Mexican smugglers, Jewish gambling syndicates, or Dixie bootleggers.

Generally, these autonomous gangs are formed along ethnic lines. Thus, when speaking of organized crime reference is made to Polish gangs, Irish gangs, Jewish, German, Puerto Rican, Cuban, and Black gangs.

Bigotry is not a factor here; it is simply a matter of fact that most of those gangs comprising the structure of organized crime are based upon ethnic or racial origin, and with good reason.

The strength of any organized crime gang lies in its cohesiveness—a Three Musketeers' attitude of "One for all, and all for one." This cohesiveness is formed through one or more "bonding links." If a gang could be conceived of as a solid cement block wall, the bonding links would be comparable to the steel reinforcing rods running throughout the wall.

The bonding links for organized crime gangs are:

1. Kinship ties
2. Neighborhood ties
3. Childhood friendships
4. Prison acquaintanceship

It is interesting to note the similarity of historical background of the countries of origin of many of the organized crime gangs. Generally, these countries are characterized by poverty, exploitation, and oppression which forced the people to turn toward the family for trust and protection. By necessity, the family unit became primary; a nucleus upon which to base all other social, economical, and political actions. Thus, although there are vast cultural differences, there remains a great deal of similarity between the Sicilians, the Corsicans, the Jews, and the Chinese. These kinship ties, so successful in fighting oppression in the mother country, were carried over to America and into organized crime.

Families immigrating to the United States were segregated into ethnic neighborhoods as much by economic necessity as by choice. Hence, the neighborhood became the focal point of all social activity and associations. Outsiders could not be trusted because there was no way to check up on them. But, in the neighborhood everybody knew everybody else. An individual's credentials could be rapidly checked by simply "asking around." The neighborhood knew who was a stand-up guy, who could be trusted, who could not. (Although for different reasons, this same attitude is prevalent in many small towns in rural areas throughout the United States, particularly in the South.)

Childhood friendships, almost always formed in the neighborhood, are another of the bonding links of organized crime gangs. These friendships continue throughout the individuals' lives. Frequently during Senate subcommittee hearings on organized crime the interrogating Senators tried to tie together a network of criminals operating in conspiracy. Witnesses were asked if they were acquainted with various organized crime figures. A common answer was, "Sure, I know him. I grew up with him."

Prison acquaintances often supplement the other bonding links, or they may substitute for them. The prison setting simulates the neighborhood, and friendships formed in prison often continue after release. Prison acquaintances are particularly important in black organized crime gangs.

Organized crime operates directly, or through franchises, vast and lucrative criminal enterprises in gambling, loan sharking, untaxed liquor, narcotics, pornography, labor racketeering and the taking over of legitimate businesses. The operator of a criminal enterprise that is franchised by organized crime pays a percentage of his gross take to the organized crime gang, and in return he receives protection. He is granted a monopoly on his activity in his locality, enforced by threats, terror, and violence directed by organized crime against possible competitors. If he is harassed or arrested by the police, the experience and legal talent that organized crime can marshal is used on his behalf to cope with the law. He has no choice in accepting this arrangement; any attempt to operate independently results in violent retribution from the forces of organized crime.

Organized crime bases its operation on corruption, force, and fear. Attempts are made to bribe public officials so that rackets, such as gambling, prostitution, and loan sharking can flourish. In 1961, for example, such a bribery attempt was successful in one eastern Pennsylvania community. In this community, one man controlled numbers, horse betting, and a crap game bankrolled at $900,000 per week. He selected the chief of police and received a substantial kickback from the official's salary.[27]

The borrower who cannot pay back the usurious loan, and the gambler in debt to organized crime, lives in fear of losing his business or even his life. Sometimes he loses both. Of even greater concern, however, is the effect that organized crime has on the lives of millions of Americans. If organized

[27] Pennsylvania Crime Commission, *Task Force Report: Goals of Justice* (Harrisburg: Pennsylvania Crime Commission, 1969), p. 8.

criminals paid income tax on their earnings, everybody's tax bill would go down. When a burglary occurs, the perpetrator may be a narcotics addict who has been intentionally hooked by a pusher who is dominated or supplied by organized crime. When the price goes up on a specific consumer item, it may result from organized crime's attempt to gain control of that particular company by price fixing. Much of the money organized crime accumulates comes from innumerable petty transactions: 50-cent bets, $3-a-month private garbage collection services, quarters dropped into racketeer-owned jukeboxes, or small price rises resulting from protection rackets.

The organization of organized crime in the United States consists of numerous gangs who are in close contact with one another. Many have direct working agreements with each other. Others (primarily small local gangs operating in rural areas) work independently and usually confine their activities to a small geographic area.

Although only a part of the overall structure in the United States, the Mafia today dominates organized crime. It is estimated that the Mafia pockets more than half the money taken in by criminal activity in America.

Because of its permanency of form, strength of organization, and vast influence, the Mafia deserves special attention.

The organization of organized crime in the United States consists of twenty-four groups operating as criminal cartels in large cities across the nation. The membership is always in frequent communication with each other, and their smooth functioning is assured by a national body of overseers.

These twenty-four groups work with a control over other racket groups, whose leaders are of various ethnic derivations. In addition, the thousands of employees who perform the street-level functions of organized crimes, gambling, and other illegal activities represent a cross-section of the nation's population groups. Organized crime in its totality thus consists of these twenty-four groups allied with other racket enterprises to form a loose confederation operating in large and small cities. In the core groups, because of

274

their permanency of form, strength of organization, and ability to control other racketeer operations, resides the power that organized crime has in America today.[28]

Each of the twenty-four groups is known as a *family* with membership varying from as many as 700 men to as few as twenty. Each family is headed by one man, normally called the "boss," whose primary functions are maintaining order and maximizing profits. Subject only to the possibility of being overruled by the National Advisory Group, which will be discussed shortly, his authority in all matters relating to his family is absolute.

Subordinate to each boss is an *underboss*, the vice-president or deputy director of the family. He collects information for the boss, relays messages to him and passes his instructions down to his own subordinates.

On the same level as the underboss, but operating in a staff capacity, is the *consiglieri*, who is a counselor or advisor. Often an older member of the family who has partially retired from a career in crime, he gives advice to family members, including the boss and the underboss, and thereby enjoys considerable influence and power.

Next in line of authority are the *caporegima*. These members serve as buffers between the top members of the family and the lower echelon personnel. To maintain their insulation from the police, the leaders of the hierarchy avoid direct communication with the workers. All commands, therefore, flow back and forth through the trusted go-between or caporegima. In fulfilling this buffer capacity, the caporegima does not make decisions or assume any of the authority of his boss. Other caporegima work as chiefs of operating units and the number of men supervised varies with the size and activities of the particular family. From a business standpoint, the caporegima is analogous to a plant supervisor or sales manager.

[28] President's Commission on Law Enforcement and Administration of Justice, *The Challenge of Crime in a Free Society*, p. 193.

The lowest level members of the family are the *soldati*, the soldiers who report to the caporegima. A soldier may operate a particular illicit enterprise such as loan sharking, a dice game, a lottery, or a book making operation on a commission basis, or he may own the enterprise and pay a portion of his profit to the organization in return for their protection or for the right to operate.

Beneath the soldiers in the hierarchy are large numbers of employees and commissioned agents who are not members of the family. These are the people who do most of the actual work in various enterprises. They have no buffers or other insulation from law enforcement and take bets, drive trucks, answer telephones, sell narcotics, tend the stills, and work in legitimate businesses. The structure and activities of a typical family are shown in the chart on page 277.[29]

The highest ruling body of the twenty-four families is the *Commission*. This body serves as a combination legislature, supreme court, board of directors and arbitration board; its principal functions are judicial. Family members look to the commission as the ultimate authority on organizational and jurisdictional disputes. It is composed of the bosses of the nation's most powerful families but has authority over all twenty-four.[30]

Public agencies and governmental officials have recently become concerned about the problem of organized crime. As a result, the federal government has reinforced the organized crime unit of the United States Justice Department so that it will have a greater striking power. Many states have also initiated special law enforcement agencies to deal with organized crime. Unfortunately, the war against organized crime is in its infant stage, and it will be some time before much is realized in terms of eliminating or eradicating this problem.

[29] President's Commission, *The Challenge of Crime.*
[30] President's Commission, *The Challenge of Crime.*

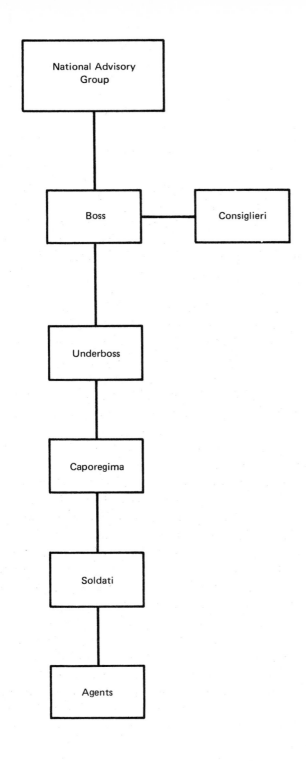

National Advisory Group

Boss

Consiglieri

Underboss

Caporegima

Soldati

Agents

THE TRAFFIC PROBLEM

The traffic problem is as old as man's first attempts to go from one place to another. Never being satisfied, man has continually searched for a faster means of reaching his destination. As he developed faster and better means of travel, he has simultaneously created problems of unparalleled magnitude. Today man has developed machines possessing power and speed beyond his needs, while he apparently does not possess the ability to adequately handle them. He has, in a sense, developed a *monster* that when improperly used leaves a trail of death, destruction, and horror.

THE TRAFFIC PICTURE

Every issue of any local newspaper will contain a multitude of stories reporting traffic accidents and the resulting deaths. Headlines read, "Playing Child Killed by Automobile," "Newsboy Struck by Auto," "Family of Six Killed in Two-Car Collision," and many similar such titles.

More people are killed and maimed in automobile accidents than by any other accident category. Traffic accidents alone cause more deaths and injuries than the combined totals of all other crimes. The number of men lost on the battlefields during our major wars has been minimal in comparison with the loss of lives on this nation's streets and highways. Each year there are more than 45 thousand people killed and 1.8 million seriously injured as a result of traffic accidents. This means that approximately one out of every 200 Americans will be killed or injured next year as a result of a traffic accident. During a person's lifetime, of course, his chances of being involved in a traffic accident become increasingly greater. In fact, one out of every two people probably can look forward to involvement in some sort of traffic accident during his or her lifetime.

It would appear that there is no letup in sight. Motor vehicle deaths and injury totals increased by more than one-

278

fourth in the decade of the sixties as compared to the fifties. In the decade from 1950 to 1959, there were 375,000 deaths and 13,350,000 injuries, while the sixties reported 475,000 deaths and 17,200,000 injuries.[31] It is anticipated that the seventies will present an even more horrible picture in terms of traffic accident deaths and disabling injuries.

Of interest is the fact that there was an increase of 850 traffic deaths in 1976 as compared to 1975. In 1976 there were 46,700 deaths as compared to 45,850 in 1975. However, the death rate per hundred million miles driven decreased from 3.45 in 1975 to 3.31 in 1976. Many police administrators attribute this decrease in deaths to the lower speed limits imposed as a result of the energy crisis. Others say, however, that accidents are often the result of many different factors— speed, driving ability, use of alcohol, and mechanical failure. There has to be something occurring other than speed for such a reduction in fatalities. It could be that higher fuel costs reduce traffic volume; keep more accident-prone drivers off the road, including the young (their parents let them drive less); discourage pleasure driving; reduce bar-hopping; and cause nonessential trips to be cancelled.

Of lesser consequence, but startling to say the least, is the economic loss due to motor vehicle accidents. At the present time this loss totals more than 24.7 billion dollars annually.[32] It has been estimated by some that in most communities the economic loss due to motor vehicle accidents is greater than the total police budget. More accidents and a higher cost per accident will certainly double the economic loss from the sixties to the seventies.[33]

[31] National Safety Council, *Accident Facts: 1970* (Chicago: National Safety Council, 1971), p. 41.
[32] National Safety Council, *Accident Facts: 1977* (Chicago: National Safety Council, 1977), p. 40.
[33] National Safety Council, 1977, p. 40.

Most of the accidents causing death and injury result directly from violations of the rules of the road. The violations most frequently causing accidents are drunk driving, speeding, failure to yield the right of way, and driving on the wrong side of the road. Of these, drunk driving and speeding contribute to the largest percentage of traffic accidents. It would seem logical for the police to particularly crack down on these two serious offenses by utilization of periodic spot checks. It certainly stands to reason the police should particularly attack those offenses which are known to be significant contributors to traffic accidents.

Every year Americans by the millions play Russian roulette on the highways, recklessly betting their lives that the spinning wheels of their automobiles won't result in death or injury. The best of automobile and highway design is of no avail if the weapon—the auto—is wielded by a reckless and careless person, and if the obvious rules of commonsense are blithely ignored by the chancetaker.

THE POLICE ROLE

As stated previously, if the police accept the responsibility of preserving lives, they must also accept the responsibility of traffic control. In fact, traffic control overshadows every other police regulatory task because it involves practically every person in the community. Automobile drivers, bicycle riders, pedestrians, the young and the old, the poor and the rich, all are affected by the diverse problems arising from the continually growing use of the automobile.

Traditionally the police have accepted a major share of this responsibility and have devoted considerable effort and time to directing traffic, enforcing traffic regulations, and investigating traffic accidents. Simply stated, the objective of the police in traffic control is *the safe and expedient movement of traffic*. This goal may sound relatively easy, but there are many ramifications that make its accomplishment quite difficult.

280

First, in spite of the serious consequences, people are apathetic to the traffic problem. Even though it is in their best interest to obey the rules of the road, many people disassociate themselves from becoming victim to a traffic accident. Many citizens view traffic violations as inconsequential nuisance rules that should apply only to other drivers. Such apathy certainly creates problems for the police.

The increasing number and growing use of automobiles further the traffic problem. Registered vehicles increased from 107 million in 1969 to 142,400,000 in 1976. Today motor vehicles are practically everywhere. There are few families without an automobile, and most have two or more. Americans average more than one million miles of travel over the nation's streets and highways every minute of the day.[34] The average car is driven ten thousand or more miles each year. There is every indication that automobile use will continue to grow.

During rush hours city streets are so jammed with automobiles that it is virtually impossible for the police to effectively handle them. In fact, when such congestion exists, the police must of necessity forget such things as enforcement and devote their full energies to traffic direction. Freeways and expressways are constantly being constructed, but not at a rate sufficient to keep up with the increasing number of vehicles.

As with crime, it is impossible for the police to eliminate traffic congestion and accidents. The task of the police, therefore, is to do the best they can under prevailing conditions. A conscientious effort on the part of the police does help, and it is this help that keeps the traffic picture from getting much worse. The police are not superhumans, and, therefore, can only do what is humanly possible to keep at a minimum death and destruction on our highways.

[34] National Safety Council, 1977, p. 40.

FRAGMENTED AND DUPLICATE POLICE SERVICES

According to the Federal document, *Task Force Report: The Police*, compiled by President Johnson's Commission on Law Enforcement and Administration of Justice, a fundamental problem confronting law enforcement today is that of fragmented crime repression efforts that result from the large number of uncoordinated local government and law enforcement agencies. The report continues by stating that it is not uncommon to find police units working at cross purposes in trying to solve the same or similar crimes. The commission's conclusion is that formal cooperation or consolidation is an essential ingredient for improving the quality of law enforcement. A workable program of formal cooperation or consolidation for law enforcement services within a "common community of interests" is a desired goal for improving the quality of law enforcement at the local level.[35]

In metropolises the demands for police service multiply disproportionately to the actual rise in population. Such demands may exceed the capacity of the several existing police agencies. As a result, the amount of tax revenue provided for law enforcement may not be sufficient to maintain several equally proficient police agencies within the same metropolitan area.

There is little doubt that over the next few years the demands of a small-town and small-city police department will be so great that all such departments will be forced into making abrupt and drastic changes which will be both expensive and chaotic unless adequate preparation is made now to get ready for the inevitability of consolidation of formal cooperative law enforcement.

Problems experienced by several police agencies in the same metropolitan area are usually quite similar in nature and severity. Many of them are common to all American

[35] Commission on Law Enforcement and Administration of Justice, *Task Force Report: The Police* (Washington, D. C.: U. S. Government Printing Office, 1968), p. 68.

New communications center capable of securing consolidated area

Courtesy of the Baltimore Police Department
Baltimore, Md.

police departments, and include difficulties of recruiting and training, rising costs of operations, growing demands for additional services, dramatic increases in traffic accidents and congestion, and literally dozens of other government-orien-

283

tated problems facing local police agencies. All of these common problems combined indicate a serious need to take immediate and decisive action toward consolidation or formal cooperative law enforcement.

The duplication of law enforcement services within most metropolitan areas tends to weaken the entire law enforcement effort. Countless hours are spent by each department in the collection, preservation, and retrieval of facts and information concerning police services, whether traffic or criminal, while neighboring agencies keep and process records in much the same manner about many of the same persons and incidents. Because of manpower and equipment shortages or overages, the deployment of police personnel geographically and by time of day varies considerably from the needs experienced by the individual departments. Citizens passing through a metropolitan area frequently experience differing quantities and quality of police service as they cross political borders. Criminals understand this and are inadvertently assisted by the problem brought about by fragmented law enforcement, which perpetuates the diffuse and often confused efforts of local police agencies.

Seldom does one find an effective central clearinghouse of information regarding police activities for metropolitan areas. Departments may appear to cooperate fully; however, there is often no coordinated, single-purpose operation which provides the efficiency and effectiveness necessary for good policing. Information concerning suspects is frequently withheld from neighboring police agencies, as much accidentally as intentionally. Wanted and missing persons bulletins and similar investigative information are unavailable on many occasions because of different methods of gathering and filing information or operational procedures used in its dissemination. In the investigation of crime, which is usually of an area-wide rather than localized nature, police of a metropolitan area are greatly handicapped by such problems as differences in public policy, specific local laws and ordinances, and the size and effectiveness of their fellow police departments.

284

As more and more police departments become involved in solving a crime, there arises a conflict relative not only to procedures and policies, but also many times to basic philosophies. Conflicts of any nature usually are detrimental to the effective provision of adequate police services, and within metropolitan areas there may be found interjurisdictional conflicts of one nature or another in all major areas of law enforcement responsibility. Areas of possible conflict in philosophy or procedures include preventative patrol and traffic enforcement, the investigation of organized crime and vice, recruiting and training police officers, the operation of detention facilities, the handling of property and evidence, the processing of records and other police related information, the handling of traffic violations, and many others. These differences may seem immaterial, or inconsequential, at first glance; however, a review of the basic responsibilities of the several law enforcement agencies may indicate that each jurisdiction may be assumed to have a common base of operations, and, generally, similar organizational goals. However, to the contrary, in many cases the methods used to achieve these goals are somewhat different. At the same time, each of the police agencies attempts in its own way to both cooperate and compete with its neighboring police departments. While not inherently bad, this frequently produces duplicated, uncoordinated, and usually inadequate efforts. The implications of the above are apparent. This situation coupled with the large number of relatively small municipalities surrounding most metropolitan areas usually contributes to higher crime rates, increased cost of police services, and disproportionate increases in traffic congestion and accidents. As these areas grow, the situation can be expected to become even more complicated and confusing, which could create additional law enforcement problems. Generally speaking, all of these problems justify the need for consolidation of police services or cooperative law enforcement.

The whole concept of consolidating police services is a new and innovative one. It is based on the premise that future demands on the police, including the development of highly sophisticated technological and professional capability, will be so exacting, so expensive, and so far-reaching that an entirely new approach to policing will be essential for the stability of the social order. Small communities will be unable to adjust for the future if their police structure remains archaic. Just as many small towns have banded together to build and administer regional high schools to provide better education for their youngsters, so too must police agencies join together to provide better, more professional, and more efficient police services for their people.

It must be recognized that before coordination and consolidation can take place, various obstacles must be overcome. One is the idea that each jurisdiction can provide at least a minimum of police service. Also legal obstacles have to be overcome. Coordination is needed and needed badly. It will lead to more effective and efficient police service; however, it must be recognized that more research must be conducted because there is not sufficient information available today to keep the public and various police units informed of the need or advantages of coordination and consolidation.

POLICE AND POLITICS

Many early police departments in the United States were characterized by corruption, incompetence, and inefficiency. Police departments became one of the favorite targets for the spoils system, and good discipline was impossible because of the political atmosphere within the ranks.

Political control of the police included such procedures as the appointment of officers for one year, the election of the chief of police, and the control of the department by local boards. Numerous attempts to remove the police from the political arena failed. One effort worthy of note was the policing of municipal agencies under state control. This occurred in New York when in 1853 a board of police commissioners was created by state law. The purpose was to eliminate the political favoritism and ward control that had dominated the department. The majority of the major cities followed suit, but this intended solution was not found to be the panacea that it was originally believed to be. Political influences and corruption would just move from the municipal to the state level. Today there are only a few city police departments remaining under state control.

Efforts to remove political corruption varied and none accomplished the desired goal. A landmark in the reform movement, however, was the passage of the United States Civil Service Act in 1883 which encouraged similar laws at the state and local level. Prior to civil service regulations, the employment of police personnel was by the patronage system. When a new mayor was elected, for example, he paid his political debts by appointing men to the police force. Civil service reform eliminated much of this procedure and gave impetus to the improvement of selection procedures and consequently the upgrading of police personnel.

Patronage positions are still found in state and local police agencies and it is still common practice in many cities for a new mayor to appoint his chief of police. In some cities the mayor still has the power to promote men at his will, particularly to management level positions. Such practices naturally lead to low morale among all police officers, and this adversely affects police efficiency. In addition, officers striving for advancement may rely more heavily upon political contacts and favors than upon improvement of their ability. In other words, *police involvement in politics breeds inefficiency*.

State police agencies are susceptible also to political manipulation. A common practice, for example, is for the newly elected governor to appoint his favorite as the police commissioner. Likewise, the new department head will appoint his favorites to high positions in the hierarchy even if new positions must be created. The department heads who are politically appointed may encourage additional political

287

manipulation and favors requested by other politicians and representatives of pressure groups.

The office of sheriff is probably the most obvious example of mixing police and politics. This office was integrated into the American police system with little change from what it was in England. Today the office of sheriff is subject to popular election in almost all counties throughout the United States. Sheriff's offices have always been prone to rapid turnover of personnel, which is directly related to the election process of the sheriff and the short term of office. Again, when a new sheriff is elected he will repay political debts by appointing new deputies and promoting others already employed. A new sheriff, because of the patronage system, knows that the chief deputy under the past sheriff may not be loyal to him. Therefore, he places his own man in that position. This constant change of leadership and manipulation of the hierarchy has not been conducive to the provision of efficient police services.

The sheriff, constable, or marshall who is subject to election is definitely and necessarily involved in politics. However, appointed police chiefs, captains, and so on down the line often depend on political assistance. They may be dependent on politics to secure the position, hold security, or perhaps avoid transfer. As stated previously, this is a system built on personalities, not merit. It is unfair, breeds low morale, and fosters an inclination toward corruption.

The above discussion supports the belief that police should not be directly involved in politics. For administrative and operational effectiveness, it is necessary that the police operate without direct political interference. As a public agency, of course, police must be responsive to public needs that ideally are defined through the ballot box. It is obvious, therefore, that there must be some involvement in politics if the police department is to be adequately responsive. It is recommended, however, that this be via the ballot box with no direct association of police in politics or politics in police operations.

POLICE UNIONISM

Although a form of police unionism can be traced back to the late 1800's, the real impetus for the growth and spread of police labor organizations did not occur until the 1960's. Initially, and for several years thereafter, police chiefs *actively resisted* their formation and refused to give them any official recognition. Most chiefs regarded unionism as a deterrent to police professionalism and sincerely believed it would thwart their attempt to deliver high quality police service. The attitude was, and still is to a large extent, one of "us versus them" so that an adversary relationship developed between the police chief and his personnel.

Perhaps this attitude by police chiefs and city administrators was the ingredient that spurred the continued development of police unionism. It would appear that the best organizer of a union is the actively resistant administrator. Due to the nature of the times, which gave us a "new breed" of police officers, they did not acquiesce as expected. Battle lines were drawn and we witnessed, among other things, strikes, work slowdowns, and "blue flu" epidemics that widened the gap between police administrators and their employees.

A recent trend has been the appearance and growth of minority police unions. They emerged primarily to redress minority officer grievances, eliminate discrimination in hiring and promotion, improve the department's relationship with minorities within the community, and address other matters of concern to minority employees. There is every indication that minority police unions will continue to grow, and perhaps the chief will find more than one minority organization within his department.

In recent years many police administrators have come to accept the inevitable. Police labor organizations are here to stay. The enlightened police chief will accept the challenge and establish a collegial relationship with police officers and union representatives. This, of course, requires the rethinking

289

of administrative philosophy and management techniques. It demands, for example, an environment for constructive participative management.

There are basically three types of police labor organizations: 1) local independent organizations; 2) organizations affiliated with a larger group at the county, state, or national level; and 3) organizations affiliated with organized labor. The most numerous are the local independent associations. This is fortunate, as they are the easiest for the chief of police and city administrator to work with in a cooperative manner. Since they are only concerned with local matters, a meeting of the minds is easier to accomplish.

Police union organizations are interested in all matters affecting their members. Initially they were concerned with pay and monetary fringe benefits. Following success with these issues, organizational leaders began to express interest in police policy areas such as disciplinary procedures, dress and hair styles, expanded political rights, assignments and transfers, promotional procedures, patrol procedures including the number of officers in a patrol car, training procedures, and the expanded use of civilians. We can expect that they will want seniority to be the primary consideration relative to promotion, vacation, and beat, shift, and job assignments.

As police unions continue to expand their power, chiefs will be confronted with increasing challenges to their authority and discretion. Some police unions have, for example, managed to include provisions in contracts which require that they be consulted before changes are made in police policies and that they be given the authority to approve such changes. There is no doubt that they will continue to strive for such contractual provisions.

The chief's first and primary responsibility is the protection of citizens and their property and the delivery of high quality police service. Therefore, policy related to police service must remain a management prerogative. The chief of police should *fight* against the loss of any prerogative that will hamper his ability to provide high quality police service to the community.

Most police chiefs agree that certain prerogatives must be vested exclusively with management. Such prerogatives, to mention a few, include the right to: 1) hire; 2) discipline and discharge; 3) decide job qualifications; 4) lay off; 5) abolish positions; 6) make rules and regulations relative to conduct and safety; 7) determine work schedules; 8) organize the department; 9) develop promotional procedures; 10) assign training; and 11) determine operational methods or procedures.

The chief of police must assume the responsibility for developing a climate conducive to employee satisfaction, open communication, participation in decision making, and trust. If he does this, the need for unionism will be minimized, and where a union does exist, smoother negotiations will exist. The most important ingredient for effective employee relations is a sound personnel program that is fair, equitable, and related to professional standards. The smart chief will be sure that personnel policies and practices are applicable to today's situation.

LEGAL RESTRICTIONS

The recognition that the police are bound by law to respect the rights of individuals has resulted from recent highly publicized Supreme Court decisions. The controversy that has arisen over these decisions has led to charges that the courts are handcuffing the police and turning offenders loose so they might strike again.

It is an established fact that criminals have been released on technicalities of the law, and this apparent injustice to society often leads the observer to overlook the possibility that justice was being served by the preservation of the individual's rights as expressed in the Constitution. Encroachment on the rights of individuals by the police and misuse of the powers vested in them is not being tolerated by the courts. For this reason, the police must be familiar with the personal liberties granted each citizen by the Constitu-

291

tion and must be aware of the instances where they most often need to take measures to extend these liberties to the suspect as accorded by the law. Failure to do this creates the possibility of the case being thrown out of court.

The parts of the Constitution that are most pertinent to civil liberties are the First, Fourth, Fifth, Sixth, and Fourteenth Amendments. These amendments embody the Constitution's expression of an individual's liberties and form the basis for many Supreme Court decisions.

The First Amendment relates to freedom of speech and assembly. During public demonstrations the law enforcement officer must be most circumspect in making arrests. It must be clear that the arrestee has engaged in unlawful conduct such as a trespass or disorderly conduct. Courts will very carefully look at the circumstances to determine whether the intent of the arrestee was to incite violence through inflammatory statements or whether his conduct otherwise created a substantial risk of a breach of the peace. Even the display of banners or placards without oral statements can be a form of expression protected by this amendment.

The Fourth Amendment protects citizens' most cherished right—the right to privacy. The writers of this amendment never envisioned that a citizen would be arrested in his house which had been searched without a warrant. Accordingly, today courts, as a general rule, require police to first obtain a warrant in the absence of some emergency circumstances justifying their failure to do so. This amendment requires that ample probable cause be shown before the right to privacy is invaded. Further, it is expected that an impartial judicial official will decide *before* the arrest or search whether probable cause exists. It requires that any invasion of privacy based on probable cause be reasonable, and that warrants describe with great particularity the person to be arrested, the place to be searched, and the thing or things to be seized. The Supreme Court has approved "stop and frisk" but has said that a "stop" may not be made unless the officer can demonstrate some justification for his actions that amounts to more than mere whim or suspicion. Further, courts reserve the "frisk" to those situations where the officer can demonstrate that it was necessary to protect himself.

The Fifth Amendment relates to the privilege against self-incrimination as illustrated by the well-known case of Miranda v. Arizona. In this case, the Supreme Court addressed itself to police interrogation under conditions described as "custodial." Assuming such conditions exist, the court said an arrestee or a suspect not yet under arrest must be advised of certain rights prior to interrogation for evidence of guilt. Such advisement is a precondition to the admissibility of any statement made by an accused, whether in the statement he admits guilt or denies guilt. In recent decisions, the Court has said that this four-point advisement is not mandated by the Constitution, but nonetheless constitute procedural safeguards to insure that the privilege is protected. The Court has held that a Miranda-defective statement that is otherwise voluntary will be admissible to attack the credibility of a testifying defendant who categorically denies all charges against him. However, even here the statement may be considered only for the limited purpose of credibility and not as evidence of guilt.

The Sixth Amendment relates to the right of a speedy and public trail by an impartial jury and the right to assistance of counsel. The attitude of the Supreme Court on failure of the state to afford an accused a speedy trial is unmistakable. The Court has said that the only suitable remedy here is to dismiss all charges against an accused. The Court has taken the position that a defendant has a right to trial by jury if charged with an offense punishable by imprisonment for more than six months. However, various state constitutions may provide for trial by jury regardless of the offense charged. Here it is important to note that Supreme Court decisions interpreting the U.S. Constitution set minimum standards for the states and do not preclude the states from adopting in their constitutions more demanding standards.

The attitude of the Court on right to counsel is equally unmistakable. It has held that an accused has a right to counsel before he may be imprisoned for the commission of any offense. It has held that an accused has such a right if put in a lineup after adversary judicial proceedings have been initiated against him by the state. The recent trend indicates that courts will insist that an accused not only be represented by counsel but by counsel who demonstrates an acceptable level of competence. In general, the courts have held that an accused is entitled to counsel at every "critical stage" of proceedings against him.

There is probably no amendment to the Constitution that has been more widely applied than the Fourteenth Amendment which relates to due process of law. It is this amendment that has resulted in the Fourth, Fifth and Sixth amendments being held applicable to the states as well as the Federal government. The Supreme Court, in a series of decisions during the 1960's, held that to violate the aforementioned rights, previously though binding only on the Federal government, was to deny an accused due process of law. The concept of due process is the cornerstone of our legal system. Embodied in this concept is the requirement of fair play, or that fundamental fairness that protects citizens from unreasonable acts of their government, be it state or federal. It prescribes certain safeguards to insure that a person charged with an offense receives that to which he is entitled as a matter of simple justice. It is interpreted as meaning that the standard of conduct required is one of reasonableness and that actions of the State must meet this standard. Otherwise, the person affected has been denied due process of law assured by this amendment. Inherent in this general concept are the following:

1. That a statute defining an offense be written in specific language which will put citizens on notice as to what constitutes criminal conduct.
2. That an accused be afforded the fullest constitutional protections during the investigation of an alleged offense and during the pretrial stage of the criminal justice process.
3. That the accused have the assistance of competent counsel during any "critical stage" of the criminal justice process.

4. That the accused be afforded a hearing before a fair and impartial court.
5. That the accused, assisted by counsel, may confront his accusers in court.
6. That the accused, assisted by counsel, may submit evidence on his own behalf and attack evidence submitted by the State.

These five amendments and the Supreme Court's decisions based upon them are important to the law enforcement officer because they set guidelines for his behavior in enforcing the law. Whether or not an individual agrees with the Court's Constitutional interpretation of these amendments, the most recent Supreme Court decisions have the effect of standardizing law enforcement procedures in police agencies across the nation. This standardization has a positive effect, because it promotes equal levels of enforcement, thus sustaining "the equal protection of the law" guaranteed each citizen by the Constitution.

The police officer himself must be well versed in these provisions of the Constitution. When the rights of an individual are violated, the case may be investigated, thrown out of court, and the criminal set free. The courts will not uphold a conviction based on evidence obtained through an unlawful violation of an individual's rights. Constitutional guarantees to the citizen must be upheld.

The policeman represents only the enforcement branch of the criminal justice system. He does not make the laws and is not free to interpret them. His only alternative if he is to preserve effective law enforcement is to perform his duties according to the Constitution and its interpretation, as formulated by the Supreme Court. His position as protector of rights is deemed of paramount importance. The only legitimate police response is to enforce the law within the framework of the Constitution and the guidelines provided by the Court.

DISORDERS AND LAW ENFORCEMENT

The decade of the sixties was one of recognition for our nation; Americans were made aware that a hunger and deprivation exists in the United States. Lyndon B. Johnson stated "Until justice is blind to color, until education is unaware of race, until opportunity is unconcerned of the color of a man's skin, emancipation will be a proclamation but not a fact, to the extent that the proclamation of emancipation is not fulfilled in fact . . . we shall have fallen short of assuring the freedom to the free."[36] The decade of the sixties showed that we as a nation have fallen short.

The poverty-stricken, black ghetto resident believes that the system or establishment has failed him. In the past ten years most of our major cities with large nonwhite populations have had serious disorders, which have been termed racial. The riots, for the most part, have occurred as a direct result of some action taken by the police.

In one city, a fifteen-year-old black schoolboy was shot by an off-duty policeman as he tried to attack the officer with a knife. In another city, rumors were spread after police arrested a black man. Another city had a similar situation over the arrest of a cab driver. In city after city, some small police action became the spark that set our cities on fire. Many ghetto blacks may resent the police as the representatives of white society's authority. This may be because the police image in the black community is a bad one. The ghetto resident may believe the primary function of the police is to protect property rights, and blacks have no property; thus, the police do not aid or represent the blacks but suppress them.

In speaking with civil rights leaders, it becomes apparent that the black ghetto resident is rebelling not against law enforcement officers but rather against what he sees law enforcement as representing: an inherently racist white society

[36] Lyndon B. Johnson, Address at Gettysburg, May 30, 1963.

that attempts to maintain a position of superiority over the subservient minorities.

In the ghetto, unemployment and underemployment are common. In the schools, segregation or defacto segregation exists today—fifteen years after the *Brown* decision. Segregated schools are inherently unequal. Our welfare system is inadequate to meet the needs of the poor, and it perpetuates welfare rather than offering meaningful ways of removing people from welfare rolls to become productive members of society. Ghetto housing remains substandard and will continue to be so until a national effort is made to improve it. This continuous lack of education, meaningful employment, and adequate housing leads to family breakups, prostitution, dope addiction, and crime that leads to the jungle of insecurity and tension that the Kerner Commission talks of as being the racial ghetto.

These are the things that cause a riot, but it is the action by the police that ignites it. The police represent the ghetto's link to the establishment, and thus are seen as being repressive. The blacks believe that they have experienced police brutality and harassment, and as long as they are subject to degrading verbal abuse they will strike out at law enforcement officials.

Allegations of police brutality, accusations of differential treatment by the police of black citizens, and denunciation of police policies and practices by spokesmen for various groups have been widespread. Whether or not these charges are valid, they have been made and have influenced public opinion, creating hostility and expression of grievances. Such unrest may lead to open clashes. And that, unfortunately, is the reality with which policemen must deal.

There has been some indication that spokesmen for protest groups have directed deliberate harassment against police departments, police administrators, and individual officers. Usually the police have not fared well when this has occurred. The police try to combat the harassment with facts, while the public is seemingly more interested in the sensational news as presented by the protest spokesmen. In addition, objective facts usually are given in response to charges and are, therefore, too late to counteract inflammatory stories.

The vast majority of our people, whether they belong to a so-called minority group or not, have no way of assessing the accuracy of what they hear or read. Even the most objective reporting is subject to individual interpretation. It is a well-known psychological fact that people "read into" and remember those aspects of events which best fit with their attitudes and beliefs. Thus, a police action which one person may regard as brutal may to another person seem overly lenient.

The strained relations between the police and the community are evidenced by the increasing number of assaults upon officers and by the increasing tendency of bystanders to offer active resistance when officers must make arrests. In addition, there is growing reluctance to aid police by giving information about crime. Recruiting is becoming more difficult, and vacancies exist within police departments all over the country.

Compounding these difficulties is another: many officers have resigned themselves to what they believe is a hopeless situation and have taken the attitude that they will do as little as possible. Many are retiring as soon as they become eligible, and many younger men are resigning.

The role of the police is controversial with many segments of the population. In addition to the many ghetto blacks who are strongly antagonistic toward the police, there are many so-called liberals—both black and white—who feel the same. Even some ultraconservative and far-rightists are highly critical of the police, although for opposing reasons. Equally discouraging and dangerous is the fact that the majority of people are more or less apathetic. The narrow views of the people at both political extremes and the apathy of the middle-of-the-roader provide a fertile field for agitators.

Within the police establishment there are two undesirable reactions to the public's hostility. First, some officers tend to meet the challenge by bending over backwards to be well

298

liked by the community. These men, in order to avoid possible criticism, may fail to take an unpopular action that they properly should take. Secondly, other officers may react by stiffening their backs and becoming overly aggressive. Neither of these reactions coincides with the impartial and impersonal police concept of police work.

The strong possibility of further deterioration in relations between the people and their police exists. It is urgent that something be done. We do not relish the prospect of dealing at sword's point with people who should be cooperative in combating crime and delinquency. We certainly do not relish the prospect of seeing any of our community's children grow up to hate the police. The problem is ours; the need is now; and we must, therefore, take the initiative in solving it.

Citizen hostility toward the police is every bit as disruptive of peace and order as police indifference to or mistreatment of citizens. Citizens, particularly those of the ghetto, will not receive adequate police protection until the police accept them as true citizens and appreciate the police role, trust them, and cooperate toward the achievement of the police goal. Basically, both the citizens and the police must recognize that the police goal is really a community goal.

THE POLICE IMAGE

Nothing is more difficult than being a police officer in a democratic society. The policeman is supposed to mediate family disputes that would tax a Supreme Court justice; maintain racial relations in a core city with little knowledge of psychology; enforce impartially literally hundreds of laws; use great discretion such as would be expected of a clergyman; and identify the elusive criminal when little or no evidence exists. The job requires a variety of extraordinary skills that no one person could possible possess.

In reality, the public's expectations of a policeman are far beyond anyone's capabilities. The policeman is supposed to resolve all the ill society has taken hundreds of years to develop. This impossible task is expected of the police, and when they fail in any minor way, the public is quick to condemn.

Plato praised the policeman's lofty forebearer as the *guardian of law and order* and placed him near the top of his ideal society, endowing him with special wisdom. The citizens of the United States have placed their guardians near the bottom. There is certainly a paradox; on one hand the citizens give the policeman the greatest responsibility of the society, and on the other hand place him in low esteem within the societal structure.

The police image in the United States today is a complicated subject to discuss. In order to clarify things as much as possible, a simple definition of what is meant by the term *image* is necessary. *Webster's Dictionary* defines image in several different ways. Perhaps the simplest meaning of image is stated as "visual picture that a phenomenon leaves in the mind of someone else." Using this definition, one could say the police image is a visual picture or impression that a policeman leaves in the mind of someone else.

The police in the United States do not present a favorable image today, and they never really have. It is difficult to determine exactly what their present-day image is, since perception differs according to the viewer. In other words, economic status, age group, occupational group, educational status, racial or ethnic membership, and sex all may influence a particular person's perception of the police.

Despite these differences in perception, there are a few criteria that are common to all groups. One common perception of the policeman is that of public servant. Generally, most people do not have a high regard for the public servant. They believe that public servants are less courteous, less competent, less intelligent, and less industrious than those in other fields of endeavor.

Another problem related to police image is that the policeman is a faceless individual. Prior to the advent of the automobile, there was a policeman on practically every street corner. Residents saw him regularly and, therefore, could relate to him. Today the street corner policeman is almost nonexistent. The policeman today is usually seen in conjunction with his vehicle, rather than as an individual. Police uniforms also add to this faceless image: the police "all look alike."

Another image presented by the policeman is that of the "enforcer." The policeman has a difficult job because, in essence, he is the one telling people what they can and cannot do. It is very difficult to perform this function and to continue to maintain an image of respect and friendliness. People don't like to be told what they can or cannot do. People may not think much about it until a contact is made with the officer, but it is often difficult to thank a policeman when he has just cited you for going through a yellow traffic light. It is hard for the police to present a good image when so often the very nature of the job is unpleasant.

Another reason for today's tarnished police image is related to their history. Early police departments were usually corrupt and inefficient. Politics was quite often involved in the selection of officers, and this frequently continues to be true today. The history of law enforcement is marked with many ugly facades of justice. Even in this century, the police often used coercive methods to extract information from suspects. An image like this is very difficult to overcome, and older citizens especially have a tendency to remember some of these poor aspects, and some relate them to today's departments.

Some experts contend that the recent Supreme Court decisions have had an adverse affect on the police image. Take the precedent case of *Miranda* v. *Arizona* as an example. When the high court ruled that policemen must inform all suspects of their constitutional rights before questioning, many people interpreted this decision as a crackdown on unethical police methods.

The mass media is quite often responsible for today's poor police image. Television programs and motion pictures that satirize the police often are very detrimental to the police

301

character. The news media often present a distorted picture of the police. Television coverage during civil disturbances, for example, often makes the police look more violent than the demonstrators. Magazines and newspapers often present articles that are slanted against the police.

In addition to the above list of reasons for the poor police image, there is another reason that probably contributes to this image: the conduct of the police officer in the field. He is the single most important creator of the police image. Every look, every word, every comment of the day communicates impressions to the public. The whole force is judged by what he says and how he says it.

It is important that every police officer recognize his role in developing the police image. The professional police officer must assume the task of improving the police image within his own police department. This will be accomplished if the officer is courteous, knowledgeable, compassionate, and truly interested in the welfare of others. Sincere interest will definitely communicate to those persons with whom he comes in contact. They will as a result perceive the police officer in the light that he wishes to be seen.

POLICE CORRUPTION

There is probably no issue that causes more anguish to police and city administrators than that of corruption in the police department. It is such a distasteful subject that few chiefs of police are even willing to talk about it, let alone admit that it might exist within their department. Yet the possibility of police corruption exists in every police department in the United States.

The police operation is a perfect setting for the emergence and feeding of corrupt activities. The opportunities, for those who do so, of buying the integrity of a police officer are numerous. The free meal at the restaurant, the burglary victim who offers the officer a bribe to record items as stolen that were not so he can collect from insurance, the payoff to ranking officers to ignore gambling activities, etc., are all forms of corruption and are opportunities presented daily to the police officer. If one officer relents and sells his integrity, the blemish of corruption is on the entire police organization.

One might ask, What is corruption? Are there degrees of corruption that can be tolerated within the police department? Is a free cup of coffee corruption or does corruption have to involve a substantial amount of money?

There is considerable controversy relative to the answers to these questions. There are the police executives who believe the free cup of coffee is a degree of corruption and cannot be tolerated within their police organization. Although accepted by most people, these executives believe that the free cup of coffee can lessen the guard of the police officer so that he is more willing to become involved in more complicated types of buying. The police executive with this philosophy says that the free cup of coffee, in reality, is buying something for that business. Normally, restaurants give the free cup of coffee because they are, in reality, receiving additional police protection while the police officers are consuming their coffee in the business establishment. The business giving the free coffee is actually receiving more police service than businesses that do not; it is believed by these police administrators that the officer is giving partial treatment to the business handing out the coffee.

Other police administrators see no harm in the so-called free cup of coffee. They believe that this is merely a courtesy that is being offered by the restaurant to the police organization. These administrators apparently believe that a department is not corrupt unless there is money involved, whereby an officer ignores a law or set of laws. One might ask, why does the restaurant not give free coffee to the mailman, milkman, and other delivery men? Why is this courtesy only extended to the police officer? *Is there something he can deliver which the others cannot?*

Generally speaking, corruption exists whenever an officer chooses to ignore a law, or set of laws, *show special considera-*

303

tion, or grant special dispensation in return for something of value which may take the form of a gift or other gratuity, even money. The important point is, that the officer did, or failed to do, something which he was required to do, and in return for his acting or not acting he received and accepted something of value from those for whom he acted. In other words, when officers accept anything other than their salary for performing their job, corruption and/or collusion is involved. Needless to say, the public is primarily concerned about corruption that causes the police to ignore certain laws to the benefit of certain individuals or that which involves any digression from the strictest standards of honesty and fairness, which every citizen has the right to expect from his police officers. However, regardless of the public's attitude, the chief administrator should have a firm policy that forbids any kind of gratuity acceptance within his police department. The chief's policy should very clearly and firmly delineate his stance relative to the acceptance of gratuities and, in fact, his philosophy relative to corruption and collusion. This stance should be communicated to every individual member of the police department so they are keenly aware, and certain, of the chief's attitude and philosophy.

Police corruption and collusion has probably been present in some degree since the beginning of law enforcement. Generally citizens, over the years, have shown genuine concern about alleged police corruption by demanding grand jury investigations, removal from office, by means of recall, of elected public officials, and also removal from office of appointed public officials as well as those who appointed them. Some of the more recent, and notable, of such actions have been the Knapp Commission investigation in New York City, the Pennsylvania Crime Commission investigation of Philadelphia, and the revelation of corruption in Chicago, Indianapolis, and other cities located throughout the United States.

In Indianapolis massage parlors paid policemen protection money so they could continue offering sex along with rubdowns. Bribes were also paid to get the police to raid competitors. Other allegations included thefts by Indianapolis policemen of money donated to police athletic league clubs, traffic cops selling parking "franchises," a detective who was identified as one of the city's top four or five drug dealers, and payoffs from $500 to $5000 to fix cases already filed against suspects.[37]

Similar cases have been reported in New York, but on a much larger scale. In one case, 16 officers were convicted in 1973 of extorting $20,000 per month from black gamblers. In super-congested Manhattan, extensive payoffs were made to allow traffic and building code violations.[38] Of course, most everyone is aware of the Knapp Commission investigation relating to payoffs from the victimless crimes. That is, the payoffs received by numerous officers throughout the department so that gambling, prostitution, narcotics violations, and other forms of vice could run rampant throughout the city. This, of course, was brought to bear as a result of the Serpico situation, which resulted in the Knapp Commission investigation.

In Chicago, 19 policemen, including a Captain, were convicted of shaking down tavern owners.[39] In a series of reports on crime in the United States, *Life* reported several instances of police corruption. In Chicago, the report said many officers tried to get on the traffic detail because of the money they could make taking bribes from traffic offenders. The report also cited corruption situations in other cities located throughout the United States.[40]

The Pennsylvania Crime Commission investigated corruption in Philadelphia and had this to say:

> The Commission found that police corruption in Philadelphia is ongoing, widespread, systematic, and occurring at all levels of the police department. Corrupt practices were uncovered during the investigation in every police

[37] *Patriot News* (Harrisburg Patriot News, July 21, 1973), p. B2.
[38] *Ibid.*, p. B2.
[39] *Ibid.*, p. B2.
[40] Herbert Brean in *Life*, 43:71, September 16, 1957.

district and involved police officers ranging in rank from policeman to inspector. . . .

Corruption and political influence in the police department are problems which have plagued the force since its inception. In the 20th century alone, there have been three previous special Grand Jury investigations, each of which found widespread corruption within the department. Difficult problems of integrity, political influence, and professionalism still continue, . . .[41]

Corruption is not limited to these cities alone. Similar activities may be occurring in any police department—large or small—in the United States. It is incumbent upon every police officer to conduct himself in such a manner that will prohibit corruptive practices within his department. It is also incumbent upon every citizen to report any indication of corruption to the police chief, the mayor, or his representative. Corruption cannot be tolerated and it is up to the professional police officers and the public to see that it is not allowed to occur.

It is believed that the new breed of police officers of today, better educated and more aware of their responsibilities in our democratic society, are making great strides in the true professionalization of police departments. The large cities are working toward removing corrupt officers from their ranks and new recruitment and selection standards are better screening out those so inclined from the service. This does not mean that corruption does not exist, but forward strides are being made.

[41] Pennsylvania Crime Commission, *Report on Police Corruption and the Quality of Law Enforcement in Philadelphia*, March, 1974, pp. 5–6.

Summary

There are two major categories of problems related to the
police. First, there are the basic problems of crime and traffic
congestion that make the existence of law enforcement
agencies necessary. Secondly, there are the multitude of
problems that hamper the police as they attempt to solve
the problems of the first category: fragmented police services,
politics, legal restrictions, ghetto disorders, the poor police
image, and many others.

The crime problem, which includes street crime, white
collar crime, and organized crime, is probably the major
problem confronting the police, and the police devote their
greatest energies to street crime, as it is the most visible
to them and to the public. The exact extent of street crime
is not known, but the most reliable statistics are those
published by the Federal Bureau of Investigation in their
uniform crime reports (UCR). Of great concern is the fact
that the rate of crime is increasing faster than the population.
Of further significance is the revelation in recent studies that
the amount of unreported crime is about twice that reported.

There are many varied direct and indirect effects of
crime, but the primary effects include injury to the victim,
hardships to the victim, economic cost, and fear. Perhaps the
most serious is injury to the victim. The probability of
becoming victim to a criminal attack in a given year is about
one in four hundred.

The traffic problem is also devastating. In 1976 there
were 46,700 deaths and 1,800,000 injuries. The economic loss
due to motor vehicle accidents totals more than 24.7 billion
dollars annually.

A serious problem that inhibits police efficiency is
fragmented police services. The duplication of law enforcement
services within most metropolitan areas tends to weaken the
entire law enforcement effort. The concept of consolidated

307

police service is based on the premise that future demands on the police will be so exacting that an entirely new approach to policing will be needed.

Involvement of police in politics or politics in police frequently breeds inefficiency. Such involvement must be kept to a minimum so that accepted administrative procedures can be utilized and professional policies established.

The police, of necessity, are restricted legally as to what they can or cannot do. These restrictions are based primarily on the First, Fourth, Fifth, Sixth, and Fourteenth Amendments to the Constitution of the United States. These amendments are important to the law enforcement officer because they set guidelines for his behavior in enforcing the law.

The police of today are faced with the problem of disorders within the cities and elsewhere. The police cannot control the things that cause a riot: poor housing, unemployment, segregation, etc., but it is often a police action that ignites the fuse.

The image of the police is not good today, and this alone creates a situation that contributes to disorder. Of course, the police image differs according to the perceiver. The poor black sees him in one light, while the wealthy white may have a completely different impression. Of importance is the fact that the police image must be improved if law enforcement is ever to enjoy a professional acceptance.

Police corruption is a problem, especially in the larger cities, but professionalization of the police service is minimizing and resolving the problem. It is incumbent upon those entering the police service to resolve that corrupt police activities will not be tolerated.

Discussion Questions

1. What are the two general categories of problems faced by law enforcement agencies? Define.
2. Discuss the scope and impact of street crime.
3. What is organized crime and what is its overall effect on society?
4. Discuss the traffic problem as it relates to police services.
5. What problems result from fragmented police services?
6. Is consolidation of police agencies feasible?
7. What is meant by police in politics and politics in police?
8. In what ways do legal restrictions benefit police efficiency?
9. Discuss police corruption—its causes and ramifications.
10. What must the police do to improve their poor image?

7

Law Enforcement
as a Career

There is probably no career with as much potential as that offered by law enforcement. The law enforcement officer serves his community, his fellow man, and gains great satisfaction from the accomplishment of his objectives: safeguarding lives and property and preservation of the public peace. Most people seek rewarding work, and there is nothing more rewarding than serving mankind. Not only does the police service offer this opportunity, but in recent years employment conditions have improved to the extent that police officers receive adequate remuneration for their efforts and dedication. In addition, each law enforcement officer has the opportunity to advance within his organization and to assume a position of leadership.

THE POLICE OFFICER

The police officer, representing the local, state, or federal government, is charged with securing compliance to the multitude of laws and regulations deemed beneficial to society. Since law is society's means of achieving conformance to desired norms, the police officer is society's agent for the maintenance of harmony within the community.

NATURE OF WORK

The hallmark of police officers is their capacity for effectively handling a large sphere of varied responsibilities.

The municipal police officer may wear a uniform and patrol a designated section of the city. On a typical day, this patrol officer may be called to a recent stabbing . . . a shooting in progress . . . a family quarrel . . . or on a complaint of a prowler. He will, of course, spend most of his time patrolling streets to insure that all laws are obeyed and to prevent crime. He will issue warnings or traffic citations to motorists

313

who violate the law. When necessary, he will make arrests and testify in court.

The patrol officer's typical day is one of great diversity, as he never knows from one minute to the next what kind of activity or situation he may be called upon to resolve. His day is often exciting and always rewarding. Of course, there are times when the patrol officer's job is rather routine. He must perform such routines as checking buildings for burglaries, directing traffic during heavy congestion, and checking peoples' homes when they are on vacation. Important, however, is the fact that at any moment a situation may arise, without warning, where the officer must respond with immediate and positive action.

Another important duty of the patrol officer is to assist people at the scene of an accident. He must give first aid to injured persons, summon ambulances and other emergency equipment, and direct traffic to avoid additional accidents. The patrol officer conducts investigations of traffic accidents and writes reports that include such information as weather conditions and causes of the accident. He must make damage estimates and execute drawings of the accident scene. This information, of course, may be used as legal evidence if someone is prosecuted for a violation of the law.

Another important duty of the municipal patrol officer is the provision of services to motorists on the highways or city streets. For example, he may assist travelers, help change a tire, radio for road service in case of mechanical trouble, direct tourists to their destinations, and provide information about lodging, restaurants, and tourist attractions.

The patrol officer also responds to the scene of crimes committed within his beat. He is usually the first to arrive at the scene of the burglary, robbery, or even the murder. He must secure and protect the crime scene, interview witnesses, and conduct the preliminary investigation so that the detective will have necessary information upon his arrival or when he picks the investigation up following the preliminary.

314

Additional duties of the patrol officer, to mention a few, include providing traffic assistance during road repair, helping at fires and during other emergencies. He is responsible for reporting hazardous road conditions to proper authorities. Patrol officers also provide assistance during special events such as parades, celebrations, and sporting events. The police officer often checks the weights of commercial vehicles and conducts driver examinations.

The police officer may be an investigator (detective) who does not wear a uniform, since he wants to appear inconspicuous as he works throughout the community. This man investigates crimes after they have been committed. He is involved in the determination as to whether a crime has been committed, the gathering of evidence to identify the perpetrator, the identification of the perpetrator, and the long search for locating the criminal. The detective also has to prepare his cases very carefully and meticulously so that evidence presented in court will support prosecution of the offender. His is a very exacting function, as careful preparation of evidence and testimony is imperative if justice is to be served within the courts.

The police officer may ride a motorcycle as he enforces traffic rules and regulations throughout the community. He will be responsible for minimizing the number of deaths and injuries that occur on the streets of his community. He will investigate traffic accidents and prepare cases for prosecution in court. Traffic officers are experienced and specially trained so they can quickly recognize traffic problems within the community and take necessary action for resolving them.

There are also behind-the-scene police officers very seldom seen by the general public. These men generally work at headquarters keeping records or updating information that is supplied by local reports and bulletins from other cities. A behind-the-scene officer may be a photographer, an identification expert, a computer technologist working in the planning and research division of his particular department, or a criminalist working in the crime laboratory. Such specialized

315

activities also include instruction of trainees in police schools and piloting police aircrafts.

There are also many federal agents who investigate violations of federal criminal and security statutes. For example, secret service agents within the United States Treasury Department are responsible for searching for and apprehending people responsible for counterfeiting money or federal documents. These same secret service agents may be assigned the task of protecting the President of the United States and his family. There are also federal officers with the Internal Revenue Department who are responsible for the enforcement of laws dealing with the illegal possession and distribution of narcotics. The federal officer may be an agent of the Federal Bureau of Investigation and responsible for the enforcement of many federal laws and regulations.

Regardless of his agency, the law enforcement officer has the duty of serving mankind, safeguarding lives and property, protecting the innocent against deception and the peaceful against disorder, and the general maintenance of law and order. The police are our first line of defense against subversive activities among those who wish to overthrow our government. In fact, if militant groups can abrogate the role of the police, they can make tremendous strides toward destroying our democratic way of life.

CAREER OPPORTUNITIES

A 1969 survey of 236 municipal police departments indicated a critical need for qualified law enforcement personnel in all areas of the country. It also illustrated that for qualified people who are seeking employment, the opportunities in law enforcement are almost unlimited. These 236 police agencies alone indicated that at that time they were 5,454 police officers short of what they were allowed by their municipal government. These 236 police departments indicated also that by 1975, they will need an additional 12,184 police officers.

Taking into consideration that municipal police departments are normally about 5 percent below authorized strength; that the authorized strength of police departments has increased at the rate of approximately 3 percent each year; that an average of 5.4 percent of existing personnel leave the departments each year; it is estimated that 50,000 new police officers will be needed each year in the United States. All this is to say that employment opportunities in law enforcement are excellent for qualified applicants. Of course, many applicants cannot meet the pre-entry requirements, thus the number of job applicants in many agencies exceeds the number of job openings.

It must be realized, however, that the competition for police positions has become considerably greater in the last two or three years. This is largely due to the economic situation and the unemployment rate. For example, many college graduates cannot find employment in that area for which they prepared themselves. Therefore, they are seeking those positions that are available, including police work, and causing a competitive situation for others who may be interested in the police profession. Having the opportunity to employ college graduates, even though their preparation is in another area, police officials are choosing them instead of noncollege people. Additionally, the unemployment situation has encouraged currently employed police officers to retain their positions. What the trend will be in the future cannot be foreseen; but currently the trend is towards increasing difficulty in obtaining a police position.

Following are agencies where opportunities exist for qualified applicants. Those interested in obtaining a law enforcement position should contact that agency with which they wish to obtain employment.

FEDERAL AGENCIES

Federal Bureau of Investigation. The Federal Bureau of Investigation is the primary investigative arm of the United States Department of Justice and, as such, its jurisdiction includes a wide range of responsibilities in the criminal, civil, and security fields. An additional responsibility is the correlation of information concerning the internal security of the United States and dissemination of such data to interested agencies in the Executive Branch of the Federal Government.

The FBI has the responsibility of investigating espionage, sabotage, treason, and other matters pertaining to the internal security of the United States. In criminal matters the FBI investigates violations of more than 170 Federal laws which, to name a few, include: kidnapping; extortion; bank robbery; crimes on Government or Indian reservations; thefts of Government property; the Fugitive Felon Act; interstate transportation of stolen motor vehicles, aircraft, cattle, or property; interstate transmission or transportation of wagering information, gambling devices or paraphernalia; election law violations; civil rights laws; and assaulting or killing the President or a Federal officer.

The FBI also administers the National Fingerprint Identification System which includes fingerprint records of thousands of known criminals and over six million other citizens. In essence, this is the national clearinghouse for fingerprint identification for the United States.

Another somewhat new, but extremely important, service performed by the FBI for all other terminalized law enforcement organizations in the United States is the National Crime Information Center (NCIC) where records of wanted persons and stolen property of nearly every sort, including securities, are data-banked. This information can be retrieved almost instantaneously at the request of any law enforcement official in even the most remote area of the nation. Many of the "hits" made on the system have been outstanding and would have probably not been made in the absence of NCIC.

Other responsibilities of the FBI include the compilation and publication of the Uniform Crime Report (UCR), the offering of crime laboratory services to law enforcement organizations, and the training of local police officers on an

318

in-field basis as well as through the National Academy.

Applicants for the position of Special Agent must possess the following qualifications:

1. They must be citizens of the United States.
2. They must be completely available for general and special assignment wherever and whenever their services are needed in any part of the United States or Puerto Rico.
3. Education and experience. Applicants must be:
    (a) Graduates from state-accredited resident law schools. Note: Graduates of law schools must have successfully completed at least two years of resident, undergraduate-level college work. A resident college is one requiring personal attendance.
    (b) Graduates from a resident four-year college with a major in accounting with at least one year of practical accounting and/or auditing experience.
    (c) Graduates from a resident four-year college with a major in a physical science for which the Bureau has a current need.
    (d) Graduates from a resident four-year college with a fluency in a language for which the Bureau has a current need.
    (e) Graduates from a resident four-year college and three years of professional, executive, complex investigative, or other specialized experience.
4. Age: They must have reached their twenty-third but not their thirty-sixth birthday on the date that the application is filed.
5. Physical ability:
    (a) Height—Must be at least 5′7 without shoes.
    (b) All applicants for the Agent position must have uncorrected vision of not less than 20/200 (Snellen) in each eye without glasses and at least 20/20 (Snellen) in each eye corrected. No applicant can be considered who has been found to be color blind.
    (c) Hearing—No applicant will be accepted if found by audiometer test to have a hearing loss exceeding a 15 decibel average in either ear in the conversational speech range (500, 1000, 2000 cycles).

All applicants must be in excellent physical condition and can have no defects which would interfere with their use of firearms or with their participation in raids, dangerous assignments, or defensive tactics. An applicant's physical and visual condition will be ascertained through a rigid physical examination conducted at a Government examining facility.

6. All applicants must have a valid license to drive an automobile.

The FBI reserves the right to waive a qualification not bearing on character and integrity when found necessary to obtain an employee with demonstrated ability in some particular skill that is unique or unusual, and for which a need exists.

Applicants who meet the basic requirements are afforded a detailed interview as well as written examinations. Any necessary travel expense incident to these tests must be borne by the applicant, and at no time should it be assumed that an appointment will be made because the opportunity for examination is offered. Prior to any appointment being made, applicants possessing the basic qualifications and who have successfully passed the necessary examinations are thoroughly investigated for the purpose of securing additional evidence of their qualifications and fitness for the position. Appointments are made on a very selective basis due to the limited number of vacancies occurring in this position.

Immigration and Naturalization Service. This organization was created in 1891, and transferred to the Department of Justice in 1940. The Immigration and Naturalization Service administers the immigration and naturalization laws related to the admission, exclusion, and deportation of aliens. They also are concerned with naturalization of aliens lawfully present in the United States. The organization investigates violations of those laws and makes recommendations for prosecution when it seems advisable. In addition, the Immigration and Naturalization Service patrols the borders of the United States through its border patrol in order to prevent the illegal entry of aliens into the United States.

320

Drug Enforcement Administration. The Drug Enforcement Administration was created on July 1, 1973, by congressional approval of a presidential reorganization plan. Prior to the establishment of DEA, the government's effort to combat the abuse of narcotics and dangerous drugs had been fragmented with several federal agencies independently pursuing courses of action.

To provide a unified leadership for a concentrated all-out global attack on narcotics trafficking and drug abuse, the presidential reorganizational plan merged under DEA, the Bureau of Narcotics and Dangerous Drugs, the Office for Drug Abuse Law Enforcement, the Office of National Narcotics Intelligence, the Drug Investigative Unit and Intelligence Units of the Bureau of Customs, and the Drug Enforcement Sections of the Office of Science and Technology.

In the field of drug law enforcement, principal emphasis is placed on the source and distribution of illicit drugs rather than on the arrest of drug abusers. The DEA's basic emphasis in enforcement of the law has been in stopping the flow of drugs at the foreign sources, disrupting the illicit and domestic commerce at the most organized level, and assisting state and local police to prevent illegal drugs from reaching the community level.

The DEA is also charged with full investigation and preparation for prosecution of suspected violators of federal drug laws and conducts relations with law enforcement officials of foreign governments, under the policy guidance of the Cabinet Committee on International Narcotics Control.

To perform its mission the DEA has stationed highly trained agents in all the major cities throughout the United States and in 45 offices in 31 countries throughout the world.

The objectives of DEA agents are to reach the highest possible source of supply and to seize illicit drugs before they reach the abuser. They achieve this goal by employing the most advanced enforcement techniques and by using modern technology and equipment.

The Drug Enforcement Administration is also responsible for regulation of the legal manufacture of drugs and other

321

controlled substances under the Controlled Substances Act of 1970.

Under this act DEA is required to establish import, export, and manufacturing quotas of various controlled drugs. Physicians, pharmacists, and other persons handling, dispensing, or prescribing controlled drugs are subject to periodic inspections by DEA representatives. These controls assure an adequate legal supply of drugs, medicine, and research needs and at the same time prevent diversion of drugs to illegal traffic.

Intelligence is also an essential element in the success in any law enforcement agency. DEA has an office of intelligence staffed by experienced criminal investigators and intelligence analysts. Each DEA regional office in the United States and in foreign countries has a regional intelligence unit. All information concerning narcotics and dangerous drugs, trafficking organizations and individuals is furnished to the office of intelligence where it is collated, analyzed, and disseminated in the form of a finished intelligence product.

The information provides the Office of Enforcement with actionable intelligence which enables them to attack the traffic in a systematic way by selecting areas of vulnerability. It also provides the administrator and other U.S. governmental agencies with strategic intelligence information for policy determination, deployment of resources, and development of an overall strategy. Intelligence on shifts in the traffic and types of drugs abused and the effectiveness of foreign and domestic programs are all a part of this intelligence process.

DEA agents also offer assistance to state and local police through task forces in metropolitan enforcement groups. The task forces are designed to concentrate enforcement efforts on drug trafficking organizations or individuals operating in a specific region. The metropolitan enforcement groups merge the efforts of various local police in planning, intelligence, and enforcement in a designated area.

U.S. Bureau of Customs. The U.S. Bureau of Customs, created in 1927, is primarily responsible for the assessment and the collection of duties and taxes on imported merchandise, the control of carriers and merchandise imported into or exported from the United States, and the prevention of smuggling and frauds on the revenue process. The U.S. Bureau of Customs cooperates closely with other federal agencies, since these agencies may have responsibilities related to the smuggling of materials either taken from or brought into the United States. Customs officials also work very closely with local law enforcement agencies in an attempt to eliminate or minimize the smuggling into the United States and various communities of such things as drugs and other contraband.

U.S. Secret Service. On July 5, 1865, the Secret Service was created as a bureau of the Department of the Treasury in order to suppress counterfeiting. It was the first general law enforcement agency of the federal government. Within less than a decade, counterfeiting was substantially reduced as a result of the work of this agency.

In addition to the suppression of counterfeiting, the Secret Service was often requested to complete assignments and conduct investigations later assigned to other governmental agencies. These included the Teapot Dome oil scandals, the Ku Klux Klan, government land frauds, and counter-espionage activity during the Spanish-American War and World War I.

After the assassination of President McKinley in Buffalo, New York in 1901 the Secret Service was assigned to protect President Theodore Roosevelt. However, legislation authorizing the President's protection by the Secret Service was not enacted by Congress until 1906. Secret Service protective responsibilities have expanded to be even greater since then.

Legislation expanding Secret Service responsibilities was signed by President Richard M. Nixon on March 19, 1970, establishing the Executive Protective Service. This increased responsibilities and the size of the former White House Police. Executive Protective Service, under supervision of the Secret Service, continues to protect the White House and it now provides security for diplomatic missions in the metropolitan area of the District of Columbia.

The specific duties of the Secret Service are to protect the

Secret Service Agent comparing forged signatures on stolen U.S. Savings Bonds

Courtesy of the U.S. Secret Service

President of the United States and members of his immediate family, the president-elect, the former president and his wife during his lifetime, the widow of a former president until her death or remarriage, minor children of a former president until they reach 16 years of age, the vice-president, and major presidential and vice-presidential candidates.

They are also responsible to detect and arrest offenders for counterfeiting the coins, the currency, stamps and other obligations and securities of the United States. They are required to suppress the forgery and fraudulent negotiation or redemption of governmental checks, bonds, and other obligations or securities of the United States. The Secret Service must also conduct investigations relating to certain criminal violations of the Gold Reserve Act of 1934, the Federal Deposit Insurance Act, the Federal Land Grant Act, the Home Owner's Loan Act, and Governmental Losses in Shipment Act.

Requirements for entrance into the Secret Service are: 1) a bachelor's degree, or 2) three years of experience, at least two of which are in criminal investigation, or 3) a comparable combination of experience and education. College-level study in any major field is acceptable, but courses in police science, criminology, and law enforcement are desirable. Applicants must also be 21 years of age, be in excellent physical condition, pass a comprehensive medical examination, possess distant vision without correction and must test at least 20/20 in one eye and no less than 20/30 in the other. Weight must be in proportion to height.

Bureau of Alcohol, Tobacco, and Firearms. The Bureau of Alcohol, Tobacco and Firearms is a federal bureau which combines law enforcement, industry regulation, and tax collection.

Special agents trained in criminal investigation form the backbone of the ATF Office of Criminal Enforcement. Through the years, many agents have died in the line of duty and many have been cited for heroism.

The Gun Control Act of 1968 and other federal firearms laws are enforced by ATF. Agents investigate violations of these laws to assure that guns do not enter illegal channels. Keeping firearms from the hands of criminals is an important task of ATF.

Special agents track down and destroy illicit distilleries. Although "moonshining" has diminished, the problem remains, especially in the southeastern United States.

The Federal Explosives Act of 1970 gave ATF jurisdiction over many types of bomb cases. ATF agents are trained to gather bomb scene evidence, which has resulted in the arrest of many bombers and arsonists. ATF will also assist any state and local law enforcement agency upon request. This free assistance ranges from joint criminal investigations to

325

training classes concerning firearms, explosives, and police methods.

ATF agents are also assigned to organized crime strike forces which operate in major cities throughout the nation. These agents investigate activities of racketeers and mobsters to uncover violations of the federal laws relating to firearms, liquor, and explosives.

The Bureau of Alcohol, Tobacco and Firearms regulates the alcohol, tobacco, firearms, and explosives industry. A major part of this regulatory effort is to ensure the collection of federal taxes on distilled spirits, beer, wine, and tobacco products. This is done so efficiently that ATF spends only $2.32 to collect each $1000 in taxes.

Inspectors stationed at many distilled spirits plants determine the taxes to be paid. Other inspectors make periodic checks of breweries, wineries, and tobacco manufacturing plants. Consumer protection programs concern advertising, packaging, correct fill, and the approval of formulas for alcoholic beverages. These programs are designed to assure that the consumer receives what he pays for and that the alcoholic beverages he drinks do not contain harmful ingredients.

ATF inspectors investigate unlawful trade practices which could lead to anticompetitive situations. They also assure that organized crime does not infiltrate the alcoholic beverage industry.

A main responsibility of ATF is to render assistance to local law enforcement agencies throughout the United States. In conjunction with this, ATF provides free technical and scientific assistance to requesting local agencies.

ATF is a central agency for all gun tracing, and approximately half of all ATF gun traces are for local law enforcement agencies. Records kept by manufacturers and dealers are valuable to the ATF tracer who tracks the gun from manufacturer to the first retail purchaser. ATF responds to all requests for criminal laboratory work; ATF lab scientists were pioneers in many forensic techniques—ink analysis, atomic absorption and neutron activation analysis to detect gunshot residue, and other important evidence.

326

Narcotics investigations account for a large part of the NIS caseload. They led to seizures by the NIS of nearly $700,000 worth of illicit drugs in 1973, and there are indications that the figure may well be exceeded this year.

The NIS serves the Navy on many fronts. As part of the investigatory process, it serves as a liaison point between the Navy and all federal law enforcement agencies, as well as state and local police departments and foreign agencies. NIS agents are also busy giving ships crews anti-drug presentations and port security briefs on what to expect from foreign intelligence activities overseas and how to avoid giving out sensitive information.

Becoming an NIS agent is no simple matter. Basic qualifications for employment as a special agent of the Naval Investigative Service are that an applicant be a U.S. citizen of unquestioned character, reputation and judgment, in excellent physical condition, between the ages of 21 and 35, with a baccalaureate degree from an accredited college. Additionally, an applicant must have the ability to communicate effectively both orally and in writing and must be willing to transfer as required.

Air Force Office of Special Investigations. The Air Force Office of Special Investigations (AFOSI), headquartered at the Forrestal Building in Washington, D.C., is a centrally directed organization controlling some 1900 AFOSI people stationed throughout the world. Recent tabulations show that slightly less than 55 percent of AFOSI special agents are enlisted men and women, slightly more than 40 percent officers, and about 5 percent civilians. In addition, there are more than 750 support personnel assigned to AFOSI. Organized into some 172 districts, detachments, and operating locations, the separate operating agency is celebrating more than 25 years of continuous service.

Initially, AFOSI was patterned after the Federal Bureau of Investigation from whose ranks came the first two directors.

Upon request, AFOSI provides professional investigative

329

services to commanders of all Air Force activities under the criminal, fraud, and counterintelligence areas. It should be noted that AFOSI, in its various directorates, functions only as a fact-finding agency. The requesting authority always determines the appropriate action to be taken.

The Criminal Directorate investigates criminal offenses committed against the Air Force and against Air Force personnel or their property. Jurisdiction is generally limited to crimes committed on Air Force installations by people subject to the uniform code of military justice. These offenses range from housebreaking to homicide. To aid in the criminal fact-finding process, AFOSI also directs the Air Force polygraph program which recruits, trains and oversees polygraph examiner activities throughout the Air Force.

In addition, the Criminal Directorate operates the Air Force terminal of the FBI National Crime Information Center. This directorate controls the criminal intelligence collections program geared to keep Air Force commanders appraised of patterns or trends in criminal activity.

The Fraud Directorate investigates criminal activity; violations of public trust involving Air Force procurement, disposal, nonappropriated fund activity; and other serious administrative irregularities.

Through this directorate, AFOSI serves as the executive agency responsible for coordinating all investigations made within the Army and Air Force exchange service.

The Directorate of Special Operations is primarily concerned with countering the threat to Air Force security posed by foreign intelligence services. To accomplish this, special operations directs offensive and defensive activities to detect, neutralize, and destroy the effectiveness of foreign intelligence agencies which target the Air Force. This includes investigating espionage, sabotage, treason, sedition, terrorism, and other major security violations.

The protection of senior Air Force and other U.S. Government officials is also under the jurisdiction of the Special Operations Directorate. In addition, the directorate supervises the collection, analysis, and dissemination of information on subversive activities affecting the security and discipline of Air Force commands.

Because of its peacemaking role in the United States and the free world, the U.S. Air Force is the primary target of foreign and domestic subversion. AFOSI is the primary means the Air Force has to counter these espionage and subversive efforts. Also, while the overall Air Force crime rate is low, some Air Force members do violate the laws. When violations occur involving Air Force personnel, their property, or crimes against the Air Force, AFOSI provides a rapid, efficient, and professional investigative service. These results are turned over to the appropriate commander, enabling him to take the appropriate action.

Military Police Units. Uniformed patrol duty in the military services is accomplished by the Military Police of the Army, by the Shore Patrol of the Navy, and by the Security Police of the Air Force. Generally speaking, the activities and services of these police units are similar to those performed by municipal police officers throughout the United States. The difference is that they enforce the law as dictated by the rules and regulations of the military service. In addition, they are only concerned with those rules, regulations, and laws that are violated by people upon a military reservation.

The police of these military units are military enlistment personnel and officers. Civilians do not serve in any capacity among the uniformed police units.

The Security Police of the Air Force and Military Police of the Army have special requirements that enlisted personnel must meet before they can don the special uniform of a Military Policeman or a Security Police Officer. Generally speaking, these requirements are that the person entering the military service must meet all the requirements of the service as well as show an aptitude for police work. The military operational officers typically attempt to get high quality personnel to serve as Military and Security Police Officers. Applicants for this assignment must pass the entrance examination with a score sufficiently high to justify their serving in that

Military police officer executing traffic stop

Courtesy of U.S. Army: U.S. Army Photograph

particular capacity. In addition, there are usually physical requirements that the applicant must meet along with the general requirements for admission into the Armed Services.

STATE AGENCIES

There are numerous opportunities at the state level for persons interested in the field of law enforcement. The major opportunity is with state highway patrols and state police agencies. Normally the state police will be primarily concerned with the enforcement of traffic regulations upon the

forcement, criminology, or criminal justice. Some police agencies pay or reimburse officers' tuition costs of the courses, and many police agencies pay an additional salary to those persons obtaining a higher education.

Police officer recruits usually serve a probationary period ranging from six months to two years, and occasionally three years. After a specified period of time, police officers then become eligible for promotion. Most states have merit promotional systems that require officers to pass a competitive examination in order to qualify for the next highest rank. The typical avenue of advancement is from patrolman to sergeant, to lieutenant, to captain, to inspector, and to chief of police.

A new trend that is becoming quite common to police agencies throughout the country is establishment of a cadet program. The cadet program usually allows the employment of eighteen-year-olds in noncritical areas until they reach age twenty-one, when they become regular police officers. While cadets, they usually attend classes to learn various aspects of police work. They are also assigned clerical, communications, and other nonenforcement duties.

SELECTION PROCESS

The process for selecting police recruits varies considerably among law enforcement agencies as do the minimum prerequisites. Generally, however, the procedure is long and tedious. Depending on the agency, it may involve all or just a few of the following steps:

1. Application
2. Meeting prerequisite requirements
3. Fingerprinting
4. Written examination
5. Medical examination
6. Physical agility test
7. Psychiatric examination
8. Lie-detector test

337

9. Oral interview
10. Background investigation
11. Training
12. Probation

The order of these steps also will vary among law enforcement agencies. Generally, however, the procedures that eliminate the largest number of applicants and are the least expensive to conduct are utilized early in the process. This is quite important administratively, as larger departments must process several hundred, or even thousands, applications each year.

Police departments that recruit from throughout the United States frequently have developed a procedure for processing the applicant, with the exception of the background investigation, within one week. In this way, applicants who reside some distance from the department will not have to make several trips in order to finish the process. Usually, however, it takes much longer to complete the entire selection process.

Because of the time involved in selection, some departments allow people to file an application prior to reaching the minimum required age. For example, a nineteen-year-old may be allowed to apply even though the minimum required age for service is twenty-one. The department may actually complete the selection process and place the applicant on the eligibility list and appoint him to the department on his twenty-first birthday.

As stated previously, procedures and requirements vary considerably among law enforcement agencies. It is suggested, therefore, that police aspirants correspond directly with agencies in which they are interested.

APPLICATION

The first step to be taken by the police aspirant is the filing of an application. The application usually can be obtained by mail, although some agencies require that it be picked up in person. The requirement that it be picked up is often utilized so that the personnel office can determine the possession of prerequisite requirements before giving the application. Normally, however, information on the application is used for this determination.

There are many purposes for the application, but paramount is to obtain information that will identify qualifications for the job, information that may be used during the oral interview, and information that will assist investigators in the background investigation. The completed application also tells the reviewers something of the applicant's ability to follow instructions.

The way an application is completed may provide some insight relative to the applicant. A neat and accurate application gives the impression of a conscientious person, while a sloppy application gives the impression of a person not really interested in the job. Whether these assumptions are correct is unimportant. What is important is that conclusions are drawn from the application that make it imperative for the applicant to carefully and accurately complete the form. It is suggested that the applicant make a working copy of the application and then transfer the information to the official form.

DETERMINATION OF MINIMUM STANDARDS

The possession of these requirements can, for the most part, be determined from information on the application form. Normally, the applicant will be asked to report to the personnel office, police department, or some other designated place where he is weighed, his height is measured, and he is asked to read an eye chart. As previously stated, this also may be done when the applicant picks up the application form or turns it in.

This usually is considered a preliminary check, and the results are verified when the applicant takes the medical examination. If, however, the applicant fails to meet the minimum standards on the first check, he will be eliminated from further consideration.

FINGERPRINTING

All law enforcement agencies require that the applicant be fingerprinted so that his record can be checked. The applicant is usually fingerprinted early in the selection process, and his prints are sent to the Federal Bureau of Investigation for processing through their records. This procedure places the applicant's prints in permanent files of the FBI for future reference.

WRITTEN EXAMINATION

The written examination usually is designed to measure aptitude and general intelligence rather than prior knowledge of practices and procedures on the job. The assumption is that a person with the necessary intelligence can learn the skills, techniques, and procedures of the job. The test also is constructed on the assumption that the applicant has a minimum of a high school education and no police experience. The applicant should expect, for example, questions concerning spelling, reading, quantitative ability, word association, definitions, and general aptitude. Entrance examinations used throughout the United States are so varied that it is virtually impossible to state specific subjects that will be covered.

The written examinations of most law enforcement agencies are rather comprehensive, and the failure rate is rather high. Actually, however, any person with a sound high school education should be able to perform adequately on examinations given by most law enforcement agencies. Of course, the present trend is to recruit people with college experience and, concurrent with this, the entrance examination will be constructed with such people in mind. Most federal agencies require a college degree, and their examinations reflect this requirement. Most departments also allow applicants who fail the examination the privilege of taking it over after the lapse of a specified amount of time.

MEDICAL EXAMINATION

It is obvious, due to the nature of police work, that applicants must be in good health. A law enforcement officer who is not medically fit may lose his own life or be responsible for the death of someone else.

Good health usually is verified by an examination by a physician. Some departments specify the examining doctor while others will accept a medical report from the applicant's family physician. The medical examination usually is quite comprehensive, and it is suggested that a person with a disabling medical deficiency not seek employment as a law enforcement officer. The work is physically demanding, and only the medically fit can withstand the demands of the job.

PHYSICAL AGILITY

Many tasks and activities of the law enforcement job depend on the officer's physical strength, coordination, agility, and endurance. These qualities cannot be measured in the written examination and, therefore, a physical agility test is imperative. Unfortunately, many departments do not require this particular test.

This test is designed to measure coordination, agility, and endurance rather than just brute strength. Typical components of the test are pull-ups, hurdles, sit-ups, standing broad jump, and running. As with all selection tests, the components and minimum standards of the physical agility test vary considerably among law enforcement agencies.

341

PSYCHIATRIC EXAMINATION

A recent trend in the selection process is the psychiatric examination. This examination is used to identify those applicants who are psychologically unsuited for the role of a law enforcement officer. The psychiatrist is looking for such things as emotional immaturity, sexual abnormalities, and deviate behavior patterns.

This examination is a very important part of the selection process, as it helps eliminate from the police service misfits, whose employment often creates very serious consequences. The examination also is beneficial to applicants deemed unsuitable for law enforcement work: they can direct their efforts toward other professions without wasting time on a job at which they can't be successful.

LIE DETECTOR TEST

Like the psychiatric, physical agility, and medical examinations, the lie detector test results are not given weight in determining the applicant's final overall score. Rather, the test is another qualifying element of the selection process. This test either eliminates the candidate or permits him to finish the selection process.

Many states prohibit the use of the lie detector as part of the selection process. In those states where it is not prohibited, only a few departments use it, which is probably due primarily to the cost and time involved.

The lie detector normally is used to determine the validity of facts recorded on the application and as an aid in the background investigation. Frequently, it is found that the candidate has concealed information that would have eliminated him from further consideration.

ORAL INTERVIEW

If properly administered, the oral interview can be one of the most effective means of determining a candidate's suitability for law enforcement work. The oral interview is designed to evaluate the applicant's work experience, attitudes, career aspirations, personal appearance, ability to express himself, and other personal traits.

The composition of the interview board differs, but usually consists of from three to five people. Many departments include a patrolman on the board along with higher ranking police officers. It also is quite common for the board to include a person unconnected with the police service. This person might be the personnel director of a local company or someone representing a citizen's group.

The oral interview results in a score that influences the candidate's overall rating. The influence of this score on the total evaluation does differ among law enforcement agencies. Some agencies give it heavy emphasis, while others make it a small portion of the overall score.

The nature of the oral interview will vary according to the individuals sitting on the board. Typically, the applicant can expect the interview to be either extremely formal or informal.

The formal interview is designed to place the applicant under some stress in order to see how she or he performs in an uncomfortable atmosphere. With this type interview the applicant may be left standing, board members from the police department will be in uniform, and they will act in a very official manner. They may ask questions that they know are impossible or extremely difficult to answer. The philosophy behind this type interview is that officers frequently have to function under stress and the formal interview will help determine the applicant's ability to do so.

The informal interview, as implied by the term, is conducted in a relaxed atmosphere. The applicant is met cordially, asked to sit down, and the initial questions are designed to put him or her at ease. Stress is not a factor and the interviewers are primarily interested in the applicant's interest, demeanor, and ability to express himself.

The oral interview is a critical stage for the applicant, as it is usually one of the last selection criteria to be used. In

343

addition, it is usually the first time the applicant has met any person connected with the decision relative to his or her employment. It is imperative, therefore, that the applicant be appropriately prepared.

The initial contact is the critical stage of the interview and, in fact, the first few seconds will probably heavily influence the outcome. First impressions are lasting ones and it is, therefore, important that the applicant be dressed appropriately. Police officers wear uniforms because the uniform gives a neat appearance. Realizing the importance police administrators place on appearance, the applicant should be clean, neat, and conservatively dressed. The male applicant should have a recent haircut that reflects the hair code of the police department. He should be clean-shaven, wear a suit and tie, and be sure his shoes are shined. The female applicant should set her hair in a conservative manner, wear a dress, hose, and fashionable shoes. Admittedly fashionable pant suits are appropriate in today's world, but the wearing of a dress may be that added ingredient that causes the board to decide in the applicant's favor. In addition, some of the officers on the Board will be older and police by nature are conservative.

When questions are asked, the applicant should respond in a positive way and keep the answers as brief as possible. Answers should be complete, but undue elaboration or discussion of irrelevant information will result in a low score. When answering a question, the applicant should look directly at the person who asked it while periodically scanning the rest of the Board members. If the applicant does not know the answer he or she should say so. Attempting to bluff one's way through will not work with police officers. It is important that the applicant answer all questions honestly and in a confident manner.

Some typical questions that will help prepare the applicant are:

1. Will you please briefly tell us about yourself and explain why you are interested in becoming a police officer?

344

2. Why are you specifically interested in this police department?

3. Do you use drugs? Have you ever experimented with drugs? Do you believe certain drugs should be decriminalized?

4. Do you drink and, if so, to what extent?

5. What do you think is the role of a police officer?

6. Are you prejudiced in any way?

7. What do you think is the biggest problem facing law enforcement today?

8. Do you mind wearing a uniform?

9. Do you object to working weekends, holidays, and swing shifts?

10. What does your spouse think of you becoming a police officer?

11. What are your feelings about the use of deadly force if it becomes necessary in the performance of official duties?

12. Under what circumstances is deadly force justified?

13. Do you believe in capital punishment? Why or why not?

These are but a few of the questions that may be asked and the applicant's responses will frequently cause clarification questions. That is why it is recommended that the applicant answer the questions completely but briefly.

In conclusion, the applicant should demonstrate honesty, moral integrity, sincere interest in law enforcement as a career, interest in the department he or she is being interviewed by, high professional standards, intelligence, confidence, and the pride he or she would have as a member of the police department.

BACKGROUND INVESTIGATION

The background investigation is another indispensable part of the selection process. There may be undesirable personal characteristics possessed by the candidate that will not be revealed by testing, but will be discovered during the background investigation. This part of the selection process is so important that many law enforcement agencies have a special unit devoting full time to this function.

The background investigation usually includes a check of the applicant's military records, high school records, references, past and present employee records, and police records from his home city. The investigators will also interview the candidate's friends, neighbors, employers, colleagues with whom he worked, distant acquaintances, teachers, relatives, and landlords. Many law enforcement agencies also have the investigator interview the candidate's spouse. It is recognized that a police officer's home situation will either adversely or favorably affect his work. A wife or husband opposed to her or his spouse going into police work would certainly place the candidate's likelihood of employment in serious doubt.

TRAINING

Training is usually considered part of the selection process, as officer trainees may not become sworn officers until they have graduated. Training is highly disciplined, and the academic and physical requirements are set quite high. It is reasonable to expect some police trainees to either drop out during training or fail to meet minimum physical or academic standards. Some also are not able to "stand up" under the strict discipline and stress of the training program. In reality, however, if the selection process is effective, few people will fail the training.

The extent and type of training varies considerably among law enforcement agencies. The length of such a training program, for example, will vary from one or two weeks to as long as six months. Regardless of the length, however, the purpose of training is to provide the trainee with the knowledge and skills necessary to perform the police function. The curriculum will include such subjects as firearms, criminal code, traffic code, laws of arrest, search and seizure, public relations, defensive tactics, patrol techniques, interpersonal relations, departmental rules and regulations, etc.

346

PROBATION

Most law enforcement agencies employ a probationary period for their new officers that generally runs from three months to one year. Basically, this means that an officer's first few months of employment are still part of the selection process. If, during this time, the "rookie" fails to meet minimum standards, he is released from the service.

This provides the department an opportunity to observe the new officer as he functions under actual working conditions. It may very well be that the officer cannot apply what he has learned in the classroom and, in spite of the previous selection steps, he is not suitable for the job. The rookie's relations with colleagues, his ability to follow instruction, his rapport with citizens, and his reaction under stress all can be observed.

During the probation period the new officer is periodically evaluated by his supervisors. Evaluations are discussed with the new officer, and then placed in his personal file. At the termination of the probation period, all evaluations are reviewed, and the man either becomes a tenured officer or is released from the service. Of course, the recruit may be released also at any time during the probationary period.

Completion of probation is the last phase of the selection process which may have begun a couple years earlier. Selection is a long process, but if properly constituted it does result in better police officers and better police service.

EARNINGS AND WORKING CONDITIONS

In recent years there has been a significant increase in the remuneration received by police officers throughout the United States. Salaries are increasing to the point that many law enforcement agencies now offer a salary that is quite competitive with other employers demanding similar qualifications. In addition, police officers usually receive a regular

347

salary increase based on experience and performance, until a specified maximum is reached. Their earnings may also increase above these levels as they are promoted to a higher rank, such as sergeant or lieutenant.

Many police agencies provide officers with uniforms, firearms, and other necessary equipment, or furnish special allowances for their purchase.

In almost all police agencies, the scheduled work week is forty hours. Police protection must be provided around the clock and, therefore, some officers are on duty over the weekends, on holidays, and at night. Of course, police officers are subject to emergency calls at any time.

Most police officers are covered by rather liberal pension plans and are able to retire at a relatively young age. Paid vacations; sick leave; and medical, surgical, and life insurance plans are frequently provided.

The work of police officers is sometimes hazardous. There is always the risk of an automobile accident during pursuit of a speeding motorist or a fleeing criminal. When controlling riots and apprehending criminals, a police officer faces the risk of bodily harm. However, the risks involved in police work are not as great as most people think. For one thing, police officers are highly trained so they are capable of handling emergency and hazardous situations. For example, the risk of a traffic accident in a high speed chase is drastically minimized because police officers have been well trained to cope with such situations. In a gun battle, the police officer is usually the better shot. Police officers are also trained in protecting themselves so that the risk of bodily harm in forceable arrest is also minimized. In fact, it is suggested that the accident rate among police officers is less than that of many other occupations.

FEMALE POLICE OFFICERS

Today's police administrators have availed themselves and their departments of many of the advantages that have automatically come with advancement toward professional status: improved salary plans, reduced work weeks, educational and training programs, and modern equipment. However, many police officials have failed to recognize the tremendous advantages of employing female officers.

Whether this failure is due to stratified thinking, lack of knowledge, or the determination to jealously guard the field of law enforcement from encroachment by females is relatively unimportant. What is important is that whatever the reason, as long as members of the police service fail to acknowledge the urgent need for female officers in their individual departments, the effectiveness and efficiency of their operations will be hampered.

To those who continue to resist the idea of women in police work, it should be pointed out that as early as 1888 New York City appointed its first full-time police matron.

Endorsements and statistics would reveal the worldwide success of the utilization of female officers. However, there are police officials, especially at the municipal level, who are reluctant to consider its merits, claiming that funds are meager, the department is extremely small, introduction of new programs of this kind would become the concern of the entire community. While these administrators have used these as excuses, the fact is that these should be some of the very reasons for instituting such a program.[1]

Recent developments in the United States have created greater opportunities for women interested in law enforcement as a career. Federal law and guidelines are quite clear; since 1972 every police department in the United States has been in the position of having to hire and assign women on an equal basis with men. No longer can police administrators discriminate in their hiring and assignment policies relative to women.

At one time women were assigned exclusively to such activities as public relations, radio dispatching, parking meter

---

[1] Felicia Shpritzer, "A Case for the Promotion of Police Women in the City of New York." *Police*, July–August, 1961, p. 57.

control, or work in the juvenile bureau. Now, however, more and more women are found serving in all areas of the police organization.

For example, it is not now uncommon to find women performing the patrol function that was once exclusively the domain of the male police officer. In essence, women now have every opportunity for positions formerly available only to policemen. Women can compete on the same basis with men for promotion to higher ranks within the police organization. In some cities women are now assigned as patrol sergeants, detective sergeants, and in some instances even higher ranks. It is quite obvious that this will have an impact upon policing in the United States. Certainly, we will see highly qualified women assuming greater roles of leadership within police organizations.

As in the case of men, the work of a female officer can be quite varied and very challenging. She may be assigned to patrol, the investigation division, or become involved in a specialized area. The female officer is also very valuable in conducting undercover investigations, as there are certain situations where only she can fit. For example, women often are used as decoys in apprehending purse snatchers and sex violators. Other assignments might include accompanying a male officer on stakeouts, participating in raids so that she can handle female prisoners, and certain kinds of public relations work. It must be remembered that female officers no longer serve only in the role of meter maids. The female officer is a professional police officer and has the same pay and benefits as her male counterparts.

There are many opportunities for qualified women in federal and state law enforcement as well. For example, the Federal Bureau of Investigation now employs women agents. So do the other federal agencies, since they are governed by the same laws that demand the eradication of discrimination in employment practices of local and federal agencies.

In today's complex world, it is imperative that more police departments seek and employ women police officers. Not only is it mandatory by law, but police administrators should recognize that certain tasks can be better performed by women, and that certain circumstances justify the presence of a woman rather than a man.

Many police administrators in the United States have questioned whether or not a woman can perform the normal police function as effectively and efficiently as a man. Numerous studies have been conducted on a formal and informal basis relative to this question. In all instances, the general findings indicate that women perform as well as, if not better than, men in some situations.

A seven-month study, financed by the Law Enforcement Assistance Administration (LEAA), studied 82 New York police officers of which half were women. The study revealed that the women generally performed as well as men in police patrol activities. The performance of women officers was found to be more like that of men officers than it was different, although the women made a better impression on the public.

Other findings of the study were as follows:

1. Citizens who encountered the female officers said they were more competent, pleasant, and respectful than the men.
2. Women officers were less likely than men to join male partners in taking control of a situation or jointly making a decision. However, when the women were with other women, they were more active, assertive, and self-sufficient.
3. Skepticism by male officers may partly explain female officers' reluctance to take control when with a male.
4. In the few incidents judged to present danger, men and women were equally likely to engage in efforts to gain control.
5. Women took more sick leave than men.

The report principally attributed the small differences to socially conditioned attitudes; that is, protectiveness or disdain by men and passivity by women.

The results of this research project offer little support either to those who hold that women are unsuited to patrol or to those who argue that women do the job better than men.

351

Because of the mandatory hiring of women, there is a whole field of service available to women who are interested in law enforcement as a career. It would seem that any woman who possesses the necessary qualifications should find little difficulty in locating employment with a municipal, state, or federal agency.

CORRECTIONAL OPPORTUNITIES

There are many varied opportunities in the correctional area and due to continual development new positions are being identified constantly. Because of the vast numbers of job titles it is best to divide the various occupations into four major correctional functions: 1) custodial personnel and group supervisors, 2) case managers, 3) specialists, and 4) technicians.

The first category, *custodial personnel*, consists of group supervisors, guards, and other institutional personnel concerned generally with the custody and care of offenders in group settings. The second category, *case managers*, consists of those persons responsible for assembling information about individual offenders, developing specific treatment programs, and supervising probationers and parolees in the community. The third category consists of *specialists*: academic and vocational teachers and therapists who work in correctional programs. The last category, *technicians*, consists of a diverse group of technical and service personnel.

CUSTODIAL PERSONNEL AND GROUP SUPERVISORS

This category of employees comprises over half of the total correctional manpower. It includes those who are variously designated as prison guards or correctional officers in adult institutions and those who are called cottage parents or group supervisors in juvenile institutions. In adult institutions, these are the guards who man the walls, supervise living units,

352

escort inmates to and from work, and supervise all group movement within an institution. In juvenile institutions, they provide the bulk of hour-by-hour supervision for youngsters.

These personnel are of critical importance, not only because of the tasks they perform directly but also because their contribution makes it possible for other programs to operate. In fact, they may be the most important persons in institutions simply by virtue of their numbers and their daily intimate contact with offenders. It is a mistake to define them as persons responsible just for control and maintenance, as they can, by their attitude, reinforce or destroy the effectiveness of almost any correctional program. They can act as effective intermediaries or become insurmountable barriers between the inmates' world and the institution's treatment personnel.

CASE MANAGERS

All conservative estimates indicate that the present number of case workers is about one-third of what is needed. For example, in 1965 there were about 17,500 case workers when the need called for approximately 55,000.[2] There has been some increase since then, but it is certain that the number is far too short of the need.

Case workers serve as juvenile counselors, juvenile probation officers, parole officers, probation officers, presentence investigators, and many other functions. Case workers must have investigative and diagnostic capacity and the ability to work with communities and institutions to obtain services for probationers and parolees. They must also be able to provide effective counseling and supervision to those with whom they work.

The desirable level of education for a case worker is generally agreed to be graduate work at least to the master's degree level. However, this is the ultimate goal and it will be

[2] *Task Force Report: Corrections* (Washington, D. C.: U. S. Government Printing Office, 1967), p. 96.

353

some time before the master's degree can become a requirement. In the meantime, individuals with a bachelor's degree will find little difficulty in obtaining a position.

SPECIALISTS

Staff members classified as specialists must possess essential professional skills that are needed in the rehabilitation of offenders. Included in this category are vocational and academic teachers, psychologists, and psychiatrists. Like other areas in corrections, the shortage of qualified people as specialists is severe. In 1965 there were 6,657 employed when the need was estimated to be approximately 20,400.[3]

TECHNICIANS AND SERVICE PERSONNEL

Employees in this category are responsible for the maintenance and operation of the correctional system as well as for providing various specialized services to offenders. This diverse group includes electricians, farm managers, foremen of industrial shops, researchers, and secretaries. The bulk of these employees work in institutions, but have no special preparation for working with offenders other than random experience, but they have potential for participating in treatment because of their close association with them.

CORRECTIONAL ADMINISTRATORS

There are also opportunities in management/administration in the correctional field. This area may, in fact, be the key to the introduction of much needed reform in the correctional profession. There are more than 17,000 middle managers and supervisors working in correction and, like other areas, the need will increase. Traditionally these positions have been

---

[3] *Task Force Report: Corrections*, p. 97.

recruited from within the ranks, but of late there is a trend to recruit people especially prepared in correctional administration.

SELECTION AND TRAINING

Many of the selection standards and requirements for correctional personnel are similar to those of police officers. Guards and custodial personnel frequently have to conform to physical and medical standards, but the more skilled positions do not. Like police, even the physical standards are being relaxed in order to avoid discrimination charges and to attract more and better people.

Salaries vary considerably in relation to the area and the position. Although salaries are rather low, recent years have seen vast improvement. In some jurisdictions salaries for custodial and case work employees are comparable to those of police officers, while in other jurisdictions they are much lower. It is unfortunate that correctional activities have not received the same attention as those of the police and, therefore, the upgrading of correctional benefits does tend to be behind.

It is believed, however, that governing officials are realizing the importance of corrections in the criminal justice system and, likewise, are becoming aware of the need for more and better resources. The next few years should witness vast improvements in corrections so that this type of career will be more attractive.

Summary

Police officers must have the unusual capacity to effectively handle a large sphere of varied activities. In any one day, a police officer may be called upon to save a child from drowning, investigate a serious traffic accident, give directions to a tourist, respond to an armed robbery, or even to inform a woman of her husband's death. Today's police officer must be carefully selected and highly trained in order to fulfill his many and awesome responsibilities.

A police officer may be assigned to patrol, serve as a detective, ride a motorcycle, or operate as a radio dispatcher. He may also be assigned to a specialized activity such as criminal identification, communications, planning and research, or working in the crime laboratory.

The need for qualified law enforcement personnel is critical. A survey of 236 police departments indicated that by 1975, they will need an additional 12,184 police officers. This clearly illustrates that employment opportunities in law enforcement are excellent for qualified applicants. These opportunities exist at all levels of government as well as with private industry and organizations.

Qualifications for police service vary from agency to agency, and court decisions resulting from charges of discrimination are influencing the requirements for entrance into the police service. Federal agencies usually require a college degree, and a few municipal agencies are raising their educational requirements beyond that of a high school degree.

Working conditions have improved considerably over the last few years to the extent that officers now enjoy competitive salaries and fringe benefits. The trend is for the continued increase of salaries.

Opportunities for women in police work are increasing, as departments across the country are becoming cognizant of their value. Generally, women are required to have a greater amount of education than their male counterparts.

356

Other than this, however, requirements are similar in that women must be in excellent physical condition, have a high moral character, and meet specified weight, height, and eyesight requirements. The female officer usually enjoys the same salary and fringe benefits as the policeman.

Discussion Questions

1. What is a policeman?
2. Describe the nature of the police officer's work.
3. How does the work of a municipal officer differ from that of a federal officer?
4. Discuss eyesight requirements for a police applicant and the trend relative to this.
5. Discuss career opportunities in law enforcement.
6. What are the general qualifications for a police applicant? Support the need for such requirements.
7. What is the fallacy of the residence requirement for a police applicant?
8. What is the purpose of the probationary period?
9. Discuss the specialized services that a police officer may perform.
10. Discuss the role of women in law enforcement.

8

Courts

Any discussion of law enforcement or the administration of justice would not be complete without including information about the American court system. The courts and their officers, as will be recalled from previous chapters, become involved in the administration of criminal justice following the arrest of the suspected law violator. It is the function of the court to mediate and adjudicate matters between the state as it represents society and individuals or between individuals.

CLASSIFICATION OF COURTS

Courts are classified in many ways, but a somewhat general classification which can be used safely is *courts of record* and *courts not of record; courts of superior jurisdiction* and *courts of inferior jurisdiction; trial courts* and *appellate courts;* and finally *civil courts* and *criminal courts.*

Courts of record, as one might expect, are those where the proceedings are recorded completely; in courts not of record no proceedings are recorded at all. Police and magistrate courts in the United States are very often courts not of record.

Courts of superior jurisdiction, frequently called higher courts, or appellate courts, are usually those to which appeals are made as a result of decisions of courts of inferior jurisdiction. These inferior jurisdiction courts are often referred to as lower or trial courts.

Civil and criminal courts deal with cases resulting from infractions of the civil and criminal law, respectively.

Courts with special, limited jurisdictions are known by the names of those jurisdictions, as probate or surrogates' courts, tribunals dealing with the probate of wills and the disposition of estates. Other courts are designated by the territorial limits of their jurisdiction. For example, included in this classification are the territorial, state, and county courts of the

United States. Municipal courts are usually courts of criminal jurisdiction only, but a few do have restrictive civil jurisdiction.

HISTORY OF THE COURTS

Archaeologists and anthropologists have established the existence of courts in primitive society over wide areas of Asia, Africa, and Europe. The existence of these primitive courts indicates that a high degree of social organization and the need for systematic adjudication of disputes on the basis of established customs and formulated rules of social conduct existed. Primitive courts comprised part of a complex social structure in which administrative, judicial, and religious functions were intermingled. Normally, these courts were held in the open and were frequently related to religion, as the judges were often priests. Those who attended were considered part of the court whether or not they had an immediate interest in the proceedings or in the judgments rendered. The proceedings normally consisted in large part of rituals designed to secure the redress of grievances presented by individuals against other individuals. At this point in history, there was no such thing as crimes against the state as we know them today, so the prosecution by the state would occur.

In the highly developed civilizations of antiquity, notably that of Egypt, judicial and executive functions were undifferentiated and were centralized in the monarch as the head of the state. An insight into the structure of Babylonian courts of the period about 2100 B.C. was obtained from the codification of the code of Hammurabi, which was discovered early in the 20th century.

In the judicial system of ancient Athens a unique feature, introduced by the law giver Solon in the 6th century B.C., was a right of aggrieved litigants to appeal from the decisions of magistrates to the people of Athens, or the judicial assembly. In later years these assemblies, referred to *heliastic courts*, became unwieldy and were divided into sections called dicasteries which were presided over by dicasts who performed the dual functions of both judge and jury. The evolution of courts in ancient Rome was marked by the development from primitive forms to a complex structure in which criminal, civil, and other jurisdictions were differentiated and were exercised by separate courts and officials. During this time violations of criminal law were prosecuted by the state, higher and lower courts were organized, the right of appeal was guaranteed, and a corps of professional jurors came into being for the first time in the history of Mediterranean civilization.

After Christianity became the state religion of Rome, the Roman legal system included the ecclesiastical courts previously established by the Christians, who had refused to have recourse to pagan courts. As the Roman empire disintegrated and its institutions declined, ecclesiastical courts survived and assumed jurisdiction over secular affairs. About 600 A.D. the jurisdictions of these ecclesiastical courts included practically all legal relations, both secular and spiritual.

When the Normans conquered England in 1066 they imposed the Carolingian judicial system on the Anglo-Saxons. In the long struggle between King and landed nobility which ensued in England, one of the principal weapons of the crown was a *curia regis*, or King's Court, which was held wherever the royal household was situated. Judicial supremacy was eventually won by the crown and from the reign of Edward I, in the 13th century, English courts have been organized on a centralized basis.

Prior to this victory of the crown, however, King John had been compelled to sign the Magna Carta in 1215. The terms of this Charter of Liberty limited the jurisdiction of common pleas as a court with a fixed location to try cases initiated by commoners against other commoners. A long step had been taken toward the separation of judicial from executive and legislative governmental powers. This process of separation continued during the reign of Edward I with the establishment of the Court of Exchequer as a tribunal with exclusive jurisdiction over revenue cases arising out of unpaid debts owed to

363

the crown; and the establishment of the Court of Kings, or Queens, bench as a supreme appellate tribunal of the realm, presided over by the King. The Court of Kings, or Queens, bench was also invested with original jurisdiction in both civil and criminal cases and thus encroached on the jurisdiction of the Court of Common Pleas. In fact, the jurisdictions of all three courts overlapped and were not definitively differentiated until much later. In later times these courts became bulwarks in the defense of civil and political liberties against the crown.

In the centuries following the granting of the Magna Carta by King John, parliament acquired appellate jurisdiction in both civil and criminal cases. This jurisdiction was subsequently confined to the House of Lords and has survived to the present day. In 1701, when parliament passed legislation establishing tenure of office for judges and made their removal from office conditional on parliament's assent, it completed the process of separating judicial from executive and legislative governmental powers. A significant restructuring of the court system which resulted in the elimination of much overlapping of jurisdictions (powers) was achieved under the Judicature Act of 1873. This established the essential features of the English judicial system, many of which were brought to the New World by the colonists from the Mother Country.

ORGANIZATION OF COURTS IN THE UNITED STATES

By the time the colonies declared their independence, each of them had developed its own court system and body of criminal law. Each colony's court system as well as its criminal law bore close resemblance to the English court system and English common law.

In order that the colonies might create a United States, much of their sovereignty had to be given up and placed in a common pool. In doing this the colonies, perforce, had to give up certain of their rights and privileges but also, because of the 9th and 10th Amendments, they retained all other rights and privileges. Even though they established a Supreme Court of the United States, the colonies retained their own supreme courts and their own court systems thereby creating a dual federal and state court system.

The Constitution does not create a federal court system; it did however give Congress power to create one, and Congress later exercised that power (Article 3, Sect. 1).

It cannot be said that there is not some overlapping of jurisdiction of the federal and state courts. At the risk of oversimplification, it can be said that basically the federal courts hear criminal cases only when the act committed has been declared a crime by the Congress of the United States. The state courts have power to try all cases involving those acts which state legislatures have declared to be criminal offenses.

The Constitution, by establishing the Supreme Court of the United States as the highest judicial power and by empowering Congress to create a court system, recognized that the Supreme Court alone was not a court system.

In accordance with the Constitutional provisions, Congress passed the Judiciary Act of 1789, and, by so doing, organized the Supreme Court and established a system of federal courts of lesser jurisdiction.

All federal judges are appointed by the President of the United States, with the consent of the Senate. They serve for life, or so long as they practice good behavior.

The Supreme Court of the United States is composed of one Chief Justice and eight Associate Justices.

The Chief Justice of the Supreme Court, in addition to the many important duties of that office, heads the federal court system which embraces more than 670 trial and appeals judges and more than 9500 other employees. The system processes nearly 160,000 cases yearly.

The Constitution declares the powers of the Supreme Court. Its jurisdiction includes:

1. All cases affecting ambassadors, other public ministers, and consuls.
2. All cases of admiralty and maritime jurisdiction.
3. All controversies over which the United States shall be a party.
4. All controversies between two or more states.
5. All controversies between one state and citizens of another state or between different states, and controversies between citizens of the same state claiming lands under grants of different states. But the 11th Amendment declares that this shall not extend to suits by a citizen of one state or a foreign state against another state.
6. All controversies between a state or the citizens thereof and foreign states, citizens, or subjects.

In many countries, the legislative body is free to enact whatever laws its members desire without any check. The whole American system is one of checks and balances. The President may veto any act of Congress, and it becomes law over his disapproval only by two-thirds vote of each house of Congress. Besides, the Supreme Court has the power to declare an act of Congress unconstitutional and therefore inoperative.

The Supreme Court has jurisdiction of two different kinds: original jurisdiction (over cases affecting ambassadors, other public ministers and consuls, and cases in which a state of the Union is a party) or the power to hear these cases in the first instance, and appellate jurisdiction over other cases as determined by Congress; that is, power to give final decisions both as to law and fact in these cases after they have been tried in other courts.

The right of appellate jurisdiction is the source of the Supreme Court's power to declare an act of Congress or a state statute unconstitutional. It has this right only by implication and by custom—the right is not definitely mentioned or given by the Constitution. It is important to bear in mind that this power comes under the head of appellate jurisdiction and that the Constitution gives the Supreme Court "appellate jurisdiction with such exceptions and under such regulations as the Congress shall make."

Other federal courts, established by Congress under powers held to be implied in other articles of the Constitution, are called legislative courts. These courts are the Court of Claims, Court of Customs and Patent Appeals, Customs Court, and the Territorial Courts established in the federally administered territories of the United States. The special jurisdictions of these courts are defined by the Congress of the United States. Except in the case of Territorial Courts, the special jurisdictions of these courts are suggested by their titles; the Territorial Courts are called Courts of General Jurisdiction.

The Constitution does not name inferior courts, but as indicated earlier does provide for such courts by giving the Congress the power to "ordain and establish them" (Article 3, Sect. 1).

The United States District Courts are trial courts with general federal jurisdiction. In the United States, district courts number more than 100 with each judicial district an entire state or part of a state. They have original jurisdiction over offenses against the laws of the United States and over certain classes of controversies between citizens of different states. Among the offenses of which district courts take cognizance are violations of federal laws connected with the revenue and postal laws, smuggling, counterfeiting, and bankruptcy. Each of the district courts has its district attorney, marshal, and other officers who prepare cases for presentation to the court and who execute the mandates of the judges.

The Circuit Courts of Appeals hear appeals from decisions in the district courts. This function relieves the Supreme Court of the United States of much of its labor, as a decision of the circuit court is usually final. In fact, usually only cases of economic and constitutional significance go on to the Supreme Court from the circuit courts.

The United States is divided into eleven judicial circuits including the District of Columbia, and there is a Court of Appeals in each circuit. The number of circuit judgeships in

THE UNITED STATES COURT SYSTEM

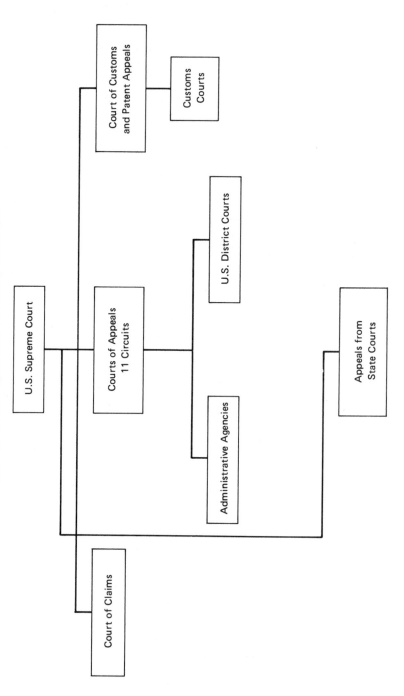

U.S. Supreme Court

Court of Customs and Patent Appeals

Customs Courts

Courts of Appeals 11 Circuits

U.S. District Courts

Administrative Agencies

Appeals from State Courts

Court of Claims

each Court of Appeals depends upon the volume of judicial work in that particular circuit.

STATE COURTS

Each state has an independent system of courts operating under the constitution and laws of the particular state. Generally speaking, the state courts are based on the English judicial system as it existed in colonial times, but modified by statutory enactments, and the character and the names of the courts differ from state to state. The state courts as a whole have general jurisdiction except in cases in which exclusive jurisdiction has been vested in the federal courts. In cases involving the United States Constitution or federal laws or treaties, the state courts are governed by the decisions of the Supreme Court of the United States, and the decisions are subject to review by that court.

Bearing in mind that any statement about state courts purporting to give a typical description of them is subject to numerous exceptions, the following may be taken as a general comprehensive statement of their jurisdictions and organization.

County courts of general original jurisdiction exercise both law and equity jurisdictions in most of the states. A few states maintain a system of separate courts of law and equity inherited from the English judicial system. Most states also maintain separate criminal and civil courts of original jurisdiction, but in a number of states the same courts of original jurisdiction deal with both civil and criminal cases.

Between the lower courts and the Supreme Appellate Courts, in a number of states, are intermediate appellate courts which, like the federal courts of appeals, provide speedier justice to litigants by disposing of a large number of cases which would otherwise be added to the overcrowded calendars of the higher courts.

The state court systems also include a number of minor courts, most of them with limited jurisdiction. These courts

Court testimony using enlarged photograph

Courtesy of Public Safety Department, Metropolitan-Dade County, Florida

dispose of minor cases, so-called lesser offenses, and relatively small civil actions. Included in this group of minor courts are police and municipal courts in cities and larger towns, as well as the courts presided over by justices of the peace in the more rural areas.

DILEMMAS OF THE COURTS

In the United States many of the courts are often poorly administered, some are woefully undermanned, and most are so inundated with cases that just keeping even is a difficult job. Some judges are somewhat less than eminent. Many judges still reach the bench through the political system, elective or appointive, and have little or no criminal court experience.

In the numerous court systems of the states of this country, there are many eminent people serving on the bench who

370

are providing outstanding service. During the past decade great progress has been made in modernizing many of the state court systems. Strides have been made in improving the quality of the courts and in the methods utilized in selecting those who administer them. Several states, through either legislatively enacted procedures or by constitutional amendment, have completely removed the selection of judges, who will serve in many of the higher courts of the state, from the political process. There still, however, remains much to be done.

The system is probably its weakest at that point where it ought to be the strongest; that is, in the juvenile and misdemeanor courts where at least there is some possibility of the first-time offender's being rehabilitated. Correct action by the judge at that particular point is more likely to result in the individual's not continuing a career of crime than perhaps at any other time.

Courts at nearly every level of the system have backlogs of cases that result in long delays for the person charged as well as for the aggrieved party. The surge in criminal activity during the last decade has overtaxed the capacity of the entire criminal justice system, particularly the courts. The so-called "victimless crimes," which some consider to be very minor offenses that should not even be prosecuted—offenses such as public drunkenness, gambling, homosexuality, prostitution, and use and possession of marijuana—have caused great backlogs of cases in the courts. In reality, these types of offenders jam up the system more than felony offenders do. However, it should be remembered that a trial of a felony offender requires a much longer period of time, sometimes several days or even weeks, whereas several of the lesser offense trials usually can be disposed of in a single day.

The new rights accorded defendants as set forth by the Supreme Court have vastly humanized the courts—particularly by assuring lawyers for the indigent—and have significantly increased the number and types of pretrial motions and postconviction appeals. Defense lawyers sometimes slow down cases by resorting to the use of all legal devices available to them as a simple matter of strategy.

371

Delay, as all defense attorneys know, puts everybody involved in the case in a bargaining mood. Courts in most large cities have many times more cases than they could handle if they all went to trial. This condition creates an environment whereby many prosecutors are more than willing to engage in plea bargaining.

Plea bargaining is a problem in the court system. The great number of cases pending before the courts is conducive to plea bargaining by defense attorneys. The prosecutor, like the judge, has a backlog of cases and is quite anxious to resolve as many as quickly as possible. Consequently, it frequently happens that people who should be charged with higher offenses are let off with a plea of guilty to a lesser offense. This does not help in the rehabilitative process either, because it tends to inject a degree of insincerity, mockery, and contempt into the entire criminal justice system. It is rather common knowledge among career criminals that the chances are quite good that they can plea bargain if brought to prosecution. Therefore, the risk of committing crime is not as great as it might otherwise be. The criminal can have less concern about being charged with the greater offense he has committed. Through plea bargaining, he has a good chance of receiving a shorter sentence for a lesser offense.

Plea bargaining is used by some prosecuting attorneys as a means of presenting a good record to the electorate when time for reelection comes around, because the more guilty pleas the prosecuting attorney can point to, generally, the better are his chances for reelection.

In this discussion of plea bargaining it should be pointed out that plea bargaining is not new. Its use has been greatly enlarged in recent years, primarily as a result of some of the conditions existing in the criminal justice system and discussed earlier in this chapter. Plea bargaining is legal; it is recognized, permitted, and participated in by the courts. However, because of abuses which have occurred in its use, state legislatures, at the urging and with the help of lawyer groups, are enacting statutory controls to limit the use of plea bargaining to certain types of offenses.

THE PROSECUTOR

The prosecutor is normally a county-elected official and may be called the District Attorney, County Attorney, or State Attorney depending upon the area of the country. Regardless of the title, however, he is the person who determines whether or not an alleged offender is to be charged, what he or she is to be charged with, and who has the responsibility of presenting the state's case in court.

The prosecutor's decisions significantly affect the arrest practices of the police, the volume of cases in the courts, and the number of offenders referred to the correctional system. Therefore, he is probably in the most favorable position to bring about needed coordination among the various law enforcement and correctional agencies in the community.

It is extremely important that the prosecutor's office and the police work closely together in preparing presentations in court. The need for closer cooperation between police and prosecutors was identified in 1967 by the President's Commission on Law Enforcement and the Administration of Justice. Over the years, however, the most common form of relationship between the chief and the prosecutor has been a personal one. Such a relationship is important, but a more formalized and systematic relationship is necessary if criminal investigations are to be more effective. The goal, of course, is to improve the quality of case investigation in order to obtain a larger number of prosecutable cases.

An improved relationship will result in many benefits to both the police and the prosecutor's office. For example, a formal system of feedback can help the police chief spot problems in investigative performance. It can also help the police manager identify training needs, evaluate managerial effectiveness, and identify areas where corruption may exist. At the same time a good relationship will help officers improve their investigations and case preparations. Similarly, police feedback to the prosecutor can provide important suggestions concerning operating policies, procedures, and practices, as well as prosecutor performance.

The following chart illustrates a formalized structure that will facilitate police/prosecutor relations.

*Police/prosecutor relations: a two-way street**

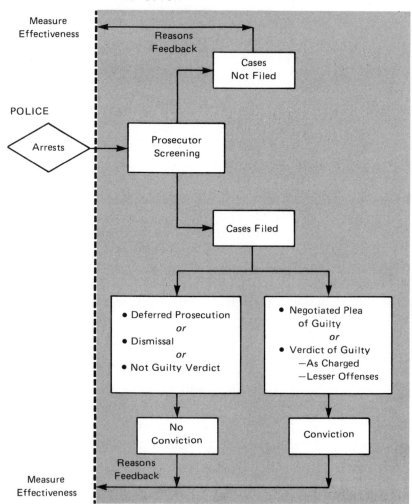

* From *Managing Criminal Investigations: Participant's Handbook,* 1977, page 100. Copyright by University Research Corporation (contract J-LEAA-022-76). Used with permission of United States Department of Justice, Law Enforcement Assistance Administration, Washington, D. C. 20531.

COUNSEL FOR THE ACCUSED

The right of a criminal defendant to be represented by counsel is a fundamental one in our democratic system of criminal justice. Counsel for the accused is important for two basic reasons. An individual forced to answer a criminal charge needs the assistance of a lawyer to protect his legal rights and to help him understand the nature and consequences of the proceedings against him.

The importance of counsel also proceeds from values transcending the interests of any individual defendant. Counsel is needed to maintain effective and efficient criminal justice. Otherwise, there would be an erosion of our whole principle of criminal justice which dictates that a person is innocent until proven guilty.

Not only is it vital that the accused have counsel, but it is equally important that he have a lawyer early in any process that makes him a defendant. Early provision of counsel is important for discovering facts bearing upon the ultimate disposition of the case, whether by trial or otherwise. The adversary system rests on the assumption that both the prosecution and defense will be prepared at the time of trial to present their respective versions of the facts by the testimony of witnesses or by other evidence. Preparation of a court case requires a considerable amount of pretrial investigation, which can be done only under the direction of a competent attorney.

The fact that a great percentage of criminal cases are disposed of without trial further increases the need for early selection or appointment of counsel. These dispositions normally result from negotiations occurring early in the process at which the prosecution agrees to dismiss or to reduce the charges or to recommend a particular sentence if the defendant agrees to plead guilty.

All this means that not only does the accused have a right to counsel, but it is important that he be represented if our criminal justice system is to work appropriately. Without defense counsel the defendant may be unjustifiably convicted or may not realize the appropriate benefit of plea

375

bargaining. In addition, because the defendant may not be familiar with courtroom procedure, more time would be required for trial. The defense attorney, therefore, plays an extremely important role in our criminal justice system.

Summary

A somewhat general classification of the various courts in the United States is: 1) courts of record; 2) courts not of record; 3) courts of superior jurisdiction; 4) courts of inferior jurisdiction; 5) trial courts and appellate courts; and 6) civil courts and criminal courts.

Archaeologists and anthropologists established the existence of courts in primitive society over wide areas of Asia, Africa, and Europe, proving there was a high degree of social organization and a need for systematic adjudication of disputes on the basis of established customs and formulated rules of social conduct. Such primitive courts comprised part of a complex social structure in which administrative, judicial, and religious functions were intermingled. The proceedings normally consisted in large part of rituals designed to redress grievances presented by individuals against other individuals.

In the highly developed civilizations of antiquity, notably that of Egypt, judicial and executive functions were undifferentiated and were centralized in the monarch as head of the state. In the judicial system of ancient Athens a unique feature was the right of aggrieved litigants to appeal from the decisions of magistrates to the people of Athens, or the judicial assembly. In later years these assemblies became courts of first resort, presided over by magistrates who prepared cases for trial. The evolution of courts in ancient Rome was marked by the development from primitive forms to a complex structure in which criminal, civil, and other jurisdictions were differentiated and were exercised by separate courts and officials.

A crossroads in the development of the court system resulted from the Magna Carta, signed in 1215. This charter limited the jurisdiction of common pleas as a court with a fixed location to try cases initiated by commoners against other

377

commoners. A long step had been taken toward the separation of judicial from executive and legislative governmental powers. Eventually, parliament acquired appellate jurisdiction of both civil and criminal cases. This jurisdiction was subsequently confined to the House of Lords and has survived to the present day.

In the United States the Constitution did not create a federal court system, but it did give Congress power to create one, and Congress later exercised that power. Basically, the federal courts hear criminal cases only when the act committed has been declared a crime by the Congress of the United States. The state courts have power to try all cases involving those acts which state legislators have declared to be criminal offenses.

In many countries the legislative body is free to enact whatever laws its members desire without any check. The whole American system is one of checks and balances. The President may veto any act of Congress and it becomes law over his disapproval only by a two-thirds vote of each house of Congress. Besides, the Supreme Court has the power to declare an act of Congress unconstitutional and therefore inoperative.

The Supreme Court has jurisdiction of two different kinds: original jurisdiction and appellate jurisdiction. The right of appellate jurisdiction is the source of the Supreme Court's power to declare an act of Congress or a state statute unconstitutional. Other federal courts, established by Congress under powers held to be implied in other articles of the Constitution, are called legislative courts. The special jurisdictions of these courts are defined by the Congress of the United States. The Constitution does not name inferior courts, but as indicated earlier does provide for such courts by giving to Congress the power to "ordain and establish them."

Each state has an independent system of courts operating on the constitution and laws of the particular state. Generally speaking, the state courts are based on the English judicial system as it existed in colonial times, but modified by statutory enactments, and the character and means of the courts differ from state to state. The state courts as a whole have general jurisdiction except in cases in which exclusive jurisdiction has been vested in the federal courts.

Generally speaking, county courts of general original jurisdiction exercise both law and equity jurisdictions in most of the states. A few states maintain a system of separate courts of law and equity inherited from the English judicial system. Most states also maintain criminal and civil courts of original jurisdiction, but in a number of states the same courts of original jurisdiction deal with both civil and criminal cases.

Between the lower courts and the Supreme Appellate Courts, in a number of states, are intermediate appellate courts which, like the federal courts of appeals, provide speedier justice to litigants by disposing of a large number of cases which would otherwise be added to the overcrowded calendars of the higher courts.

The state court systems also include a number of minor courts, most of them with minor jurisdictions. These courts dispose of minor cases, lesser offenses, and relatively small civil actions. Included in this group of minor courts are police and municipal courts in cities and larger towns, as well as courts presided over by justices of the peace in the more rural areas.

In the United States many of the courts are often poorly administered, some are woefully undermanned, and most are so inundated with cases that just keeping even is a difficult job. However, there has been much revision of the state and local court systems so that improvement in the criminal justice process is being realized.

One of the major problems with the courts as identified by the police is the practice of plea bargaining. Its use has been greatly enlarged in recent years, primarily as a result of some of the conditions existing in the criminal justice system. The problem with plea bargaining is that it is often used by prosecuting attorneys to gain a good record of convictions and, at the same time, criminals are becoming confident that they will be charged with a crime lesser than that committed.

Discussion Questions

1. List the general classification of courts.
2. Describe the difference between trial courts and appellate courts.
3. Describe the difference between civil courts and criminal courts.
4. How does a court of superior jurisdiction differ from other courts?
5. Briefly describe the history of the development of the American court system.
6. Describe the court system in your specific state.
7. What are the two jurisdictions of the United States Supreme Court?
8. What is the function of the circuit courts of appeal?
9. Describe the relationship between the police and local courts.
10. Discuss the various dilemmas facing our courts.

9

Corrections

To most law abiding citizens, corrections is an invisible, virtually unknown, and unappreciated part of the criminal justice system. But its operations are extensive and are vital in society's fight against crime. Corrections involves much more than the mere temporary protection of society by institutionalizing offenders for varying periods of time. Nearly all offenders are eventually released, and so the crime rate of the future depends greatly upon the success of the corrections system in performing its rehabilitative functions.

The number and characteristics of offenders are influenced by numerous factors over which corrections has little control. The career criminal, because he is skilled in avoiding arrest and conviction, often remains outside the corrections system. For example, of the 142 members of the national organized crime syndicate who live or operate in Pennsylvania, 92 have records totaling 495 arrests for indictable offenses; only one is in prison. Offenders of sufficient finances to make bail and hire able defense counselors may often escape prison sentences.

High employment and expanded military service have contributed to a decline in state prison populations. Other contributing factors are long trial delays and postponements and U.S. Supreme Court decisions which have created a backlog of court cases and caused the release of many prisoners since 1963. With the strengthening of probation services and the development of other community-based programs, it is reasonable to expect that greater numbers will be diverted from imprisonment in the future. As a result, the prison population may continue to decline or level off.

EFFECTIVENESS

Prisoners in the United States represent society's ills and its failure to eradicate them. The violence of city street gangs, the bitterness of the ghetto, and the damaging effects of alcoholism are everywhere in evidence. In most instances the offenders come from the cities, from broken homes, and from minority groups. They are predominantly young, poor, unskilled, and unmarried. Although their average intelligence is usually normal, many are not even high school dropouts; they are junior high school dropouts with even lower levels of academic achievement and comprehension.

What success has been achieved in "correcting" offenders? Unfortunately, because of gaps in information, this cannot be answered precisely. Compiled statistics cover the offender while he is in the corrections system but no coordinated information exists on the offender's behavior after he leaves. It has been generally determined, however, that the further an offender is entrenched in the corrections system, the less his chances for successful rehabilitation. For example, more than one-third of paroled offenders violate their parole.

EVOLUTION

History has left the United States with outdated buildings and the remnants of outmoded thinking, but has pointed out past mistakes and enabled corrections to begin progress toward a new and more hopeful future.

Our legacy of corrections evolves from medieval beliefs that criminals were possessed by devils which could be driven out by flogging or execution. Colonial America was dominated by harsh criminal codes until William Penn's Pennsylvania Assembly passed "The Great Law" in 1682. Based on a more humane Quaker code, the law spared many offenders the torture and death that had been traditional. However, the law was repealed in 1718, and penology in Pennsylvania reverted to the practice of vengeance against the criminal.

A new school of thought emerged with the growth of western democracy in the late 18th and early 19th centuries. It maintained that man's actions are based on seeking pleasure and avoiding pain. It was reasoned that imprisonment would

Pennsylvania Eastern State Penitentiary

Courtesy of the Department of Justice, Commonwealth of Pennsylvania

deter crime by making it more painful than pleasant to break the law. At the same time, it would afford a place for the criminal to penitently contemplate his sins and work at a craft. During this era, the United States evolved a penal philosophy based on Quaker beliefs which espoused the individual isolation of prisoners to avoid harmful influences on others. Known as the Pennsylvania System, or Separate System, this approach to corrections was symbolized by the Eastern State Penitentiary erected in 1829 at Cherry Hill in Philadelphia. Resembling a medieval fortress and containing an individual, walled-in exercise yard at the rear of each cell, the prison was deliberately adapted to the principle of "separate and solitary confinement at labor, with instruction in labor, in morals, and in religion." To further insure isolation and anonymity, prisoners were enshrouded in hoods.

The benefits expected from punishment through impris-

387

Inside Pennsylvania Eastern State Penitentiary

Courtesy of the Department of Justice, Commonwealth of Pennsylvania

onment failed to materialize. Crime did not decrease; prisons became overcrowded; and imprisonment created more problems than it solved. By the turn of the century it was recognized that restraint alone could not accomplish the purposes of correction. Beliefs were then advanced that criminal behavior is a response to environmental conditions and emotional problems rather than the consequence of moral deficiency. This gave rise to a variety of specialized methods of fitting treatment to an offender's individual needs: indeterminate sentences, probation, psychotherapy, prisons with graded degrees of security, vocational training, etc. The rationale of individualized treatment opposed the idea that criminals are all alike and can be corrected by some common approach. It brought awareness of the fact that criminal behavior has no single cause or universal pattern and requires diverse approaches for its understanding and correction.

It is becoming dramatically clear that treatment programs carried out in the artificial world of the prison do not sufficiently recognize that crime is a symptom of the failure of the community as well as of the individual, or that success in resocializing the offender is necessarily limited when he is isolated from those community institutions that motivate law-abiding conduct. Today's knowledge imposes a dual task for corrections in achieving its basic goal of protecting the public by aiding in the prevention of crime:

1. To correct the individual so that he lives within the limits of the law—reformation and rehabilitation.
2. To develop the offender's links with the community to the maximum extent compatible with protecting society— reintegration.

ORGANIZATIONAL PROBLEMS

The involvement of this nation's city and county governments, along with their state government, and various phases of the adult corrections process produces a multilevel administrative maze. There is similar fragmentation in juvenile corrections. Juvenile detention is usually a county function, and juvenile probation and parole are usually local court functions, while the juvenile training schools are many times operated or supervised by other offices within the state government. In many instances these segments are only loosely tied to the community resources which can affect the offender's life.

A second undesirable division is the traditional barrier between institutional and community programs that has persisted in keeping probation and parole services isolated from the prisons. Waste and duplication occur, for example, when prison classification personnel must gather information that has been previously compiled in presentencing reports in previous probation case histories, but is not available because of inadequate communication between agencies. With increasing emphasis on community programs and reintegration of the offender into the community, close organizational structuring between institutional and field services is needed more than ever.

A third split is between local and state facilities, engendering a wide variation in the quality and quantity of rehabilitative programs. The problem is most acute in local jails, which have few resources compared to the state institutions. The jails are often seriously overcrowded with antiquated, meager physical facilities. Programs for rehabilitation are almost completely lacking. Consequently, the opportunity to correct those who have committed minor crimes, particularly first-offenders most prone to successful rehabilitation, is crippled by inadequate facilities and programs. In addition, most convicted offenders who are held in local jails are short termers serving from two or three days to no more than ninety days. Certainly little rehabilitative work can be accomplished within such restrictive time restraints. This should not imply, however, that programs should not be developed for the short termers. Qualified individuals should develop appropriate programs and work with these people.

Another unfortunate organizational separation is the frequent administration of correctional services in almost complete isolation from the total health and welfare spectrum. One cause has been the inward-directed perspective of some corrections administrators who fail to consider corrections as part of the total community picture. A second factor is that many social agencies have traditionally screened out clients manifesting criminal behavior, apparently in the belief that the offender is incapable of being aided as part of society as a whole.

During the course of a criminal career it is entirely possible for an individual to be shunted through many different and separate substrata in the correctional process, from juvenile detention to adult parole. Each substratum gathers information, makes decisions about the offender's fate, and affects

390

rehabilitation. Fragmented administration hinders continuity in handling the offender, since any one segment of the system often knows little of what other segments have done. The same fragmentation also works against a unified approach in planning for balanced and full utilization of correctional services, and developing comprehensive training and research programs, and in sharing skills of personnel.

To attain maximum administrative and functional efficiency, a number of states have consolidated their correctional services into state departments of correction. Such structures have been established in at least 18 states, with Delaware, Oklahoma, and Connecticut being the most recent. In other states, including New York and New Jersey, new forms of organization are under consideration. All states must evaluate the specific revisions in correctional management that are best suited to a criminal justice system.

Most authorities believe that planning and administration of correctional services should be consolidated, and the plans to implement an optimum unified organizational structure for institutional corrections, probation, and parole on a state and county level should be formulated immediately.

THE CORRECTIONAL PROCESS

Corrections administrators today generally agree that prisons serve most effectively in protecting society against crime when the major emphasis is on rehabilitation. However, there is no such agreement on methods of rehabilitation, and various unproven theories will persist until they are scientifically tested. Opinions differ because academic concepts are rejected by some administrators, and because the disciplines engaged in correctional practice differ ideologically. Since crime has many causes, correctional treatment requires a range of programs provided by a multidisciplinary approach in a therapeutic institutional climate.

Systematic diagnosis and classification is essential to

analyzing the individual's problems and adapting treatment programs to his needs. Prisoners should be classified early in the correctional process and information gathered from various sources, including presentencing reports. New inmates should be given IQ and standard educational tests, vocational tests, and training assignments based upon an in-depth analysis of the best approach to their rehabilitation. The process utilized in determining treatment based upon classification should be done as quickly as possible so that the individual can be put on the road to reintegration into the community.

If a well-balanced program of rehabilitation is to be attained, treatment services must be provided to help inmates deal with emotional problems that may interfere with lawful conduct. Services need to be provided for treating pre-psychotic cases; for effectively handling the aggressive, acting-out, hard-core inmate; and for offering individualized therapy for special problem cases. If criminal attitudes and values are left unchanged, an inmate subculture that breeds antisocial behavior remains an accepted way of institutional life, and the offender is likely to fail in his ultimate objective, his adjustment to the community upon his release. Effective counseling service requires professionally trained personnel in psychiatry, psychology, social case work, and group work, and requires them in sufficient numbers to limit caseloads to manageable levels.

Correctional administrators should also fully explore the use of corrections officers and work supervisors in working with inmates toward rehabilitative goals. By reason of their numbers and close contact with inmates, they are in a particularly good position to exert a positive influence. This relationship has been utilized in institutions throughout the United States, with the result that increased understanding has helped to maintain order by relying on morale and cooperation rather than repression. By contributing more directly to the rehabilitative process, rather than functioning simply as a keeper, the corrections officer achieves an increased sense of personal worth. Simultaneously, the inmate's attitude toward authority improves. More extensive and uniform informal and formal procedures must be developed throughout the United States system. As this is done, corrections officers will need to be better trained.

VOCATIONAL TRAINING

It is important that correctional institutions provide vocational training suited to each individual's needs. Without such training, the inmate will find it difficult to re-enter society and serve a fruitful and beneficial life. The majority of inmates enter prison without employment skills or stable work records. Because of the correlation between unemployment and crime, the correctional process has an important contribution to make in providing offenders with opportunities to acquire good work habits and training in a marketable craft or trade. While this is a primary goal of prison employment, its achievements have

Residents learning a trade

Courtesy of the Department of Justice, Commonwealth of Pennsylvania, Pennsylvania Eastern State Penitentiary

393

not been evaluated except in terms of production and maintenance. What is the actual value of the prison work programs as vocational preparation for today's labor market? How relevant, for example, are grinding coffee, making soap, or operating sewing machines for male prisoners? What new forms of training are needed to help offenders to meet society's changing technological needs? Are pay scales that average 50¢ per day realistic incentives for inmate motivation? What should be the role of private industry in employing and training prisoners? Answers are needed to attain maximum usefulness from institutional programs. Correctional administrators generally agree that all prison work programs should be evaluated to determine their relevance to the training and rehabilitation needs of inmates and the labor market to which the inmate, upon release, will be returning.

EDUCATION

In gaining employment, most prisoners are handicapped by educational deficiencies. They are, therefore, more prone to pursuing illegitimate activities. In recent years correctional institutions have made significant strides in acquiring accreditation for their educational courses and in upgrading the academic levels of prisoners. Educational programs at all correctional institutions are one of the most important ingredients for successful reintegration.

COMMUNITY-BASED CORRECTIONS

The importance to both the offender and the community of the offender's social adjustment is now being recognized as an essential ingredient of the rehabilitative process. Inherent in the concept of community-based corrections is a closer confrontation between the offender and his environment. Most offenders, including a great many young and first-time offenders, can benefit from these community-based programs with minimal risk to the community. However, the offender's activity must be controlled. Also, his exposure to the environment must be controlled, and his ability to adapt will determine the kind and amount of such control.

Whenever possible, it is most effective to treat the offender in his social and cultural atmosphere, rather than in the unreal and often socially sterile environment of the prison. This approach constantly exposes the offender not only to his personal problems, but also to his responsibilities in the community. The concept is diametrically opposed to the old philosophies of penology, which envisioned reform through the offender's social isolation and disassociation from his peers.

There are, of course, many offenders who cannot tolerate or be tolerated in the open environment of the community and who must be held in custody for intensive treatment within institutions. The corrections system must be able to screen out those offenders who are dangerous to the community and must be incarcerated. This capability calls for highly trained persons, sensitive to the needs of the community as well as to the needs of the individual offenders.

The new community-centered approach to corrections requires a new correctional philosophy, not merely new methods for approaching old objectives. The core of the correctional process is moved away from the institutions and back to the community. The following principles characterize the operational philosophy of community-based corrections:

1. Restraint, whether in the form of physical custody or some other control, should be used only to the degree necessary to protect the public, deter the offender, or contribute to his treatment. Punishment for its own sake only reinforces the pattern of criminal behavior.
2. Traditional long-term incarceration should be reserved for those dangerous and violent offenders who cannot be handled safely in the free community or by community-based facilities.

3. Placing the offender closer to the social, cultural, emotional roots of his life enhances the treatment process, making it more relevant to the offender's normal situations and conditions and the society into which he must reintegrate.
4. Decentralization of correctional services permits specialized services and meaningful programs to be individually fitted to the needs of each offender.
5. The "convict" stigma, which psychologically thwarts attempts at rehabilitation and which is inherent in the large prison-type institution is less pronounced in community-based corrections.
6. Even though the cost of clinical services is high, community-based programs and facilities are less expensive than the operation and maintenance of large correctional institutions.

PROBATION

Probation is a procedure under which a defendant, having been found guilty of a crime upon verdict or plea, is released by the court without institutionalization. He is subject to conditions imposed by the court and to supervision by the probation service.

Generally, probation may be used in all cases with exception of first degree murder. The specified term of probation usually cannot exceed the maximum prison term to which the offender would have been sentenced.

Probation is the most appropriate, economical, and effective method of handling the vast majority of offenders. This has been clearly demonstrated by the Saginaw Project which showed that 68 percent of first-time felons could be safely supervised in the community.[1] With adequate probation services, 80 percent of those placed on probation did not commit crimes during the course of the three-year study. Several other

[1] John G. Jaeger, *Pennsylvania Judicial Statistics: 1967*, Report J-11, Department of Justice, Bureau of Criminal Justice Statistics, October 1968.

studies on probation effectiveness show success rates varying from 60 to 90 percent.

It is evident that probation has been significantly underused and that the field service agencies have not been provided with the necessary resources to handle the present load. Unnecessary institutionalization of offenders is an economic waste; typically the imprisonment of an offender is much more expensive than the provision of probation services.

Part of the reason for the underuse of probation is public ignorance of what probation really is and what can be accomplished through its use. In an overwhelming majority of instances, probation and parole officers are overloaded and undertrained. Probation has never been given the opportunity to work. The report of the President's Commission on Law Enforcement and Administration of Justice states:

> The best data available indicates that probation offers one of the most significant prospects for effective programs and corrections. It is also clear that at least two components are needed to make it operate well. The first is a system that facilitates effective decision making as to who should receive probation; the second is the existence of good community programs to which offenders can be assigned. Probation services now available in most jurisdictions fall far short of meeting either of these needs.[2]

PAROLE

Parole is a release of a prisoner to the community by the parole board prior to the expiration of his term, subject to conditions imposed by the board and to its supervision. Parole is a conditional release. Eligibility for consideration for parole involves such factors as the type of crime upon which the conviction

[2] President's Commission on Law Enforcement and Administration of Justice, Task Force Report, *Corrections*, U.S. Government Printing Office, 1967, p. 27.

was based and the length of sentence imposed.

Sooner or later nearly all prisoners are released: most of all those who enter the prison system eventually are returned to free society, and only those who are paroled receive assistance in the transition from prison life to life in the community.

The advantage of parole is that the released individual does have assistance in reintegrating into his community and living a rewarding life. It is suggested by most corrections administrators that pre-release centers be provided at the community level to supervise all released offenders, assist in their readjustment, and minimize the possibility of recidivism.

PRESENTENCE INVESTIGATION

The presentence investigation is a comprehensive study of the relevant legal, social, and psychological factors that affect the offender. It is then expanded into a complete study of the offender during the time he is in the corrections system. It can be used as a basis for an effective treatment plan for the probation agent. If the offender is in prison, it forms a comprehensive instrument for use by the institution in the classification process. Finally, it is used by parole personnel in planning for the release and supervision after release.

Most judges advocate presentence investigations. Judge Lorain L. Lewis of the Court of Common Pleas, Pittsburgh has said:

> . . . I have long been an advocate of presentence investigation. I don't see how a judge can sentence a defendant intelligently unless he has the benefit of such an investigation.
>
> I use presentence investigation reports in practically all cases where a first offender is involved except cases that are of a very minor nature.

In spite of such testimony, the percentage of presentence investigations ordered for cases going through the criminal courts throughout the United States is amazingly low. Typically the excuse for this is the low number of trained staff available for doing the presentence investigation.

In the long run, the additional staff needed for a full program of presentence investigation will probably more than pay for itself. Lack of presentence investigation results in sentencing without sufficient information. This is probably responsible for substantial numbers of offenders being in the adult prison system today who do not belong there. Diverting them from incarceration would decrease instituional expenditures, and the funds could be used to hire the necessary staff for additional presentence investigations. Further savings to the community would result from the prevention of crimes by the imprisonment of dangerous offenders who in the absence of presentence investigation might have been paroled.

PRE-PAROLE INVESTIGATION

The pre-parole investigation can be utilized in the same way that the judge uses a presentence investigation. It is a highly useful instrument for making parole decisions. An updated evaluation of the offender, his home, community environment, family relationships, and potential for and probability of gainful employment upon release, along with the institutional reports, can determine readiness for parole.

Corrections administrators generally agree that presentence and pre-parole investigations should be conducted in all cases where they can be useful in assessing risk to the community and the criminal's behavior pattern. They also believe that maximum use should be made of their content by the courts and paroling authorities and that qualified manpower should be increased to satisfy the investigative needs that exist.

SUPERVISION OF PROBATION AND PAROLE

In probation or parole supervision, the officer operates under continuing multifaceted responsibilities. The most important of these are to: 1) protect the community; 2) assist the released offender in avoiding further violations of the law; and 3) guide and assist the released offender in reintegration into society.

In addition to certain personal attributes, those crucial responsibilities call for the use of special knowledge, skills, and techniques. Supervision is more than routine reporting, collecting fines and support monies, surveillance, or police work. It must be based on an understanding of the individual's emotional and environmental situation and the effect of his life history upon his present reactions. It calls for diagnostic insight gained through the presentence and pre-parole investigations, and for the utilization of a treatment plan that considers the offender's strengths and weaknesses. This quality of supervision cannot be provided when: 1) caseloads are excessive; 2) necessary information and knowledge is lacking due to absence of a presentence and pre-parole investigation; 3) judges or parole authorities do not accept, or do not realize, the potential of quality supervision; 4) agents are overloaded with clerical routines or assigned to other unrelated tasks; or 5) agents are inadequately prepared and trained.

PROBATION SUPERVISION

Successful probation is determined by: 1) the selection process (presentence investigation), and 2) the quality of supervision. The present county probation system typically produces significant inequities in the administration of criminal justice. The quality of service available to the offender or the court is inconsistent. This adversely affects the welfare of the public as well as that of the individual offender and his family.

Nonuniform services often result from lack of funds in the less affluent counties, or when too few cases are assigned by the courts to justify the cost of good probation services. Probation services in many states and counties remain inert because they are politically oriented rather than being related to human and societal needs. There are, of course, many meritorious exceptions where individual counties or states are aware of the need and are developing quality probation operations.

It is not enough, however, to have such services available. The courts must make meaningful use of these services. Many times the courts choose to ignore the availability of such services and, consequently, little is achieved. In addition, the intensity of probation supervision by counties or states varies widely. In the majority of cases, supervision amounts to routine and superficial reporting by the offender, rather than the use of case work or counseling techniques. Moreover, many cases are "on probation" in name only, or solely for the purpose of collecting fines, court costs, or family support money.

PAROLE SUPERVISION

The success of parole supervision depends largely on the effectiveness of the prison system in which the offender has been incarcerated and the quality of the process used in determining the readiness for parole.

In addition to focussing on the readjustment of the offender from antisocial to socially acceptable behavior, parole supervision involves helping the parolee make the often difficult transition from institutional life to the free community. Supervision during this transition is a sensitive problem. The agent must help the parolee adjust to the community stigma which exists in such areas as employment, church, and school. In addition, the parolee must be helped to rebuild the interpersonal and family relationships which often deteriorate with imprisonment. And, of course, the agent must work with the parolee on the specific problems that caused his arrest in the first place.

These social problems and interpersonal conflicts, often

further aggravated by incarceration, cannot be resolved through routine supervision alone. Effective supervision calls for the knowledge and experience of a trained and skilled practitioner, with a manageable case load. In general, probation and parole services do not have the capacity to satisfy either of these conditions.

PRE-TRIAL RELEASE

The increasing number of offenders awaiting trial or detained in jail because of delays in legal procedures has added costly burdens to jail operations. It has become imperative that officials and planners consider alternatives that may reduce this problem.

Detention in jail for safekeeping is an essential security measure with some offenders. But is justice really served and the community better protected through the extensive use of pre-trial detention? Must the length of stay or the time required for final disposition of a case be so long?

Traditional bail procedures do not keep dangerous offenders in jail or release those who are not dangerous. These procedures are based upon the financial resources of the accused rather than on more relevant factors. Those who are detained prior to trial simply because they are not well known or cannot raise bail are severely and unfairly penalized. They suffer loss of earnings and the stigma and discomfort of being in jail. It has been shown by several surveys that those who are not able to post the required bail are more likely to be convicted and imprisoned than those who can.

Increasing numbers of jurisdictions have implemented bail reform, permitting the release of selected persons on their own recognizance or under special conditions rather than posting a money or property bond. A relatively simple screening process can enable the court to reliably determine who may be released by his own signature. In one project where this was tested, a default rate of less than .7 of one percent was realized. Experiments are also being made with "partial" detention—the procedure that permits the accused to work at his regular job but requires confinement in jail during non-working hours. The selective use of summons in place of arrest for certain offenses is another means of extending the scope of pre-trial liberty.

The few studies that have been made indicate that exercise of the guarantee of a speedy trial varies according to jurisdiction, the nature of the plea, and the nature of the offense itself. Since it is the primary responsibility of the courts to provide the right to speedy trial, a statistical monitoring system within existing court structures would permit the exercise of control over the time required for the successive steps in the criminal justice process.

PREVENTIVE DETENTION

The subject of preventive detention is a natural corollary to that of pre-trial release. It can be argued that if we release the nondangerous offender whether or not he can afford bail, we should detain the dangerous individual even when he can make bail.

Preventive detention is pre-trial detention on the basis that the alleged offender may otherwise commit additional offenses, harm witnesses, or tamper with evidence while awaiting trial. There are strong indications that the federal government is contemplating a preventive detention proposal for the federal judicial system, including the municipal courts of Washington, D.C., where it is being used in a limited way.

A number of unresolved problems become apparent when the use of preventive detention is considered. There are no known statistics on the incidents or severity of crimes committed by persons awaiting trial or sentencing for early offenses. Clogged court calendars result in unreasonably long delays prior to trial. Any plan for preventive detention would

403

have to include prompt scheduling of trials for those who are so detained to assure an absolute minimum of pre-trial custody. In addition, more and rapid evaluations would be needed immediately after each arrest to decide whether preventive detention should be used.

WORK RELEASE

The concept of work release dates back to the Huber law enacted in Wisconsin in 1913. This law sought to reform the prisoner and at the same time provide means of financial support, other than public relief, for the prisoner's dependents. Work release permits selected offenders to leave their place of custody for specified times to pursue gainful employment or, in some cases, to attend school.

Work release is not a panacea in correctional treatment. Rather, it is one promising alternative to full-time institutional care. It is not an alternative to probation, nor should it take the place of various kinds of treatment programs which many offenders need. It has, however, extensive application for less serious offenders who require control beyond that provided under probation supervision. The partial release privilege may be extended for purposes other than work, including educational or vocational training or home visits.

COMMUNITY RESIDENTIAL CORRECTIONAL CENTERS

A great majority of the released offenders who have failed have done so within the first few months following their release. Motivation for change, if it exists at all, is strongest in the offender at the moment of release. Based on this, it becomes evident that too much blame is directed at the institution for its failure to rehabilitate offenders. Instead, we should examine the failure of the correctional systems to provide a bridge between the institution and the community at the critical point of the offender's return to the community.

One such attempt at this is the pre-release center. The pre-release center is a residence for the housing of prisoners of institutions who are released to work in the community or are on their way out of the institution. Prisoners may become eligible for placement in a center for periods up to ninety or more days before completing their sentences. They will live under supervision in a home setting and be provided with supportive professional services. Their wages will be disbursed toward their living expenses, support of dependents, and payment of obligations.

Another attempt is the halfway house. Like pre-release centers, these act as "decompression chambers" in the social reintegration of the offender into the community. Administered under public or private auspices, the halfway house is designed for parolees who do not have a substantial plan for living independently in the community. Halfway houses are being considered also as an alternative to institutionalization, as a "halfway in" facility between probation and parole or as a "halfway back" station for parolees attempting to make the adjustment. Both pre-release centers and halfway houses feature individual as well as group counseling and other services; the chief distinction between them is the status of the offenders.

Summary

Corrections involves much more than the mere temporary
protection of society by institutionalizing offenders for varying
periods of time. Nearly all offenders are eventually released,
and so the crime rate in the future depends greatly upon the
success of the corrections system in performing its
rehabilitative functions.

Prisoners in the United States represent society's ills and
its failure to eradicate them. The violence of city street gangs,
the bitterness of the ghetto, and the damaging effects of
alcoholism are everywhere in evidence. In most instances, the
offenders come from the cities, from broken homes, and from
minority groups. They are predominantly young, poor,
unskilled, and unmarried.

Our legacy of corrections evolves from medieval beliefs
that criminals were possessed by devils which would be driven
out by flogging or execution. Colonial America was dominated
by harsh criminal codes until William Penn's Pennsylvania
Assembly passed "The Great Law" in 1682. Based on a more
humane Quaker Code, the law spared many offenders the
torture and death that had been traditional. However, the law
was repealed in 1718 and penology in Pennsylvania reverted to
the practice of vengeance against the criminal.

A new school of thought emerged in the late 18th and
early 19th centuries, which maintained that man's actions are
based on seeking pleasure and avoiding pain. It was reasoned
at that time that imprisonment would deter crime by making it
more painful than pleasant to break the law. At the same time,
it would afford a place for the criminal to penitently
contemplate his sins and work at a craft. However, the benefits
expected from punishment through imprisonment failed to
materialize. Eventually, it was realized that the primary
function of corrections must be to correct the individual so that
he can live within the limits of the law; the offender has to be

linked with the community to the maximum extent compatible with protecting society.

One of the primary problems with corrections is the multitude of governmental levels and agencies dealing with the problem. This creates a multilevel administrative maze which hinders the accomplishment of correctional objectives.

Corrections administrators today generally agree that prisons serve most effectively in protecting society against crime when the major emphasis is on rehabilitation. However, there is no such agreement on the methods of rehabilitation, and various unproven theories will persist until they are scientifically tested. Obviously, correctional treatment requires a range of programs provided by a multidisciplinary approach in a therapeutic institutional climate.

It has long been recognized that vocational training is a basic ingredient in the proper rehabilitation of offenders. Therefore, most correctional programs do include vocational training so that an individual can pursue a productive life upon his release from prison.

Correctional officials recognize that the transition from prison life to open society is difficult. Therefore, various community-based correctional programs have been instituted to help offenders bridge that gap.

Probation is a procedure under which a defendant, having been found guilty of a crime upon verdict or plea, is released by the court without institutionalization. He is, of course, subject to conditions imposed by the court and to supervision by the probation service.

Parole is a release of a prisoner to the community by the parole board prior to expiration of his term. Such release is subject to conditions imposed by the board and to its supervision.

In recent years, it has become apparent that presentence investigation is an important process, as it provides information to the judge in deciding the best type of sentence to impose upon the offender. Most judges do advocate such an investigation, as it does provide information which makes their function in the criminal justice process more effective. Pre-parole investigation is also very important, as it provides correctional officers information for the proper rehabilitation and reintegration of the offender into society.

1. Describe the purpose of corrections.
2. Briefly describe the evolution of the correctional process.
3. Describe the organizational problems that adversely affect the rehabilitation of offenders.
4. What is the importance of appropriate diagnosis and classification of offenders?
5. Describe the type of vocational training program that will best rehabilitate the offender.
6. Describe the basic principles that characterize the operational philosophy of community-based corrections.
7. What is probation and how can it most effectively be utilized?
8. What is parole and how can it most effectively be utilized?
9. Discuss the importance of presentence and pre-parole investigations.
10. Develop your concept of an effective work release program.

10

Process of Justice

The process of criminal justice involves a large number of separate and sequential steps. It involves the many activities of the police, judicial proceedings, and correctional agencies. The process begins with the commission of a crime and ends, hopefully, with rehabilitation of the offender and his return to a normal and productive life. This is, of course, an over-simplification of the process, as several activities occur sub-sequent to the commission of an offense and before the reha-bilitation of the offender. In addition, outcomes of various steps determine what will or will not follow.

For clarification and ease of understanding, the steps in the administration of justice are grouped into: 1) police proc-ess, 2) pre-trial judicial process, 3) the trial, and 4) correc-tional process.

THE POLICE PROCESS

Within the scope of the administration of justice, the police process involves the: 1) determination that a crime has been committed, 2) crime scene investigation, 3) identification of the offender, 4) arrest of the offender, 5) booking of the offender, and 6) investigation and case preparation. With the possible exception of an on-sight arrest, this represents the normal sequence of events. In an on-sight arrest, the crime scene investigation may follow the arrest, and the identifica-tion of the offender will occur simultaneously with the deter-mination that a crime actually has been committed. There may be other exceptions to this, but the above listed se-quence usually holds true.

DETERMINING THAT A CRIME HAS BEEN COMMITTED

One of the first responsibilities of the police upon arrival at the scene of a reported crime is to determine whether a crime has in fact been committed. Frequently, people call the police on the premise that "There ought to be a law." This is especially true in the case of civil disputes over which the police have no authority. Good examples are the person who calls the police because his neighbor has planted a hedge over the property line or the woman who complains about her husband's late hours.

Concurrent with determining that a crime has been committed is the decision as to what the crime is. Both determinations must be based on law. This clearly illustrates why it is imperative that police officers be knowledgeable in criminal law and know the elements of a crime.

In burglary, for example, the essential elements necessary to constitute the offense may be the *breaking* and *entering* the house of another, with *intent* to *commit* a *felony* therein. (Definition of burglary will vary among states.) All of these elements must exist before the police officer can conclude that a crime has been committed and that the crime is burglary.

This determination may not be as simple as it sounds, as there are other considerations. The officer must know the legal definitions of *breaking, entering,* and *intent.* Is it considered breaking if there is no forcible entry? Does the perpetrator have to enter with his whole person or does reaching into the premises to obtain an object constitute entering? Is intent implied if a theft has occurred? Is asportation necessary for a theft to occur? All of these questions and more must be answered before the final determination can be made.

As can be seen, the determination that a crime has been committed involves some investigatory work. In the case of burglary this would involve, among other things, discovering the means of entry and whether or not something was stolen. A good example of how the investigation determines the crime is the question of murder or suicide. Does the evidence support a suicide or does it indicate murder?

CRIME SCENE INVESTIGATION

The crime scene investigation has three general objectives: 1) to assist in determining that a crime has been committed and the identification of what the specific crime is, 2) to secure evidence that provides proof relative to the perpetration of the crime and the identity of the offender, and 3) to identify the criminal. In the case of an on-sight arrest of a criminal during the commission of a crime, these objectives are quickly and easily achieved. In other instances, however, the investigation can be quite involved and an arrest may occur weeks, months, or even years after the commission of the crime.

One crime scene investigation may involve the patrol officer who is the first to arrive, detectives who may be summoned by the patrol officer, crime-scene evidence technicians, and crime laboratory specialists. All have very important roles, and the success of the investigation is dependent upon the ability of each in the performance of his tasks. Their efforts must also be well coordinated.

In most situations, the patrol officer is the first to arrive at the crime scene, but his responsibility will vary from department to department. In some departments, he will merely protect the scene and summon detectives. In other departments, the patrol officer will conduct the entire preliminary investigation unless it is a serious crime. In a few departments, he will conduct the investigation to its conclusion. This third alternative is, however, rather rare.

It is becoming more common for the beat officer to assume major responsibility for the preliminary investigation. The preliminary investigation consists of: 1) protecting the crime scene, 2) preserving the crime scene, 3) searching the scene for evidence, 4) packaging evidence and transporting it to the crime laboratory, 5) interviewing witnesses, and 6) preparing a detailed investigation report that will be forwarded to the detective division for necessary follow-up investigation.

It should be understood that whether detectives or beat officers are responsible for the preliminary investigation they will usually utilize the service of specialists such as a police photographer and fingerprint expert. In larger departments, evidence technicians will search the scene, serve and package evidence, and transport it to the laboratory.

415

IDENTIFYING THE OFFENDER

As stated previously, one of the primary objectives of the investigation is the identification of the offender. In many cases, the victim can name the person responsible. This is frequently true in the case of an assault, as most assaults are committed by a person known by the victim. In other situations, however, the identification is not so easily accomplished.

Identification of the offender is usually accomplished by information given by the victim and witnesses. Frequently, the police have just descriptions to go on, but this is often sufficient. The police may be able to develop a composite from the description, or someone may be able to identify the suspect from pictures in the police file.

The offender may also be identified by physical evidence, such as fingerprints, that may be found at the scene. Admittedly, however, this means of identification is not as common as many people believe. If the offender is identified, the next step in the administration of justice is finding the responsible person and effecting the arrest.

THE ARREST

Arrest is defined as "taking, under real or assumed authority, custody of another for the purpose of holding or detaining him to answer a criminal charge or civil demand."[1] In many instances, the actual arrest is made on the scene subsequent to the commission of the crime. Frequently, however, the arrest will not be made until a thorough investigation has been made and a legal warrant issued for the arrest of the perpetrator.

There are two types of arrests: 1) with a warrant, and 2) without a warrant. A police officer can legally make an arrest without a warrant when he observes the commission of a misdemeanor or when a felony is committed and he has reasonable grounds to believe that a certain person has com-

[1] Henry Campbell Black, *Black's Law Dictionary* (St. Paul, Minnesota: West Publishing Company, 1951), p. 140.

mitted that felony. Police officers must know the legal status of arrest without a warrant within their particular jurisdiction, as it may vary slightly from state to state.

A warrant of arrest is defined as "a written order issued and signed by a magistrate, directed to a peace officer or some other person specially named, and commanding him to arrest the body of a person named in it, who is accused of an offense."[2] Generally, it is best if the police department can obtain a warrant of arrest prior to making an arrest, as this provides a legal document supporting that arrest. Generally, criminal investigations will end with the obtaining of a warrant that is served by a police officer.

The manner in which an arrest is accomplished will depend upon the situation. In some cases, the officer can control the conditions, but in other cases the officer must use force; in such cases the force used should be only the amount necessary to overcome the resistance of the offender.

BOOKING

Following the arrest, the suspect is taken to the jail where he is "booked." Booking refers to making positive identification of the suspect before he is actually placed in detention. This procedure consists of fingerprinting the suspect, photographing him, and verifying his name.

The booking procedure also develops additional records that show the time of arrest, the person arrested, the charge against the suspect, the name of the officer making the arrest, and additional information. These records often are of great importance during the trial of the suspect, and it is imperative that they be accurate.

INVESTIGATION AND CASE PREPARATION

The final role of the police is the continuation of the criminal investigation to ascertain all facts relative to the case for presentation in court. The final report on the case must be as complete as possible if the process of justice is to work effectively.

[2] *Ibid*, p. 141.

417

This phase of the process entails a close working relationship between the police and the prosecutor's office. In fact, many police departments assign one or more detectives to the prosecutor's office for the phase of the investigation. Many prosecutors also have their own investigators who work very closely with the police.

The prosecutor frequently indicates what additional information he needs and, to a degree, helps direct this phase of the investigation. The objective, obviously, is to gather information that will assist in the prosecution of the case.

This should not imply that the police concern themselves with gathering only those facts that will help convict the person charged with a crime. *The police role is to gather all facts that will assist the court in rendering a just verdict.* It may very well be that some information will actually help the defense if they are able to obtain it through cross examination. This is acceptable and good.

Police officers involved in the investigation usually will appear in court as witnesses for the prosecution. Their responsibility is to answer the prosecutor's questions as accurately as possible. All information must, of course, be based on facts that are known by the police officer. Appearing as a witness for the prosecution should not imply, however, a lack of cooperation with the defense attorney. The police have fulfilled their responsibility in the process, and it is now the court's responsibility to arrive at a just verdict. Testifying police officers must answer all questions impartially and cooperate fully with the defense attorneys if the process of justice is to work effectively.

PRE-TRIAL JUDICIAL PROCESS

DECISION TO PROSECUTE

The normal procedure is for the county or city prosecutor to receive a copy of the booking slip and subsequent field investigation report. The prosecutor has the responsibility of de-

418

termining if there is sufficient evidence to bring charges against the suspect. The prosecutor, if he decides to prosecute, will prepare the complaint which contains the name of the person and the offense that the person has committed and is charged with. The complaint is usually signed by the arresting officer or complaining witness as well as by the prosecutor.

THE PRESENTMENT

The second step in the pre-trial judicial process is taking the offender before a magistrate without unnecessary delay. The magistrate then informs the suspect of the charge against him as well as his constitutional rights relative to that charge and the criminal justice procedure. He is also informed of his right for preliminary examination as well as his right to legal counsel. If the suspect is indigent, the magistrate or court may appoint counsel for him. The magistrate may also set bail at this initial appearance of the suspect.

PRELIMINARY HEARING

The preliminary hearing is not a trial for determining the guilt or innocence of the suspect, but an open hearing to determine if there is sufficient evidence to hold the accused for trial. If, in the opinion of the judge, the evidence is sufficient, the accused will be bound over for trial by a court that possesses general jurisdiction. Many people accused of a felony waive the right to a preliminary hearing, and their case automatically advances to the trial.

GRAND JURY INDICTMENT

A grand jury is a large group of jurers, usually twelve to twenty-three members, which examines accusations of criminal charges as a preliminary to the trial. The grand jury is a county institution, and hears the evidence presented by the state. Their duty is to receive complaints and accusations in

419

criminal cases, hear the evidence presented by the state, and file bills of indictment when they are satisfied that a trial should be held.

An indictment is defined as "an accusation in writing found and presented by a grand jury, legally sworn, to the court in which it is impanelled, charging that a person therein named has done some act, or been guilty of some omission, which by law is a public offense, punishable on indictment."[3]

The use of grand juries varies considerably from state to state. It is suggested, therefore, that the reader consult his own state judicial processes to determine the activities, responsibilities, and use of the grand jury. Some states have abolished the grand jury or limited its activities.

ARRAIGNMENT

In the arraignment, the accused or defendant appears before the trial court, is informed of the crime he is charged with, and is asked to enter his plea. He may plead guilty, not guilty, or nolo contendere. Nolo contendere means that the person will not contest the charge. This is the name of a plea in a criminal action, having the same legal effect as the plea of guilty, with regard to all proceedings on the indictment, and on which the defendant may be sentenced. This plea admits, for the purposes of the case, all the facts which are well pleaded, but is not to be used as an admission elsewhere.[4]

THE TRIAL PROCESS

All people have the right to a speedy trial as guaranteed by the Sixth Amendment and the right to a trial by jury as guaranteed by the Seventh Amendment of the Constitution

[3] *Ibid*, p. 912.
[4] *Ibid*, p. 1198.

of the United States. The accused may, however, waive his right to a trial by jury and be tried by the judge. In this instance, the judge hears the evidence and decides by himself whether the accused is guilty or not guilty. Generally, the accused will receive a trial by jury and the following processes will be in effect.

JURY SELECTION

The first order of business is the selection of the jury. Both the defense attorney and the prosecutor have a specified number of "peremptory challenges," which means each can refuse prospective jurors for any reason. After twelve jurors and from one to four alternates are selected, the judge outlines their responsibilities, and the trial is ready to begin.

OPENING STATEMENTS

The purpose of the opening statements is to advise the jury of facts of the case and the issues involved. This provides the jury with a general picture of the total situation so they will better understand the evidence to be presented.

The prosecutor usually opens the case by explaining how he is going to present the case for the prosecution. He may outline the evidence to be presented that will prove the guilt of the accused. The defense attorney then gives his statements which will explain his method of action. He usually will explain how he will show the defendent innocent of the crime charged.

THE PROSECUTOR'S CASE

The prosecutor begins his case by presenting his witnesses. Witnesses for the prosecution present testimony that will support a verdict of guilty. The prosecutor begins with direct examination of his witnesses with questions that will bring out the facts in chronological order. After he has brought out all necessary information, the prosecutor rests. The defense counsel then cross-examines the prosecution's witnesses. His purpose is to challenge the witness relative to his testimony and, if possible, show where inconsistencies in testimony exist. He then rests. If the prosecutor believes it necessary, he may engage in redirect examination of the witness for material that may have been overlooked or that is new. Following the redirect, the defense can also ask additional questions.

THE DEFENSE CASE

Following the presentation of all prosecution witnesses, the defense calls its witnesses. The same procedure is used in this process, with the exception that the defense counsel asks for testimony and the witnesses are cross-examined by the prosecution. The purpose of the defense is, of course, to prove that the defendent is innocent of the charges lodged against him.

PROSECUTOR'S REBUTTAL

The prosecutor then engages in the rebuttal and may call previous or additional witnesses in order to strengthen any part of his case that may have been weakened by the defense counsel. The same order of testimony and cross-examination follows during this rebuttal.

DEFENSE SURREBUTTAL

The defense then engages in a surrebuttal and brings forth previous and additional experts and witnesses to strengthen his case. The same procedure as in the prosecutor's rebuttal is followed.

SUMMATIONS BY DEFENSE AND PROSECUTOR

The defense counsel and the prosecutor then are allowed to give their closing arguments or summations. Each reviews the laws and the facts involved for the jury and summarizes the important facts of his case. Of course, each attempts to discuss the facts as they support their own interests.

INSTRUCTION TO JURY

The judge reads to the jury certain written instructions relative to the legal principles involved in the case. The judge also will explain to the jury their responsibility relative to arriving at a "true and just verdict."

DELIBERATION AND VERDICT

The jury then adjourns to a private chamber where it deliberates the facts and issues of the case. The jury elects a foreman who acts as chairman of the whole group. The jury will remain in deliberation as long as it takes to reach a unanimous verdict. After a unanimous verdict is reached, the judge is notified, and the jurors return to the court where the verdict is read by the foreman. If the verdict is guilty, the final sentencing decision rests with the judge. If the verdict is not guilty, the defendant is released.

MOTIONS

If the defendant is found guilty, the defense may move for a new trial or for a mistrial. There are several possible motions for a new trial, such as a wrong courtroom procedure, prejudice or bias on the part of witnesses, etc. If any of these motions can be proved, then a new trial will be granted.

THE SENTENCE

The sentence rests with the judge, who follows guidelines set up by the state legislature. The defendant may be sentenced to imprisonment or to a correctional institution, or he may be put on probation.

423

APPEALS

The defendant may appeal his case to a reviewing court by having his defense counsel prepare a brief repealing the decision of the court on the grounds of prejudice or some other injustice to him. If the defense counsel and his client are granted a new trial, it goes to the next higher court where the same procedures are utilized. An appeal case may go as high as the state supreme court, and very special cases may go as high as the United States Supreme Court. If the lower court's decision is reversed and remanded, the decision is nullified and the defendant may be tried over on the same indictment but have a different jury. If the decision is reversed, in other words, there is not sufficient evidence, the prosecuting attorney probably will not make a second attempt to convict the defendant.

CORRECTIONS

After the trial has concluded, and if the verdict of guilty has been rendered, the judge has several alternative actions to take relative to the guilty party. The two most common alternatives are sentencing to a penitentiary for a specified length of time or probation. There may be other alternatives, but these are the most common. Of course, in some situations the judge has no power to elect probation for the offender, as punishment may be specified in the state's criminal statutes.

IMPRISONMENT

The "old school" of penology advocated "lock-up" of the offender, so that he was removed from society and could do it no harm. The theory was that such punishment would discourage the individual from committing additional crimes upon release for fear of additional incarceration. Little attention was given rehabilitation or treatment, and the offender merely served his time, while his basic survival needs were met.

424

Today, the emphasis is on treatment of the offender so that he can pursue a useful life upon release. Theoretically, the prison staff will design an individualized program for each inmate that will develop his potential for rehabilitation and reintegration into the mainstream of society. This, of course, requires a staff of professional people who can analyze each individual's sociological, psychological, and medical makeup. Background information in these areas is absolutely necessary before a treatment program can be tailored to fill the individual's specific needs.

In conjunction with such treatment are the provision of additional formal and informal educational opportunities as well as social, cultural, and recreational activities. In other words, the professional staff of the prison is interested in developing a program that treats the "whole" person rather than just isolated specifics. The ultimate goal, of course, is to release a well-adjusted individual who will still maintain individual integrity.

In theory, also, prison officials are interested in keeping offenders for as short a time as possible. That is, the prisoner should be released as soon as possible after he has been rehabilitated. To incarcerate a prisoner beyond this may actually perpetuate additional problems in his treatment. It can be quite frustrating for a prisoner to know he is ready, but held back by unreasonable policy or regulations.

There are two methods by which a prisoner may be released from prison. These are the nonconditional and the conditional release. A nonconditional release may be obtained by serving the full sentence, by a court reversing its sentence, or by receiving a full pardon from the chief executive. The most common form of a conditional release is parole.

PAROLE

Parole is the process whereby the inmate is conditionally released from prison prior to serving his full sentence. This occurs when the professional prison staff determines that the person is ready to satisfactorily reintegrate into the community. Such release usually is not given until a parole board evaluates all records of the individual and agrees that he is ready for release.

The parolee is always under the supervision of a parole officer who provides necessary counseling and guidance. The parole officer also has supervisory powers and continually monitors the parolee's activities and conduct. As long as the parolee's conduct meets or excels acceptable standards during parole, he remains free. If, however, he violates the requirements of parole he may be returned to prison to serve the remainder of his sentence.

It should be realized that parole is not necessarily available to all prisoners. In many states perpetrators of serious crimes, such as murder and rape, are not eligible for parole. It should be realized also that a person may not be paroled just because he is deemed ready by the prison professional staff. Usually, the person must serve a certain portion of his sentence before he is eligible for parole. This time requirement generally runs from one-third to one-half of the sentence.

As stated earlier, parole is a conditional release. These conditions, to mention a few, may include: 1) scheduled or periodic meetings with the parole officer, 2) not fraternizing with known criminals, 3) not using alcoholic beverages, 4) not breaking any law, and 5) not leaving the jurisdiction without prior approval. These are just a few examples and conditions, which will vary among jurisdictions and according to the original crime committed.

PROBATION

Probation is the other possible alternative of the sentencing judge. This means that the person will not be sent to prison, but will remain at liberty under certain conditions prescribed by law. In granting probation the judge may, and usually does, prescribe conditions that must be met by the probationer. If the probationer does not comply with the

426

specified conditions, his probation can be revoked and the individual incarcerated.

As in the case of parole, the conditions may vary according to the jurisdiction, the crime committed, and the age of the offender. In addition to those of parole, the probationers' conditions may include the payment of court costs or restitution to the victim.

During the probation period, the individual is usually assigned a probation officer who provides general supervision, guidance, and counseling services. The relationship with the probation officer is obviously quite important as he can, to a large degree, determine the destiny of the probationer.

The utilization of probation as an alternative to incarceration is continually becoming more widespread as correctional people recognize its value. It seems quite appropriate and beneficial not to incarcerate those people who can be rehabilitated without serving time in prison.

Of course, persons convicted of certain crimes, as determined by the state, do not have the alternative of probation available to them. Many states also restrict the use of probation to first offenders only.

Summary

The administration of justice involves the many activities of the police, judicial proceedings, and correctional agencies. What happens from the commission of a crime to the rehabilitation of the offender is referred to as the process of the administration of justice. The steps in this process are divided into four groups: 1) police process, 2) pre-trial judicial process, 3) the trial, and 4) corrections.

The police process involves the determination that a crime has been committed, the crime scene investigation, the identification of the offender, the arrest of the offender, and the booking. These may be accomplished very quickly as in the case of an on-sight arrest, but more often the process is very systematic, and involves a considerable length of time.

The pre-trial judicial process consists of a decision by the prosecutor to prosecute, the presentment, a preliminary hearing, and the arraignment. Many states use the grand jury to examine accusations of criminal charges as a preliminary to the trial. The use of the grand jury does vary from state to state.

The trial process usually involves a trial by jury even though in certain situations the judge may decide guilt or innocence on the basis of evidence presented. This second alternative is effected only when the accused waives a jury trial. The trial process can be rather lengthy, starting with the selection of a jury and concluding with either an acquittal or the sentencing of the guilty party.

The final process involves correctional personnel and agencies who are responsible for the rehabilitation of the offender. The judge may place the guilty person on probation so that he is under the supervision of a probation officer. Many people are released on parole prior to serving their entire sentence and, therefore, come under the jurisdiction of a parole officer. Prisons have many ongoing programs designed for inmates during their incarceration.

Discussion Questions

1. What is meant by the "administration of justice"?
2. How is justice achieved?
3. Discuss the police responsibility in the administration of justice.
4. What are the two types of arrest? Discuss legal restrictions.
5. What is the purpose of the crime scene investigation?
6. What is the police role in the trial process?
7. What is the authority and responsibility of the grand jury?
8. Under what conditions can a trial be held without a jury?
9. Discuss the trial sequence of activities.
10. Discuss the responsibility of correctional agencies and personnel in the administration of justice.

11

Government and
Constitutional Rights

Since the police officer is both a representative of government and a community leader, it is important that he understand the units of government and the constitutional rights guaranteed all citizens. He certainly should know the framework within which he works, and he may have occasion to explain such divisions and rights to people with whom he comes in contact.

DIVISION OF CIVIL GOVERNMENT

The American system of government divides governmental powers and functions into three branches: 1) the legislative, 2) the executive, and 3) the judicial. The legislative branch enacts the laws, the executive branch administers and enforces them, and the judicial branch interprets the laws and judges whether persons are guilty of law violations.

The American system of government also divides governmental powers and functions into three areas: 1) the federal government, 2) the state government, and 3) the local units of government. Under the American system, every citizen in a state, for example, is a citizen of two governments: the government of the United States and of the state within which he resides.

The federal government and state government each have their own laws. Each of these governments is sovereign or supreme in the functions and powers reserved to it. The powers of the federal government are limited by the United States Constitution; state government powers are limited by the constitutions of each state. The federal government may exercise only powers that are delegated to it by the United States Constitution. The states have a reservoir of authority, in the sense that they can do anything that is not forbidden to them by the Constitution of the United States or by their own constitution.

Local government units are divisions within the state. The primary division of the state is the county. Other local

433

government units within the state include cities, towns, and in some states boroughs and townships. These are incorporated units to which a charter has been given under authority of an act of the state legislature. The local governments have no sovereign power, but exist at the pleasure of the state government. Individuals holding office enforce the law in the manner prescribed and approved by state law. In other words, the police receive their authority from the state constitution or legislature rather than from local governmental units.

The authors of the United States Constitution set up a most complex government. Each of the three branches is independent and coordinate, and yet each is checked by the other. The judiciary hears all cases arising under the laws and the Constitution and, therefore, interprets both the fundamental law and the statute law. The federal judiciary is appointed by the President and confirmed by the Senate, and is subject to impeachment by Congress. The election of Senators for six-year terms and the appointment of federal judges assure that parts of the federal government are exposed to little direct public pressure. The lower house of Congress is more subject to such pressure. Officers of government are chosen for terms of such varying length, ranging from two years to life, that a complete change in personnel would not be possible except by a revolution.

The states are also strong, especially as they were the original sovereignties who created the United States Constitution that made the federal government. Schools, local courts, policing, the chartering of towns and cities, incorporation of banks and stock companies, the care of bridges, roads, canals, are all matters under state control.

THE LEGISLATIVE BRANCH

The legislative branch of the federal government is the Congress, composed of the Senate and House of Representatives.

434

The Congress is responsible for making laws, and also for representing the interests of state governments.

In the state, the legislative branch may be called the general assembly or the state legislature. This, too, is composed of a Senate and a House of Representatives, with the exception of Nebraska, which has a unicameral state legislature. The state legislature or general assembly enacts the laws which govern the particular state. Like the President, the governor has a veto power. This power closely associates him with the legislative branch of the state government.

Counties, being subdivisions of the state, have no legislative branch. Generally speaking, the state legislature is the legislative authority of all counties within the state.

The legislative branch of most cities is the city council. It is usually a single-chambered body, and is responsible for the enactment of city ordinances which do not fall in the classification of misdemeanors or felonies, since the state authority establishes crimes. In some cities, legislation is enacted by city managers. The legislative body of certain towns is the town meeting.

THE EXECUTIVE BRANCH

The executive branch of the United States Government carries the law into effect and applies it directly to the people. The executive branch makes most of the contacts between government and the people, and these personal contacts determine the value of government in aiding or protecting citizens. Executive officials may direct only the operations of officials and offices within the executive branch. The chief executive of the nation is the President of the United States. The administrative offices and agencies of the various federal police are under his executive authority. He is also the commander-in-chief of the armed forces.

The governor is the state's chief executive officer and the head of the law enforcement agencies of the state. In coun-

435

ties, the Board of County Commissioners is the principal executive body. Usually, law enforcement officers of the county who do not report to the courts directly or to the district attorney are under the authority of the sheriff.

THE JUDICIAL BRANCH

The judicial department interprets and applies the laws. The lower courts are independent of the higher courts, but the higher court may inject itself into the lower courts through the processes of appeal, supersedeas, habeas corpus, or other direct court orders. The federal Constitution states that the judicial branch shall be on the same level with the executive and legislative branches. The judicial power of the United States will be vested in one Supreme Court and such lower courts as Congress shall establish from time to time.

The extensive federal court system has grown from this authority. There are district courts, circuit courts of appeals, and special courts in Washington, D. C. These federal courts have jurisdiction in all cases arising under the federal Constitution, including: federal laws, admiralty law, cases where the United States is a party, cases between states, and cases between citizens of different states.

Federal courts have no jurisdiction in cases involving state affairs after they have been heard by the state supreme court. If the case has some connection with the federal Constitution, the Supreme Court decides if it has jurisdiction when a citizen appeals a state court decision or procedure.

Most states have a supreme court, a superior court, and justice courts. The district courts or superior courts are commonly called county courts because the district lines usually coincide with the county lines.

Magistrates, aldermen, and justices of the peace comprise the minor judiciary. In some respects, their powers are countywide, but their court trials are confined to the city, or jurisdiction which they represent.

436

CONSTITUTIONAL RIGHTS

Legal rights are bestowed by the federal Constitution. Police administration is directly related to constitutional rights. An important part of police training is to clarify the shadowy line between the legality and illegality of an officers's procedure.

The fundamental rights of personal freedom guaranteed citizens by the Constitution should never be infringed upon by public officials. A public official must know what the rights of the citizen are and he is duty bound to protect these rights at all times.

FREEDOM OF RELIGIOUS PRACTICE

The Constitution of the United States safeguards religious freedom by forbidding Congress to pass any law concerning "an establishment of religion." All religious expression must be kept separate from the state, and no special privileges, rights, or immunities are granted any religious body. Thus, everyone is free to worship his god or gods in his own way—or not to worship at all. Provision for protection of religious freedom is now part of all state constitutions.

FREEDOM OF SPEECH AND OF THE PRESS

Every citizen may freely speak or write on any subject, but he is responsible for what he says or what he writes.

FREEDOM OF ASSEMBLY AND THE RIGHT OF PETITION

It is very difficult for a government to enforce regulations on the right of people to assemble and discuss actions. Citizens have a right to assemble in a peaceful manner and to criticize the government, so long as they do not advocate change by unlawful means. Unlawful in this sense would usually apply to seditious or treasonable acts. The freedom of speech and

437

the right of assembly and petition are closely bound together.

Streets and public places belong to the state or an agency of the state. Therefore, the regulation of their use for the general welfare is a responsibility of the state or its agencies. The only limitation on this power is that it be used in a reasonable, lawful, and constitutional manner.

The preservation of the public peace and order is a primary police function. The authority to investigate a breach of the peace, preserve the peace and order of the municipality, prevent an unlawful exercise of violence, and compel citizens to abstain from riot, rout, and unlawful assembly, is regarded as an inherent municipal power essential to municipal life.

FREEDOM FROM UNREASONABLE SEARCH AND SEIZURE

The right of the people to be secure in their persons, houses, papers, and effects, against unreasonable search and seizure shall not be violated, and no warrant shall be issued, but upon probable cause, supported by oath or affirmation, in particular describing the place to be searched, and the persons or things to be seized.

It is not a violation of this clause for an officer making an arrest, with or without a warrant, to discover and seize any evidence found on the prisoner or the premises in his immediate vicinity if it is directly connected with the offense charged.

FREEDOM FROM DEPRIVATION WITHOUT DUE PROCESS OF LAW

In no criminal prosecution can the accused be deprived of his life, liberty, or property unless by the judgment of his equals or the law of the land. The key to correct legal functions is found in the phrase *due process of law*—an orderly, recognized legal procedure enforced, and within jurisdictional limits.

438

FREEDOM FROM SELF-INCRIMINATION

An accused person is always innocent until the court renders a verdict of guilty, and only then may he be punished. In no criminal prosecutions can the accused be compelled to give evidence against himself. There is no legal way of forcing him to talk except in a court trial, but a court can order a witness to talk under certain restrictions or the witness may be punished for disobedience.

FREEDOM FROM UNKNOWN AND UNSEEN ACCUSERS AND ACCUSATIONS

In all criminal prosecutions, the accused has a right to demand the nature and cause of the accusation against him and to meet the witness face to face. Witnesses meet face to face in a court hearing. This clause forms the basis for requiring a signed complaint in connection with arrest. In all criminal cases, the witness must be examined in the presence of the accused and be subject to cross-examination.

RIGHT TO BAIL AND THE USE OF WRIT OF HABEAS CORPUS

All prisoners shall be bailable by sufficient security except for capital offenses where the proof is evident or presumption of guilt great. The privilege of the writ of habeas corpus shall not be suspended unless the public safety may require it in a case of rebellion or invasion. Bail is the delivery of the accused to others upon their giving, with himself, sufficient security for his appearance when called. It also means that those persons agree to produce the accused when called upon to do so or to forfeit the security. Such security is properly called the bail bond. There is some serious consideration for revising statutes and legislation relative to the use of bail bonds.

Habeas corpus is a writ or an order to the person detaining another, commanding him to produce the prisoner at a certain time and place, with the day and the cause of his arrest detention indicated, in order to comply with whatever the judge who awarded the writ shall consider proper. The true use of the writ is to insure a legal inquiry in to the cause of imprisonment, and to produce the release of the prisoner if his imprisonment is found illegal.

RIGHT TO A SPEEDY TRIAL BY AN IMPARTIAL JURY

Basically, this means that in all criminal prosecutions the accused has the right to a speedy, public trial by an impartial jury of the vicinity, whether the prosecution be by indictment or by information. Jury of the vicinity does not require trial in the county where the crime was actually committed, as there is an allowance for change in venue. There may be instances where neither the prosecution nor the defense can expect a fair trial in the local county and, therefore, they agree that a change of venue would be important if justice is to be achieved.

FREEDOM FROM EXCESSIVE BAIL AND FINES AND FROM CRUEL AND UNUSUAL PUNISHMENT

Excessive bail shall not be required, nor excessive fines imposed, nor cruel punishment inflicted, the judiciary having the responsibility of setting the bail and assessing the fines and other punishments. An accused person is innocent until a verdict of guilty is pronounced by the court; therefore, punishment is a function reserved to the judicial branch, and must not be inflicted until after the accused has been found guilty, and the law has affixed a certain punishment. Police or accusers have no right to inflict any kind of punishment on the accused before he is convicted. The American system of law presumes a man to be innocent until he is proven guilty. This presumption attends all proceedings against the defendant from their initiation until their resolution in a verdict which either finds the party guilty, or converts the presumption of innocence into a fact.

440

DOUBLE JEOPARDY

A person is protected by the Constitution of the United States from being tried for the same crime twice. When a person has been tried in court and found innocent, he cannot again be tried for that same offense.

Summary

The government of the United States is divided into three branches: 1) the legislative, 2) the executive, and 3) the judicial. The legislative branch enacts law, the executive branch administers and enforces law, and the judicial branch interprets law. The American system of government also divides government powers and functions into three levels: 1) federal, 2) state, and 3) local.

The powers of the federal and state governments are limited by their respective constitutions. The federal government may exercise only powers that are delegated to it by the United States Constitution. All powers not delegated to the federal government by the Constitution are reserved to the states. By virtue of this, the states have a reservoir of authority, in the sense that they can do anything which is not forbidden to them by the Constitution of the United States or by their own constitution. Each state, therefore, has the authority to establish state and local police agencies.

The Constitution of the United States guarantees certain fundamental rights to all citizens that cannot be denied them. It is in these fundamental rights of personal freedom that many of the rights, duties, and obligations of the police and courts are found. Public officials must guarantee these rights, and should not be in a position to be accused of infringing upon them.

Discussion Questions

1. Why should police officers be familiar with the organization of government?
2. What are three branches of the federal government?
3. Explain the function of each branch of the federal government.
4. What relationship exists between the branches of the federal government?
5. From what source do local and state police derive their authority?
6. What level of government has the primary police authority?
7. Discuss the various levels of government as they relate to the police function.
8. What is the police responsibility in guaranteeing fundamental rights to citizens?
9. How does the guarantee of freedom from unreasonable search and seizure affect the police function?
10. What is "due process of law"?

Bibliography

Adam, Hargrave L. *The Police Encyclopedia*, vol. 1. Waverly Book Company, Ltd., 1925.

Brown, Douglas G. *The Rise of Scotland Yard*. New York: G. P. Putnam's Sons.

Cross, Wilbur L. *The History of Henry Fielding*, vol. 1. New York: Russell & Russell, Inc., 1963.

Feiling, Keith. *A History of England*. London: Macmillan and Co., Ltd., 1963.

Fosdick, Raymond B. *American Police Systems*. New York: The Century Company, 1920.

Mays, Katherine. *Justice To All: The Story of the Pennsylvania State Police*. New York and London: G. P. Putnam's Sons, The Knickerbocker Press, 1917.

Morrell, W. P. *British Colonial Policy in the Age of Peel and Russell*. New York: Barnes and Noble, Inc., 1930.

Rowell, Henry Thompson. *Rome in the Augustan Age*. Norman: University of Oklahoma Press, 1962.

Wells, J., and Barrow, R. H. *A Short History of the Roman Empire*. New York: Barnes and Noble, Inc., 1958.

Appendixes

APPENDIX A

LEGAL PHRASES AND DEFINITIONS

The following legal terms and words frequently arise in police work, and all students should be familiar with their meaning. The definitions listed are clear and as devoid of legal phraseology as is consistent with accuracy. It must be realized, however, that some definitions will vary from state to state. The definitions are, therefore, given in rather general terms. Where questions arise, the student should consult his state's criminal code.

Accessory before the fact.   One who helps another to commit a crime, though he is absent when the crime actually is committed.

Accessory after the fact.   One who harbors, assists, or protects another person when he knows that person has committed a crime.

Accomplice.   One who is directly concerned in the commission of a crime with another person, or persons, whether he actually commits the crime or abets others. The term *principal* means the same thing, except that one may be a principal if he commits a crime without being aided by others.

Acquit.   To legally free a person from an accusation of criminal guilt.

Adjournment.   Termination or postponement of a session or hearing to some other time or place.

Adult.   Any person who is twenty-one years of age or older.

Adultery.   Voluntary sexual intercourse where one or both of the participants is married, but not to each other. Prosecution usually is commenced only on complaint of spouse.

Affidavit.   A voluntary written or printed declaration or statement of facts confirmed by the oath or affirmation of the person making it, taken before an officer having the authority to administer such oath.

Affirmation.   An oath which means that one calls upon God to witness the truth of what he says. So we generally swear on the *Bible*. However, some people, because of their religious beliefs or their lack of religion, refuse to swear in such a manner. Such people are allowed to swear on their conscience that what they say is true. This may be called an *affirmation* or an *asseveration*. It has the same legal force and effect as an oath.

Alias. Any name by which a person is known other than his true name.

Alibi. A claim that one was in a place different from that claimed.

Appeal. A case carried to a higher court, in which it is asked that the decision of the lower court, in which the case originated, be altered or overruled completely.

Arraign. When a person is arrested and brought before a court, the complaint is read to him and he pleads guilty or not guilty to the charge.

Arrest. To take a person into custody so that he may be held to answer for a crime.

Arson. The willful or malicious setting afire of a building with the intent to defraud.

Asportation. The moving of an object from its original position.

Assault. An unlawful attempt to hurt another person physically. If the person is actually beaten, the additional act is called *battery*.

Bail. To release a person from jail by guaranteeing that he shall remain within the jurisdiction and call of the court.

Battery. Wrongful physical force inflicted on another without his consent. It is associated with an assault, which is the attempt to inflict the force. If the attempt is completed, the result is a battery.

Blackmail. To extort something of value from another by the threat of accusation or exposure.

Brief. A summary of the law relating to a case, which is prepared by the attorneys for both parties to a case, and given to the judge.

Burden of proof.   The burden of proving the fact in issue. The prosecution must prove beyond a reasonable doubt that the defendant is guilty.

Burglary.   Breaking into another person's house or other building with the intention of committing a felony or stealing something of value. The laws relative to burglary vary from state to state.

Capital crime.   Any crime punishable by death.

Coercion.   Compelling a person to do that which he does not have to do, or to omit what he may legally do, by an illegal threat, force, intimidation, etc.

Complaint.   A sworn written allegation that a specified person committed a crime. It is the complaint that gives the court jurisdiction to try the case.

Conspiracy.   A combination of two or more persons for the purpose of committing a crime.

Corporeal.   Relating to the body. Thus, corporeal punishment is force used against the body of another.

Corpus delicti.   The body or essence of a crime; all things necessary to constitute a crime.

Defraud.   To withhold from another what is justly due him, or to deprive him of a right by artifice or deception.

Defendant.   The party against whom an action at law or in equity is brought.

Deposition.   The written testimony of a witness given under oath.

Domicile.   The place where a person has his permanent residence.

Duress.   To influence by force or by imparting fear of injury.

Embezzlement.   Misappropriating the personal property of another person who has given one the property for a specified purpose.

Eminent domain.   The power of the state, or a political subdivision, to acquire private property for public use through appraisal, court action, and payment of a fair price.

Evidence.   All the means used to prove or disprove a fact and issue.

451

Extortion.   The obtaining of property from another with his consent induced by wrongful use of force or fear, or under color of official right.

Extradition.   The surrender of a fugitive from justice from one nation to another. A similar surrender between states is known technically as *rendition*, although by common usage, both types are called extradition.

Felony.   An offense punishable by death or by imprisonment in a state prison.

Fence.   A term applied to a professional receiver of stolen goods.

Grand jury.   A jury of inquiry who is summoned and returned by the sheriff to each session of the criminal courts, and whose duty it is to receive complaints and accusations in criminal cases, hear the evidence adduced on the part of the state, and file bills of indictment in cases where they are satisfied a trial ought to be held. They are first sworn, and instructed by the court. This is called a grand jury because it comprises a greater number of jurors than the ordinary trial jury or petit jury.

Homicide.   Killing of one human being by another.

Indict.   To accuse of crime, in writing, by a grand jury. The indictment gives a court jurisdiction to try the case.

Injunction.   An order by a court prohibiting a defendant from committing an act which is injurious to the plaintiff.

Intent.   A design or determination of the mind to do or not to do a certain thing. Criminal intent is the intent to break the law. Intent usually is determined by the nature of one's act.

Justifiable homicide.   The excused killing of a human being by accident, in performance of a legal duty, in self-defense, in defense of one's home or family, etc.

Larceny.   Unlawful taking of property belonging to another.

Malum prohibitum.   A wrong prohibited; a thing which is wrong because it is prohibited; an act which is not inherently immoral, but becomes so because its commission is expressly forbidden by positive law; an act involving an illegality resulting from positive law.

Malum in se.   A wrong in itself; an act or case involving illegality from the very nature of the transaction, upon

452

principles of natural, moral, and public law.

Manslaughter. The unlawful killing without malice of another.

Misdemeanor. An indictable offense not amounting to a felony.

Modus operandi. Method of operation by criminals.

Parole. A conditional release from prison.

Perjury. The act of willfully swearing falsely.

Petit jury. The ordinary jury of twelve men for the trial of a civil or criminal action. So called to distinguish it from the grand jury, a petit jury is a body of twelve men impanelled and sworn to try and determine, by true and unanimous verdict, any questions or issues of fact, in any civil or criminal action or proceeding according to law and the evidence given them in the court.

Plaintiff. In a criminal case, the complainant.

Postmortem. Meaning after death. Commonly applied to examinations of a dead body. An *autopsy* is a postmortem examination to determine the cause of death.

Preliminary hearing. A hearing before a magistrate to decide if there is sufficient evidence to hold the defendant for further action.

Probation. The type of penalty whereby a convicted person is put under the jurisdiction of probation officers for a stated time, instead of being sent to prison.

Sentence. The judgment formally pronounced by the court or judge upon the defendant after his conviction in a criminal prosecution, awarding the punishment to be inflicted. In civil cases, the terms *judgment, decision, award, finding,* etc., are used.

Subpoena. A written order to appear at a trial as a witness.

Summons. A signed request directing a person to appear in court at a specified time to explain a charge made against him.

Venue. A neighborhood; the neighborhood, place, or county in which an injury is declared to have been done.

Verdict. The decision of a jury.

Warrant. A writ issued by a court or magistrate ordering a peace officer to arrest the one named therein for a crime.

APPENDIX B

The Constitution of the United States of America

We the people of the United States, in order to form a more perfect union, establish justice, insure domestic tranquility, provide for the common defense, promote the general welfare, and secure the blessings of liberty to ourselves and our posterity, do ordain and establish this Constitution for the United States of America.

ARTICLE I

Section 1. All legislative powers herein granted shall be vested in a Congress of the United States, which shall consist of a Senate and House of Representatives.

Section 2. 1. The House of Representatives shall be composed of members chosen every second year by the people of the several States, and the electors in each State shall have the qualifications requisite for electors of the most numerous branch of the State legislature.

2. No person shall be a representative who shall not have attained to the age of twenty-five years, and been seven years a citizen of the United States, and who shall not, when elected, be an inhabitant of that State in which he shall be chosen.

3. Representatives and direct taxes[1] shall be apportioned among the several States which may be included within this Union, according to their respective numbers, which shall be determined by adding to the whole number of free persons, including those bound to service for a term of years, and excluding Indians not taxed, three fifths of all other persons.[2] The actual enumeration shall by made within three years after the first meeting of the Congress of the United States, and within every subsequent term of ten years, in such manner as they shall by law direct. The number of representatives shall not exceed one for every thirty thousand, but each State shall have at least one representative; and until such enumeration shall be made, the State of New Hampshire shall be entitled to choose three, Massachusetts eight, Rhode Island and Providence Plantations one, Connecticut five, New York six, New Jersey four, Pennsylvania eight, Delaware one, Maryland six, Virginia ten, North Carolina five, South Carolina five, and Georgia three.

4. When vacancies happen in the representation from any State, the executive authority thereof shall issue writs of election to fill such vacancies.

5. The House of Representatives shall choose their speaker and other officers; and shall have the sole power of impeachment.

Section 3. 1. The Senate of the United States shall be composed of two senators from each State, chosen by the legislature thereof,[3] for six years; and each senator shall have one vote.

2. Immediately after they shall be assembled in consequence of the first election, they shall be divided as equally as may be into three classes. The seats of the senators of the first class shall be vacated at the expiration of the second year, of the second class at the expiration of the fourth year and of the third class at the expiration of the sixth year, so that one third may be chosen every second year; and if vacancies happen by resignation, or otherwise, during the recess of the legislature of any State, the executive thereof may make temporary appointments until the next meeting of the legislature, which shall then fill such vacancies.[4]

3. No person shall be a senator who shall not have attained to the age of thirty years, and been nine years a citizen of the United States, and who shall not, when elected, be an inhabitant of that State for which he shall be chosen.

4. The Vice President of the United States shall be President of the Senate, but shall have no vote, unless they be equally divided.

5. The Senate shall choose their other officers, and also a president pro tempore, in the absence of the Vice President, or when he shall exercise the office of the President of the United States.

6. The Senate shall have the sole power to try all impeachments. When sitting for that purpose, they shall be on oath or affirmation. When the President of the United States is tried, the chief justice shall preside: and no person shall be convicted without the concurrence of two thirds of the members present.

7. Judgment in cases of impeachment shall not extend further than to removal from office, and disqualifications to hold and enjoy any office of honor, trust or profit under the United States: but the party convicted shall nevertheless be liable and subject to indictment, trial, judgment and punishment, according to law.

Section 4. 1. The times, places, and manner of holding elections for senators and representatives, shall be prescribed in each State by the legislature thereof: but the Congress may at any time by law make or alter such regulations, except as to the places of choosing senators.

2. The Congress shall assemble at least once in every year, and such meeting shall be on the first Monday in December, unless they shall by law appoint a different day.

Section 5. 1. Each House shall be the judge of the elections, returns and qualifications of its own members, and a majority of each shall constitute a quorum to do business; but a smaller number may adjourn from day to day, and may be authorized to compel the attendance of absent members, in such manner, and under such penalties as each House may provide.

[1] Altered by the 16th Amendment.
[2] Altered by the 14th Amendment.
[3] Superseded by the 17th Amendment.

[4] Altered by the 17th Amendment.

2. Each House may determine the rules of its proceedings, punish its members for disorderly behavior, and, with the concurrence of two thirds, expel a member.

3. Each House shall keep a journal of its proceedings, and from time to time publish the same, excepting such parts as may in their judgment require secrecy; and the yeas and nays of the members of either House on any question shall, at the desire of one fifth of those present, be entered on the journal.

4. Neither House, during the session of Congress, shall, without the consent of the other, adjourn for more than three days, nor to any other place than that in which the two Houses shall be sitting.

Section 6. 1. The senators and representatives shall receive a compensation for their services, to be ascertained by law, and paid out of the Treasury of the United States. They shall in all cases, except treason, felony, and breach of the peace, be privileged from arrest during their attendance at the session of their respective Houses, and in going to and returning from the same; and for any speech or debate in either House, they shall not be questioned in any other place.

2. No senator or representative shall, during the time for which he was elected, be appointed to any civil office under the authority of the United States, which shall have been created, or the emoluments whereof shall have been increased, during such time; and no person holding any office under the United States shall be a member of either House during his continuance in office.

Section 7. 1. All bills for raising revenue shall originate in the House of Representatives; but the Senate may propose or concur with amendments as on other bills.

2. Every bill which shall have passed the House of Representatives and the Senate, shall, before it become a law, be presented to the President of the United States; If he approves he shall sign it, but if not he shall return it, with his objections, to that House in which it shall have originated, who shall enter the objections at large on their journal, and proceed to reconsider it. If after such reconsideration two thirds of that House shall agree to pass the bill, it shall be sent, together with the objections, to the other House, by which it shall likewise be reconsidered, and if approved by two thirds of that House, it shall become a law. But in all such cases the votes of both Houses shall be determined by yeas and nays, and the names of the persons voting for and against the bill shall be entered on the journal of each House respectively. If any bill shall not be returned by the President within ten days (Sundays excepted) after it shall have been presented to him, the same shall be a law, in like manner as if he had signed it, unless the Congress by their adjournment prevent its return, in which case it shall not be a law.

3. Every order, resolution, or vote to which the concurrence of the Senate and the House of Representatives may be necessary (except on a question of adjournment) shall be presented to the President of the United States; and before the same shall take effect, shall be approved by him, or being disapproved by him, shall be repassed by two thirds of the Senate and House of Representatives, according to the rules and limitations prescribed in the case of a bill.

Section 8. The Congress shall have the power

1. To lay and collect taxes, duties, imposts, and excises, to pay the debts and provide for the common defense and general welfare of the United States; but all duties, imposts, and excises shall be uniform throughout the United States;

2. To borrow money on the credit of the United States;

3. To regulate commerce with foreign nations, and among the several States, and with the Indian tribes;

4. To establish an uniform rule of naturalization, and uniform laws on the subject of bankruptcies throughout the United States;

5. To coin money, regulate the value thereof, and of foreign coin, and fix the standard of weights and measures;

6. To provide for the punishment of counterfeiting the securities and current coin of the United States;

7. To establish post offices and post roads;

8. To promote the progress of science and useful arts, by securing for limited times to authors and inventors the exclusive right to their respective writings and discoveries;

9. To constitute tribunals inferior to the Supreme Court;

10. To define and punish piracies and felonies committed on the high seas, and offenses against the law of nations;

11. To declare war, grant letters of marque and reprisal, and make rules concerning captures on land and water;

12. To raise and support armies, but no appropriation of money to that use shall be for a longer term than two years;

13. To provide and maintain a navy;

14. To make rules for the government and regulation of the land and naval forces;

15. To provide for calling forth the militia to execute the laws of the Union, suppress insurrections and repel invasions;

16. To provide for organizing, arming, and disciplining the militia, and for governing such part of them as may be employed in the service of the United States, reserving to the States respectively, the appointment of the officers, and the authority of training the militia according to the discipline prescribed by Congress;

17. To exercise exclusive legislation in all cases whatsoever, over such district (not exceeding ten miles square) as may, by cession of particular States, and the acceptance of Congress, become the seat of the government of the United States, and to exercise like authority over all places purchased by the consent of the legislature of the State in which the same shall be, for the erection of forts, magazines, arsenals, dockyards, and other needful buildings; and

18. To make all laws which shall be necessary and proper for carrying into execution the foregoing powers, and all other powers vested by this Constitution in the government of the United States, or any department or officer thereof.

Section 9. 1. The migration or importation of such persons as any of the States now existing shall think proper to admit, shall not be prohibited by the Congress prior to the year one thousand eight hundred and eight, but a tax or duty may be imposed on such importation, not exceeding ten dollars for each person.

2. The privilege of the writ of habeas corpus shall not be suspended, unless when in cases of rebellion or invasion the public safety may require it.

3. No bill of attainder or ex post facto law shall be passed.

4. No capitation, or other direct, tax shall be laid, unless in proportion to the census or enumeration hereinbefore directed to be taken.[5]

5. No tax or duty shall be laid on articles exported from any State.

6. No preference shall be given by any regulation of commerce or revenue to the ports of one State over those of another: nor shall vessels bound to, or from, one State be obliged to enter, clear, or pay duties in another.

7. No money shall be drawn from the treasury, but in consequence of appropriations made by law; and a regular statement and account of the receipts and expenditures of all public money shall be published from time to titne.

8. No title of nobility shall be granted by the United States: and no person holding any office of profit or trust under them, shall, without the consent of the Congress, accept of any present, emolument, office, or title, of any kind whatever, from any king, prince, or foreign State.

Section 10. 1. No State shall enter into any treaty, alliance, or confederation; grant letters of marque and reprisal; coin money; emit bills of credit; make any thing but gold and silver coin a tender in payment of debts; pass any bill of attainder, ex post facto law, or law impairing the obligation of contracts, or grant any title of nobility.

2. No State shall, without the consent of the Congress, lay any imposts or duties on imports or exports, except what may be absolutely necessary for executing its inspection laws: and the net produce of all duties and imposts laid by any State on imports or exports, shall be for the use of the treasury of the United States; and all such laws shall be subject to the revision and control of the Congress.

3. No State shall, without the consent of the Congress, lay any duty of tonnage, keep troops, or ships of war in time of peace, enter into any agreement or compact with another State, or with a foreign power, or engage in war, unless actually invaded, or in such imminent danger as will not admit of delay.

ARTICLE II
Section 1. 1. The executive power shall be vested in a President of the United States of America. He shall hold his office during the term of four years, and, together with the Vice President, chosen for the same term, be elected, as follows:

2. Each State shall appoint, in such manner as the legislature thereof may direct, a number of electors, equal to the whole number of senators and representatives to which the State may be entitled in the Congress: but no senator or representative, or person holding an office of

trust or profit under the United States, shall be appointed an elector.

The electors shall meet in their respective States, and vote by ballot for two persons, of whom one at least shall not be an inhabitant of the same State with themselves. And they shall make a list of all the persons voted for, and of the number of votes for each; which list they shall sign and certify, and transmit sealed to the seat of the government of the United States, directed to the president of the Senate. The president of the Senate shall, in the presence of the Senate and House of Representatives, open all the certificates, and the votes shall then be counted. The person having the greatest number of votes shall be the President, if such number be a majority of the whole number of electors appointed; and if there be more than one who have such majority, and have an equal number of votes, then the House of Representatives shall immediately choose by ballot one of them for President; and if no person have a majority, then from the five highest on the list the said House shall in like manner choose the President. But in choosing the President, the votes shall be taken by States, the representation from each State having one vote; a quorum for this purpose shall consist of a member or members from two thirds of the States, and a majority of all the States shall be necessary to a choice. In every case, after the choice of the President, the person having the greatest number of votes of the electors shall be the Vice President. But if there should remain two or more who have equal votes, the Senate shall choose from them by ballot the Vice President.[6]

3. The Congress may determine the time of choosing the electors, and the day on which they shall give their votes; which day shall be the same throughout the United States.

4. No person except a natural born citizen, or a citizen of the United States, at the time of the adoption of this Constitution, shall be eligible to the office of President; neither shall any person be eligible to that office who shall not have attained to the age of thirty-five years, and been fourteen years a resident within the United States.

5. In case of the removal of the President from office, or of his death, resignation, or inability to discharge the powers and duties of the said office, the same shall devolve on the Vice President, and the Congress may by law provide for the case of removal, death, resignation or inability, both of the President and Vice President, declaring what officer shall then act as President, and such officer shall act accordingly, until the disability be removed, or a President shall be elected.

6. The President shall, at stated times, receive for his services a compensation, which shall neither be increased nor diminished during the period for which he shall have been elected, and he shall not receive within that period any other emolument from the United States, or any of them.

7. Before he enter on the execution of his office, he shall take the following oath or affirmation:—"I do solemnly swear (or affirm) that I will faithfully execute the office of President of the United States, and will to the best of my

---

[5] Superseded by the 16th Amendment.

[6] Superseded by the 12th Amendment.

ability, preserve, protect, and defend the Constitution of the United States."

Section 2. 1. The President shall be commander in chief of the army and navy of the United States, and of the militia of the several States, when called into the actual service of the United States; he may require the opinion, in writing, of the principal officer in each of the executive departments, upon any subject relating to the duties of their respective offices, and he shall have power to grant reprieves and pardons for offenses against the United States, except in cases of impeachment.

2. He shall have power, by and with the advice and consent of the Senate, to make treaties, provided two thirds of the senators present concur; and he shall nominate, and by and with the advice and consent of the Senate, shall appoint ambassadors, other public ministers and consuls, judges of the Supreme Court, and all other officers of the United States, whose appointments are not herein otherwise provided for, and which shall be established by law: but the Congress may by law vest the appointment of such inferior officers, as they think proper, in the President alone, in the courts of law, or in the heads of departments.

3. The President shall have power to fill up all vacancies that may happen during the recess of the Senate, by granting commissions which shall expire at the end of their next session.

Section 3. He shall from time to time give to the Congress information of the state of the Union, and recommend to their consideration such measures as he shall judge necessary and expedient; he may, on extraordinary occasions, convene both Houses, or either of them, and in case of disagreement between them with respect to the time of adjournment, he may adjourn them to such time as he shall think proper; he shall receive ambassadors and other public ministers; he shall take care that the laws be faithfully executed, and shall commission all the officers of the United States.

Section 4. The President, Vice President, and all civil officers of the United States, shall be removed from office on impeachment for, and conviction of, treason, bribery, or other high crimes and misdemeanors.

ARTICLE III

Section 1. The judicial power of the United States shall be vested in one Supreme Court, and in such inferior courts as the Congress may from time to time ordain and establish. The judges, both of the Supreme and inferior courts, shall hold their offices during good behavior, and shall, at stated times, receive for their services, a compensation, which shall not be diminished during their continuance in office.

Section 2. 1. The judicial power shall extend to all cases, in law and equity, arising under this Constitution, the laws of the United States, and treaties made, or which shall be made, under their authority;—to all cases affecting ambassadors, other public ministers and consuls;—to all cases of admiralty and maritime jurisdiction;—to all cases of admiralty and maritime jurisdiction;—to controversies to which the United States shall be a party;[7]—to controversies between two or more

States;—between a State and citizens of another State;—between citizens of different States;—between citizens of the same State claiming lands under grants of different States, and between a State, or the citizens thereof, and foreign States, citizens or subjects.

2. In all cases affecting ambassadors, other public ministers and consuls, and those in which a State shall be party, the Supreme Court shall have original jurisdiction. In all the other cases before mentioned, the Supreme Court shall have appellate jurisdiction, both as to law and fact, with such exceptions, and under such regulations as the Congress shall make.

3. The trial of all crimes, except in cases of impeachment, shall be by jury; and such trial shall be held in the State where the said crimes shall have been committed; but when not committed within any State, the trial shall be at such place or places as the Congress may by law have directed.

Section 3. 1. Treason against the United States shall consist only in levying war against them, or in adhering to their enemies, giving them aid and comfort. No person shall be convicted of treason unless on the testimony of two witnesses to the same overt act, or on confession in open court.

2. The Congress shall have power to declare the punishment of treason, but no attainder of treason shall work corruption of blood, or forfeiture except during the life of the person attainted.

ARTICLE IV

Section 1. Full faith and credit shall be given in each State to the public acts, records, and judicial proceedings of every other State. And the Congress may by general laws prescribe the manner in which such acts, records and proceedings shall be proved, and the effect thereof.

Section 2. 1. The citizens of each State shall be entitled to all privileges and immunities of citizens in the several States.[8]

2. A person charged in any State with treason, felony, or other crime, who shall flee from justice, and be found in another State, shall on demand of the executive authority of the State from which he fled, be delivered up to be removed to the State having jurisdiction of the crime.

3. No person held to service or labor in one State under the laws thereof, escaping into another, shall, in consequence of any law or regulation therein, be discharged from such service or labor, but shall be delivered up on claim of the party to whom such service or labor may be due.[9]

Section 3. 1. New States may be admitted by the Congress into this Union; but no new State shall be formed or erected within the jurisdiction of any other State; nor any State be formed by the junction of two or more States, or parts of States, without the consent of the legislatures of the States concerned as well as of the Congress.

2. The Congress shall have power to dispose of and make all needful rules and regulations respecting the

[7] Cf. the 11th Amendment.

[8] Superseded by the 14th Amendment, Sec. 1.
[9] Voided by the 13th Amendment.

territory or other property belonging to the United States; and nothing in this Constitution shall be so construed as to prejudice any claims of the United States, or of any particular State.

Section 4. The United States shall guarantee to every State in this Union a republican form of government, and shall protect each of them against invasion; and on application of the legislature, or of the executive (when the legislature cannot be convened) against domestic violence.

ARTICLE V

The Congress, whenever two thirds of both Houses shall deem it necessary, shall propose amendments to this Constitution, or, on the application of the legislatures of two thirds of the several States, shall call a convention for proposing amendments, which in either case, shall be valid to all intents and purposes, as part of this Constitution, when ratified by the legislatures of three fourths of the several States, or by conventions in three fourths thereof, as the one or the other mode of ratification may be proposed by the Congress; Provided that no amendment which may be made prior to the year one thousand eight hundred and eight shall in any manner affect the first and fourth clauses in the ninth section of the first article; and that no State, without its consent, shall be deprived of its equal suffrage in the Senate.

ARTICLE VI

1. All debts contracted and engagements entered into, before the adoption of this Constitution, shall be as valid against the United States under this Constitution, as under the Confederation.

2. This Constitution, and the laws of the United States which shall be made in pursuance thereof; and all treaties made, or which shall be made, under the authority of the United States, shall be the supreme law of the land; and the Judges in every State shall be bound thereby, any thing in the Constitution or laws of any State to the contrary notwithstanding.

3. The senators and representatives before mentioned, and the members of the several State legislatures, and all executive and judicial officers, both of the United States and of the several States, shall be bound by oath or affirmation to support this Constitution; but no religious test shall ever be required as a qualification to any office or public trust under the United States.

ARTICLE VII

The ratification of the conventions of nine States shall be sufficient for the establishment of this Constitution between the States so ratifying the same.

Done in Convention by the unanimous consent of the States present the seventeenth day of September in the year of our Lord one thousand seven hundred and eighty-seven, and of the independence of the United States of America the twelfth. In witness whereof we have hereunto subscribed our names.

[Names omitted]

*   *   *

Articles in addition to, and amendment of, the Constitution of the United States of America, proposed by Congress, and ratified by the legislatures of the several States, pursuant to the fifth article of the original Constitution.

AMENDMENT I [First ten amendments ratified December 15, 1791]
Congress shall make no law respecting an establishment of religion, or prohibiting the free exercise thereof; or abridging the freedom of speech, or of the press; or the right of the people peaceably to assemble, and to petition the government for a redress of grievances.

AMENDMENT II
A well regulated militia, being necessary to the security of a free State, the right of the people to keep and bear arms, shall not be infringed.

AMENDMENT III
No soldier shall, in time of peace be quartered in any house, without the consent of the owner, nor in time of war, but in a manner to be prescribed by law.

AMENDMENT IV
The right of the people to secure in their persons, houses, papers, and effects, against unreasonable searches and seizures, shall not be violated, and no warrants shall issue, but upon probable cause, supported by oath or affirmation, and particularly describing the place to be searched, and the persons or things to be seized.

AMENDMENT V
No person shall be held to answer for a capital, or otherwise infamous crime, unless on a presentment or indictment of a grand jury, except in cases arising in the land or naval forces, or in the militia, when in actual service in time of war or public danger; nor shall any person be subject for the same offense to be twice put in jeopardy of life or limb; nor shall be compelled in any criminal case to be a witness against himself, nor be deprived of life, liberty, or property, without due process of law; nor shall private property be taken for public use, without just compensation.

AMENDMENT VI
In all criminal prosecutions, the accused shall enjoy the right to a speedy and public trial, by an impartial jury of the State and district wherein the crime shall have been committed, which district shall have been previously ascertained by law, and to be informed of the nature and cause of the accusation; to be confronted with the witnesses against him; to have compulsory process for obtaining witnesses in his favor, and to have the assistance of counsel for his defense.

AMENDMENT VII
In suits at common law, where the value in controversy shall exceed twenty dollars, the right of trial by jury shall be preserved, and no fact tried by a jury shall be other-

wise reëxamined in any court of the United States, than according to the rules of the common law.

AMENDMENT VIII

Excessive bail shall not be required, nor excessive fines imposed, nor cruel and unusual punishments inflicted.

AMENDMENT IX

The enumeration in the Constitution of certain rights shall not be construed to deny or disparage others retained by the people.

AMENDMENT X

The powers not delegated to the United States by the Constitution, nor prohibited by it to the States, are reserved to the States respectively, or to the people.

AMENDMENT XI [Ratified January 8, 1798]

The judicial power of the United States shall not be construed to extend to any suit in law or equity, commenced or prosecuted against one of the United States by citizens of another State, or by citizens or subjects of any foreign State.

AMENDMENT XII [Ratified September 25, 1804]

The electors shall meet in their respective States, and vote by ballot for President and Vice President, one of whom, at least, shall not be an inhabitant of the same State with themselves; they shall name in their ballots the person voted for as President, and in distinct ballots, the person voted for as Vice President, and they shall make distinct lists of all persons voted for as President and of all persons voted for as Vice President, and of the number of votes for each, which lists they shall sign and certify, and transmit sealed to the seat of the government of the United States, directed to the President of the Senate;—The President of the Senate shall, in the presence of the Senate and House of Representatives, open all the certificates and the votes shall then be counted;—The person having the greatest number of votes for President, shall be the President, if such number be a majority of the whole number of electors appointed; and if no person have such majority, then from the persons having the highest numbers not exceeding three on the list of those voted for as President, the House of Representatives shall choose immediately, by ballot, the President. But in choosing the President, the votes shall be taken by States, the representation from each State having one vote; a quorum for this purpose shall consist of a member or members from two thirds of the States, and a majority of all the States shall be necessary to a choice. And if the House of Representatives shall not choose a President whenever the right of choice shall devolve upon them, before the fourth day of March next following, then the Vice President shall act as President, as in the case of the death or other constitutional disability of the President. The person having the greatest number of votes as Vice President shall be the Vice President, if such number be a majority of the whole number of electors appointed, and if no person have a majority, then from the two highest numbers on the list,

the Senate shall choose the Vice President; a quorum for the purpose shall consist of two thirds of the whole number of Senators, and a majority of the whole number shall be necessary to a choice. But no person constitutionally ineligible to the office of President shall be eligible to that of Vice President of the United States.

AMENDMENT XIII [Ratified December 18, 1865]

Section 1. Neither slavery nor involuntary servitude, except as a punishment for crime whereof the party shall have been duly convicted, shall exist within the United States, or any place subject to their jurisdiction.
Section 2. Congress shall have power to enforce this article by appropriate legislation.

AMENDMENT XIV [Ratified July 28, 1868]

Section 1. All persons born or naturalized in the United States, and subject to the jurisdiction thereof, are citizens of the United States and of the State wherein they reside. No State shall make or enforce any law which shall abridge the privileges or immunities of citizens of the United States; nor shall any State deprive any person of life, liberty, or property, without due process of law; nor deny to any person within its jurisdiction the equal protection of the laws.
Section 2. Representatives shall be apportioned among the several States according to their respective numbers, counting the whole number of persons in each State, excluding Indians not taxed. But when the right to vote at any election for the choice of electors for President and Vice President of the United States, representatives in Congress, the executive and judicial officers of a State, or the members of the legislature thereof, is denied to any of the male inhabitants of such State, being twenty-one years of age, and citizens of the United States, or in any way abridged, except for participating in rebellion, or other crime, the basis of representation therein shall be reduced in the proportion which the number of such male citizens shall bear to the whole number of male citizens twenty-one years of age in such State.
Section 3. No person shall be a senator or representative in Congress, or elector of President and Vice President, or hold any office, civil or military, under the United States, or under any State, who having previously taken an oath, as a member of Congress, or as an officer of the United States, or as a member of any State legislature, or as an executive or judicial officer of any State, to support the Constitution of the United States, shall have engaged in insurrection or rebellion against the same, or given aid or comfort to the enemies thereof. But Congress may by a vote of two thirds of each House, remove such disability.
Section 4. The validity of the public debt of the United States, authorized by law, including debts incurred for payment of pensions and bounties for services in suppressing insurrection or rebellion, shall not be questioned. But neither the United States nor any State shall assume or pay any debt or obligation incurred in aid of insurrection or rebellion against the United States, or any claim for the loss or emancipation of any slave; but all such debts, obligations, and claims shall be held illegal and void.

Section 5. The Congress shall have power to enforce, by appropriate legislation, the provisions of this article.

AMENDMENT XV [Ratified March 30, 1870]
Section 1. The right of citizens of the United States to vote shall not be denied or abridged by the United States or by any State on account of race, color, or previous condition of servitude.
Section 2. The Congress shall have power to enforce this article by appropriate legislation.

AMENDMENT XVI [Ratified February 25, 1913]
The Congress shall have power to lay and collect taxes on incomes, from whatever source derived, without apportionment among the several States, and without regard to any census or enumeration.

AMENDMENT XVII [Ratified May 31, 1913]
The Senate of the United States shall be composed of two senators from each State, elected by the people thereof, for six years; and each senator shall have one vote. The electors in each State shall have the qualifications requisite for electors of the most numerous branch of the State legislature.
When vacancies happen in the representation of any State in the Senate, the executive authority of such State shall issue writs of election to fill such vacancies: *Provided,* That the legislature of any State may empower the executive thereof to make temporary appointments until the people fill the vacancies by election as the legislature may direct.
This amendment shall not be so construed as to affect the election or term of any senator chosen before it becomes valid as part of the Constitution.

AMENDMENT XVIII[10] [Ratified January 29, 1919]
After one year from the ratification of this article, the manufacture, sale, or transportation of intoxicating liquors within, the importation thereof into, or the exportation thereof from the United States and all territory subject to the jurisdiction thereof for beverage purposes is thereby prohibited.
The Congress and the several States shall have concurrent power to enforce this article by appropriate legislation.
This article shall be inoperative unless it shall have been ratified as an amendment to the Constitution by the legislatures of the several States, as provided in the Constitution, within seven years from the date of the submission hereof to the States by Congress.

AMENDMENT XIX [Ratified August 26, 1920]
The right of citizens of the United States to vote shall not be denied or abridged by the United States or by any State on account of sex.
Congress shall have the power to enforce this article by appropriate legislation.

AMENDMENT XX [Ratified January 23, 1933]
Section 1. The terms of the President and Vice President shall end at noon on the 20th day of January, and the

[10] Repealed by the 21st Amendment.

terms of Senators and Representatives at noon on the 3d day of January, of the years in which such terms would have ended if this article had not been ratified; and the terms of their successors shall then begin.
Section 2. The Congress shall assemble at least once in every year, and such meeting shall begin at noon on the 3d day of January, unless they shall by law appoint a different day.
Section 3. If, at the time fixed for the beginning of the term of President, the President-elect shall have died, the Vice President-elect shall become President. If a President shall not have been chosen before the time fixed for the beginning of his term, or if the President-elect shall have failed to qualify, then the Vice President-elect shall act as President until a President shall have qualified; and the Congress may by law provide for the case wherein neither a President-elect nor a Vice President-elect shall have qualified, declaring who shall then act as President, or the manner in which one who is to act shall be selected, and such person shall act accordingly until a President or Vice President shall have qualified.
Section 4. The Congress may by law provide for the case of the death of any of the persons from whom the House of Representatives may choose a President whenever the right of choice shall have devolved upon them, and for the case of the death of any of the persons from whom the Senate may choose a Vice President whenever the right of choice shall have devolved upon them.
Section 5. Sections 1 and 2 shall take effect on the 15th day of October following the ratification of this article.
Section 6. This article shall be inoperative unless it shall have been ratified as an amendment to the Constitution by the legislatures of three-fourths of the several States within seven years from the date of its submission.

AMENDMENT XXI [Ratified December 5, 1933]
Section 1. The Eighteenth Article of amendment to the Constitution of the United States is hereby repealed.
Section 2. The transportation or importation into any State, Territory, or possession of the United States for delivery or use therein of intoxicating liquors in violation of the laws thereof, is hereby prohibited.
Section 3. This article shall be inoperative unless it shall have been ratified as an amendment to the Constitution by conventions in the several States as provided in the Constitution, within seven years from the date of the submission thereof to the States by the Congress.

AMENDMENT XXII [Ratified March 1, 1951]
No person shall be elected to the office of the President more than twice, and no person who has held the office of President, or acted as President, for more than two years of a term to which some other person was elected President shall be elected to the office of the President more than once.
But this article shall not apply to any person holding the office of President when this article was proposed by the Congress, and shall not prevent any person who may be holding the office of President, or acting as President, during the term within which this article becomes operative from holding the office of President or acting as President during the remainder of such term.

461

This article shall be inoperative unless it shall have been ratified as an amendment to the Constitution by the legislatures of three-fourths of the several States within seven years from the date of its submission to the States by the Congress.

AMENDMENT XXIII [Ratified March 29, 1961]
Section 1. The District constituting the seat of Government of the United States shall appoint in such manner as the Congress may direct:

A number of electors of President and Vice President equal to the whole number of Senators and Representatives in Congress to which the District would be entitled if it were a State, but in no event more than the least populous State; they shall be in addition to those appointed by the States, but they shall be considered, for the purposes of the election of President and Vice President, to be electors appointed by a State; and they shall meet in the District and perform such duties as provided by the twelfth article of amendment.
Section 2. The Congress shall have power to enforce this article by appropriate legislation.

AMENDMENT XXIV [Ratified January 23, 1964]
Section 1. The right of citizens of the United States to vote in any primary or other election for President or Vice President, for electors for President or Vice President, or for Senator or Representative in Congress, shall not be denied or abridged by the United States or any State by reason of failure to pay any poll tax or other tax.
Section 2. The Congress shall have power to enforce this article by appropriate legislation.

AMENDMENT XXV [Ratified February 10, 1967]
Section 1. In case of the removal of the President from office or of his death or resignation, the Vice President shall become President.
Section 2. Whenever there is a vacancy in the office of the Vice President, the President shall nominate a Vice President who shall take office upon confirmation by a majority vote of both Houses of Congress.
Section 3. Whenever the President transmits to the President pro tempore of the Senate and the Speaker of the House of Representatives his written declaration that he is unable to discharge the powers and duties of his office, and until he transmits to them a written declaration to the contrary, such powers and duties shall be discharged by the Vice President as Acting President.
Section 4. Whenever the Vice President and a majority of either the principal officers of the executive departments or of such other body as Congress may by law provide, transmit to the President pro tempore of the Senate and the Speaker of the House of Representatives their written declaration that the President is unable to discharge the powers and duties of his office, the Vice President shall immediately assume the powers and duties of the office as Acting President.

Thereafter, when the President transmits to the President pro tempore of the Senate and the Speaker of the House of Representatives his written declaration that no inability exists, he shall resume the powers and duties of his office unless the Vice President and a majority of either the principal officers of the executive departments or of such other body as Congress may by law provide, transmit within four days to the President pro tempore of the Senate and the Speaker of the House of Representatives their written declaration that the President is unable to discharge the powers and duties of his office. Thereupon Congress shall decide the issue, assembling within forty-eight hours for that purpose if not in session. If the Congress, within twenty-one days after receipt of the latter written declaration, or, if Congress is not in session, within twenty-one days after Congress is required to assemble, determines by two-thirds vote of both Houses that the President is unable to discharge the powers and duties of his office, the Vice President shall continue to discharge the same as Acting President; otherwise, the President shall resume the powers and duties of his office.

APPENDIX C

The Code of Hammurabi

(The Code of Hammurabi, the earliest known Code, consists of 282 sections, certain selections from which follow.)

1. If a man weaves a spell about another man (i. e. accuses him) and throws a curse on him, and cannot prove it, the one who wove the spell shall be put to death.

2. If a man weaves a spell about another man, and has not proved it, he on whom suspicion was thrown shall go to the river, shall plunge into the river. If the river seizes hold of him, he who wove the spell shall take his house. If the river shows him to be innocent, and he is uninjured, he who threw suspicion on him shall be put to death. He who plunged into the river shall take the house of him who wove the spell on him.

3. If a man has accused the witnesses in a lawsuit of malice and has not proved what he said, if the suit was one of life (and death), that man shall be put to death.

4. If he has sent corn and silver to the witnesses, he shall bear the penalty of the suit.

5. If a judge has delivered a sentence, has made a decision and fixed it in writing, and if afterwards he has annulled his sentence, that judge for having altered his decision shall be brought to judgment; for the penalty inflicted in his decision, twelve-fold shall he pay it, and publicly shall they remove him from his judgment seat. He shall not come back and shall not sit in judgment with the other judges.

6. If a man has stolen property from the god or palace, that man shall be put to death.

7. If a man has bout or received in deposit, silver, gold, a man or woman slave, an ox, a sheep, an ass, or whatever it may be, from the hands of a son of another or a slave or another, without witness or contract, that man shall be put to death as a thief.

8. If anyone has stolen an ox, a sheep, an ass, a pig, or a boat, if it belongs to the god or to the palace, he shall return it thirty-fold; if it belongs to a noble he shall return it ten-fold; if the thief has nothing with which to repay, he shall be put to death.

9. If anyone who has lost something, finds his something that was lost in the hand (possession) of another; if the man in whose hand the lost object was found says: "A trader sold it to me, before witnesses I paid for it," and if the owner of the lost object says: "Witnesses who know my lost object I will bring," then shall the purchaser bring the seller who sold it to him, and the witnesses before whom he bought it, and the owner of the lost object shall bring witnesses who know his lost goods; the judge shall consider their words, and the witnesses before whom the purchase was made, and the witnesses who know the object shall bear testimony before God. The seller is a thief and shall be put to death. The owner of the lost object shall get back the money he paid from the house of the seller.

10. If the buyer does not bring the seller who sold it to him and the witnesses before whom he bought it; if the owner of the lost object brings the witnesses who know his object, the buyer is a thief and shall be killed; the owner shall get his lost object.

11. If the owner of the lost object does not bring his expert witnesses, then he is a miscreant; he has accused falsely, he shall die.

12. If the seller has gone to his fate, the buyer shall receive from the house of the seller five times the costs of the suit.

13. If that man has not his witnesses at hand, the judge shall give him a respite of six months. If in six months his witnesses do not come, that man is a miscreant and shall bear the costs of the suit.

14. If anyone steals the minor son of a man, he shall be put to death.

15. If anyone has caused a male slave of the palace or a female slave of the palace, the male slave of a noble or the female slave of a noble, to go out of the gate, he shall be put to death.

16. If anyone harbours in his house a runaway male or female slave from the palace or the house of a noble, and does not bring them out at the command of the majordomo, the master of the house shall be put to death.

17. If anyone has caught a runaway male or female slave in the field, and brings him back to his master, the master of the slave shall give him two shekels of silver.

18. If that slave will not name his owner, to the palace he shall bring him; his case shall be investigatted; to his owner one shall bring him.

19. If he retains that slave in his house, and if, later, the slave is found in his hands, that man shall be put to death.

20. If the slave escapes from the house of the one who caught him, that man shall swear to the owner of the slave in the name of God and he shall be quit.

21. If anyone has broken a hole in a house, in front of that hole one shall kill him and bury him.

22. If anyone has committed a robbery and is caught, he shall be killed.

23. If the robber is not caught, the man who has been robbed shall make claim before God to everything stolen from him, and the town and its governor within the territory and limits of which the robbery took place shall give back to him everything he has lost.

24. If it was a life, the city and governor shall pay one mina of silver to his people.

25. If a fire breaks out in the house of a man, and some one who has gone thither to put it out raise his eyes to the goods of the master of the house and take the goods of the master of the house, that man shall be thrown into that fire.

42. If anyone has taken a field to cultivate, and has not made grain to grow in the field, he shall be charged with not having done his duty in the field; he shall give grain equal to that yielded by the neighboring field to the owner of the field.

43. If he has not tilled the field, has let it lie, he shall give to the owner of the field grain equal to the yield of the neighbouring field; and the field which he left untilled, he shall harrow, sow, and return to its owner.

44. If any one has hired an unreclaimed field for three years, to open (cultivate) it, but has neglected it, has not opened the field, in the fourth year he shall harrow the field, hoe it, and plant it and return it to the owner of the field, and 10 GUR of grain for every 10 GAN he shall measure out.

45. If a man has rented his field to a cultivator for the produce and he has received his produce, and then a storm has come, and destroyed the harvest, the loss is the cultivator's.

46. If he has not received the produce from his field, but has given his field on a half or a third share, the grain which is in the field shall the owner and cultivator share according to their contract.

47. If the cultivator, because in the first year he did not obtain his living (?), had the field cultivated by another, the owner of the field shall not blame this cultivator, his field has been cultivated; at the time of harvest he shall receive grain according to his contract.

48. If a man has a debt and a storm has devastated his field, and carried off the harvest, or if the grain has not grown on account of lack of water, in that year he shall give no grain to the creditor; he shall soak his tablet (in water, i. e., alter it), and shall pay no interest for that year.

49. If anyone has borrowed money from a merchant and given a ploughed field sown with grain or sesame to the merchant and said to him: "Cultivate the field, harvest and take the grain or sesame which is thereon;" when the cultivator has raised the grain or sesame in the field, at the time of harvest the owner of the field shall take the grain or sesame which is in the field, and shall give to the merchant grain in return for the money with its interest, which he took from the merchant, and for the support of the cultivator.

50. If he has given him an (already) cultivated field (of grain) or a field of sesame, the grain or sesame which is in the field shall the owner of the field receive; money and interest to the merchant he shall give.

51. If he has no money with which to pay him, he shall give to the merchant sesame equal to the value

of the money which he received from the merchant, with interest according to the king's tariff.

52. If the cultivator has not raised grain or sesame in the field, his contract is not altered.

53. If anyone is too lazy to keep his dikes in order and fails to do so, and if a breach is made in his dike and the fields have been flooded with water, the man in whose dike the breach was opened shall replace the grain which he has destroyed.

54. If he is not able to replace the grain, he and his property shall be sold, and the people whose grain the water carried off shall share (the proceeds).

55. If anyone opens his irrigation canals to let in water, but is careless and the water floods the field of his neighbour, he shall measure out grain to the latter in proportion to the yield of the neighbouring field.

56. If any one lets in the water and it floods the growth of his neighbour's field, he shall measure out to him 10 GUR of grain for every 10 GAN (of land).

109. If a wine merchant when rebels meet in her house does not arrest them and take them to the palace, that wine merchant shall be put to death.

110. If a votary who does not live in the temple shall open a tavern or enter a tavern to drink, she shall be burned.

116. If the confined man has died in the house of his confinement as a result of blows or ill-treatment, the owner of the prisoner shall call his merchant to account. If the man was free-born, his son (of the merchant) one shall kill; if he was a slave, he shall pay one-third of a mina of silver, and shall lose possession of everything which he gave him.

117. If anyone has an indebtedness, sells wife, son, or daughter, for gold or gives them into bondage, three years in the house of their buyer or their task-master shall they labour; in the fourth year shall he let them go free.

118. If he gives away a man or woman slave into servitude, and if the merchant passes them on, sells them for money, there is no protest.

119. If anyone has contracted a debt and sells a slave who has borne him children, the money which the merchant paid, the owner of the slave shall pay back to him and buy back his slave.

120. If anyone has stored his grain in the house of another for keeping and a disaster has happened in the granary, or the owner of the house has opened the granary and taken out the grain, or if he disputes as to the whole amount which was deposited with him, the owner of the grain shall pursue (claim) his grain before God, and the master of the house shall return undiminished to its owner the grain which he took.

127. If anyone has caused a finger to be pointed at a votary or the wife of a man and has not proved (his accusation against) that man, one shall bring him before the judge and brand his forehead.

128. If anyone has married a wife but has not drawn up a contract with her, that woman is not a wife.

464

141. If a man's wife, who lives in his house, sets her face to go out, causes discord, wastes her house, neglects her husband, to justice one shall bring her. If her husband says "I repudiate her," he shall let her go her way, he shall give her nothing for her divorce. If her husband says, "I do not repudiate her," her husband may take another wife; that (first) wife shall stay in the house of her husband as a slave.

148. If anyone has taken a wife and a sickness has seized her, and if his face is set towards taking another wife, he may take (her), but his wife whom the sickness has seized he may not repudiate her, she shall live in the house he has built, and as long as she lives he shall support her.

149. If that woman does not desire to live in the house of her husband, he shall give her the marriage portion she brought from her father's house, and she shall go.

150. If anyone has given his wife, field, garden, house, or property, and has left her a sealed tablet; after (the death of) her husband, her children shall contest nothing with her. The mother shall leave her inheritance to the child whom she loves; to a brother she shall not give it.

163. If anyone has married a wife and she has borne him no children; if that woman has gone to her fate, if the dowry which that man took from the house of his father-in-law his father-in-law has returned; on the marriage portion of that woman the husband shall make no claim, it belongs to the house of her father.

164. If his father-in-law has not returned him the dowry, from her marriage portion he shall deduct all her dowry; and her marriage portion he shall return to the house of her father.

165. If any man to his son, the first in his eyes, has given a field, garden, and house, and has written a tablet for him; if afterwards the father has gone to his fate, when the brothers make a division, the present which the father gave him he shall keep; in addition, the goods of their father's house in equal parts they shall share (with him).

166. If a man has taken wives for his sons, for his little son a wife has not taken, if afterwards the father has gone to his fate, when the brothers divide the goods of their father's house, to their little brother, who has not taken a wife, besides his portion, money for a dowry they shall give him, and a wife they shall cause him to take.

167. If a man has married a woman, if she has borne him children, if that woman has gone to her fate; if afterwards he has taken another wife, who has borne him children, and if afterwards the father has gone to his fate; the children shall not divide the property according to their mothers; they shall take the marriage portion of their mother; their father's property they shall share in equal parts.

168. If anyone has set his face to cut off his son and say to the judge, "I cut off my son," the judge shall inquire into the matter; and if the son has no grievous offence, which would lead to being cut off from sonship, the father shall not cut off his son from sonship.

169. If he has a grievous crime against his father to the extent of cutting him off from sonship, for the first time he (the father) shall turn away his face; but if he commit a grievous crime a second time, the father shall cut off his son from sonship.

170. If to a man his wife has borne children, and if his servant has borne him children; if the father during his life has said: "You are my children," to the children which his servant bore him, and has counted them with his wife's children; afterwards if that father has gone to his fate, the goods of the father's house shall the children of the wife and the children of the servant share on equal terms. In the division the children of the wife shall choose (first) and take.

171. And if the father, during his life to the children which his slave bore him has not said, "You are my children," and afterwards when the father has gone to his fate, the property of the father's house the children of the servant shall not share with the children of the wife. The freedom of the servant and her children shall be assured. The children of the wife cannot claim the children of the servant for servitude. The wife shall take her marriage portion and the gift which her husband gave her and wrote on a tablet for her, and shall remain in the house of her husband. As long as she lives she shall keep them, and for money she shall not give them; after her they belong to her children.

172. If her husband has not given her a gift, her marriage-portion she shall receive entire; and of the property of her husband's house, a portion like a son she shall take. If her children force her to go out of the house, the judge shall inquire into the matter, and if a fault is imputed to the children, that woman shall not go out of the house of her husband. If that woman has set her face against the gift which her husband gave her she shall leave it to her children. The marriage portion which came from her father's house she shall keep, and the husband of her choice she shall take.

173. If that woman, there where she has entered, to her second husband has borne children, and if afterwards that woman dies, her marriage portion shall her earlier and her later children divide between them.

174. If to her second husband she has borne no children, her marriage portion shall the children of her first husband take.

175. If a free-born woman has married a palace slave or the slave of a noble, and has borne children; the owner of the slave on the children of the free-born woman shall make no claim for servitude.

176. And if a free-born woman marries a slave of the palace or the slave of a noble, and if when he married her she entered the house of the palace slave or of the nobleman's slave with a marriage portion from the house of her father, and from the

time that they set up their house together have acquired property; if afterward either the slave of the palace or the slave of the nobleman has gone to his fate, the free-born woman shall take her marriage portion, and whatever her husband and she since they began housekeeping have made, into two parts they shall divide; one-half the owner of the slave shall take, one-half the free-born woman shall take for her children.

176a. If the free-born woman had no marriage portion, everything which her husband and she had acquired since they kept house together, into two parts they shall divide. The owner of the slave one-half shall take; one-half shall the free-born woman take for her children.

177. If a widow whose children are still young, has set her face to enter the house of another without consulting the judge, she shall not enter. When she enters another house the judge shall inquire into that which was left from the house of her former husband; and the goods of her former husband's house to her later husband and to that woman (herself) one shall confide, and a tablet shall make them deliver. They shall keep the house and bring up the little ones; no utensil shall they give for money. The buyer who shall buy a utensil belonging to the children of the widow, shall lose his money; the property shall return to its owner.

178. If a votary or a vowed woman to whom her father has given a marriage portion, a tablet has written, and on the tablet he wrote for her did not write, "After her she may give to whom she pleases," has not permitted her all the wish of her heart; afterwards when the father has gone to his fate, her field and garden shall her brothers take, and according to the value of her portion they shall give her grain, oil, and wool, and her heart they shall content. If her brothers have not given her grain, oil, and wool according to the value of her portion, and have not contented her heart, she shall give her field and garden to a cultivator who is pleasing to her, and her cultivator shall sustain her. The field, garden, and whatever her father gave her she shall keep as long as she lives, but for money she shall not give it, to another she shall not part with it; her sonship (inheritance) belongs to her brother.

179. If a votary of a vowed woman to whom her father has given a marriage portion, and has written her a tablet, and on the tablet which he wrote her has written, "property where (to whom) it seems good to her to give (let her give)," has allowed her the fulness of her heart's desire; afterwards when the father has gone to his fate, her property after her death to whomever it pleases her she shall give; her brothers shall not strive with her.

180. If a father to his daughter, a bride or vowed woman, a marriage portion has not given; after the father has gone to his fate, she shall receive of the possession of the father's house a share like one son. As long as she lives she shall keep it. Her property after her death shall belong to her brothers.

181. If a father has vowed to God a hierodule or a temple virgin, and has gone to his fate, she shall have a share in the possession of the father's house

equal to one-third her portion as one of his children. As long as she lives she shall keep it. Her property after her death shall belong to her brothers.

182. If a father to his daughter, a votary of Marduk of Babylon, has not given a marriage portion, a tablet has not written; after the father has gone to his fate she shall share with her brothers in the possession of her father's house; a third of her share as his child (she shall receive). Control over it shall not go from her. The votary of Marduk shall give her property after her death to whomever it pleases her.

183. If a father to his daughter by a concubine has given a marriage portion, and has given her to a husband and has written her a tablet; after the father has gone to his fate, in the goods of the father's house, she shall not share.

184. If a man to his daughter by a concubine a marriage portion has not provided, to a husband has not given her; after the father has gone to his fate, her brothers shall provide her a marriage portion according to the value of the father's house, and to a husband they shall give her.

185. If a man has taken a small child as a son in his own name and has brought him up, that foster child shall not be reclaimed.

186. If a man has taken a small child for his son, and if when he took him his father and his mother he offended, that foster child shall return to the house of his father.

187. The son of a familiar slave in the palace service, or the son of a vowed woman, cannot be reclaimed.

188. If an artisan has taken a child to bring up, and has taught him his handicraft, no one can make a complaint.

189. If he has not taught him his handicraft, that foster child shall return to the house of his father.

190. If a man, a small child whom he took for his son and brought him up, with his own sons has not counted, that foster son shall return to his father's house.

191. If a man who has taken a small child for his son and brought him up, has afterwards made a home for himself and his acquired children, if he sets his face to cut off the foster child; that child shall not go his way. His adopted father shall give him of his goods one-third of a son's share, and then he shall go. Of the field, garden, and house he shall not give him.

192. If the son of a favourite slave or the son of a vowed woman to the father who brought him up and to the mother who brought him up say, "Thou art not my father, thou art not my mother," one shall cut out his tongue.

193. If the son of a palace favourite or the son of a vowed woman has known the house of his father and has hated the father who brought him up and the mother who brought him up, and has gone to the house of his father, one shall tear out his eyes.

194. If a man has given his son to a nurse and if his son has died in the hand of the nurse, and if the nurse, without the consent of his father or mother, another child has nourished, she shall be

brought to account and because she nourished another child, without the consent of the father and mother, one shall cut off her breasts.

195. If a son has struck his father, one shall cut off his hands.

196. If one destroys the eye of a free-born man, his eye one shall destroy.

197. If anyone breaks the limb of a free-born man, his limb one shall break.

198. If the eye of a nobleman he has destroyed, or the limb of a nobleman he has broken, one mina of silver he shall pay.

199. If he has destroyed the eye of the slave of a free-born man or has broken the limb of the slave of a free-born man, he shall pay the half of its price.

200. If he knocks out the teeth of a man who is his equal, his teeth one shall knock out.

201. If the teeth of a freedman he has made to fall out, he shall pay one-third of a mina of silver.

202. If anyone has injured the strength of a man who is high above him, he shall publicly be struck with sixty strokes of a cowhide whip.

203. If he has injured the strength of a man who is his equal, he shall pay one mina of silver.

204. If he has injured the strength of a freedman, one shall cut off his ear.

205. If the slave of a man has injured the strength of a free-born man, one shall cut off his ear.

206. If a man has struck another in a quarrel and has wounded him, and that man shall swear, "I did not strike him wittingly," he shall pay the doctor.

207. If he dies of the blows, he shall swear again, and if it was a free-born man, he shall pay one-half mina of silver.

208. If it was a freedman, he shall pay one-third a mina of silver.

215. If a doctor has treated a man for a severe wound with a lancet of bronze and has cured the man, or has opened a tumour with a bronze lancet and has cured the man's eye; he shall receive ten shekels of silver.

216. If it was a freedman he shall receive five shekels of silver.

217. If it was a man's slave, the owner of the slave shall give the doctor two shekels of silver.

218. If a physician has treated a free-born man for a severe wound with a lancet of bronze and has caused the man to die, or has opened a tumour of the man with a lancet of bronze and has destroyed his eye, his hands one shall cut off.

219. If a doctor has treated the slave of a freedman for a severe wound with a bronze lancet and has caused him to die, he shall give back slave for slave.

220. If he has opened his tumour with a bronze lancet and has ruined his eye, he shall pay the half of his price in money.

221. If a doctor has cured the broken limb of a man, or has healed his sick body, the patient shall pay the doctor five shekels of silver.

222. If it was a freedman, he shall give three shekels of silver.

223. If it was a man's slave, the owner of the slave shall give two shekels of silver to the doctor.

224. If the doctor of oxen and asses has treated an ox or an ass for a grave wound and has cured it, the owner of the ox or the ass shall give to the doctor as his pay one-sixth of a shekel of silver.

225. If he has treated an ox or an ass for a severe wound and has caused its death, he shall pay one-fourth of its price to the owner of the ox or the ass.

226. If a barber-surgeon, without consent of the owner of a slave, has branded the slave with an indelible mark, one shall cut off the hands of that barber.

227. If anyone deceives the barber-surgeon and makes him brand a slave with an indelible mark, one shall kill that man and bury him in his house. The barber shall swear, "I did not mark him wittingly," and he shall be guiltless.

228. If a builder has built a house for some one and has finished it, for every SAR of house he shall give him two shekels of silver as his fee.

229. If a builder has built a house for some one and has not made his work firm, and if the house he built has fallen and has killed the owner of the house, that builder shall be put to death.

230. If it has killed the son of the house-owner, one shall kill the son of that builder.

231. If it has killed the slave of the house-owner, he (the builder) shall give to the owner of the house slave for slave.

232. If it has destroyed property, he shall restore everything he destroyed; and because the house he built was not firm and fell in, out of his own funds, he shall rebuild the house that fell.

233. If a builder has built a house for some one and has not made its foundations solid, and a wall falls, that builder out of his own money shall make firm that wall.

234. If a boatman has caulked (?) a boat of 60 GUR for a man, he shall give him two shekels of silver as his fee.

235. If a boatman has caulked a boat for a man, and has not made firm his work, if in that year that ship is put into use and it suffers an injury, the boatman shall alter that boat and shall make it firm out of his own funds; and he shall give the strengthened boat to the owner of the boat.

236. If a man has given his boat to a boatman on hire, if the boatman has been careless, has grounded the boat or destroyed it, the boatman shall give a boat to the owner of the boat in compensation.

237. If a man has hired a boatman and a boat, and has loaded it with grain, wool, oil, dates, or whatever the cargo was; if that boatman has been careless, has grounded the ship and destroyed all that was in it, the boatman shall make good the ship which he grounded and whatever he destroyed of what was in it.

241. If a man has forced an ox to too hard labour, he shall pay one-third a mina of silver.

242. If a man hires (the ox) for one year he shall pay 4 GUR of grain as the hire of a working ox.

243. For the hire of an ox to carry burdens (?) he shall give 3 GUR of grain to its owner.

244. If anyone has hired an ox or an ass and if in the field a lion has killed it, the loss is its master's.

250. If a furious ox in his charge gores a man and

kills him, that case cannot be brought to judgment.

251. If an ox has pushed a man (with his horns) and in pushing showed him his vice, and if he has not blunted his horns, has not shut up his ox; if that ox gores a free-born man and kills him, he shall pay one-half a mina of silver.

253. If a man has hired a man to live in his field and has furnished him seed grain (?) and oxen, and has bound him to cultivate the field; if that man has stolen grain or plants and they are seized in his possession one shall cut off his hands.

255. If he has given out the man's oxen on hire or has stolen the grain, has not caused it to grow in the field; one shall bring that man to judgment, for 100 GAN of land he shall measure out 60 GUR of grain.

261. If a man has hired a herdsman to pasture cattle and sheep, he shall pay him 8 GUR of grain a year.

264. If a herdsman, to whom oxen and sheep have been given for pasturing, has received his wages, whatever was agreed upon, and his heart is contented; if he has diminished the oxen, or the sheep has lessened the offspring, he shall give offspring and produce according to the words of his agreement

265. If a herdsman, to whom oxen and sheep have been given for pasturing, has deceived, has changed the price, or has given them for money; he shall be brought to judgment and he shall return to their owner oxen and sheep ten times that which he stole

271. If anyone has hired oxen, a cart, and driver he shall pay 180 KA of grain for one day.

278. If anyone has bought a man or woman slave and before the end of the month the bennu-sickness has fallen upon him, he shall return him to the seller and the buyer shall take back the money which he paid.

279. If anyone has bought a man or woman slave and a complaint is made, the seller shall answer for the complaint.

282. If a slave has said to his master, "Thou art not my master," one shall bring him to judgment as his slave, and his master shall cut off his ear.

468

APPENDIX D

Declaration of Independence

In Congress, July 4, 1776.

The unanimous declaration of the thirteen United States of America. When in the course of human events, it becomes necessary for one people to dissolve the political bands which have connected them with another, and to assume among the powers of the earth, the separate and equal station to which the Laws of Nature and of Nature's God entitles them, a decent respect to the opinions of mankind requires that they should declare the causes which impel them to the separation.

We hold these truths to be self-evident, that all men are created equal, that they are endowed by their Creator with certain unalienable Rights, that among these are Life, Liberty and the pursuit of Happiness. That to secure these rights, Governments are instituted among Men, deriving their just powers from the consent of the governed, That whenever any Form of Government becomes destructive of these ends, it is the Right of the People to alter or to abolish it, and to institute new Government, laying its foundation on such principles and organizing its powers in such form, as to them shall seem most likely to effect their Safety and Happiness. Prudence, indeed, will dictate that Governments long established should not be changed for light and transient causes; and accordingly all experience hath shewn, that mankind are more disposed to suffer, while evils are sufferable, than to right themselves by abolishing the forms to which they are accustomed. But when a long train of abuses and usurpations, pursuing invariably the same Object evinces a design to reduce them under absolute Despotism, it is their right, it is their duty, to throw off such Government, and to provide new Guards for their future security. Such has been the patient sufferance of these Colonies; and such is now the necessity which constrains them to alter their former Systems of Government. The history of the present King of Great Britain is a history of repeated injuries and usurpations, all having in direct object the establishment of an absolute Tyranny over these States. To prove this, let Facts be submitted to a candid world.

He has refused his Assent to Laws, the most wholesome and necessary for the public good.

He has forbidden his Governors to pass Laws of immediate and pressing importance, unless suspended in their operation till his Assent should be obtained; and when so suspended, he has utterly neglected to attend to them.

He has refused to pass other laws for the accommodation of large districts of people, unless those people would relinquish the right of Representation in the Legislature, a right inestimable to them and formidable to tyrants only.

He has called together legislative bodies at places unusual, uncomfortable, and distant from the depository of their public Records, for the sole purpose of fatiguing them into compliance with his measures.

He has dissolved Representative Houses repeatedly, for opposing with manly firmness his invasions on the rights of the people.

He has refused for a long time, after such dissolutions, to cause others to be elected; whereby the Legislative powers, incapable of Annihilation, have returned to the People at large for their exercise; the State remaining in the meantime exposed to all the dangers of invasion from without, and convulsions within.

He has endeavored to prevent the population of these States; for that purpose obstructing the Laws of Naturalization of Foreigners; refusing to pass others to encourage their migrations hither, and raising the conditions of new Appropriations of Lands.

He has obstructed the Administration of Justice, by refusing his Assent to Laws for establishing Judiciary Powers.

He has made Judges dependent on his Will alone, for the tenure of their offices, and the amount and payment of their salaries.

He has erected a multitude of New Offices, and sent hither swarms of Officers to harass our people, and eat out their substance.

He has kept among us, in times of peace, Standing Armies without the Consent of our legislature.

He has affected to render the Military independent of and superior to the Civil power.

He has combined with others to subject us to a jurisdiction foreign to our constitution, and unacknowledged by our laws; giving his Assent to their Acts of pretended Legislation:

For quartering large bodies of armed troops among us:

For protecting them, by a mock Trial, from punishment for any Murders which they should commit on the inhabitants of these States:

For cutting off our Trade with all parts of the world:

For imposing Taxes on us without our Consent:

For depriving us in many cases of the benefits of Trial by jury:

469

For transporting us beyond Seas to be tried for pretended offences:

For abolishing the free System of English Laws in a neighboring Province, establishing therein an Arbitrary government, and enlarging its Boundaries so as to render it at once an example and fit instrument for introducing the same absolute rule into these Colonies:

For taking away our Charters, abolishing our most valuable Laws, and altering fundamentally the Forms of our Governments:

For suspending our own Legislatures, and declaring themselves invested with power to legislate for us in all cases whatsoever.

He has abdicated Government here, by declaring us out of his Protection and waging War against us.

He has plundered our seas, ravaged our Coasts, burnt our towns, and destroyed the lives of our people.

He is at this time transporting large Armies of foreign Mercenaries to complete the works of death, desolation and tyranny, already begun with circumstances of Cruelty and perfidy scarcely paralleled in the most barbarous ages, and totally unworthy the Head of a civilized nation.

He has constrained our fellow-Citizens taken captive on the high Seas to bear Arms against their Country, to become the executioners of their friends and Brethren, or to fall themselves by their Hands.

He has excited domestic insurrections amongst us, and has endeavored to bring on the inhabitants of our frontiers, the merciless Indian Savages, whose known rule of warfare, is an undistinguished destruction of all ages, sexes and conditions.

In every stage of these Oppressions We have Petitioned for Redress in the most humble terms: Our repeated Petitions have been answered only by repeated injury. A Prince, whose character is thus marked by every act which may define a tyrant, is unfit to be the ruler of a free people.

Nor have We been wanting in attentions to our British brethren. We have warned them from time to time of attempts by their legislature to extend an unwarrantable jurisdiction over us. We have reminded them of the circumstances of our emigration and settlement here. We have appealed to their native justice and magnanimity, and we have conjured them by the ties of our common kindred to disavow these usurpations, which would inevitably interrupt our connections and correspondence. They, too, have been deaf to the voice of justice and of consanguinity. We must, therefore, acquiesce in the necessity, which denounces our Separation, and hold them, as we hold the rest of mankind, Enemies in War, in Peace Friends.

We, Therefore, the Representatives of the United States of America, in General Congress, Assembled, appealing to the Supreme Judge of the world for the rectitude of our intentions, do, in the Name, and by authority of the good People of these Colonies, solemnly Publish and Declare, That these United Colonies are, and of Right, ought to be Free and Independent States; that they are absolved from all Allegiance to the British Crown, and that all political connection between them and the State of Great Britain, is and ought to be totally dissolved; and that as Free and Independent States, they have full Power to levy War, conclude Peace, contract Alliances, establish Commerce, and to do all other Acts and Things which Independent States may of right do. And for the support of this Declaration, with a firm reliance on the protection of Divine Providence, We mutually pledge to each other our Lives, our Fortunes, and our sacred Honor.

(The foergoing declaration was, by order of Congress, engrossed, and signed by the following members.)   JOHN HANCOCK

New Hampshire—Josiah Bartlett, Wm. Whipple, Matthew Thornton.

Massachusetts Bay.—Saml. Adams, John Adams, Robt. Treat Paine, Elbridge Gerry.

Rhode Island, etc.—Step. Hopkins, William Ellery.

Connecticut—Roger Sherman, Sam'el Huntington, Wm. Williams, Oliver Wolcott.

New York—Wm. Floyd, Phil. Livingston, Frans Lewis, Lewis Morris.

New Jersey—Richd. Stockton, Jno. Witherspoon, Fras. Hopkinson, John Hart, Abra. Clark.

Pennsylvania—Robt. Morris, Benjamin Rush, Benja Franklin, John Morton, Geo. Clymer, Jas. Smith, Geo. Taylor, James Wilson, Geo. Ross.

Delaware—Caesar Rodney, Geo. Read, Theo M'Kean.

Maryland—Samuel Chase, Wm. Paca, Thos. Stone, Charles Carroll of Carrolton.

Virginia—George Wythe, Richard Henry Lee, Th Jefferson, Benja. Harrison, Thos. Nelson, Jr., Francis Lightfoot Lee, Carter Braxton.

North Carolina—Wm. Hooper, Joseph Hewes, John Penn.

South Carolina—Edward Rutledge, Thos. Heyward Jr., Thomas Lynch, Jr., Arthur Middleton.

Georgia—Button Gwinett, Lyman Hall, Geo Walton.

APPENDIX E

The Twelve Tables

TABLE I. THE SUMMONS BEFORE THE MAGISTRATE.

1. If the plaintiff summon a man to appear before the magistrate and he refuses to go, the plaintiff shall first call witnesses and arrest him.

2. If the defendant attempt evasion or flight, the plaintiff shall take him by force.

3. If the defendant be prevented by illness or old age, let him who summons him before the magistrate furnish a beast of burden, but he need not send a covered carriage for him unless he choose.

4. For a wealthy defendant only a wealthy man may go bail; any one who chooses may go bail for a poor citizen of the lowest class.

5. In case the contestants come to an agreement, the magistrate shall announce the fact.

6. In case they come to no agreement, they shall before noon enter the case in the comitium or forum.

7. To the party present in the afternoon the magistrate shall award the suit.

9. Sunset shall terminate the proceedings.

10. . . . sureties and sub-sureties. . . .

TABLE II. JUDICIAL PROCEDURE.

2. A serious illness or a legal appointment with an alien . . . should one of these occur to the judge, arbiter, or either party to the suit, the appointed trial must be postponed.

3. If the witnesses of either party fail to appear, that party shall go and serve a verbal notice at his door on three days.

TABLE III. EXECUTION FOLLOWING CONFESSION OR JUDGMENT.

1. A debtor, either by confession or judgment, shall have thirty days grace.

2. At the expiration of this period the plaintiff shall serve a formal summons upon the defendant, and bring him before the magistrate.

3. If the debt be not paid or if no one becomes surety, the plaintiff shall him away, and bind him with shackles and fetters of not less than fifteen pounds weight, and heavier at his discretion.

4. If the debtor wish, he may live at his own expense; if not, he in whose custody he may be shall furnish him a pound of meal a day, more at his discretion.

6. On the third market day the creditors, if there are several, shall divide the property. If one take more or less, no guilt shall attach to him.

TABLE IV. PATERNAL RIGHTS.

3. If a father shall thrice sell his son, the son shall be free from the paternal authority.

TABLE V. INHERITANCE AND TUTELAGE.

3. What has been appointed in regard to the property or tutelage shall be binding in law.

4. If a man die intestate, having no natural heirs, his property shall pass to the nearest agnate.

5. If there be no agnate, the gentiles shall succeed.

7. . . . If one be hopelessly insane, his agnates and gentiles shall have authority over him and his property. . . . in case there be none to take charge.

8. . . . from that estate . . . into that estate.

TABLE VI. OWNERSHIP AND POSSESSION.

1. Whenever a party shall negotiate a nexum or transfer by mancipatio, according to the formal statement so let the law be.

5. Whoever in presence of the magistrates shall join issue by manuum consertio. . . .

7. A beam built into a house or vine-trellis shall not be removed.

9. When the vines have been pruned, until the grapes are removed.

TABLE VII. LAW CONCERNING REAL PROPERTY.

5. If parties get into dispute about boundaries. . . .

7. They shall pave the way. If they do not pave the way with stones a man may drive where he pleases.

8. If water from rain gutters cause damage. . . .

TABLE VIII. ON TORTS.

1. Whoever shall chant a magic spell. . . .

2. If a man maim another, and does not compromise with him, there shall be retaliation in kind.

3. If with the fist or club a man break a bone of a freeman, the penalty shall be three hundred asses; if of a slave, one hundred and fifty asses.

4. If he does any injury to another, twenty-five asses; if he sing a satirical song let him be beaten.

5. . . . If he shall have inflicted a loss . . . he shall make it good.

8. Whoever shall blight the crops of another by incantation . . . nor shalt thou win over to thyself another's grain. . . .

Appendix E

12. If a thief be caught stealing by night and he be slain, the homicide shall be lawful.

13. If in the daytime the thief defend himself with a weapon, one may kill him.

15. . . . with a leather girdle about his naked body, and a platter in his hand. . . .

16. If a man contend at law about a theft not detected in the act . . .

21. If a patron cheat his client, he shall become infamous.

22. He who has been summoned as a witness or acts as libripens, and shall refuse to give his testimony, shall be accounted infamous, and shall be incapable of acting subsequently as witness.

24. If a weapon slip from a man's hand without his intention of hurling it . . .

TABLE IX.

(No fragments of this table are extant.)

TABLE X. SACRED LAW.

1. They shall not inter or burn a dead man within the city.

2. . . . more than this a man shall not do . . . a man shall not smooth the wood for the funeral pyre with an axe.

4. Women shall not lacerate their faces, nor indulge in immoderate wailing for the dead.

5. They shall not collect the bones of a dead man for a second interment.

7. Whoever wins a crown, either in person or by his slaves or animals, or has received it for valor . .

8. . . . he shall not add gold . . . ; but gold used in joining the teeth . . . This may be burned or buried with the dead without incurring any penalty

TABLE XI.

(No fragments of this table are extant.)

TABLE XII. SUPPLEMENTARY LAWS.

2. If a slave has committed theft, or has done damage . . .

3. If either party shall have won a suit concerning property by foul means, at the discretion of the opponent . . . the magistrate shall fix the damage at twice the profits arising from the interim possession.

472

APPENDIX F

Magna Charta

JOHN, by the grace of God king of England, lord of Ireland, duke of Normandy and Aquitaine, and count of Anjou, to his archbishops, bishops, abbots, earls, barons, justiciaries, foresters, sheriffs, governors, officers, and to all bailiffs, and faithful subject, greeting. Know ye, that we, in the presence of God, and for the salvation of our soul, and the souls of our ancestors and heirs, and unto the honour of God and the advancement of Holy Church, and amendment of our Realm, by the advice of our venerable Fathers, STEPHEN, Archbishop of Canterbury, primate of all England, and cardinal of the Holy Roman Church, HENRY, Archbishop of Dublin, WILLIAM of London, PETER of Winchester, JOCELIN of Bath and Glastonbury, HUGH of Lincoln, WALTER of Worcester, WILLIAM of Coventry, BENEDICT of Rochester, Bishops; of Master PANDULF, Sub-Deacon and Familiar of our Lord the Pope, Brother AYMERIC, Master of the Knight-Templars in England; and of the Noble Persons, WILLIAM MARESCALL, Earl of Pembroke, WILLIAM, Earl of Salisbury, WILLIAM, Earl of Warren, WILLIAM, Earl of Arundel, ALAN de GALLOWAY, Constable of Scotland, WARIN FITZ GERALD, PETER FITZ HERBERT, and HUBERT DE BURGH, Seneschal of Poitou, HUGH de NEVILLE, MATTHEW FITZ HERBERT, THOMAS BASSET, ALAN BASSET, PHILIP of ALBINEY, ROBERT de ROPPELL, JOHN MARESCHALL, JOHN FITZ HUGH, and others our liegemen, have, in the first place, granted to God, and by this our present Charter confirmed, for us and our heirs forever:

1. That the Church of England shall be free, and have her whole rights, and her liberties inviolable; and we will have them so observed, that it may appear thence, that the freedom of elections, which is reckoned chief and indispensable to the English Church, and which we granted and confirmed by our Charter, and obtained the confirmation of the same from our Lord the Pope Innocent III. before the discord between us and our barons, was granted of mere free will; which Charter we shall observe, and we do will it to be faithfully observed by our heirs forever. We also have granted to all the freedom of our kingdom, for us and for our heirs forever, all the underwritten liberties, to be hand and holden by them and their heirs, of us and our heirs forever.

2. If any of our earls, or barons, or other, who hold of us in chief by military service, shall die, and at the time of his death, his heir shall be of full age, and owes a relief, he shall have his inheritance by paying the ancient relief; that is to say, the heir or heirs of an earl, for a whole earldom, by a hundred pounds; the heir or heirs of a baron, for a whole barony, by a hundred pounds; the heir or heirs of a knight, for a whole knight's fee, by a hundred shillings at most; and whoever oweth less shall give less, according to the ancient custom of fees.

3. But if the heir of any such shall be under age, and shall be in ward, when he comes of age, he shall have his inheritance without relief and without fine.

4. The keeper of the land of such an heir, who shall be under age, shall take of the land of the heir none but reasonable issues, reasonable customs, and reasonable services, and that without destruction and waste of his men and his goods; and if we commit the custody of any such lands to the sheriff, or any other who is answerable to us for the issues of the land, and he shall make destruction and waste of the lands which he hath in custody, we will take of him amends, and the land shall be committed to two lawful and discreet men of that fee, who shall answer for the issues to us, or to him to whom we shall assign them; and if we sell or give to anyone the custody of any such lands, and he therein make destruction or waste, he shall loose the same custody, which shall be committed to two lawful and discreet men of that fee, who shall in like manner answer to us aforesaid.

5. Moreover the keeper, so long as he shall have the custody of the land, shall keep up the houses, parks, warrens, ponds, mills, and other things pertaining to the lands, out of the issues of the same land; and shall deliver to the heir, when he comes of full age, his whole land, stocked with ploughs, and carriages, according as the time of wainage shall require and the issues of the land can reasonably bear.

6. Heirs shall be married without disparagement, and so that before matrimony shall be contracted those who are near in blood to the heir shall have notice.

7. A widow, after the death of her husband, shall forthwith and without difficulty have her marriage portion and inheritance; nor shall she give anything for her dower, or her marriage portion or her inheritance which her husband and she held at the day of his death; and she may remain in the mansion house of her husband forty days after his death, within which term her dower shall be assigned to her.

8. No widow shall be distrained to marry again, so long as she has a mind to live without a husband; but yet she shall give security that she will not marry without our assent, if she holds of us; or without the consent of the lord of whom she holds, if she hold of another.

473

9. Neither we nor our bailiffs shall seize any land or rent for any debt so long as the chattels of the debtor are sufficient to pay the debt; nor shall the sureties of the debtor be distrained so long as the principal debtor is sufficient for the payment of the debt; but if the principal debtor shall fail in the payment of the debt, not having wherewithal to pay it, then the sureties shall answer for the debt; and if they will they shall have the lands and rents of the debtor, until they shall be satisfied for the debt which they paid for him, unless the principal debtor can show himself acquitted thereof against the said sureties.

10. If anyone have borrowed anything of the Jews, more or less, and die before the debt be satisfied, there shall be no interest paid for that debt, so long as the heir is under age, of whomsoever he may hold; and if the debt fall into our hands we will only take the chattel mentioned in the deed.

11. And if anyone shall die indebted to the Jews, his wife shall have her dower and pay nothing of that debt; and if the deceased left children under age, they shall have necessaries provided for them, according to the tenement of the deceased; and out of the residue the debt shall be paid, saving however the service due to the lords; and in like manner shall it be done touching debts due to others than the Jews.

12. No scutage or aid shall be imposed in our kingdom, unless by the general council of our kingdom; except for ransoming our person, making our eldest son a knight, and once for marrying our eldest daughter; and for these shall be paid only a reasonable aid. In like manner it shall be concerning the aids of the City of London.

13. And the City of London shall have all its ancient liberties and free customs, as well by land as by water; furthermore we will and grant that all other cities and boroughs, and towns and ports, shall have all their liberties and free customs.

14. And for holding the general council of the kingdom concerning the assessment of aids, except in the three cases aforesaid, and for the assessing of scutages, we shall cause to be summoned to the archbishops, bishops, abbots, earls, and greater barons of the realm, singly by our letters. And furthermore we shall cause to be summoned generally by our sheriffs and bailiffs, all others who hold of us in chief, for a certain day, that is to say, forty days before their meeting at least, and to a certain place; and in all letters of such summons we will declare the cause of such summons. And summons being thus made, the business of the day, shall proceed on the day appointed, according to the advice of such as shall be present, although all that were summoned come not.

15. We will not for the future grant to anyone the right to take aid of his own free tenants, unless to ransom his body, and to make his eldest son a knight and once to marry his eldest daughter; and for this there shall be only paid a reasonable aid.

16. No man shall be distrained to perform more service for a knight's fee, or other free tenement, than is due from thence.

17. Common pleas shall not follow our court, but shall be holden in some certain place.

18. Assizes of novel disseisin, and of mor d'ancestor, and of darrien presentment, shall be taken but in their proper countries, and after this manner: We, or, if we should be out of the realm our chief justiciar, shall send two justiciaries through every county every four times a year, who, with four knights, chosen out of every shire by the people, shall hold the said assizes, in the count, or the day, and at the place appointed.

19. And if any matters cannot be determined on the day appointed for holding the assizes in each county, so many of the knights and freeholders as have been at the assizes aforesaid, shall stay to decide them as is necessary, according as there is more or less business.

20. A freeman shall not be amerced for a small offence, except according to the measure of the offence; and for a great crime according to the heinousness of it, saving him his contentment; and after the same manner a merchant, saving to him his merchandise. And a villain shall be amerced after the same manner, saving to him his wainage, if he falls under our mercy; and none of the aforesaid amerciaments shall be assessed save upon the oath of honest men in the neighborhood.

21. Earls and barons shall not be amerced, but by their peers, and according to the degree of the offence.

22. No ecclesiastical person shall be amerced for his lay tenement, except according to the proportion of the others aforesaid, and not according to the value of his ecclesiastical benefice.

23. Neither a town nor any tenant shall be distrained to make bridges or banks unless anciently and of right they are bound to do it.

24. No sheriff, constable, coroner, or other of our bailiffs, shall hold pleas of the crown.

25. All counties, hundreds, wapentakes, and tithings, shall stand at the old rents, without any increase, except in our demesne manors.

26. If anyone holding of us a lay-fee shall die, and the sheriff, or our bailiffs, can show our letters patent, containing our summons for the debt which the dead man did owe to us, it shall be lawful for the sheriff or our bailiff to attach and inroll the chattels of the dead, found upon his layfee, to the value of the debt, by the view of lawful men, so however, that nothing be removed until our whole clear debt be paid; and the rest shall be left to the executors to fulfil the testament of the dead, and if there be nothing due from him to us, all the chattels shall go to the use prescribed by the dead, saving to his wife and children their reasonable shares.

27. If any freeman shall die intestate, his chattels shall be distributed by the hands of his nearest relations and friends, by view of the church; saving to everyone the debts which the deceased owed to him.

28. No constable or bailiff of ours shall take corn or other chattels of any man, unless he presently give him money for it, or hath respite of payment by the good-will of the seller.

474

29. No constable shall distrain any knight to give money for castle ward, if he himself will do it in his person, or by another able man in case he cannot do it through any reasonable cause. And if we lead him, or send him in any army, he shall be free from such ward for the time he shall be in the army by our command.

30. No sheriff or bailiff of ours, or any other, shall take horses or carts of any freeman for carriage, but by the good-will of the said freeman.

31. Neither shall we nor our bailiffs take any man's timber for our castles or other uses, unless by the consent of the owner of the timber.

32. We will retain the lands of those convicted of felony only one year and a day, and then they shall be delivered to the lord of the fee.

33. All weirs for the time to come shall be done away with in the rivers of the Thames and throughout all England, except upon the sea coast.

34. The writ which is called praecipe, for the future, shall not be served upon anyone, of any tenement, whereby a freeman may lose his court.

35. There shall be one measure of wine and one of ale through our whole realm; and one measure of corn, that is to say, the London quarter; and one breadth of dyed cloth, and russets, and haberjects, that is to say, two ells within the lists; and it shall be of weights as it is of measures.

36. Nothing from henceforth shall be given or taken for a writ of inquisition of life or limb, but it shall be granted freely, and not denied.

37. If any do hold of us by fee-farm, or by socage, or by burgage, and he hold also lands of any other by knight's service, we will not have the custody of the heir or land, which is holden of another man's fee by reason of that fee-farm, socage, or burgage; neither will we have the custody of such fee-farm, socage, or burgage; except knight's service was due to us out of the same fee-farm. We will not have the custody of an heir, nor of any land which he holds of another by knight's service, by reason of any petty serjeanty that holds of us, by the service of paying a knife, an arrow, or the like.

38. No bailiff from henceforth shall put any man to his law upon his own bare assertion, without credible witnesses to prove it.

39. No freeman shall be taken or imprisoned, or disseised, or outlawed, or banished, or any ways destroyed, nor will we pass upon him, nor will we send upon him, save by the lawful judgment of his peers, or by the law of the land.

40. We will sell to no man, we will not deny to any man, either justice or right.

41. All merchants shall have safe and secure conduct, to go out of, and to come into England, and to stay there, and to pass as well by land as by water, for the purpose of buying and selling according to the ancient and allowed customs, without any evil tolls; except in time of war, or when they are of any nation at war with us. And if there be found any such in our land, in the beginning of the war, they shall be held, without damage to their bodies or goods, until it be known unto us or of our chief justiciar, how our merchants be treated in the nation at war with us; and if ours be safe there, the others shall be safe in our dominions.

42. It shall be lawful, henceforth, for anyone to go out of our kingdom, and return safely and securely, by land or by water, saving his allegiance to us; unless in time of war, for some short space, for the common benefit of the realm; but prisoners and outlaws, according to the law of the land, shall be excepted, and people at war with us, and merchants who shall be in such condition as is above mentioned.

43. If any man hold of any escheat, as of the honour of Wallingford, Nottingham, Boulogne, Lancaster, or of other escheats which be in our hands, and are of baronies, and shall die, his heir shall give no other relief, and perform no other service to us, than he would to the baron, if it were in the baron's hand; we will hold it after the same manner as the baron held it.

44. Those men who dwelt without the forest, from henceforth shall not come before our justiciaries of the forest, upon common summons, but such as are impleaded, or are pledges for any that are attached for something concerning the forest.

45. We will not make any justices, constables, sheriffs, or bailiffs, unless they are such as know the law of the realm and mean duly to observe it.

46. All barons who have founded abbeys, and have the kings of England's charters of advowson, or the ancient tenure thereof, shall have the keeping of them, when vacant, as they ought to have.

47. All forests that have been forests in our time, shall forthwith be disforested; and the same shall be done with the river banks that have been fenced in by us in our time.

48. All evil customs concerning forests, warrens, foresters, and warreners, sheriffs and their officers, rivers, and their keepers, shall forthwith be inquired into in each county, by twelve sworn knights of the same shire, chosen by creditable persons of the same county; and within forty days after the said inquest, be utterly abolished, so as never to be restored; so that we are first acquainted therewith, or our justiciar, if we should not be in England.

49. We will immediately give up all hostages and charters delivered unto us by our English subjects, as securities for their keeping the peace, and yielding us faithful service.

50. We will entirely remove from our bailiwicks the relations of Gerard de Atheyes, so that for the future they shall have no bailiwick in England; we will also remove Engelard de Cygnes, Andrew, P. Peter, and Ryon de Chanceles; Gyon de Cygnes, Geoffrey de Martyn and his brothers; Philip Mark and his brothers, and his nephew, Geoffrey, and their whole retinue.

51. As soon as peace is restored, we will send out of the kingdom all foreign soldiers, crossbowmen, and stipendiaries, who are come with horses and arms to the prejudice of our people.

52. If anyone has been dispossessed or deprived by us, without the legal judgment of his peers, of his lands, castles, liberties, or right, we will forthwith

restore them to him; and if any dispute arises upon this head, it shall be decided by the five-and-twenty barons hereafter mentioned, for the preservation of the peace. As for all those things of which any person has, without the legal judgment of his peers, been dispossessed or deprived, either by King Henry our father, or our brother King Richard, and which we have in our hands, or are possessed by others, and which we are bound to warrant and make good, we shall have a respite till the term usually allowed the crusaders; excepting those things about which there is a plea depending or whereof an inquest hath been made, by our order, before we undertook the crusade, but when we return from our pilgrimage, or if perchance we tarry at home and do not make our pilgrimage, we will immediately cause full justice to be administered therein.

53. The same respite we shall have (and in the same manner about administering justice, disafforesting the forests, or letting them continue) for disafforesting the forest, which Henry our father, and our brother Richard have afforested; and for the keeping of the lands which are in another's fee, in the same manner as we have hitherto enjoyed those wardships, by reason of a fee held by us by knight's; and for the abbeys founded in any other fee than our own, in which the lord of the fee says he has a right; and when we return from our pilgrimage, or if we tarry at home, and do not make our pilgrimage, we will immediately do full justice to all complaints in this behalf.

54. No man shall be taken or imprisoned upon the appeal of a woman, for the death of any other than her husband.

55. All unjust and illegal fines made by us, and all amerciaments imposed unjustly and contrary to the law of the land, shall be entirely given up, or else be left to the decision of the five-and-twenty barons hereafter mentioned as sureties of the peace, or of the major part of them, together with the aforesaid Stephen, archbishop of Canterbury, if he can be present and others whom he shall think fit to associate with him; and if he cannot be present, the business shall notwithstanding go on without him; but so that if one or more of the aforesaid five-and-twenty barons be plaintiffs in the same cause, they shall be set aside as to what concerns this particular affair, and others shall be chosen in their room, out of the said five-and-twenty, and sworn by the rest to decide the matter.

56. If we have disseised or dispossessed the Welsh, of any lands, liberties, or other things, without the legal judgment of their peers, either in England or in Wales, they shall be immediately restored to them; and if any dispute arise upon this head, the matter shall be determined in the March by the judgment of their peers; for tenements in England according to the law of England, for tenements in Wales according to the law of Wales, for tenements of the March according to the law of the March; the same shall the Welsh do to us and our subjects.

57. As for all those things of which a Welshman hath, without the legal judgment of his peers, been disseised or deprived of by King Henry our father, or our brother King Richard, and which we either have in our hands, or others are possessed of, and for which we are obliged to give a guarantee, we shall have a respite till the time generally allowed the crusaders; excepting those things about which a suit is depending, or whereof an inquest has been made by our order, before we undertook the crusade; but when we return, or if we stay at home without performing our pilgrimage, we will immediately do them full justice, according to the laws of the Welsh and of the parts before mentioned.

58. We will without delay dismiss the son of Llewelyn, and all the Welsh hostages, and release them from the engagements they have entered into with us for the preservation of the peace.

59. We will treat with Alexander, King of the Scots, concerning the restoring his sisters and hostages, and his right and liberties, in the same form and manner as we shall do to the rest of our barons of England; unless by the charters which we have from his father, William, late King of the Scots, it ought to be otherwise; but this shall be left to the determination of his peers in our court.

60. All the aforesaid customs and liberties, which we have decreed to be observed in our kingdom, as far as it belongs to us, towards our people of our kingdom, the clergy as well as laity shall observe, as far as they are concerned, towards their own dependents.

61. And whereas, for the honour of God and the amendment of our kingdom, and for the better quieting the discord that has arisen between us and our barons, we have granted all these things aforesaid; willing to render them firm and lasting, we do give and grant our subjects the underwritten security, namely, that the barons may choose five-and-twenty barons of the kingdom, whom they think worthy; who shall take care, with all their might, to hold and observe, and cause to be observed, the peace and liberties we have granted them, and by this our present charter confirmed; so that if we, our justiciar, our bailiffs, or any of our officers, shall in any circumstance fail in the performance of them, towards any person, or shall break through any of these articles of peace and security, and the offence be notified to four barons chosen out of the five-and-twenty before mentioned, the said four barons shall repair to us, or our justiciar, if we are out of the realm, and, laying open the grievance, shall petition to have it redressed without delay; and if it be not redressed by us, or if we should chance to be out of the realm, if it should not be redressed by our justiciar, within forty days, reckoning from the time it has been

notified to us, or to our justiciar (if we should be out of the realm), the four barons aforesaid shall lay the cause before the rest of the five-and-twenty barons; and the said five-and-twenty barons, together with the cummunity of the whole kingdom, shall distrain and distress us in all possible ways, by seizing our castles, lands, possessions, and in any other manner they can, till the grievance is redressed according to their pleasure; saving harmless our own person, and the persons of our queen and children; and when it is redressed, they shall obey us as before. And any person whatsoever in the kingdom may swear that he will obey the orders of the five-and-twenty barons aforesaid, in the execution of the premises, and will distress us, jointly with them, to the utmost of his power; and we give public and free liberty to anyone that shall please to swear to this, and never will hinder any person from taking the same oath.

62. As for all those of our subjects who will not, of their own accord, swear to join the five-and-twenty barons in distraining and distressing us, we will issue orders to make them take the same oath as aforesaid, And if any one of the five-and-twenty barons dies, or goes out of the kingdom, or is hindered any other way from carrying the things aforesaid into execution, the rest of the said five-and-twenty barons may choose another in his room, at their discretion, who shall be sworn in like manner as the rest. In all things that are committed to the execution of these five-and-twenty barons, if, when they are all assembled together, they should happen to disagree about any matter, and some of them, when summoned, will not, or cannot come, whatever is agreed upon, or enjoined, by the major part of those that are present, shall be reputed as firm and valid as if all the five-and-twenty had

given their consent; and the aforesaid five-and-twenty shall swear that all the premises they shall faithfully observe, and cause with all their power to be observed. And we will not, by ourselves, or by any other, procure anything whereby any of these concessions and liberties may be revoked or lessened; and if any such thing be obtained, let it be null and void; neither shall we ever make use of it, either by ourselves or any other. And all the ill-will, indignations, and rancours that have arisen between us and our subjects, of the clergy and laity, from the first breaking out of the dissensions between us, we do fully remit and forgive; more over all trespasses occasioned by the said dissensions, from Easter in the fifteenth year of our reign, till the restoration of peace and tranquillity, we hereby entirely remit to all, both clergy and laity, and as far as in us lies do fully forgive. We have, moreover, caused to be made for them the letters patent testimonial of Stephen, lord archbishop of Canterbury, Henry, lord archbishop of Dublin, and the bishops aforesaid, as also of Master Pandulf, for the security and concessions aforesaid.

63. Wherefore we will and firmly enjoin, that the Church of England be free, and that all the men in our kingdom have and hold all the aforesaid liberties, rights, and concessions, truly and peaceably, freely and quietly, fully and wholly to themselves and their heirs, of us and our heirs, in all things and places, forever, as is aforesaid. It is also sworn, as well on our part as on the part of the barons, that all the things aforesaid shall be observed in good faith and without evil intent. Given under our hand, in the presence of the witnesses above named, and many others, in the meadow called Ruming-meade, between Windsor and Staines, the 15th day of June, in the 17th year of our reign.

APPENDIX G

Petition of Right (1628 A.D.)

THE PETITION EXHIBITED TO HIS MAJESTY BY THE LORDS SPIRITUAL AND TEMPORAL AND COMMONS. IN THIS PRESENT PARLIAMENT ASSEMBLED, CONCERNING DIVERS RIGHTS AND LIBERTIES OF THE SUBJECTS, WITH THE KING'S MAJESTY'S ROYAL ANSWER THEREUNTO IN FULL PARLIAMENT.

To the King's Most Excellent Majesty.

Humbly shew unto our Sovereign Lord the King, the Lords spiritual and temporal, and Commons in Parliament assembled, that whereas it is declared and enacted be a statute made in the time of the reign of King Edward I., commonly called 'Statutum de tallagio non concedendo,' that no tallage or aid shall be laid or levied by the King or his heirs in this realm, without the good will and assent of the archbishop, bishops, earls, barons, knights, burgesses, and other the freemen of the Commonalty of this realm; and by authority of Parliament holden in the five-and-twentieth year of the reign of King Edward III., it is declared and enacted, that from henceforth no person shall be compelled to make any loans to the King against his will, because such loans were against reason and the franchise of the land; and by other laws of this realm it is provided, that none should be charged by any charge or imposition called a benevolence, nor by such like charge; by which statutes before mentioned and other the good laws and statutes of this realm, your subjects have inherited this freedom, that they should not be compelled to contribute to any tax, tallage, aid, or other like charge not set by common consent in Parliament.

II. Yet nevertheless, of late, divers commissions directed to sundry commissioners in several counties, with instructions, have issued; by means whereof your people have been in divers places assembled, and required to lend certain sums of money unto your Majesty, and many of them, upon their refusal so to do, have had an oath administered unto them not warrantable by the laws or statutes of this realm, and have been constrained to become bound to make appearance and give utterance before your Privy Council and in other places, and others of them have been therefore imprisoned, confined, and sundry other ways molested and disquieted; and divers other charges have been laid and levied upon your people in several counties by lord lieutenants, deputy lieutenants, commissioners for musters, justices of peace and others, by command or direction of your Majesty, or your Privy Council, against the laws and free customs of the realm.

III. And whereas also by the statute called 'The Great Charter of the Liberties of England,' it is declared and enacted, that no freeman may be taken or imprisoned, or be disseised of his freehold or liberties, or his free customs, or be outlawed or exiled, or in any manner destroyed, but by the lawful judgment of his peers, or by the law of the land.

IV. And in the eighth-and-twentieth year of the reign of King Edward III, it was declared and enacted by authority of Parliament, that no man, of what estate or condition that he be, should be put out of his land or tenements, not taken, nor imprisoned, nor disherited, nor put to death without being brought to answer by due process of law.

V. Nevertheless, against the tenor of the said statutes, and other the good laws and statutes of your realm to that end provided, divers of your subjects have of late been imprisoned without any cause shewed; and when for their deliverance they were brought before justices by your Majesty's writs of habeas corpus, there to undergo and receive as the court should order, and their keepers commanded to certify the causes of their detainer, no cause was certified, but that they were detained by your Majesty's special command, signified by the lords of your Privy Council, and yet were returned back to several prisons, without being charged with anything to which they might answer according to law.

VI. And whereas of late great companies of soldiers and mariners have been dispersed into divers counties of the realm, and the inhabitants, against their wills, have been compelled to receive them into their houses, and there to suffer them to sojourn, against the laws and customs of this realm, and to the great grievance and vexation of the people.

VII. And whereas also by authority of Parliament, in the five-and-twentieth year of the reign of King Edward III., it is declared and enacted that no man should be forejudged of life or limb against the form of the Great Charter and the law of the land; and by the said Great Charter and other the laws and statutes of this your realm, no man ought to be adjudged to death but by the laws established in this your realm, either by the customs of the same realm, or by Acts of Parliament; and whereas no offender of what kind soever is exempted from the proceedings to be used, and the punishments to be inflicted by the laws and statutes of this your realm; nevertheless, of late times, divers commissions under your Majesty's great seal have issued forth, by which certain persons have been assigned and appointed commissioners with power and authority to proceed within the land, according to the justice of marshal law, against such soldiers or mariners, or other dissolute persons joining with them, as should committ any murder, robbery, felony, mutiny, or other outrage or misdemeanor whatsoever, and by such summary course or other as is agreeable to martial law, and as is used in armies in time of war, to proceed to the trial and condemnation of such offenders, and them to cause to be executed and put to death according to the law martial.

VIII. By pretext where of some of your Majesty's subjects have been by some of the said commissioners put to death, when and where, if by the laws and statutes of the land they had deserved death, by the same laws and statutes also they might, and by no other, ought to have been judged and executed.

IX. And also sundry grievous offenders, by colour thereof claiming an exemption, have escaped the punishments due to them by the laws and statutes of this your realm, by reason that divers of your officers and ministers of justice have unjustly refused or forborne to proceed against such offenders according to the same laws and statutes, upon pretence that the said offenders were punishable only by martial law, and by authority of such commissions as aforesaid, which commissions, and all other of like nature, are wholly and directly contrary to the said laws and statutes of this your realm.

X. They do therefore humbly pray your mos excellent Majesty that no man hereafter be compelled to make or yield any gift, loan, benevolence tax, or such like charge, without common consent by Act of Parliament; and that none be called to make answer, or to take such oath, or to give attendance, or be confined, or otherwise molested or disquieted concerning the same, or for refusa thereof; and that no freeman, in any such manner as is before mentioned, be imprisoned or detained and that your Majesty would be pleased to remove the said soldiers and mariners, and that your people may not be so burthened in time to come; and that the aforesaid commissions, for proceeding by martia law, may be revoked and annulled; and that hereafter no commissions of like nature may issue forth to any person or persons whatsoever to be executed as aforesaid, lest by colour of them any of your Majesty's subjects be destroyed or put to death contrary to the laws and franchise of the land.

XI. All of which they most humbly pray of your most excellent Majesty as their rights and liberties, according to the laws and statutes of this realm and that your Majesty would also vouchsafe to declare that the awards, doings, and proceedings, to the prejudice of your people in any of the premises, shall not be drawn hereafter into consequence or example; and that your Majesty would be also graciously pleased, for the further comfort and safety of your people, to declare your royal will and pleasure, that in the things aforesaid all your officers and ministers shall serve you according to the laws and statutes of this realm, as they tender the honour of your Majesty, and the prosperity of this kingdom.

Quà quidem petitione lectá et plenius intellectá per dictum dominum regem taliter est responsum in pleno parliamento, viz., Soit droit fait comme est desiré.

Index

490

Night watch, 51, 67–68, 69,
  70–71
Nixon, Richard M., 323

Oath, 44
Office of Law Enforcement
  Assistance (OLEA),
  111–112, 208–209
Office of Naval Intelligence,
  328–329
Office of Special Investigations, Air Force, 329–
  331
Omnibus Crime Control and
  Safe Streets Act of
  1968, 109, 112–113,
  119, 140, 208–209
Ordeal, trial by, 44–45
Organization, police, 210–217,
  285–286, 289–291
  defined, 210–211
  principles, 216–222
Organizations:
  community, 183–186, 261
  professional, 115–118
Organized crime, 269–277,
  326, 385
Overlapping shifts, 160–161

Parker Center, 86
Parker, William H., 84–87
Parliament, 53–55, 56, 61, 364
Parole, 397–398, 425–426

investigation before, 399
  supervision, 400–402
Patrol, Kansas City experi-
  ment, 174–175
Patrol system, 51, 156–180
  efficiency, 173–175
  organization, 156–167,
    176–186
  origin, 70–73, 165
  types, 162–166
Patronage, 87, 107, 286–288
  origin, 40
Peel, Robert, 61–63, 71
Pennsylvania Crime Commis-
  sion, 304, 406
Pennsylvania Eastern State
  Penitentiary, 387
Pennsylvania system, 387
Petition, right of, 437–438
Petition of Right, 55–56, 479–
  480
Philosophy of law enforce-
  ment, 140–143
Pfiffer, John M., 210
Pinkerton, Allan, 74–77
Pisistratus, 38
Plato, 300
Platoon, 160–162, 215
Plea bargaining, 272, 375–376
Police:
  accountability, 22
  administration, 61–62, 78–
    87, 133, 138, 167, 190–
    193
  authority, 17–20, 291–295,
    413–414